SO-AZG-755

THE ORDEAL OF
NATIONHOOD

THE ORDEAL OF
NATIONHOOD

A Social Study of India
Since Independence, 1947-1970

KRISHAN BHATIA

NEW YORK

ATHENEUM

1971

DS
480.84
B4894

To Kanta

60007

Map by Ava Morgan

Copyright © 1971 by Krishan Bhatia
All rights reserved
Library of Congress catalog card number 71–139300
Published simultaneously in Canada by McClelland and Stewart Ltd.
Manufactured in the United States of America by
H. Wolff, New York
Designed by Kathleen Carey
First Edition

CONTENTS

THE ORDEAL OF
NATIONHOOD

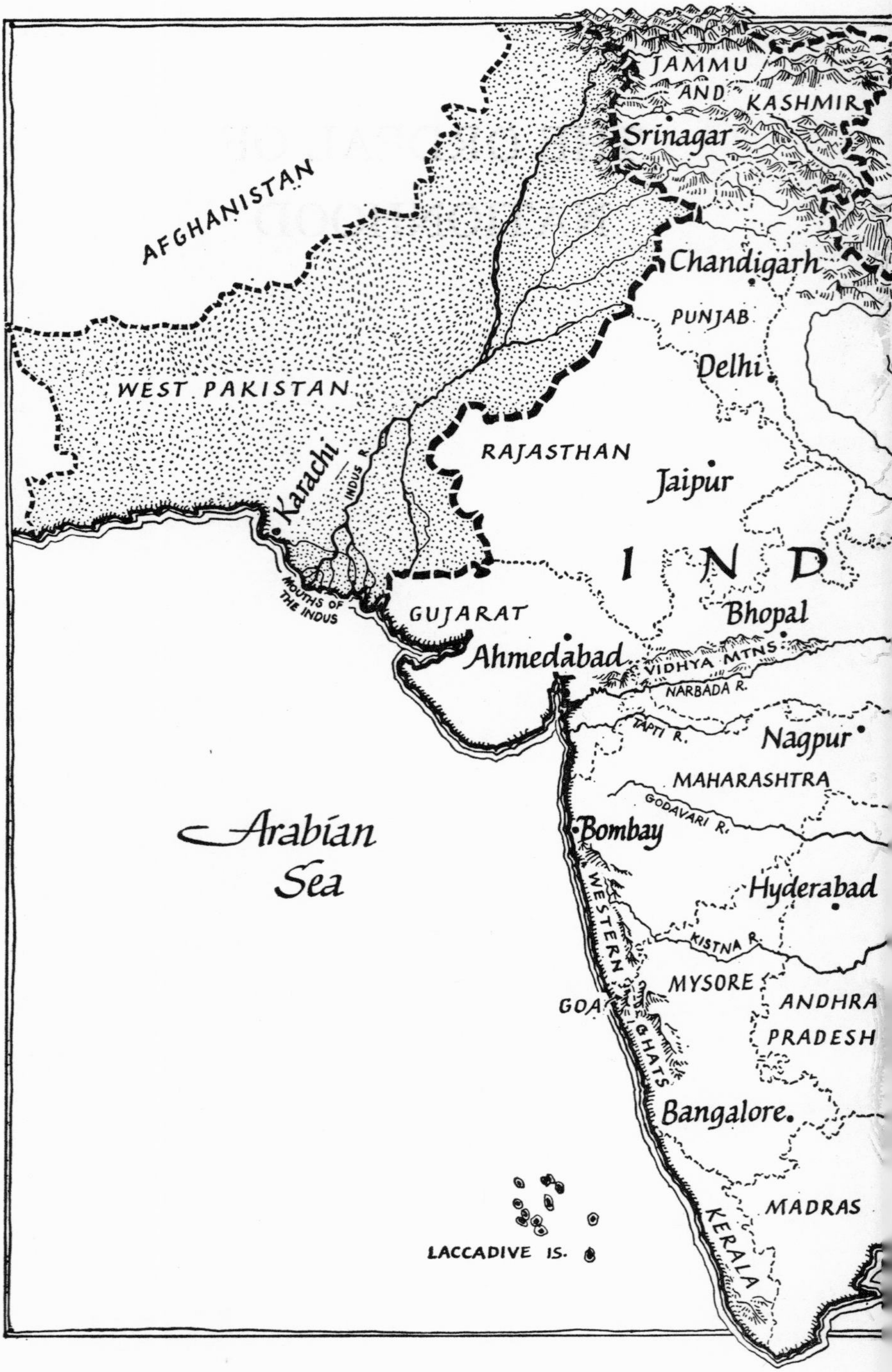
JAMMU
AND
KASHMIR
Srinagar
AFGHANISTAN
Chandigarh
PUNJAB
Delhi
WEST PAKISTAN
RAJASTHAN
Karachi
INDUS R.
Jaipur
I N D
MOUTHS OF THE INDUS
GUJARAT
Bhopal
Ahmedabad
VIDHYA MTNS.
NARBADA R.
TAPTI R.
Nagpur
MAHARASHTRA
GODAVARI R.
Arabian
Sea
Bombay
WESTERN
GHATS
Hyderabad
KISTNA R.
MYSORE
GOA
ANDHRA
PRADESH
Bangalore
MADRAS
KERALA
LACCADIVE IS.

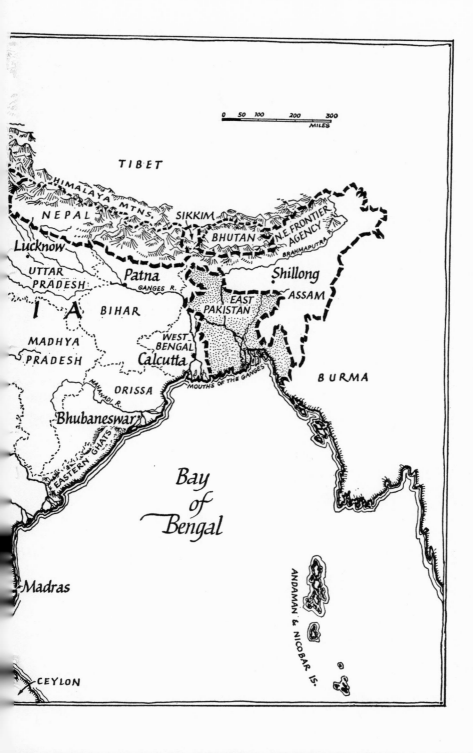

I

A GORY CURTAIN CALL

ON AUGUST 15, 1947, after ruling the subcontinent for over 150 years, the British surrendered power and India became a nation. Though divided officially from that morning into Indians and Pakistanis, nearly one-fifth of the human race had attained freedom from foreign rule.

In New Delhi, India's imperial capital, it was a bright, hot and humid morning. Tens of thousands of sweating Indians stood outside the circular Parliament House shouting euphorically as the Constituent Assembly met inside to hear the message of greetings from His Majesty King George VI. "Freedom-loving people everywhere will wish to share in your celebrations," the message said. "It is inspiring to think that all this has been achieved by means of peaceful change."

The significance of the change and of the means by which it had come about was demonstrated more dramatically moments later when, after delivering the King's message, Earl Mountbatten, India's last Viceroy, emerged from the circular red stone building with its massive Roman pillars built by a latter-day empire. As the horse-drawn coach carrying Lord and Lady Mountbatten left the Parliament House porch, its way was almost barred by the surging crowd. Despite ranks of sturdy bodyguards around it, men held onto the ornate coach, some even clambering onto its steps in an exuberant attempt to shake Lord Mountbatten's hand or merely to touch his wilting Naval uniform. At the same time, those at the back who could not come near broke out in prolonged cheers and shouted *"Mountbatten zindabad"*—Long live Mountbatten!"

For anyone who had watched the freedom movement in the preceding quarter of a century and noted the pervasive bitterness it had generated, this spontaneous expression of affection for a British ruler was a remarkable phenomenon. That a crowd of Indians would ever shout slogans for the long life of a former Viceroy was beyond imagining. The sense of alienation nurtured over so long a period melted away in that singular moment of triumph. The Jallianwala Bagh shooting incident ordered by an arrogant foreign power in 1919, when several hundred unarmed Indians had been mowed down, the extensive police firing and wholesale arrests of political workers following the Quit India movement of 1942, and so many other humiliations in the intervening period appeared suddenly to have been erased from the public mind by the British action of renouncing power voluntarily. Seldom before had such deep wounds healed so quickly. It was a measure of the extent to which the Indian mind had been purged of bitterness toward the British that Lord Mountbatten had been persuaded to stay on for a while as the Governor-General, a position without executive authority in the new "Dominion of India" but carrying much prestige.

India was transformed from a colony to a dominion at the stroke of midnight, August 14–15. It had become a member of the British Commonwealth—as sovereign as Canada or Australia. The Constituent Assembly of India, engaged in framing the constitution in anticipation of the freedom, met that night to inherit power formally for the Indian part of the subcontinent. M. A. Jinnah, whose powerful agitation for a separate homeland for the Muslims had led to the country's partition, had already left New Delhi for Karachi to take over as the Governor-General of the Dominion of Pakistan. As representative of the British Crown, Lord Mountbatten had conveyed similar royal greeting to the Pakistanis before flying back to New Delhi to end his role as the all-powerful Viceroy of the subcontinent and becoming a mere figurehead.

On the eve of independence, New Delhi seemed in a mood of gaiety and celebration. The minarets and domes of the Viceroy's imposing palace as well as those of the two stately wings of the Central Secretariat were wreathed in multicolored bunting and lights. All-India Radio, the state-owned broadcasting network, had assembled some of the nation's most gifted artists to usher in freedom with joyful music and patriotic songs. Before they drove to the Constituent Assembly session that night, several members of the new government held ceremonies, devout if somewhat noisy, in the gardens of their palatial official residences and chanted Mantras around the sacred fire as an expression of thanks for what had been bestowed on their country —and themselves.

While waiting for midnight, Jawaharlal Nehru, Prime Minister designate of India and an idol of the people, spoke feelingly in the Assembly of what the new age meant to him. "Long years ago we made a tryst with destiny, and now the time comes when we shall redeem our pledge, not wholly or in full measure, but very substantially. At the stroke of the midnight hour, when the world sleeps, India will awake to life and freedom. A moment comes, which comes but rarely in history, when we step out from the old to the new, when an age ends, and when the soul of a nation, long suppressed, finds utterance."

Behind all the festivities and political rhetoric, however, there was a distinct sense of national anguish. Even as firecrackers were being exploded in parts of the capital to herald the beginning of the new age, old tensions and hatred were manifesting themselves. Thousands had been arriving daily in Delhi as refugees, driven out of their ancestral homes in Pakistan by mass terror perpetrated by those who shared their language, culture and history but not their religion. The harrowing tales of massacre, looting, rape and arson that the fleeing Hindu refugees brought to India had touched off a series of retaliations in which equally heinous crimes were committed against Muslims on the Indian side of the border. On July 22, nearly three weeks before the subcontinent's formal partition, the Partition Council, at which both future governments were represented, had formally stated that "all citizens will be regarded as equal, and both the governments will assure to all people within their territories the exercise of liberties." Both governments also pledged that "there shall be no discrimination against those who before August 15 may have been political opponents." The Pakistani delegation at the Council was led by Jinnah himself, whom the Pakistanis hailed as the Qaid-e-Azam ("the great leader"), while the future Government of India was represented by Sardar Patel, its Home Minister and the strong man of Indian politics. Though offered by the foremost leaders and in acknowledged sincerity, the promises of security and freedom to the minorities in both countries were of no avail against the communal hatred that had been brewing like lava inside the people. A boundary force of nearly 50,000 soldiers, led largely by British officers, could not contain the fury with which minorities in the two dominions were attacked.

Even before the country was actually partitioned, many parts had witnessed serious communal rioting. Exactly a year earlier, some 5,000 people were killed in the streets of Calcutta. Muslims, who were then in the majority in Bengal and who controlled the government, started the massacre while the provincial government and its police pretended to restrain them. On the third day of the killing, however, the Hindus of Calcutta retaliated with an anger that, coming from a supposedly meek people, surprised nearly everyone and, despite energetic police intervention, could be contained only after hundreds of Muslims had been butchered. The riots then spread to Noakhali in the eastern part of Bengal, and so distressing was the display of passion that

Mahatma Gandhi left the important constitutional negotiations in progress with the British government in New Delhi to undertake a village-by-village walking tour of the area in an effort to restore calm and sanity. Even as he finished his Noakhali tour, riots broke out in Punjab. In the beginning of March 1947, while leaders were fiercely debating the issue of partition, street fighting started in Lahore, the capital of Punjab. Stabbing, killing and arson spread to other big cities of Punjab such as Rawalpindi, Lyallpur, Multan and Amritsar. As the date of partition and independence approached, more areas erupted in orgies of violence. Calcutta and Lahore were particularly prone to the virus because they were the capitals of the two major provinces that Jinnah had demanded as part of the Muslim homeland, though each had had large Hindu-majority areas. Gandhi returned to Calcutta to implore both sides to stop the killing. When freedom came to India, the Mahatma, who had led the fight for it since 1920, was not in New Delhi to celebrate India's awakening "to life and freedom." To associates he said, "What is there to celebrate? I see nothing but rivers of blood."

What happened in the weeks after independence made the earlier rioting look like fisticuffs among schoolchildren. Two days after the transfer of power, Sheikhupura, a prosperous border town in Pakistan, witnessed a massacre of Hindus in which several thousand were killed. Amritsar, a large city on the Indian side of the border and for long the stronghold of militant Sikhs and Hindus, reacted by committing acts of unspeakable barbarity toward the Muslim minority. This retaliatory action set into motion a process of action-and-reaction massacres that engulfed all of West Pakistan on one side and the whole of East Punjab on the other side, besides affecting Delhi and western Uttar Pradesh and princely states like Patiala, Alwar and Bharatpur. In the holocaust, railway trains carrying terror-stricken refugees from one side to the other were stopped and the bulk of the passengers were mercilessly butchered.

The minorities in both countries passed through a period of utter horror and misery. They had not only had to abandon their hearths and homes but had seen their relatives and dear ones slaughtered by erstwhile friends and neighbors, their women abducted and raped. Many had to flee for their lives without knowing what had happened to other members of their families. Thousands trudged long distances in hostile territory only to be ambushed and slaughtered within sight of the border that promised safety. It would be small exaggeration to say that the magnitude and sheer barbarity of the partition massacres on both sides of the border made the slaughter ordered by Genghis Khan, Tamerlane, Nadir Shah and other bloodthirsty conquerers in history appear, by comparison, insignificant and inconsequential. It is estimated that as many as 100,000 men, women and children were killed in the orgy of communal anger as nearly five million refugees crossed into India from Pakistan and an almost equal number of Muslims journeyed in the opposite direction. Within weeks of independence, the whole of West Pakistan, where Hindus had held positions of political influence and enjoyed a measure of economic power, was completely without them. On the Indian side, almost no Muslim was left in the state of East Punjab. Even in New Delhi the killing of Muslims lasted several days, and for months to come they lived terror-stricken, huddled together in a temporary camp in an old fort, the Purana Qila, protected from the insane hatred of the Hindus by the massive walls built to withstand aggression of a different kind. At the same time, Hindu temples were desecrated on a scale and with a degree of venom that even the inconoclasts like Mahmud of Ghazni, who destroyed (1025–26 A.D.) the idol in the famous Somnath temple, had not displayed. The fanatics among the Hindus of East Punjab and Delhi damaged the mosques with equal abandon. East Pakistan as well as West Bengal and Bihar in India witnessed a similar ghastly drama of Hindu-Muslim hatred and violence, although the carnage there did not lead to a complete exchange of population between the two countries. At the time of independence more than one million fled from East Pakistan in the face of terror. East Pakistan suffered periodic fits of violence and communal passion that caused tens of thousands of Hindu families to flee in waves in the following years. The size and frequency of their exodus brought the two governments almost to the brink of war in 1951.

The distress of the Indian leaders over the killing of the Muslims was deep and genuine. In his book *India Wins Freedom,* Maulana Azad, himself then a senior member of the Central Cabinet, describes the deep shock that Nehru and Gandhi experienced over the developments. "The whole of the Punjab, East and West, was becoming a graveyard of destruction and death," he recorded. The virus of communal hatred had affected the police force and the administration, which often failed to offer the Muslim citizens even meager protection amid the mass hysteria. Azad suggests—and not without justification—that even Sardar Patel, then Home Minister, displayed noticeable callousness in protecting the Delhi Muslims, but he acknowledges the distress that Gandhi and Nehru suffered. Azad recalls a meeting with Gandhi at which "Jawaharlal said with deep sorrow that he could not tolerate the situation in Delhi, where Muslim citizens were being killed like cats and dogs. He felt humiliated that he was helpless and could not save them."

Once, on a tour with local officials, Nehru came to Connaught Place, New Delhi's fashionable shopping area, and saw a band of looters plundering a Muslim store while a pair of policemen stood idly about fifty yards away. Obviously moved by what he had already seen of the death and destruction in other parts of the city, Nehru was so upset by this relatively minor exhibition of lawlessness that he jumped from the jeep in which he was traveling and ran toward the looters, angrily shaking his fist. When his personal bodyguards were able to restrain him, Nehru was still trembling with rage and his eyes were brimming with tears of frustration. Gandhi was not less frustrated. Every evening after prayers he beseeched his people to regain their sanity, but he knew his words were having little effect. His sense of helplessness in trying to control communal passions later drove him to undertake a fast unto death, a weapon he used only in extreme situations.

The storm of religious fanaticism and animus gave way in time to relative calm as a sense of shame pervaded the majority community in Delhi and the adjoining states of Uttar Pradesh, East Punjab, Bharatpur and Alwar, but only when the Muslims had fled to Pakistan or been evacuated to officially protected camps, or when passion had temporarily exhausted itself. Those in authority realized that they had looked the other way for far too long.

It is a measure of the vehemence of Hindu–Muslim anger that the people would not heed even leaders like Gandhi and Nehru, who were then their idols. At their command many had left lucrative or promising careers to join the freedom movement, challenged the might of the British Empire and, as a result, gone to jail. In 1942, Gandhi's Quit India movement against British rule had led to the imprisonment of more than 50,000 people besides the unnumbered hordes who fell before police firing. Yet the same people would not listen to Gandhi and Nehru five years later on the issue of religious tolerance: the charisma of these two men was remarkable, but the mass hatred of Muslims proved an even stronger force.

The total abandon with which the Hindus and Muslims indulged in mutual killing, arson, rape and abduction was probably the most convincing argument for the country's partition. Those who opposed the creation of Pakistan had pointed out the cultural affinities between the two communities. Hindus as well as Muslims of Punjab spoke Punjabi, just as members of the two communities in Bengal spoke Bengali, and in Sind they spoke Sindhi. Hindus and Muslims had also lived in reasonable amicability over long periods, and individual friendships often overcame religious barriers. But this cordiality was obviously superficial, a thin cover for deep hostilities.

The emotional and psychological factors dividing the Hindus and Muslims were not merely the creation of British strategy to divide and rule or the result of political covetousness of leaders like Jinnah, who was accused by his critics of wanting to carve out a modern sultanate for himself. The idea of Pakistan (meaning "Land of the Pure")—a separate homeland for the Indian

Muslims—did not originate with Jinnah. The Pakistan resolution, as it came to be generally known, was adopted by the Muslim League in March 1940 at Lahore, where it met under Jinnah's presidency. But the idea embodied in that resolution was first put forward by Dr. Mohammed Iqbal, the noted Urdu poet, when he presided over the League session in 1930 at Lucknow. Three years later Chaudhri Rehmat Ali, a lawyer, gave the concept the name of Pakistan National Movement to seek a separate state of Pakistan, comprising the Muslim-majority areas of Punjab, Kashmir, Baluchistan, Sind and North-West Frontier Province. The Lahore resolution went a step further by including as part of the proposed homeland the Muslim-majority areas of Bengal and Assam.

Though the idea failed to strike roots when proposed by Dr. Iqbal or Chaudhri Rehmat Ali, Jinnah was able to set the Muslims afire with it a decade later. In the early Thirties the prospects of British withdrawal from the subcontinent were still distant and the question of a Muslim state seemed academic. But by 1940, when the Muslim League met in Lahore, the end of the empire and independence for India were around the corner. What position the Muslims would hold in an independent India had by then become a matter of genuine concern. With the impending withdrawal of the umbrella of British power, the Muslims felt vulnerable to what Jinnah and other Muslim League leaders feared as Hindu oppression. From a privileged, favored minority, they saw themselves being reduced to a minority with which the majority had many old scores to settle. Their fears— exaggerated up to a point—made the demand for a separate homeland not merely a bargaining ploy for assurances and guarantees about the position of the Muslims in a united India but an essential goal if they were to survive with dignity. The Muslims, the League therefore insisted, must have a separate state of their own. They were entitled to this state, it was argued, because they constituted a separate "nation" distinct from the Hindus, and what made them a separate nation was their state of mind and the will to be separate.

The division of India into two states was by no means the

perfect solution. The areas in which the Muslims were in clear majority were not contiguous. Muslims were dominant in the northwestern region outlined in the Rehmat Ali scheme and in parts of Bengal and Assam in the east. Jinnah demanded the western region and the two eastern provinces in their entirety. The two wings of the new state were thus to be separated by a thousand miles of Hindu-majority areas, and Jinnah seriously entertained the fantastic idea of securing a long corridor to connect them. Aside from their lack of contiguity, the creation of Pakistan did not solve the problem of religious minorities. Even in the truncated form in which it was finally created, Pakistan contained eighteen million Hindus, Sikhs and Christians, while thirty-five million Muslims were left in India to exist as virtual hostages between two hostile countries. Sacred shrines would fall into adverse possession. The Sikhs were barred from the holiest of their shrines at Nankana Sahib in West Pakistan, while Muslims of Pakistan lost some of their historic mosques in Delhi and Ajmer.

The problem of religious minorities was not solved by partition. In 1970 the number of Muslims in India is estimated to have risen to nearly fifty-five million. Even though their proportion had been reduced from nearly 33 percent before partition to only 10 percent, the Muslims were too numerous to be ignored or taken for granted or kept in a state of subservience. Also, the cancerous animosity between the two communities was too deep-rooted to disappear as a result of the territorial amputation that the British had carried out. In their elation over attainment of independence and their preoccupation with Pakistan, few Indian leaders visualized the chauvinism of which a majority community, repressed and humiliated for nearly a thousand years, was capable when power passed into its hands.

In the subcontinent, religion plays a far more dominant role in the lives of the people than it does in the West. On the surface, the Hindus and Muslims of India seem deeply religious. Few would describe themselves as nonbelievers or conscientiously object to any important tenets of their respective faiths.

These adherents to their faiths are quick to rise in their defense at the slightest challenge. The slogan that their religion is in danger has traditionally roused Hindus and Muslims even if the nature of the supposed danger is not clearly specified. Politicians pander unashamedly to the religious sentiments of both peoples. Some openly seek votes on the basis of religion; others exploit it less blatantly. Even important official occasions such as the opening of a new institute or inauguration of an irrigation project is often preceded by a religious ceremony.

On closer scrutiny, however, the average Indian's zeal is more for the form than the substance of his religion. A Muslim would scarcely understand the prayer in Arabic, but he must recite it five times a day; a Hindu would recite the Sanskrit Mantras with equal fervor and equal lack of comprehension of their meaning. Even an educated Muslim will vehemently question any move to modernize the "Shariat," the personal law prescribed by the Prophet, although in private he would admit that it is outmoded and no longer serves his needs; his counterpart among the Hindus would willingly eat beef when abroad, but would angrily rebuke anyone at home who might suggest that the ban on cow slaughter be lifted to tackle the country's enormous problem of stray cattle. Such passionate dedication to formal religion combined with a nearly total disregard of the charity and humanism that the two religions preach make a bigot of the average Hindu or Muslim in the subcontinent. Theirs is a bigotry heightened by the confrontation between Islam and Hinduism for the past several centuries. Subconsciously, therefore, a Hindu feels affronted by the "Muazzin's" call for prayers, while the Muslim is irritated by the tolling of temple bells. In such circumstances, the existence of millions of Hindus in Pakistan and the Muslims in India promised continuance of the very bitterness and strife that had led to partition.

If, despite its obvious flaws, the dominant Congress Party ultimately accepted partition, it was because there seemed to be no alternative. Several proposals had been offered by the British government, which, with the coming to power of the Labour

Party in 1945, was genuinely eager to fulfill its promise to surrender power in the subcontinent. There were efforts to create a loose federation with a center exercising only limited authority and the federating units enjoying enormous autonomy. There were other suggestions for averting division. A Constituent Assembly had actually been elected and an interim government formed in 1946, but the demand for the creation of Pakistan did not abate. The Muslim League boycotted the Constituent Assembly, and during the brief period that its representatives joined the interim government their presence only demonstrated their incompatibility with the Congress Party. A force to reckon with, the League had captured the imagination of the Muslim masses, the bulk of whom undoubtedly stood behind it. It had won office in the Muslim-majority provinces where previously the Congress Party's secular ideals were widely accepted and succeeded in weaning away the followers of Muslim leaders like Azad, who remained in the Congress Party. Gandhi firmly declined to accept partition, but the rest of the party leadership, wearied by the protracted agitation for freedom, read the omens and agreed to opt for the country's division rather than delay the transfer of power indefinitely. When Lord Mountbatten outlined the proposal for partition on June 3, 1947, its acceptance by both parties was prompt and caused little surprise.

Once the Muslim League had achieved its objective, the Congress Party's claim to inherit power from the British in India was beyond challenge. Most people idolized Nehru, Patel, Rajendra Prasad and other Congress leaders and retained full confidence in their integrity. (Indeed, lesser leadership could not have taken the unpopular decision to divide the country and survived the holocaust that it caused.) They were already in office as members of the interim government, and transferring into the government of independent India was only a routine matter. Legislatures elected in 1946 were in position to receive power at the provincial levels. The Constituent Assembly conferred upon itself the status of a sovereign legislature until the new constitution was completed and the regular Parliament elected. The Muslim League's right to succeed British power in what constituted the new state of Pakistan was similarly undisputed. But Jinnah's moment of triumph was dimmed by the realization that Pakistan as actually carved out was much less imposing a state than he had demanded. Not only was the corridor demand rejected outright, but Pakistan did not include Kashmir and received only half of Punjab and Bengal and a small portion of Assam. Having argued in favor of the Muslims' right for self-determination, the British could not deny the same right to the Hindus of Punjab, Bengal and Assam, particularly when they happened to be in the majority in large parts of those provinces contiguous to India. Jinnah therefore complained bitterly that he had been given a "moth-eaten" Pakistan. Pakistani leaders charged that in agreeing to partition the Congress leaders had insincerely accepted an unavoidable and unpleasant necessity; they had not subscribed to the Two-Nation Theory on which the Muslim League had based its claim to a separate homeland. In India's adherence to secularism the Pakistanis saw an affront and a challenge.

Leaders of India, on the other hand, suspected that partition was part of a British plot. They could not imagine that the Muslims could feel insecure in a united India and that an outgoing colonial power could have such deep concern for the sentiments of the minorities as to go to the extent of dividing the country. They believed that division was a Machiavellian device to keep India weak and give Britain a foothold in the region even after leaving it. Many therefore tended to look upon Pakistan not as a neighbor with which India must live in cordiality but as the backyard of British—and later western—power. Even Nehru, who was responsible for Lord Mountbatten's continuance as Governor-General after independence and who vehemently opposed any demand for India's exit from the British Commonwealth, was not entirely free of such suspicions. On the eve of independence, he justified his acceptance of partition by saying that it was better to have at least three-fourths of India free rather than none at all.

Whatever its weaknesses at the time and whatever dangers lay ahead of it, India seemed like a colossus in 1947. Nehru frequently described the attainment of independence by India as the rising of a giant. Never before in history had such a vast body of human beings changed from colonial subjugation to complete freedom overnight.

Although only one-third the size of Brazil, India, even after ceding some of its populous areas to Pakistan, had a population second only to China's. The 1941 census, the latest before independence, estimated India's population at 318 million. In 1951, when the next census was held, the population of the truncated India was found to be 361 million. History and nature had combined to give the country multitudes that at the time of independence were regarded as its strength but that are now acknowledged as its biggest handicap. India's Neolithic technology —which it acquired long before Europe did—provided the basis for a "thickly settled population" probably as early as seven thousand years ago. In his book on India's population, Kingsley Davis argues that the Harappa and Mohenjo-daro excavations in the Indus Valley reveal that "as far back as the third or fourth millennium B.C. and probably much earlier still, India was in possession of a highly developed civilization with large and populous cities." Apparently this long history of settled existence of its people and the temperate climate have combined to create what is now an overpopulated nation. Except for a short period in its distant history, when some of its people sallied forth to parts of Southeast Asia, India has led a self-contained, inward-looking existence. It has received and absorbed large numbers of invaders at various times, but seldom have Indians emigrated to other parts in sizable numbers. In modern times the only group of Indians who left home were the indentured laborers whom the British prodded into going to such areas as South Africa, Ceylon and the Caribbean, and their number was too small to have any impact on the country's population.

Thus, the India that emerged on August 15, 1947, as a free nation was buoyant yet harassed, massive yet weak, loudly proclaiming its nationhood yet plagued by doubts about its viability.

II

STAMINA FOR SURVIVAL

1: *A History of Diversity*

JAWAHARLAL NEHRU once remarked that "fostering the unity of India is my profession." As one surveys his long years of leadership before and after independence, it is obvious that Nehru regarded the preservation of India's unity as his biggest challenge. While conscious of the enormity of the challenge, he did not visualize the outcome of his endeavor pessimistically. Even in 1961, when he was deeply distressed by a renewed outbreak of bloody riots between Hindus and Muslims, he asserted at a meeting of State Chief Ministers and top party leaders that he did not believe "some great and imminent danger of disintegration or disruption is facing us."

Not everyone, of course, shared Nehru's optimism. A decade after independence, Chakravarti Rajagopalachari, who had held important cabinet posts in Nehru's government and whose sense of history was in no way inferior to that of the Prime Minister he served, darkly predicted that "centrifugal forces will ultimately prevail" and that the nation "may be compelled to go through a period of political anarchy."

Rajagopalachari was being unduly gloomy. It is possible that personal anger and political frustration (he terminated his thirty-eight-year association with the ruling Congress Party to organize one of the principal opposition parties) had imparted to his assessment an edge of pessimistic bitterness. If Rajagopalachari was moved by personal pique, Nehru struck a nonchalant pose in response to the need for him, as the country's Prime Minister, to view things optimistically and hopefully.

Doubts had always existed about India's capacity to preserve its unity and territorial integrity after British power was withdrawn from the subcontinent. Not only those among the British who resented the end of the Empire but others sympathetic to Indian freedom entertained misgivings about India's future. The country had no history of unity, nor any strong binding forces. If anything, it had always tended to pull apart; and even during the few brief periods of apparent political unity, divisive tendencies had lurked close to the surface. Many, like Sir John Strachey, felt that "there is not and never was an India, no Indian nation, no people of India" and that India was something that British colonial power had created. Many took it for granted that India would revert to its pre-British fragmented form as soon as the adhesive force of foreign rule was withdrawn.

That historically India had no marked tradition of political unity is true. Occasionally, powerful monarchs were able to extend their authority to distant parts of the country, but such periods were short and were followed by centuries during which power was exercised over rather small geographical regions. In the third century B.C. Ashok Maurya extended his empire to cover the entire Gangetic plains and parts of the Deccan plateau, thereby controlling almost two-thirds of India, only to have it crumble soon after his death. It was six centuries later that the Gupta dynasty brought a large part of India under its hegemony, but by the end of the fifth century A.D. the period of their dominance had come to an end. The next thousand years saw only a brief phase of consolidation under Alauddin Khilji (1296–1316 A.D.) until the emergence of the Moghul empire in the sixteenth century.

Even when a large part of the country was ruled by a powerful king whose overlordship was widely acknowledged, his effective power did not extend to every part of his domain. The Hindu concept of kingship was largely one of aggrandizement, not of annexation of territory. Accompanied by his troops, a king would occasionally visit distant parts of his domain and secure acknowledgment of his superior authority. There was seldom an attempt to displace the weaker regional ruler and bring his domain under the king's direct administration. This apart, even the most extensive of empires covered only a portion of the country. The Mauryan empire under Ashok left out almost the whole of the southern peninsula. The Gupta empire was even smaller. The Turk and Moghul rulers of Delhi made some feeble attempts to extend their power beyond the Deccan plateau, but were discouraged by the physical enormity of the undertaking. Even the British, the emergence of whose power was greatly facilitated by the tremendous developments in the means of communication and transportation, ruled in a rather messy pattern in which half the country was under their direct day-to-day administration while the other half was divided into over 500 princely states of varying sizes whose rulers enjoyed a fair measure of autonomy in domestic matters. Some of the distant border areas, such as the tribal areas of North-West Frontier Province (now in Pakistan) and extensive parts of the country adjoining Tibet, were administered only lightly and through a generous distribution of subsidies and political bribes to tribal chiefs, punctuated occasionally with a demonstration of repressive force.

Perhaps if better means of communication had been available to them and their armies had been more mobile, the rulers of the pre-British era, too, would have established control over the entire subcontinent, from the southern tip of Madras State to the Himalayan ranges in Kashmir nearly 1,500 miles away, and from the marshlands of Kutch in the west to the distant forests and mountains of Assam. But would their control have been durable? What is more relevant is to ask whether the availability of modern means of communication adequately mitigates the national characteristics and political forces that have historically tended to pull India asunder.

Nehru once bemoaned the tendency on the part of the people to resurrect their "ancient historical memories." These memories are replete with visions of glory and power, but invariably there are also harsh reminders of past humiliations suffered at the hands of one or another people of another part of India.

There was almost no period of political power and upsurge that affected the entire land. Often the golden age of one region was the dark age of another. If, for example, the rise of Shivaji, the great Maratha warrior of the 17th century, is proudly enshrined in the folklore of the western region of Maharashtra, the adjoining state of Gujarat remembers him as an invader whose agents robbed the state of its riches and subjected it to much harsh treatment. People of northern regions like to remind themselves of the power they achieved under the Mauryas and the Guptas, while in the eastern state of Bengal they sing songs of the Pala kings. The people of Orissa, similarly, speak nostalgically of the beginning of the Christian era, when they are believed to have dominated the surrounding areas. In the other extreme of the northern region, the Sikhs remember little of Indian history except the time when they challenged the declining power of the Moghul emperors and carved out a sizable kingdom under their ruler Ranjit Singh. In South India, the Andhra patriots speak of the time when their ancestors conquered the neighboring Karnatak, Maharashtra and Tamil-nad areas, just as people of those states proudly remember the time they ruled Andhra.

Such lines of division drawn by the "ancient historical memories" were deepened by divergence in cultural heritage, economic inequalities, diversity of temperaments and multiplicity of languages, religions and races.

There are at least three distinct racial strains to be found in India. The people of the north are descendants of the Aryans from Central Asia who occupied the vast Gangetic plains, or of the subsequent foreign invaders from the north who were absorbed by the region. In the south, the dominant strain is Dravidian—the original inhabitants of the country who moved to the Deccan plateau and beyond under the pressure of the Aryan power. In the east, beyond the tablelands of Chota Nagpur, the people of India steadily acquire distinctly Mongoloid characteristics. This racial divergence, aided by a series of other factors relating to religion and language, accentuates the tendency on the part of the people to raise a network of mental and emotional barriers.

To indulge in a measure of generalization, people of each region believe excessively in their own superiority and have an undisguised scorn for Indians living in other parts of the country. In the north, particularly in Punjab, the people are hardworking, outward-looking and innovative, with enormous capacity for initiative in work and warmth in personal relationship. Bengalis have a rich cultural heritage, an extraordinary talent for artistic pursuits, a deep sense of pride and a volatile temperament. South Indians have as rich a culture as that of Bengal or any other part of the country and a high degree of intellectual attainment. They are industrious, rather simple in their living style, conservative in thinking and not as adventurous in spirit as the Punjabis. These varying characteristics deserve praise, but seemingly, in assessing them, fellow Indians find scope only for self-esteem. Qualities somehow do not look the same when viewed from another region. The northern Indians in general and the Punjabis in particular are widely considered by others as crude and flashy. Other regions tend to regard the Bengalis not as sensitive and artistic but as quarrelsome and lazy. The simplicity of southern living is similarly derided elsewhere, and the people of that region, who have produced some of the most prominent intellectuals of this century, are often dismissed as capable of little better than being good clerks and steno-typists.

Even common religious mythology changes from region to region, making demons of one area into saints and gods of another. In the Hindu epic of *Ramayana,* the central figure, Rama, belongs to the royal family of Ayodhya somewhere in the Gangetic plains of the north, while Ravana, the demon king who kidnaps Rama's wife, is from the south. In the Tamil and Telegu versions of the *Ramayana,* however, Ravana sheds many of his villainous traits and is portrayed as a man of deep wisdom and nobility. Similarly, in translating the *Ramayana* into Bengali, the poets and writers of that language imparted to the ancient heroes and heroines markedly Bengali features and characteristics. In an Oriya translation of the epic, the entire action was set on the narrow stage of Orissa, and so determined was the translators' endeavor to shut out references to other parts of India in the Oriya version that the Ganges was converted into the Mahanadi, a relatively small river that flows in the area. Even credit for developing Hindu religion and culture is diversely claimed. In the north it is taken for granted that Hinduism was the by-product of the superior Aryan civilization, but many in the south are convinced, and frequently assert in their books and pamphlets, that the Aryans were "barbarians who developed into civilized beings on coming into contact with the highly civilized Dravidians."

India's sense of nationhood thus has to contend with deeply ingrained religious and regional narrow-mindedness, memories of ancient indignities that various regions inflicted on each other at different times in history, and the excessive demands that the caste system makes on the loyalty of an average Indian. Instinctively, most Indians regard themselves as Rajputs, Brahmins or members of some other caste, or as belonging to a linguistic group such as Punjabis, Biharis, Oriyas, Gujaratis, Maharashtrians or Bengalis. It is only rarely and usually with conscious effort that they think of themselves as Indians.

Until the British succeeded in consolidating various parts of the subcontinent into a single political unit, the popular concept of what comprised India was imprecise and somewhat limited. The Indus, which gives the country its English name of India, is a northwestern river flowing in what is now West Pakistan. "Aryavart," the name used in some early Sanskrit works, related mainly to India north of the Vindhya mountain range. Bharat, the country's ancient name drawn from the name of a legendary king who ruled parts of northern India, is now formally adopted by the Constitution. The term covers the entire country "north of the ocean and south of the snowy mountains," but in the public mind it has traditionally meant the Indo-Gangetic plains in which the invaders from Central Asia had settled in prehistoric times. Bengal and Assam in the east and the areas to the south of the Narbada were always virtually the areas beyond Bharat and were considered as part of India mainly because they lacked a clearly established, separate national identity of their own.

Before the impact of British colonialism, Hinduism was the principal—perhaps the only—unifying factor in India. Its influence extended to all parts of the subcontinent. That was the religion professed by those who came from Central Asia as also of those who were forced by the invasion to move to the southern parts of the subcontinent. When Shankaracharya rose in the ninth century A.D. to give battle to Buddhism and work for the revival of Hinduism, he campaigned from Kanya Kumari on the southernmost tip of the peninsula to Mansrover in the Himalayas in the distant north. A good Hindu, whatever his caste or regional affiliations, is required to undertake several pilgrimages in his lifetime—perhaps to Varanasi and Haridwar in the northern state of Uttar Pradesh, to Kamarup in Assam, to Kanya Kumari and Rameshwaram in the south and to the famous Dwarka temple in the western state of Gujarat. In his mind, the location of these temples delineates the boundaries of India. Unlike Islam, which is the dominant faith in countries as far apart as Indonesia and Egypt, Hinduism has traveled no farther than the neighboring country of Nepal. That the frontiers of Hinduism were so confined has tended to give India a certain sense of identity as well as cohesiveness.

2: The British Influence

If in the nineteenth century Indian nationalism took a precise form and grew to considerable strength, it was not because of British rule, as is commonly believed, but in spite of it. The British undoubtedly created a single political unit and a unified administration, but its role in stimulating Indian nationalism has been exaggerated. Since its conquest by the British in 1885, Burma was administered by the government of India and politically was a part of India, yet the fact of common administration prompted few in India to think of Burma as an integral part of the country. No objections were raised when an act of British Parliament in 1935 separated Burma from India. That kind of indifference was not displayed in 1947 when Muslim-majority areas were separated from India. There was thus a geographical concept of India that was not necessarily identical with the unified administration set up by the British.

Actually, under the general umbrella of British control, divisiveness was not only tolerated but carefully nurtured. The religious differences between Hindus and Muslims were calculatedly accentuated and exploited. The Communal Award of 1932 provided special rights, protections and legislative representation for various communities. The minorities were encouraged to feel that they were not only different from the majority community but that they were vulnerable to its high-handedness and therefore needed protection. Where religious differences did not exist traditionally or were of a minor nature, they were assiduously created. The Sikhs, for example, previously regarded as a reformist, militant segment of Hinduism, were persuaded through preferential treatment in the civil and armed services and the offer of other similar privileges to regard themselves as a separate community. On the plea that they needed special assistance and care, the tribal communities in the northwest, northeast and central India were virtually sealed off from the rest of the country and prompted to continue with their primitive way of life. Within the Hindu community, where divisions were already complex and extensive, further barriers were raised through the creation of a special group of what were called "Scheduled Classes" comprising certain socially backward sections. Constituting nearly 20 percent of the community, the "Scheduled Classes" enjoyed preferential treatment in recruitment to services and dispensation of certain welfare benefits, and thus acquired a kind of vested interest in remaining apart from the main body of Hinduism. As far as the armed forces were concerned, the British divided the Indians into "martial" and "nonmartial" classes and, by restricting the recruitment almost entirely to the former, created a new privileged group. The formation of various units of the armed forces was customarily based on religious, regional and even caste lines, and various parts of the armed forces were made to lead a firmly segregated life.

Even the unified administration with the creation of which the British were credited was unified rather superficially. As representative of the British Crown, the Viceroy ruled supreme, but his domain was divided into what were popularly called British India and Princely India. In terms of political advancement, the two segments were poles apart. While the former had attained a high degree of political consciousness and had a large cadre of qualified legislators, administrators and leaders to assume power from the departing British, the princely segment, comprising nearly one-third of the country, was still burdened with autocratic, almost medieval, institutions. What was readily accepted as law in the British India was not so in a princely state if it did not conform to the personal whims and fancies of the ruler. The states, as they were called, varied enormously in size. Some, such as Hyderabad and Kashmir, were nearly as large as France and pre-war Germany, but many, particularly in the hill region, were not much bigger than Monaco. Even British India was divided into provinces whose boundaries were drawn on an *ad hoc,* often incoherent, basis cutting across physical, cultural and linguistic lines.

The British contribution to the strengthening of the idea of India as single nation rather than a collection of princely states, linguistic and tribal groups, and divergent faiths was largely unintentional. It was the by-product of certain decisions they took to achieve ends totally unrelated to Indian unity and nationalism. The enforced study of English produced the large clerical staff that Lord Macaulay had hoped it would, but it also created an elite class which could appreciate Western thought and was inspired by the growth of nationalism in Europe. The development of an extensive railway network enabled a relatively small British army—less than 200,000 in 1939—to control a country of India's size, but it also broke the shell of narrow parochialism inside of which the average Indian had traditionally lived. Above all, the British dominance of the subcontinent led to the freedom movement during which several of the divisive tendencies from which the Indians had always suffered were subordinated to the common desire to achieve independence.

The desire for freedom was undoubtedly the principal factor responsible for creating unprecedented unity and a sense of nationalism among the Indian people, but other developments of the past hundred years or so tended to buttress it. By the end of the nineteenth century, India had as many as 300 newspapers in different languages, which helped demolish some of the ancient mental barriers among the people. The rise of an educated middle class provided the nationalistic leadership the country needed. The process of modernization created a class of industrialists that saw in the united vastness of India an attractive market. Significantly, the owners of Ahmedabad and Bombay textile mills offered generous financial support to the freedom movement, and the boycott of British textiles was one of the principal weapons that Gandhi used for the attainment of freedom from Britain.

The nationalistic fervor created by the Indian fight against British dominance turned out to be somewhat short-lived. It had pushed the various forms of domestic strife into the background, but only temporarily—a situation not realized in 1947. Linguistic fanaticism, for example, raised its head only some years after independence. Also, once the trauma of partition and the accompanying blood-bath was over, it was felt that communal divisiveness had exhausted itself and the threat that it posed to national unity had passed. The Muslims had acquired the homeland they wanted, and in India the proportion of the Hindus had risen from 65 percent (1941 census) to 85 percent (1951 census). This, it was presumed, met the political aspirations of both communities. In India, communal rage and fanaticism had led to the assassination of Gandhi in January 1948 and had shocked the public conscience. It had also isolated and seemingly shamed the Rashtriya Swayamsevak Sangh (RSS) and other elements which practiced an extreme form of Hindu communalism or dreamed of establishing a state in which Hindus exercised political power exclusively. Subsequent events were to prove these assumptions to be grievously over-optimistic, but in the spring of 1948 it seemed that the perils of communal conflict were behind India.

In the first year of independence, therefore, the principal threat to India's solidarity appeared to come from the direction of Indian princes, more than 500 of whom had enjoyed varying degrees of autonomy under the broad umbrella of British paramountcy and whose states were generally regarded as bastions of political reaction. During the eighteen months before independence, when India's constitutional future was being discussed by Indian leaders and representatives of the British government, many princes had clearly indicated that they were entertaining visions of independence and power—aspirations that, before they were proved unrealistic in execution and unacceptable to the people, seemed likely to do India's unity irreparable harm. The Nawab of the central Indian state of Bhopal was then the Chancellor of the Chamber of Princes, an advisory group of the state rulers which generally watched their interests. He bluntly told the British Cabinet mission, headed by Lord Pethick-Lawrence, in April 1946 that Indian states wished to continue their existence with the maximum degree of "sovereignty." He also pleaded with the mission not to transfer the paramountcy of British power to the successor government of India after independence. The Raja of Bilaspur, a small hill state of less than 500 square miles in Punjab, even opposed the grouping of small states to form viable units and threatened to "fight" if his tiny domain was merged with other states. Sir C. P. Ramaswami Aiyar, Prime Minister of Travancore, a sizable state in southern India facing the Arabian Sea, similarly told the mission that paramountcy "could not be transferred to a successor government." The Nizam of Hyderabad, who controlled India's largest princely domain (82,000 square miles), sent his Prime Minister to the mission to demand return of the territories ceded a century ago to the East India Company and a free outlet to sea. The intention to assert his independent status after the withdrawal of British power was implicit in this demand. The Nizam's representative made it clear that, in the event of the country's partition, Hyderabad would accede neither to India nor to Pakistan. Much of this talk, of course, was political bargaining. Some of it was pipe dreams on the part of the princes, but, as the actions of the rulers of several important states such as Kashmir, Hyderabad, Indore and Travancore subsequently confirmed, the threat to Indian unity that they posed was not small.

That the confusing pattern of princely states had become an anachronism by 1947 was not widely realized among the princes. The states which occupied nearly 40 percent of Indian territory numbered 601. They came into being as a result of the "policy of subsidiary alliances" that the East India Company followed in the beginning of the nineteenth century. In its endeavor to establish itself as the paramount power in the subcontinent to the total exclusion of the French influence, the company embarked on this policy in addition to military annexation of territory. Under such "subsidiary alliances," princes were offered the company's protection against external aggression in return for the promise not to enter into negotiations with any other state without the company's knowledge and approval. The bigger states in the alliance maintained their own armies, but under British officers. The policy admirably served the purpose of the British empire builders, who were in a hurry to establish their power and could not always afford the expensive method of gaining control through military means.

In the century that followed, the British authority over the princely states grew enormously. A succession, for example, was not valid unless approved by the British, who also maintained a Resident to oversee the state's administration and whose wishes were virtually a command for the prince. At the same time, the British authority indulged the princes tremendously in the use of their states' revenues for personal pleasures and aggrandizement and overlooked a degree of autocracy, even highhandedness, on their part. There were some enlightened conscientious rulers, but they were few in number; most deservedly acquired a reputation for profligacy and extravagance. Lord Curzon, who was the British Viceroy in the beginning of the century, once sternly told a gathering of princes that a prince's "figure should not be merely known on the playground or on the race course or in the European hotel." Actually, many a princely figure was seen at places much less reputable than those the Viceroy could publicly mention. Most of them took little interest in the welfare of their people and good governance of their states. The British Residents watched the local administrations, but their patience was immense. Occasionally a prince would be rebuked by the Resident or even deposed by the Viceroy, but, as a close study of such drastic action would reveal, such measures would be taken usually because the prince had earned the British government's displeasure for political reasons. Bad administration, extravagance and misuse of public funds, highhandedness in petty domestic matters and constant disregard of basic moral values seldom brought a prince to grief.

The princely dreams of real power after the withdrawal of British rule were stimulated by Prime Minister Clement Attlee's announcement in the House of Commons on February 20, 1947, that "His Majesty's Government do not intend to hand over their powers and obligations under paramountcy to any government of British India." By this he meant that the government of independent India would not automatically inherit the outgoing authority's constitutional powers over the princely part of the country. This intention was reiterated by Lord Mountbatten, who took over as Governor-General and Viceroy a month later with the explicit direction from London to liquidate the empire. But the mere end of paramountcy when the British quit did not satisfy all the rulers. On June 3, when he announced the plan to partition the country into two separate "dominions" of India and Pakistan, Mountbatten spoke to a negotiating committee set up by the princes. At this meeting, Sir C. P. Ramaswami Aiyar, Prime Minister of Travancore, urged that paramountcy be allowed to lapse even before freedom came to the subcontinent so that states could negotiate with the prospective governments of the new dominions "on equal terms." The Viceroy did not favor this course, though the princes were assured that British power over the states was already in the "process of retraction." Mountbatten also explained that the entry of every state into either country's Constituent Assembly was a matter of free choice.

The immediate impact of the British announcement regarding lapse of paramountcy was disturbing for Nehru and others in the country who were hoping to lead a strong, united India to freedom and whose hopes had already been seriously shaken by the impending partition. The ruler of Bhopal, a relatively small state in central India, wrote to Mountbatten that "Bhopal state would, as soon as paramountcy is withdrawn, be assuming an independent status" and announced his intention to negotiate directly with the successor governments in regard to its interests and future "political relationship with Pakistan and Hindustan." A few days later Travancore announced its intention to set itself up as an independent, "sovereign" state. The Nizam of Hyderabad acted similarly a day later. The Maharaja of Kashmir did not make a pronouncement then, but subsequent developments revealed that he, too, was visualizing his beauteous Himalayan state as an independent, neutral "Switzerland of Asia." Other princes had similar, if undeclared, intentions. Two months before independence, the danger of India's "Balkanization" seemed real.

3: *Muslims and Princes*

Another dangerous element in the situation was added by the attitude of the Muslim League, which was to inherit power in Pakistan. Nehru, unhappy as he was over the lapse of paramountcy and the excessively legalistic stand that the British government was taking on its obligations to the princes, asserted that the withdrawal of British power did not mean total independence for all states and a complete severance of relationship with the successor government. At a meeting with Mountbatten attended by leaders of all communities, Nehru repeatedly argued that in his view the British government's proposal for Indian independence as studied in the context of the Cabinet mission's memorandum did not confer independence on princely states. Jinnah, who was also present at the meeting, differed strongly and argued that every princely state was "sovereign" and fully entitled to decline joining either of the two Constituent Assemblies. A few days later the Muslim League leader issued a press statement in which he declared without any ambiguity that on the termination of paramountcy every state would be free to remain independent if it so desired. For princely ears, this was sweet music, particularly because, in addition to offering a constrictive interpretation of the states' rights after the end of paramountcy, the Congress Party had made no secret of its view that it did not regard the rulers as the real inheritors of power and that the people—and not the princes—must decide the future pattern of the states' political relationship with India.

There is evidence to suggest that, in addition to offering this generous view of princely powers and privileges after independence, the League made other efforts to win the states over to Pakistan. According to V. P. Menon, who, as Secretary to the

60007

Ministry of States, supervised the gigantic task of integrating the states with "British India," Pakistan was playing with the idea of getting some of the border Hindu states to join it. In this connection, he specifically mentions the rulers of Jodhpur and Jaisalmir, who, though they themselves and the majority of their people were Hindus, were inclined to cast their lot with Pakistan. Maharaja Hanwant Singh of Jodhpur claimed that Jinnah had signed a blank sheet of paper and authorized him to fill in the conditions should he choose to join his state with Pakistan. This was obviously not a bogus assertion intended to extract the maximum price for acceding to India, for only three weeks before transfer of power Jinnah again publicly criticized the Congress for its insistence on the states' accession to one dominion or the other and announced that "he would guarantee the independence of the states in Pakistan."

Despite all these political, constitutional and emotional obstacles which on the eve of independence caused concern and nervousness among Indian leaders, the task of integrating the princely states with the rest of India and stripping their rulers of power proved to be relatively simple and was accomplished remarkably quickly. Barring Kashmir, which triggered a war between India and Pakistan and continues to be a serious source of friction between the two countries, the last of the states had come under New Delhi's control by the end of 1948. The Nizam, the Muslim ruler of Hyderabad, encouraged presumably by the prevailing atmosphere of uncertainty and instability, and prodded by Pakistani leaders, fought tenaciously to keep his authority and to secure a sovereign status for his state. Mountbatten used his influence to make him accede to India, but the Nizam was adamant. He surrendered only when the Indian Army moved in on September 13, a year after independence, to carry out what was officially described as "police action." The Nizam had spent over 200 million rupees (approximately 60 million dollars in terms of the then prevailing currency exchange rate) on the purchase of weapons for Hyderabad's Army, but that enabled it to resist the Indian forces for no more than four days. By September 18 the commander of the Indian Army had entered the city of Hyderabad and assumed control of the state.

The Nizam's case was hopeless from the very start. The Asaf Jah dynasty to which he belonged had ruled Hyderabad for more than two centuries, but its power had been sustained first by the French and then by the British. The latter had bestowed on the Nizam the special title of "Faithful Ally of the British Government" and had permitted him to distinguish himself from other Indian princes by styling himself as "His Exalted Highness" (other princes were entitled to be referred to only as "His Highness"). But at no stage in history did the Nizam enjoy anything approximating independence. In 1925 the Nizam had asserted that except for foreign affairs, his government was independent—a position sternly repudiated by Lord Reading, then the Viceroy, who informed the Nizam that the British government enjoyed the right to intervene in the state's internal affairs and brusquely reminded him that British supremacy was "based not only on treaties and engagements but that it existed independently of them."

The two decades following Lord Reading's blunt epistle had not improved Hyderabad's claim to independence. Hyderabad occupied a territory as large as Britain and had substantial economic resources, but these positive factors were mitigated by certain harsh political and geographical realities. A landlocked state, Hyderabad was surrounded on all sides by territory that did not accept the Nizam's claim to independence. Within the state there was even less public enthusiasm for an entity distinct from the rest of India. Almost 85 percent of Hyderabad's 16 million people were Hindus to whom continuance of the Nizam's rule and the dominance of the Muslim minority were an anathema. At a time when the country had been partitioned on the basis of religion, it was impossible for Hyderabad to exist as a seeming citadel of Muslim power in the heart of Hindu-majority India. Pakistani leaders shouted encouragement to the Nizam and his advisers, but, separated by hundreds of miles of land and sea and engrossed in the difficult task of establishing its own national identity and a functioning administration, Pakistan could offer no real help. These political facts, more than the incompetence of the Nizam's army, led to the collapse of his plans for power. It is a measure of the large-heartedness of Sardar Patel, who held the States Portfolio in the Indian government, that the Nizam's personal interests did not suffer in the settlement that followed the conflict. He virtually received the terms that Lord Mountbatten had vainly tried for over a year to induce him to accept. To the disappointment of many in India then, his threat to accede to Pakistan at one stage and to take the issue to the U.N. at another and his action in precipitating a clash of arms costing 800 lives brought him no punishment. Besides receiving the title of Rajparmukh, he was allowed to retain much of his vast riches and estates and was awarded an annual privy purse or a tax-free grant of five million rupees (nearly 1.5 million dollars). What irritated many princes who had acceded willingly was the fact the privy purse granted the Nizam, despite his intransigence, was the largest granted to any ruler.

There were other princes who had entertained dreams of unfettered power and for whom the Congress Party's democratic ideals constituted a personal menace. But they saw the writing on the wall, accepted the offer to accede to India and gave up their power, whatever it was. In return, they received a host of personal privileges, such as the grant of a generous annual pension, retention of personal jewelry and extensive property including palaces and resort villas, and permission to use their titles. Most princes realized that their hopes of independence were untenable and impractical and that they should settle with India while its leaders were in a mood to offer them an attractive price for their cooperation.

Several other factors facilitated the process of the states' integration with the rest of India. Under the British, the princes had led a sheltered life. British power protected them not only from external aggression but also from the wrath of their own subjects. Once the umbrella of foreign power was withdrawn, the rulers felt exposed and vulnerable. Their desire to preserve their personal power did not blind them to the hollowness of the base on which their authority rested. Though the Congress Party had formally confined its political agitation to British India, a sister political organization, the States' People's Conference, had been active in the princely domain and drew much sustenance from the national freedom movement. In the years preceding independence, Nehru had maintained close personal links with the conference and had even participated, somewhat impulsively, in some of its movements. The ruler of Faridkot, a small Sikh state in Punjab, had expelled Nehru from the state in 1945, and the Maharaja of Kashmir had actually ordered his arrest for defying the order prohibiting his entry into the state. On which side Nehru's sympathies would lie after independence was, thus, obvious. Patel's personality, too, offered no comfort to the princes. He had a reputation for ruthlessness and a total lack of patience with obstacles in his way, and it was he who had taken on the task of welding the princely India to the rest of the country. In his negotiations with the princes, V. P. Menon, who was known to enjoy Patel's confidence, deftly played upon their fears about the future and highlighted the advantages of coming to terms while Patel was in a friendly, generous mood. The Nawab of Bhopal, who was the first prince to announce his state's intention to be independent, acknowledged the realities of the situation shortly before the end of paramountcy and assured Patel that he would be a "loyal and faithful ally." The Maharaja of Indore, an important central Indian state, held back his state's accession till the last moment and then, in a seemingly sulky gesture of resignation, forwarded the instrument of accession by ordinary mail without even a covering letter.

The fear of public anger was a major inducement in many cases. The Muslim Nawab of Bhopal could not have held out against the state's merger without inviting upon himself the anger of his people, a majority of whom were Hindus and had lived without political power until then. The Hindu Maharajas of Jodhpur and Jaisalmir, whose desert states were contiguous to Pakistan, were dissuaded from acceding to Pakistan by the realization that their Hindu subjects would rise against them should the rulers try to break away from India. Significantly, even Travancore, which as a maritime state could entertain dreams of independence with somewhat greater justification than most other states, was made to fall in line by a strong public agitation in which Sir C. P. Ramaswami Aiyer, who symbolized the move for the states' independence, was attacked and wounded.

Patel and V. P. Menon have earned much public praise for masterminding the country's integration, but Lord Mountbatten's contribution to Indian unity has been diversely assessed. Was he a friend who worked for India's unity, with sincerity if not always with success, or did he act in a Mephistophelian manner and plant seeds of future conflict while seeming to work for India's consolidation and strength? The criticism of Lord Mountbatten's role is based on two specific developments. First, it was he who insisted on the end of British paramount power over the princes and thereby encouraged them to entertain thoughts of independence. Second, it was he who advised Nehru to volunteer to hold a plebiscite in Kashmir even though at the time of the state's accession neither its ruler nor its popular leader, Sheikh Mohammed Abdullah, wished to make the relationship temporary and conditional. The offer was legally unnecessary and subsequently caused India tremendous difficulty.

Much of the criticism of Lord Mountbatten's actions was the result of a general suspicion of British motives. Somehow, the average Indian regards the British as capable of a degree of deviousness in action that is borne out neither by their long history of blundering through situations nor by the weakness of their position in postwar Europe. It is true that the Viceroy advised Nehru to make Kashmir's accession subject to future ratification through a plebiscite, but it is too much to believe that he could then visualize that a situation would develop six years later in which the state's principal leader, Sheikh Abdullah, would be estranged from Nehru and the plebiscite offer would become a serious political embarrassment to India. Mountbatten's action was seemingly intended to demonstrate India's good faith in the face of Pakistani charges that India had brought about Kashmir's accession through fraud. In his letter to the Maharaja accepting the latter's request for accession, Mountbatten wrote that "as soon as law and order have been restored in Kashmir and her soil cleared of the invader, the question of the state's accession should be settled by a reference to the people." By this declaration Mountbatten made the state's union with India conditional and thereby introduced into the situation an element of uncertainty. His offer to ascertain the wishes of the people reflected the mood of the new government of independent India. Nehru himself was anxious that the Maharaja's decision to accede to India, though legally sound, should be backed by an endorsement from the people of Kashmir. He was confident of a favorable verdict in such a test and believed that it would silence Pakistan, which had its eye on Kashmir. In fact, he went so far as to refuse the Maharaja's offer of accession and request for military assistance against Pakistani raiders and changed his mind only when Sheikh Abdullah interceded. On November 2, 1947, five days after Kashmir's accession, Nehru publicly stated that "we are prepared when peace and law and order have been established to have a referendum in Kashmir under international auspices." Nor was offer of a referendum made only in the case of Kashmir. In the protracted negotiations with the Nizam which preceded military action, an offer of a referendum in Hyderabad was similarly made. Nehru and his Cabinet colleagues took this stand in complete certainty that the verdict of the people in Hyderabad as well as Kashmir would go in favor of India. The government, particularly Nehru, also had an attitude of stern rectitude and propriety then and did not wish to appear to be indulging in the imperialistic practice of grabbing territory for India. If it had not been for Patel's impatience, the Indian Army would not have marched even into Hyderabad. In these circumstances, if Mountbatten promised a reference to the people, he was hardly plotting future difficulties for India in sinister fashion, but merely reflecting the mood of confidence and political self-righteousness that prevailed in the government of the new India.

On the issue of lapse of paramountcy, Mountbatten was similarly expressing not his own preferences and predilections but the views of the British government that he was supposed to represent until the transfer of power. Attlee's statement in Parliament on February 20 left no room for ambiguity. If, therefore, Mountbatten insisted that on the withdrawal of British power the princes would be free to chart their own course of action, he was merely adhering to the rather legalistic attitude the British Cabinet had adopted. But while accepting that view of the British obligations, he used all his personal influence to make Indian princes act realistically and, as V. P. Menon's account of the states' integration clearly suggests, brought much pressure to bear upon the Nizam to overcome his unwillingness to join India.

With princely dreams of independence fading rather rapidly, India, notwithstanding its enormous problems, presented a heartening picture of national unity. It was true, of course, that nearly one-third of Kashmir had been occupied by Pakistan; that several million Hindus had fled from Pakistan, representing an enormous problem of refugee rehabilitation; that a great leader, Gandhi, had been assassinated by a Hindu fanatic; and that there were harsh economic realities facing the country. But in the years following independence India seemed remarkably united and well-knit. Its common national identity did not appear to be in doubt. Forces of disunity and discord that later surfaced appeared distant—in fact, unreal.

Other factors, besides the dominoes-like fall of the princes, contributed to the sense of coalescence. The fight against foreign domination had pushed regional and sectional considerations into the background, and the euphoria of success in that struggle had withstood even such painful aspects of freedom as the country's partition and the uprooting of millions from their homes. The war with Pakistan over Kashmir and the constant threat posed by the new neighbor tended to make people in India ignore their differences and move closer to each other. The country's division, though a traumatic experience, gave a feeling of greater cohesion to what was left as India. The Muslims who could not live with the Hindus had got their own homeland, and those who had remained in India were overwhelmed by the unforeseen realities of partition and felt too weak and vulnerable to assert themselves against the majority community. The Hindus, on the other hand, had finally found themselves free of Muslim and British domination and after centuries stood in unchallenged control of the country. After the first few months of independence had been marked by hate and anger over the plight of their co-religionists fleeing from Pakistan, Gandhi's assassination at the hands of a Hindu had a cathartic effect that blunted the edge of their communal rage.

But the biggest factor in the swift achievement of unity then was the presence of a strong national party and a leadership whose writ ran in every part of the country and with almost every sector of the people. The Congress Party ruled the Centre (the term commonly used to designate the national government) as well as all states. Even in princely states merged into India, where the party had not formally existed before independence, power was inherited by the All-India States' People's Conference and its affiliates, like the Kashmir National Conference, which were distinct from the Congress Party only in name. The political apparatus ruling the country was, thus, a monolith that faced no challenge from a rival party and had as yet not developed strong internal dissensions and jealousies of the kind that would mar its functioning in later years. Nehru, who headed the government, and Patel, the Deputy Prime Minister, often disagreed with each other, but they carefully avoided a confrontation that might precipitate a split. Despite the fact that one was a liberal and the other a conservative in outlook, they were united in their concern for national good, and what infected the people in the country was the two leaders' idealism and not their mutual suspicions.

4: *Language Barriers*

When history is being viewed from close range, it is often almost impossible to discern a clear watershed. At precisely what stage India's fragile unity began to break apart is difficult to say, but certain landmarks are noticeable. The first was the language agitation in 1953 which led to the creation of a separate Telugu-speaking state of Andhra. It also began a process of India's division into linguistic units and churned up forces that have since weakened its sense of integration and have once again raised the danger of balkanization. A comparable event occurred in 1959 when Nehru, with remarkable foresight, offered in Parliament a compromise on the issue of an official national language which, if it had been implemented then in the spirit in which it was offered, would have allayed South India's fears of northern domination and prevented the arson, bloody riots and political bitterness over language that various parts of the country have since periodically experienced. The other significant development with a direct bearing on India's capacity to acquire a sense of nationhood was the Hindu-Muslim clash in Jabbalpore in 1961, which brought to the surface the communal animosities of pre-independence days and which has been followed by even bloodier conflicts in various parts of India with distressing frequency.

The seeds of linguistic divisiveness were sown almost twenty-five years before independence, when the Congress Party accepted the redrawing of provincial boundaries as one of its objectives after independence. In British India, provinces came into being as the East India Company acquired territory and parceled it into administratively convenient units. Their boundaries were drawn with scant heed to linguistic or cultural considerations. The Congress Party under Gandhi, however, chose to follow a different pattern. It organized its provincial committees almost entirely on a linguistic basis.

There was no precedent for a division of this type. India has always had numerous languages—the Indian Constitution formally lists as many as fourteen, each with its distinctive vocabulary, script and literature. Under the British, English was the official language at the Centre and the provincial headquarters. At the district level, however, whichever happened to be the predominant regional language was used alongside English. Since British rule did not intrude upon the individual's life to any meaningful extent, this arrangement caused no serious hardship.

In promising to discard this system after independence, the Congress leadership was moved as much by political considerations as by its concern for the survival of the cultural traditions borne by the various regional languages. The leadership of the freedom movement was provided by the Western-educated, English-speaking elite of the time, but English could build no bridges with the masses, the majority of whom spoke only one of the numerous regional languages. If the agitation for independence was to acquire a mass character, emphasis on regional languages—in fact, a certain amount of pandering to linguistic chauvinism—was unavoidable. Britain was then blamed for thrusting English on the people and ignoring the cultural richness that each regional language possessed. The Congress Party promised to redraw the provincial boundaries in such a way as to give each language an area in which it could reign supreme and flourish.

At the time the promise was made, such reorganization of boundaries seemed eminently reasonable and attractive. The establishment of party units on a linguistic basis also widened the base of the Congress movement. But it was not realized then that the creation of linguistic units would encourage the growth of "subnationalities" which might place additional strain on India's still fragile sense of national identity. Those who visualized the danger were told that India's unity lay in diversity and that acceptance of the individuality of the various linguistic regions would lead to a willing and happy union. In any case, by the time independence came, the promise to give every principal language a homeland of its own had been repeated too often for the Congress leaders to go back on it. Most of them were themselves so afflicted by regional parochialism that they had little desire to get out of the commitment. In its manifesto for the 1946 and 1952 elections, the party unambiguously reiterated its determination to create linguistic states to enable "each group and territorial area within the nation to develop its own life and culture."

Nehru, however, did not have his heart in this political promise. He had never been enthusiastic about linguistic provinces, and he seemed to realize the threat their creation posed to India's unity. But his was a lone voice. As he told Parliament in July 1952, he agreed with the proposal, but he had "not taken any aggressive or positive step in regard to the formation of linguistic provinces." He had been "overburdened with the thought" that he must give topmost priority to the "development of a sense of unity in India" and any decision "that might come in the way of that unity should be delayed till we have laid a strong foundation for it." It seemed to him "extraordinarily unwise" to unsettle and uproot the whole of India on the basis of "a theoretical approach or linguistic division."

Despite this unambiguous and seemingly stern stand, Nehru gave in to pressures from chauvinistic elements and short-sighted party colleagues and acquiesced in seeing the map of India "cut up anew on the basis of language." The years following 1953 present a sad story of Nehru correctly foreseeing hazards ahead and forecasting the harmful implications of the country's linguistic division but surrendering to the wishes of the mob. The reorganization ignored almost every safeguard that the Prime Minister had suggested. He felt that a linguistic state ought to be carved out only where there was a genuine demand for it and where it could be undertaken with mutual goodwill between the parties involved in the operation. He did not favor reorganization on a national scale. Yet in many places the redrawing of new boundaries was preceded or followed by clashes between rival groups and by police firing, in which many lives were lost. He had argued that in creating new units, economic, administrative and financial factors must also be taken into consideration, but the states were created entirely in accordance with the compulsions of narrow regionalism, while economic and other considerations were ignored. The States' Reorganization Commission recommended that the state of Bombay be bilingual so that it would preserve its economic unity; Nehru agreed, only to rescind this wise decision in the face of violence and create the separate states of Gujarat and Maharashtra and weaken the region's economic unity.

Perhaps the time to take a firm, unbending stand would have been in 1953, when the Telugu-speaking people of Madras demanded a separate state of their own. The Central Government turned down the demand, but it suffered sharp tremors of nervousness within a short time because Potti Sriramulu, a local leader, fasted himself to death on the issue and his passing was followed by extensive mob violence in parts of the state. In the later stages of his fast, Sriramulu was a virtual prisoner in the hands of a group of self-seeking political agitators who would not let him end his ordeal even though he was known to be anxious to. If the government had really wanted the sense of national unity to take firm root and be strong enough not to resist being choked by weeds of linguistic narrow-mindedness, it should have sternly faced the riots that erupted in the Telugu area. Instead, it conceded the demand with an alacrity that surprised even the organizers of the agitation.

Once a separate Telugu state of Andhra was carved out, it was too late to stop similar agitations in other parts of the country, or even to let the new boundaries be drawn at a carefully measured pace and with the goodwill of the people concerned. The separation of the Telugu-speaking areas from Madras was like an operation that checks a malignancy temporarily, only to divert it with even greater malevolence to other parts of the body. After Andhra there was nothing to stop linguistic parochialism. A commission presided over by a former judge of India's Supreme Court was set up to suggest a rational and orderly pat-

tern of state boundaries, but the course that the States' Reorganization actually followed was marked not by judicial wisdom but
by conflict and bitterness. Almost all recommendations of the
commission not in conformity with the passions of the street
mobs fell by the wayside. Nehru had opposed the disintegration
of the state of Hyderabad, but he confessed later that "circumstances" (by which he apparently meant mob violence and parochial pressures within his own party) had been "too strong for
me." The bilingual state of Bombay gave way to Maharashtra
and Gujarat. The tiny state of Nagaland, with a population of
300,000, was created to appease the insurgent Nagas demanding independence and separation from India.

The only aspect of reorganization on which Nehru had taken
an uncompromising posture and had not been overawed by the
fierceness of public agitation related to the creation of a small
Sikh majority state on the border with West Pakistan. "I am not
going to play about with our frontiers in the north," he declared.
The Punjabi-speaking Sikhs had a legitimate claim to a linguistic
state, since all other languages listed in the constitution had acquired a home of their own, but economic and security considerations stood in the way. On a strictly linguistic basis, the small
community (1.75 percent of the total national population)
would have received a state economically weak and woefully
lacking in depth for a political unit situated on a sensitive border
with a hostile neighbor. But what Nehru refused to concede was
allowed after his death, and the state of Punjab was bifurcated
to create a small Sikh-majority state.

The "Pandora's Box," which Nehru had warned would open
with linguistic states, continues to produce vexatious problems
and situations. If the Nagas, numbering less than .01 percent of
the country's population and with no distinctive language, can
be given a state, why should the homes of the Khasi and Mizo
tribes continue to be an insignificant part of Assam? Actually,
not only the Khasi and Mizo tribes but the entire hill region of
Assam feel they have no cultural affinity with the people in the
plains of Assam and assert their right to separation. In the

Nagpur region there is a movement for separation from Maharashtra and creation of a state of Vidharbha. In the Jammu Region of Kashmir, where Hindus are in a majority, there is a movement for the area's separation from the Muslim-dominated vale and for its merger with adjoining state of Himachal Pradesh. The move has the blessings even of Karan Singh, for long the constitutional head of the state and later a Cabinet minister at the Centre. Since the spring of 1969 the demand for a state of Telengana has erupted in a violent form and on a mass scale leading to widespread arson in parts of Andhra and frequent police firing.

Quite apart from the continuous demands for creation of new state boundaries, the existing barriers are rising steadily, restricting people's mental horizons and encouraging a selfish, narrow outlook. Assam indulged in an orgy of linguistic hate in 1960 when its people massacred hundreds of Bengalis and burned their villages, even though the latter had lived and worked in the state for generations. Authorities in Bihar and Bengal have sponsored what is described as the "sons-of-the-soil policy," which in reality means only that workers from other states should not compete with local residents for jobs in the large industrial complex or big commercial houses located in the two states. In Orissa, students were on the rampage in the summer of 1967, opposing the screening of Telugu films and thereby demonstrating their hostility toward the neighboring state of Andhra. They also demanded that non-Oriyas be denied employment facilities in the state. In Maharashtra, and particularly in the capital city of Bombay, a militant near-Fascist organization, Shiv Sena, has become a factor to reckon with by merely feeding on parochial hate directed against the people of the South who come to Bombay to work as factory labor or junior clerks or to run small business. In 1969 the Sena gave the city of Bombay the worst experience of mob violence in a century and organized arson and terror against South Indians living in the metropolitan city. Economic compulsions undoubtedly play a part in forming this kind of restrictive attitude, but apparently a sense of national cohesion is not strong enough to mitigate them. A movement similar to Shiv Sena was launched in 1925 by the father of Bal Thakre, currently the supreme leader of the Sena. Jobs were scarcer then and the economic situation generally was far worse; yet the senior Thakre's efforts had almost no impact in Bombay.

The second decade of independence has given increasing evidence of a tendency on the part of political leaders to subordinate national interests to the requirements of their states or regions. In the mid-Sixties, India experienced what was described as the worst drought in a hundred years. Its reported severity prompted schoolchildren of distant Italy and Denmark to give up their lunch money to buy food for starving millions in India, but, tragically, the Indian states with surplus food were unwilling to part with it to help other areas in their own nation that were afflicted with drought. In some parts of India, people subsisted on a six-ounce daily ration per person while other parts had either no rationing or had more than double that quota of cereals. Even when public and political pressure compelled the surplus areas to share some of the sorrows and hardships of regions victimized by the elusiveness of the monsoon, they did so with visible reluctance. Immediately after a meeting of State Chief Ministers in Delhi, at which the Prime Minister had presided and at which they had pledged themselves to share and share alike, the Chief Minister of Punjab, an important surplus state, frankly remarked to newsmen that he had no intention of parting with his state's extra food. If necessary, he would get the police to stop food trucks from leaving the state boundaries on false traffic charges, he confessed.

States have also quarreled pettily and interminably over matters other than food. Relations between two of the country's major states, Maharashtra and Mysore, are embittered over a small border area. Years of negotiations at the initiative of the Central Ministry of Home Affairs have failed to solve the problem. So strong are the sentiments on this issue that in November 1966, when Indira Gandhi decided to give the Home Portfolio to Y. B. Chavan, a Maharashtrian, her decision led to a strong private protest from the then Mysore Chief Minister, Siddhavanahalli Nijalingappa, who feared that Chavan's presence in that ministry would adversely affect the Mysore case. Successive commissions and protracted talks over more than a decade have similarly failed to produce an agreement among the states of Andhra, Mysore and Maharashtra over sharing the waters of the Krishna and the Godavari, while Madhya Pradesh, Andhra and Orissa are tangled inextricably in another river-water dispute. In 1956, when the states were reorganized on a linguistic basis, an effort was launched to counter the divisiveness that such an arrangement encouraged. Four regional councils were to be created, each comprising chief ministers of the states in the region and headed by the Home Minister of the Central Government. The councils were to discuss important administrative and economic matters in which the states could act jointly for common good of the region. The councils were supposed to blur the state boundaries and create among the council members a sense of common purpose. With the passing of the years, however, the councils have languished, their meetings become steadily less frequent, and their agenda been overburdened with trivialities. In 1957–58 there were over ten meetings of the various councils; in 1967–68 there were only two such meetings.

Some of the decline of nationalistic fervor might have been mitigated if the compromise on official language that Nehru had offered in 1959 had been implemented then and not in 1968, by which time attitudes had hardened and blood had flowed in the streets in Hindi as well as non-Hindi areas.

Of India's fourteen recognized languages, the framers of Indian constitution chose Hindi to be the country's national official language in place of English, which, as a foreign language, could not be allowed to continue. The deadline for enthronement of Hindi was fixed as January 26, 1965, to allow for a fifteen-year period of transition after the introduction of the constitution. The urge for national unity and the antipathy to all symbols of foreign rule was strong in 1949, when the Constituent Assembly chose Hindi, but how divided opinion was on this delicate subject even then is indicated by the fact that the Congress Party in the Assembly made its decision in favor of Hindi in a private caucus with a majority of a single vote.

That English must give place to an Indian language was not seriously disputed then, but enthusiasm for Hindi was limited to the northern region. Apart from the fact it was an alien language and a reminder of foreign colonial domination, English was understood by less than 2 percent of the people at the time of independence. It was too much to expect that it would ever become a language of mass communication or a vehicle of creative thought on any extensive scale. Gandhi, Nehru and others who led the freedom movement, many of whom themselves spoke and wrote English remarkably well, were as anxious to free the Indian mind of the domination of English as they were to rid the country of British power.

Hindi's claim to be the national language was undoubtedly the strongest among the Indian languages. On the basis of the census data, the government claims that Hindi is the language of 43 percent of the people of India. As such, it is spoken by a larger number than any other language. In its claim to take the place of English, however, it suffered from two drawbacks. First, it had almost no vocabulary of modern political and scientific terms, and, second, it was the language of the north; to the people of the south and east it symbolized northern domination over the rest of the country. The latter was the more serious of the two handicaps.

The single-vote majority by which it was accepted by the Congress Party in the Constituent Assembly indicates the volume of opposition to Hindi. The antipathy to Hindi's elevation as the national official language was particularly strong in the southern states. The south had always looked at the north with a degree of hostility and nursed the grievance that the latter exercised political power well beyond its due and that the south was not allowed to play the role to which it was entitled by its cultural superiority. The Vindhya mountain range, which divides the north from the south, constituted not only a physical but also an emotional barrier between the two regions. On the eastern side, the Bengalis felt overwhelming pride in the superiority of their language, particularly the richness of its literature. If in recognition of Hindi as the successor to English the south saw yet another imposition from the traditional direction, the people of Bengal in the eastern section of the nation regarded it as a cultural affront.

The south had another reason to be wary of Hindi as the official language for communication between states and the Centre and among the states themselves. Possibly because Madras was among the first footholds of British power, the people of the south attained a greater and more extensive mastery over English. Consequently, they secured a substantially larger proportion of Central Government jobs at all levels than people from the other areas. The replacement of English by Hindi would deprive them of that superiority and place them at a decided disadvantage in their competition with the north Indians for whom Hindi was the mother tongue.

Resistance to Hindi was, thus, considerable. Only a sense of party discipline made Congress members who had opposed Hindi in the party caucus support it later in the Constituent Assembly. The party whip, however, could not dispel the mental reservations that they nurtured.

Several of the fourteen languages formally listed in the constitution as the languages of India had more extensive vocabulary and richer literature than Hindi. Bengali, for example, is acknowledged to be considerably more expressive and melodious than Hindi. Similarly, Marathi, the language spoken in Maharashtra, and Tamil, one of the four principal languages of the south, could justifiably claim qualitative superiority over Hindi. Some of the languages had grown out of different sources and had their own scripts. The south Indian languages—Tamil, Telugu, Kanari and Malayali—had a pre-Aryan origin and, as such, claimed a distinctive history and background. Hindi, like many other Indian languages, had not had the time to ac-

quire an impressive literature of its own or even develop a pronounced literary tradition. An outgrowth of Sanskrit, it was
born in its present form not more than two or three centuries
ago as the language of the man in the street in the Gangetic
region. Indeed, its strength lay in its plebeian character.

Because of the reservations non-Hindi-speaking areas entertained about accepting Hindi as the national official language
and because of Hindi's verbal limitations, the replacement of
English was deferred for fifteen years—a compromise between
the protagonists of Hindi and its opponents. By 1965, it was
hoped, Hindi could overcome its inadequacies through concerted government efforts. Furthermore, any immediate establishment of Hindi as the national official language would have
created an administrative chaos, since the non-Hindi states
would have no means of communication with the Centre and
with each other. Even where Hindi was spoken, not many administrators knew the language with any degree of proficiency.

Thus, Hindi should have moved forward to take its place
modestly and slowly—almost surreptitiously. It did not have the
backing of an autocratic regime, as English did, and it should
have become the official or "link" language through a gradual
process of acceptability. But this is precisely what did not happen. The progress of Hindi as successor to English was marked
by lack of political foresight and by administrative ineptness and
remarkable aggressiveness and arrogance on the part of its protagonists.

If he had been alive during this period, Gandhi would have
been shocked and distressed by the course that the issue of a
national language took after independence. He had always suggested Hindustani as the country's official language. Hindustani
was a confluence of Hindi and Urdu (the two languages have a
large common vocabulary). He even favored two scripts for
Hindustani—the Devanagri script based on Sanskrit and the
Persian script in which Urdu was customarily written. To his
mind, such a two-script language, apart from being widely acceptable, would also promote communal unity, since Hindi had

acquired strong cultural meaning with the Hindus while Urdu had similar associations for Muslims. By the time the Constituent Assembly of India came to decide the language issue, however, Gandhi had died, Muslims had won a homeland in Pakistan, and the urge to placate them and reassure them against the cultural domination of the majority community had virtually disappeared. Hindi, and not Hindustani, was chosen as the official language.

It was not realized at the time, or even later, that even if the creation of Pakistan had canceled the Muslims' right to be reassured against linguistic domination, there were other sections of the nation that might entertain similar fears that needed to be allayed. Nehru perceived this aspect of the problem when he argued that Hindi as the national language would be different from Hindi as a regional language. Like all regional languages, Hindi should develop into a rich language with extensive vocabulary, but as the "link" between the Centre and the states and among the states themselves, Hindi should have a simple, practical form in which people of the non-Hindi areas might acquire proficiency quickly. If, as Nehru had suggested, Hindi had developed two distinct identities, much of the bitterness over this issue might have been avoided. But, as in several other situations, Nehru charted the right course and yet would not compel people to move along it when they seemed unwilling.

Far from developing a simple, common language for the entire people and allowing it to accumulate a large vocablary of widely understood words, the Hindi protagonists abandoned many of the words the language already had and overburdened it with heavy words, little known or specially manufactured, based on Sanskrit vocabulary. New expressions, unwieldy and unnatural, were incorporated by the thousand, replacing ordinary words like "engine," "ticket" and "railway station" which Hindi had acquired from English and other popular expressions it had accepted from Urdu during the previous century and which were understood even by the illiterate. Committees of experts attended to this task of enriching the language, and their efforts, the sheer ludicrousness of which caused occasional mirth, had the unfortunate effect of making many even in the Hindi region feel linguistic aliens and causing deep resentment in other areas. The state-owned All-India Radio took to new Sanskritized Hindi with the zeal of a crusader and made it necessary for the average listener in the north to switch to English news instead of Hindi. In the south, the reaction was so adverse that the movement for voluntary study of Hindi, which had made impressive progress in the early years of independence, came almost to an end. The attitudes hardened to such an extent that those who had previously pleaded for the study of Hindi began calling vociferously for the continuation of English. As a political writer remarked of the way the language issue was handled, "nothing could be a more pathetic demonstration of academic bumbling combined with political fatuousness."

In 1959, during a debate in Parliament, Nehru sought to reassure the non-Hindi areas by offering to retain English as an "associate" official language even after 1965, when Hindi would assume the status of national language, and for as long as even a single non-Hindi state felt it was not ready to give up the foreign language. But the Prime Minister's offer was quietly sabotaged by the Hindi lobby in Parliament and the government. The President's order on official language, issued some months later, made no reference to the Prime Minister's offer. In February 1965 Prime Minister Shastri invited the state Chief Ministers to review the language problem—Madras had greeted Hindi's formal emergence as the national language with an extensive orgy of arson and violence—and the Indian leaders found themselves repeating arguments and suggesting solutions offered six years earlier. But even the trauma of the Madras riots did not make them implement the compromise that Nehru had proposed. It was only in 1968, after many more lives had been lost and much property destroyed in anger throughout north and south, that Nehru's promise about continuance of English as an optional official language was given a statutory basis.

This compromise may discourage future conflict and mass vi-

olence, but it is doubtful that it will dismantle the mental and
emotional barriers erected in the two decades following independence. Even without the intervention of interested parties,
language is almost certain to retain its divisive character because
of an allied decision. In placating local chauvinism, the government has gone to the extent of ordering that the medium of in-
struction even at the university level be the regional language. It
has also directed the Union Public Service Commission, which
recruits officials for all important all-India services, including
the Indian Foreign Service, Indian Administrative Service and
the Indian Educational Service, to conduct its examinations in
all of the fourteen Indian languages. The results of this decision
in terms of national solidarity are not difficult to imagine. The
movement of students, teachers and bureaucrats from one state
to another will almost stop. Most civil servants will lack proficiency in any language other than their own and will not be
equipped linguistically to serve at the Centre as they do at present. Even senior civil servants will have to confine themselves
to the states to which they belong, and the flow of administrative
experience between the Centre and the states will be greatly restricted. State government officials will not, as they have in the
past, bring to the Centre an awareness of regional problems and
predilections and carry back to the states at the end of their
tenure in Delhi a wider perspective and a consciousness of India's
identity as a nation.

5: *Kafirs, Untouchables and the Limits of Tolerance*

On the question of Hindu-Muslim understanding, Nehru's
thinking was marked by the same acute awareness of the threat
to national unity from this direction that he displayed over the
language problem. He pleaded with people to give up thinking in
restrictive religious terms. Religion, he argued, should be one's
personal business and not permitted to influence political and
administrative decisions. But many in the government and the

party seemingly did not have their hearts in what he prescribed. Constitutionally, India is a secular state in which all citizens, whether Hindu, Muslim, Sikh or Christian, have equal rights. Discrimination on the basis of religion, creed, race or sex is strictly forbidden. The laws are quite clear on this point, and should there be any case of discrimination, the victim would be entitled to legal redress. But secularism is also a state of mind, and neither the Hindus, the majority community constituting nearly 85 percent of the country's population, nor the Muslims, who form the principal religious minority, have succeeded in acquiring that attitude. The prospects of their developing a secular mind have been diminishing steadily since Nehru's death.

The violence exhibited by the Hindus at the time of partition assumes added dimension when considered in the context of the emphasis that their religion places on practice of nonviolence and preservation of life. That life—not only human life, but all life, including animals and insects—is sacred is accepted by most Hindus unquestioningly as part of the basic fabric of their beliefs. Many among the more orthodox Hindus place rice or wheat flour near ant-hills every morning as part of their duty to preserve life. The average Hindu would hesitate to swat a fly or kill a cockroach that might be bothering him. Even those among the Hindus who eat meat would not kill a chicken or a goat themselves. Many cannot bear to see an animal being slaughtered or even buy meat from the local butcher. Yet many Hindus committed acts of unspeakable brutality against fellow human beings when roused by hatred and suppressed anger. Helpless Muslims, including women and children, were slain mercilessly or subjected to atrocities.

Similar acts of brutality were committed on an even wider scale and perhaps with greater callousness by the people in Pakistan. Hindu refugee tales of atrocities committed in Pakistan undoubtedly provided the immediate provocation for the retaliatory action on the Indian side.

But reports of these incidents only supplied the spark; the combustible material in the form of communal strife and animosity had always been there. What the instinctive respect for the sacredness of life and the exhortations of charismatic national leaders had to contend with was not merely a spate of disturbing, provocative reports from across the border, but almost seven centuries of humiliation that the Hindus had suffered during the Muslim rule of India and the attitudes of insecurity and hostility which that rule had created in them.

The first violent impact of Muslim power on India was felt at the beginning of the eleventh century, when Mahmud of Ghazni carried as many as seventeen raids deep into the Gangetic plains, plundering India's wealth, laying waste its beautiful cities such as Thanesar (1014) and Kanauj (1018) and desecrating its temples. In the centuries that followed, other Muslim kings established their power over a vast part of India. Occasionally some enlightened ruler such as Akbar tried to treat them with consideration, but by and large the Hindus received harshness and were regarded with contempt as "kafirs" (nonbelievers) for whom Islam prescribed no mercy. There were long periods of repression, forcible conversions, imposition of harsh levies specifically on the Hindus, plundering of temples and destruction of Hindu libraries and cultural centers. Tales are constantly told of how women of Hindu princely families burned themselves alive on a common pyre after their menfolk were defeated and killed on the battlefield at the hands of the Muslim kings. Today, centuries later, these memories of past humiliation still influence the attitude of the average Hindu.

At the same time, the Muslims, now reduced to a 10-percent minority, nostalgically think of centuries of dominance they exercised before the advent of the British. One characteristic that several scholars of Islamic history have noted is the Muslims' inability to blend with another religious group or live in a position of equality with it. Muslims, they point out, are fiercely jealous of their communal identity, and when confronted with another group, they either dominate it or allow themselves to be subjugated by it. The situation in present-day India challenges both these instincts. The predominantly Hindu environment is constantly trying to engulf them and deprive them of their Islamic identity. Other religious groups, such as the Buddhists and Jains, have been devoured by the quicksands of Hinduism, and Islam feels similarly threatened. The democratic processes based on adult franchise and devoid of civil-service job allocations and other privileges the minorities enjoyed under the British reduce the Muslims to the position of minor, ineffective shareholders in political power.

In strictly religious terms, Hinduism and Islam have little in common. They have grown out of totally different historical and social backgrounds, have no common deities and profess widely divergent basic tenets. According to Dr. B. R. Ambedkar, a scholar of repute and one of the foremost leaders of the "Untouchable" community (the lowest stratum of the caste-structured Hindu society), the past of the Hindus and Muslims "is embedded in their religion, and for each to give up its past is to give up its religion." And what was their past? In Ambedkar's words, "they have been just two armed battalions warring against each other. There was no common cycle of participation for a common achievement. Their past is a past of mutual destruction—a past of mutual animosities, in the political as well as in the religious fields."

It is a measure of the protracted nature of this conflict between the Hindus and Muslims that those whom the latter regard as heroes are considered by the former as tyrants and oppressors, while the Hindu heroes are almost always those who challenged Muslim power and contributed to its ultimate weakening. A sense of mutual hostility is, thus, deeply rooted in the psyche of the two communities and explains the hysterical way in which each tends to react to any provocation from the other.

Before independence, whenever there was a Hindu-Muslim riot in India, Indian leaders pointed an accusing finger at the British rulers for dividing the two principal communities. Communal tension, it was consolingly suggested, was the creation of the British, who wished to perpetuate their dominance over the country by dividing its people. The British undoubtedly exploited the tension between the two communities, but, as continuance of communal rioting in the years following independence confirms, they did not create this phenomenon.

In fact, even if partition riots be dismissed as the by-product of an unusual political upheaval, seldom did the Hindu-Muslim conflict assume the intensity and scale under the British that it has done at times in recent years. The British employed methods typical of any foreign power that intends to make its rule last as long as possible. In their endeavor to prevent Indian nationalism from confronting them as a united force, they tended to play one community against the other and occasionally even to foment religious conflict. During the last three decades of their rule, which coincided with the growth of a powerful urge for independence among the Indian masses, the British concern for religious minority groups seemed to deepen suddenly. At all stages of the constitutional reforms during this period, the British government stubbornly insisted on maintaining the separate identity of the various religious groups and encouraging them to stand apart from the Hindus. In all services—from the Indian Civil Service at the top to revenue staff at the level of the village— special quotas were fixed for Muslims, Sikhs and Christians. This privilege was also extended to the "untouchables," or the "Scheduled Castes," as they were described, even though technically they were Hindus. Similarly, seats were reserved for various groups in legislatures, whether elected or nominated. In the elections held under the Government of India Act of 1935, a person could cast his vote only for a candidate belonging to his own religious group.

Such analysis of British maneuvers to divide the people of India would be in perspective only if one also mentioned the futile efforts that Gandhi and other national leaders constantly made to bring them together. The Congress Party was avowedly secular, and its leaders genuinely tried to enlist the support of all communities, particularly Muslims, but with indifferent success. Gandhi associated the party energetically with the Khilafat movement of 1920, not because the end of the Caliphate in

Turkey had any bearing on the Indian independence movement, but because the Muslims of India were distressed over the dismemberment of the Turkish empire; by making common cause with them on that issue, Gandhi sought to build a bridge of understanding and amity between the two communities. While the movement lasted, there was much demonstration of Hindu-Muslim unity, but by 1922 their traditional divisiveness had reasserted itself. In 1940 the Muslim League had passed the resolution for the country's partition to create for the Muslims a separate "homeland." The league was then a small body and its supreme leader, M. A. Jinnah, a grand but lonely figure. In the long period between the Khilafat movement and the rise of the Muslim League, the Muslim masses had no strong party nor any towering leader nor any appealing slogan to rival the Congress Party and its movement, and yet they were not drawn into the party on any significant scale. Muslims like Dr. Ansari, Maulana Azad, Khan Abdul Ghaffar Khan and Asaf Ali attained positions of eminence in the Congress Party and freedom movement, but they did not bring into the party many Muslim followers or involve them in the agitation against the British. If the British endeavor was to keep the Muslims away from the Hindus, Gandhi and other Congress leaders were constantly trying to bring the two communities together and give them a sense of common purpose. But it was the British who succeeded.

It was not the offer of a few reserved jobs at various levels or other enticements of a similar nature that enabled the British to keep the Muslims away from the Congress Party. The Muslims had no particular reason to be drawn to the foreign rulers or be excessively influenced by them, for it was the British who had deprived them of political power and ended their seven-century period of dominance. The Mutiny of 1857, essentially a Muslim effort to regain some of that power, was ruthlessly crushed and the Muslim sense of pride suffered the humiliation of seeing Bahadur Shah, the last of the Moghul emperors, deposed and exiled to Burma to die in pathetic circumstances. For decades after the Mutiny, the British power regarded the Muslims with suspicion, while the latter tended to cut themselves away from the reigning authority and withdraw into a shell of hopelessness and indifference. If, despite this background of hostility and antagonism, the British were able to keep the Muslims separated from the Hindus, it was because their prompting was in harmony with the sense of estrangement that had traditionally existed between the two communities. It was the same inherent alienation that frustrated the Congress Party's concerted efforts to win over the Muslims and turned a seemingly rootless political party, the Muslim League, into a massive force and Jinnah, for long a neglected, lonesome figure in Indian politics, into a power whom the combined charisma of Gandhi and Nehru could not challenge.

The riots which broke out in the city of Jabbalpore in 1961 represent a landmark, as far as independent India's communal problem is concerned. They ended a fourteen-year period in which, notwithstanding what the Pakistani propaganda machine alleged at home and in the United Nations, India was virtually free from serious Hindu-Muslim clashes. Since Jabbalpore, though, and despite the soul-searching at the top and conscious efforts to integrate the communities following the outbreak, the country has witnessed a succession of riots at points as distant from one another as Meerut in western Uttar Pradesh, Ranchi in eastern Bihar and Nagpur in northern Maharashtra. In some of them—for example, at Ranchi in the spring of 1964 and at Ahmedabad in 1969—hundreds were killed and the army had to be called in to quell mass violence. They reflected a measure of venom that few clashes had displayed before partition, when Hindu-Muslim relations were supposedly more abrasive and when a foreign power was at hand to exploit them.

In the years immediately following independence it seemed as if relations between the two communities were on the mend. Perhaps, as many thought, the massacres in which the two communities had indulged on both sides of the India-Pakistan border had purged them of mutual hatred and suspicion. This conclusion was unduly optimistic. The real reasons for the respite in communal clashes were different and temporary. Partition had left the Muslims who could not move to Pakistan dazed and bewildered. The country's division had provided a "homeland" for only those Muslims who belonged to the Muslim-majority parts of India and had left over thirty-five million Muslims as a minority in the new, truncated India. After the heady feeling of success when Pakistan was conceded and Jinnah and other Muslim League leaders had departed to Karachi to assume power came the depressing realization that Pakistan had not brought the promised land for every Muslim in the subcontinent. How perverse and irrational some people's involvement in political agitation can be is demonstrated by the fact that the most spirited support for the concept of Pakistan had come from the Muslims of Uttar Pradesh and Bihar, who formed minority pockets in overwhelmingly Hindu areas and whose home states could by no stretch of imagination have been ceded to the new country. While agitating for Pakistan, they had formed in their minds a picture of Pakistan that had no relevance to the real political or geographical situation. Later their bitterness made them lament that Jinnah had deceived them. In the first years of independence, therefore, the harshness of political realities, the sense of vulnerability and fear of reprisals for their earlier aggressiveness made the Indian Muslims withdraw defensively into a shell.

The clashes in Jabbalpore marked the end of the period in which the Muslims stayed huddled together stoically and defensively while the majority community lived through the catharsis brought on by the murder of a saintlike leader. These moods, based as they were on temporary factors, were bound to change.

In recent years, therefore, the basic attitudes of conflict between the two religious communities have asserted themselves again. What is more, the display of communal distrust and antagonism shows little evidence that Nehru's efforts to strengthen communal bonds have had any effect.

As a community, the Muslims broke their silence about their grievances at a conference in Delhi in 1960. Muslim leaders—including some, such as Maulana Hifz-ur-Rehman and Dr. Syed

Mahmud, whose credentials as opponents of partition were impeccable—complained that the members of the community were living in the new India as second-class citizens. Some of the allegations were exaggerated, for those who leveled them were playing to a Muslim gallery. There was a distinct endeavor on their part to win followers from among people who were just emerging from a sort of political hibernation. But the charge was not without substance. Partly because they had withdrawn into a shell and partly owing to communal prejudice, economic and education opportunities had passed the Muslims by in the first decade of independence. Politically their voice counted for little because their leaders had either migrated to Pakistan or had been rendered inactive by their past association with the demand for the creation of Pakistan. The opening years of independence had seen an enormous increase in national economic activitity, but the Muslims had received only a very small portion of the benefits flowing from it. The government, under Nehru, bravely tried to bring Muslims into the services, but its hands were tied because it could no longer offer them the protection and deferential (if not preferential) treatment that the community had enjoyed under the British. In open competitive examinations for recruitment to government services, the Muslims inevitably lagged behind the Hindus, who had taken to Western education earlier and with greater enthusiasm. As plans to modernize the economy were launched, the bulk of new opportunities arose in the field of commerce and industry, traditionally dominated by the Hindus. As far as the Muslims were concerned, leadership and political power had normally come from the landed aristocracy, a class whose influence and power shriveled under the impact of socialist concepts like the abolition of landlordism. The Muslims thus saw the gap between themselves and the majority community grow visibly, and they complained bitterly.

The Hindu reaction to the Muslim charge was wholly along expected lines. By the time the Muslim voice was raised, Gandhi and his assassination had become vague memories, but the generation of Hindus that had been driven out of its homes and forcibly deprived of its property in Pakistan was still in positions of power and influence in India. The Muslim grievance, therefore, appeared to the average Hindu as unfair—in fact, as bordering on impertinence—and it invited anger, not sympathy. The element of exaggeration in the community's complaint of being reduced to second-class citizenship tended to obscure even the valid aspects of its grievance. In many a Hindu mind, the Muslim conference stirred memories of past conflict and roused fears that, instead of living in political docility, the Muslims intended to live aggressively and assertively. Since 1960, therefore, the two communities have moved steadily toward confrontation, bitterness and periodic bloodshed.

To suggest, as many in India do, that the recent communal tensions are the work of mischievous *agent provocateurs* is to oversimplify the problem and miss the forest in spotting a few trees. There have, of course, been occasions when riots were the outcome of baseless rumors mischievously spread, but such rumors would not work or at least not lead to such bloody consequences as the riots in Calcutta, Ranchi, Allahabad, Nagpur and Meerut if the basic attitudes of suspicion and antagonism did not exist. A study by the central Ministry of Home Affairs in the summer of 1968 clearly acknowledged that the real causes of the tension went deep into "the thinking and attitudes of the two communities."

There is no evidence that these attitudes are changing or even softening. The clash of economic interests could be averted through some careful planning but cultural and religious hostilities are perhaps rooted too deep to eradicate. Additionally, there are psychological factors that make the process of conciliation nearly an impossibility. Hinduism has just emerged from centuries of political domination and helplessness. For the first time it is in a position to lay down the law to those outside the faith, and consequently there is a tendency to act arrogantly and irrationally. Legislative action to ban cow slaughter and the attempts by "Sadhus" and other orthodox elements among the Hindus to browbeat the states that were unenthusiastic in this respect is a manifestation of that aggressive and intolerant state of the Hindu mind. Islam, on the other hand, retains its attitude of contempt and intolerance toward the Hindus, and the Muslims are not prepared to come to terms with the Hindus by acknowledging their political supremacy. For a religion that does not advocate conversions from other faiths, Hinduism has a strangely acquisitive instinct and capacity to absorb other sects. It has assimilated Buddhism and Jainism. Christianity in India is increasingly acquiring Hindu characteristics. Islam, on the other hand, is fiercely individualistic and proud and has refused to become part of an amorphous culture. To Hinduism, Islam is a challenge; to Islam, Hinduism today seems a renewed threat. What equation they would ultimately develop is difficult to imagine, but before they learn to coexist in harmony they may greatly enfeeble the forces striving to build Indian unity.

POLITICS: IMPORTED
AND DOMESTIC

1: *A Cumbersome Transplant*

INDIAN POLITICAL LEADERS and columnists seldom miss an opportunity to express satisfaction over how well the nation's political institutions have been functioning since independence. After every general election—five have been held so far—there are extensive references to the genuineness of India's democracy, the maturity of the electorate and the degree of sophistication that political processes have attained despite 76-percent illiteracy. Every change of prime minister is similarly greeted with smug declarations about the ability of Indian politicians to keep the struggle for power within bounds of democratic proprieties. Parliament is praised for its vigilance in keeping the executive on its toes while the "panchayats" (elected councils of village elders) are lauded for providing roots to democracy.

The claims that commentators make on behalf of India's political system are sometimes exaggerated, but they are not untrue. For the first two decades of independence India has presented a spectacle of political stability uncommon in Asia. It has held elections to national and state legislatures at regular intervals prescribed in the constitution, preserved the independence of its judiciary, and permitted its press to function freely and vocally, and its Parliament has been as assertive as and noticeably less susceptible to vested interests than the legislatures of some older democracies. Even changes in national leadership were effected in considerable calm. Many Western observers who had predicted the "deluge" after Nehru were surprised at the placid and dignified manner in which the succession issue was settled.

The expressions of satisfaction by Indians and wonderment by foreigners over the working of the political system is, in fact, only a reflection of the doubts that both had entertained about its likely durability. Pakistan, which formed part of the subcontinent, had suffered a succession of ineffective regimes and finally come under military dictatorship in 1958 without holding an election or adopting a democratically debated constitution. Neighboring Burma, which attained freedom at virtually the same time as India, had similarly come under the authoritarian rule of an army general in 1962. India, which shared its neighbors' temperament and limitations as well as their history, was naturally expected to undergo similar tribulations and perhaps move in the same direction. And while these fears have not been realized, they have increased markedly since the 1967 general election, in which the setback the Congress Party suffered exposed the constitutional structure to severe stresses for the first time. The organizational split in the Congress in the autumn of 1969, the frequency with which governments have changed in certain states and the multiplicity of political parties have sustained and strengthened these doubts.

The principal criticism of the system was that it was foreign and unsuited to India's temperament and needs. The parliamentary institutions that the constitution-makers chose to set up were a more or less exact copy of the British system. That it was alien made many doubt it would endure. India's needs and circumstances were radically different from those of Britain, and it seemed unlikely that what had grown up in Britain over centuries would take root in a virtually arid soil. Except for brief periods during the last decade of the British Raj, when semi-autonomous legislatures were set up, Indians had had no experience of the working of parliamentary institutions. They also had almost no traditions of democracy. The "panchayat," often described as an embodiment of grass-root democracy, was in reality nothing more than a council of village elders who dispensed justice in an *ad hoc* manner. The sense of personal rights and individual dignity basic to a democracy was seldom evident in Indian society. Indians, in fact, though highly individualistic in temperament, have traditionally respected stern authoritarian administrations. What they yearn for is a just society, not a democratic one. To combine justice with almost total personal freedom, as the Indian constitution adopted in 1950 sought to do, therefore seemed a daring venture with uncertain chances of success.

The constitution goes to considerable length in enumerating and safeguarding personal rights and freedoms. It specifically lists "fundamental rights" that include, besides the right to work and own property, the right to free speech and association and elections on the basis of universal adult franchise. At the time the constitution was being framed, universal suffrage appeared a privilege of doubtful value in a country where eighty percent of the people could not even write their names. Their illiteracy, combined with the state of abject poverty in which they lived, seemed liable to render them pawns in the hands of unscrupulous political manipulators. But the suggestion that the franchise be limited in the initial stages and enlarged as education spread and political consciousness grew was not favored. Nehru argued in the Constituent Assembly—and others agreed with him—that adult suffrage would hasten the process of consciousness. Prevailing views regarded the danger of the illiterate masses misusing their vote as less ominous than the possibility that those who might acquire power on the basis of a limited franchise would prove unwilling to share it with others later.

In the choice of the particular legislative system, Nehru's personal predilections and the influence of British thought and experience on other leaders undoubtedly played its part. For a country of India's size and diversity, the presidential system of government might have been more meaningful. The direct election of an individual to exercise top authority might have been easier for a villager to comprehend than voting for an individual who seeks his support in the name of an intangible entity such as a party. In a country where extensive illiteracy makes it necessary for each party to be described by a picture symbol on the ballot paper, the parliamentary system asks the voter to understand such complexities as the role of the individual candidate in a party, a party's relationship with its leader, the leader's prospects of becoming the country's chief executive and his dual responsibility to his party on the one hand and to the entire Parliament on the other. But such considerations received scant attention. The British system was the one that the leaders understood, and they unhesitatingly chose it for India. Many years later, when an interviewer tried to argue with him about the suitability of the British system, Nehru reportedly cut short the discussion by saying that "we wanted it, we got it, and we have grown up with it."

Like the British Parliament, the Indian Parliament is comprised of two houses. The lower house—the Lok Sabha, or the House of the People, made up of 525 members—is directly elected and, like the House of Commons in Britain, exercises the real legislative authority. The Rajya Sabha, the upper house, is almost half the size of the Lok Sabha, is indirectly elected by the state legislatures and, in the manner of the House of Lords, is intended principally to provide a healthy check on the lower house. On a smaller scale, the same arrangement exists in the states, except that the legislatures are bicameral only in the larger states.

The first Speaker of the Lok Sabha, the late G. V. Mavalankar, once described the British parliamentary practice as the "ideal" and then added with obvious reverence that that could only be "reached in the course of time." In an endeavor to attain that "ideal," the Indian legislators imitate the British procedures almost slavishly. Having had the advantage of modern planning, the parliamentary chambers in New Delhi are more suitably designed than those occupied by the "Mother of Parliaments"; there is no traditional "despatch box" in front of the Prime Minister's seat and the Speaker does not wear a wig, but there the dissimilarity ends. The rules of procedure are virtually the same as in British Parliament, and May's Parliamentary Practices is as much a bible in New Delhi as in London. Even the terminology, form of address ("Will the Honourable Member on the Treasury benches . . .") and mannerisms are typically British. The similarity between the two parliaments was considerably more pronounced in the earlier years, when the Lok Sabha membership had a substantial percentage of Western-educated professional classes (more than 20 percent of the members in the first Lok Sabha were lawyers). Many of them had functioned in the pre-independence Central Assembly or were otherwise familiar with the British legislative system. They spoke fluent English and observed the British parliamentary idiom and style strictly. Nehru himself practiced the form devotedly. Over the years, the membership has become more diffused, and its composition has demonstrated the impact of adult franchise. More members now express themselves in Hindi than in English, and there is a tendency on their part to be indifferent to the verbal refinements and the formalism of the British system. But the essentials are still carefully preserved.

As in Britain, the leader of the party or coalition commanding majority in the Lok Sabha becomes the country's Prime Minister. He may—again as in Britain—pick his Cabinet from among members of either house of Parliament. If a minister is not a member of Parliament he must, under the constitution, get himself elected within six months of his appointment. Such appointments of nonmembers are made infrequently and in unusual circumstances. Mrs. Gandhi, for example, was appointed a minister on her father's death, although she was not an M.P. She was elected to the Rajya Sabha within the prescribed period.

An apparent similarity to the American system is that the head of the state in India is designated President. The likeness, however, is superficial. Chosen by an electoral college comprising legislators at the Centre or the Federal level and in the states, the President in India is only a ceremonial head. He exercises no authority. His presence is intended to provide the administration with a sense of continuity and stability in a system in which governments could well change frequently. All his duties are ritualistic. Like the monarch in Britain, he formally inaugurates the budget session of Parliament, but his address is prepared for him by the government and enunciates the policy of the party in office. The pronouncements and orders that he may sometimes issue must represent the decisions of the administration and not his own judgment. He is supposed to act only on the Prime Minister's advice. If no party is in a position to form the government in a state, the state is placed temporarily under what is described as the President's rule. But the President exercises the authority only nominally; in fact, the state is administered by the Central Government until fresh elections are held and constitutional processes can be resumed.

Thus far, the President has exercised influence in accordance with his personal equation with the Prime Minister and the strength of his personality. India's first President, Rajendra Prasad, was a leader of considerable stature, but he wielded no influence over the government, for Nehru was critical—almost contemptuous—of his orthodoxy. Support for Prasad in the Congress Party was so extensive that despite Nehru's opposition he held the Presidency for twelve years, but the impact of his views on the administration was negligible. Sarvepalli Radhakrishnan, who succeeded him in 1962, on the other hand, received much greater consideration from the government, though he had almost no political service to his credit. Inevitably, an assertive President wields power when the Prime Minister is weak or on the defensive. Radhakrishnan publicly spoke out against Krishna Menon when the latter's mishandling of affairs as Defense Minister caused India humiliation at the hands of the

Chinese. He tended to treat Shastri with unconstitutional stern-ness—indeed, almost bullied him—when the latter succeeded Nehru as Prime Minister and seemed somewhat unsure of him-self. Later, a more confident Shastri virtually ignored Radha-krishnan.

As long as Nehru was Prime Minister, discussion about the President's authority and the extent to which he may or may not disregard the "advice" of the Prime Minister was purely an aca-demic exercise. The possibilities for confusion and diverse inter-pretation were, however, always there. Prasad, as first President, never chose to disagree with the Council of Ministers, but aca-demically he once argued that since conditions in India differed from those in Great Britain, "it may not be desirable to treat ourselves as strictly bound by the interpretations which have been given from time to time . . . in England." Himself a law-yer, Prasad had presided over the Constituent Assembly deliber-ations and seemingly spoke in awareness of the spirit in which the constitution was framed. K. M. Munshi, another eminent lawyer and politician who had served in the Constituent Assem-bly, argued that the President's powers included "dismissal of a Prime Minister who does not enjoy leadership of his party; dis-missal of a ministry which has lost the confidence of Parliament. . . ." Others, including on one occasion the Supreme Court, have expressed the belief that the constitution is vague regarding some aspects of Presidential authority and responsibility be-cause it assumed that the British pattern would prevail and that the President, though elected, would function strictly as a mon-arch.

The conclusion that one may draw from these periodic argu-ments is that in general the British convention in regard to the acceptance of ministerial advice must prevail, but that there are some areas, still uncharted either by the written constitution or by precedent, in which the President may possess discretionary powers.

For a country moving steadily toward legislative instability, multi-party coalitions and narrow-majority or even minority governments, the uncertainty over the President's discretion could be a serious factor. In fact, it was this imponderability about the President's role that prompted an otherwise diffident Mrs. Gandhi to have a showdown with her rivals led by the old-guard leaders. The clash was caused when the latter selected N. Sanjiva Reddy as a candidate for the Presidency. The post had fallen vacant in mid-term due to the sudden death of Dr. Zakir Hussain, whom Mrs. Gandhi had trusted and for whose election in 1967 she had worked energetically. Reddy, on the other hand, though an old member of her own party, was a committed opponent. In his selection by the party executive as the Congress nominee for the Presidential election, she and her advisers saw the beginning of a plan by which Reddy would take advantage of the undefined nature of the President's authority to remove her from the Prime Ministership. She therefore chose to oppose Reddy by putting up against him V. V. Giri, who enjoyed her confidence. To get her nominee elected President, she acted as if she was fighting for survival and was undeterred even by the prospect of a major split in the Congress Party.

As in Britain, real authority is vested in the Prime Minister, who enjoys total freedom in choosing his Cabinet and devising the policies of the government. The President may formally issue some orders, but they represent the decisions of the government over which the Prime Minister presides. For his power, the Prime Minister looks not upward to the President, but toward members of Parliament and through them to the electorate. He stays in office as long as he enjoys the goodwill of the majority of the members of the Lok Sabha. While he has that support, he is supposed to wield tremendous authority. All members of the government retain office at his discretion, and he may exclude any minister from the Cabinet without explanation or summarily overrule his decisions. In 1969, for example, Mrs. Gandhi suddenly took the important Finance Portfolio from Morarji Desai, without any convincing explanation. When Desai protested and tendered his resignation, she advised the President to accept it. Thus she virtually dismissed one who ranked in the government next only to the Prime Minister and was acknowledged as a leader of considerable standing.

Actually, however, the Prime Minister's authority is not so extensive as such stray incidents may suggest. A Prime Minister must carry his party with him in the Lok Sabha. His party must have the majority strength or, if it does not, the Prime Minister must secure the support of other parties and factions in the Parliament to give him the necessary majority. He must, therefore, constantly see that his government does nothing which would alienate any group within his own party and prompt them to withdraw their support. If his own party lacks the necessary majority, he must additionally watch the mood of other groups in the Lok Sabha and endeavor to win over a sufficient number of members to secure the majority support he must have on all issues before the legislature. Since October 1969, when a split in the Congress Party she headed deprived her of a clear majority, Mrs. Gandhi had continued in office, but in order to do so she had had to depend on the goodwill of opposition groups such as the Communists and right-wing Akali Dal. The constant need to appease groups with divergent ideologies had inevitably restricted her freedom of action to a great extent.

Even if the Prime Minister commands a majority in the Lok Sabha, his exercise of authority is subjected to certain subtle restraints. The Congress Parliamentary Party, which has run the federal government since independence, meets regularly to discuss the party's program and decide what the government's stand on specific legislative proposals should be. It does not always impose its will on the Prime Minister, but the latter must carefully take note of its mood and decide how far he can go against its wishes on a specific issue. Often it is not very far. The executive committee of the party, composed of less than twenty-five members, meets more frequently—sometimes twice a week —and has customarily expressed itself fairly bluntly on government policies. It was the executive that virtually compelled Nehru to dismiss Krishna Menon as Defense Minister in 1962. On other occasions it has even forced the government to abandon or postpone measures that were known to have the Prime Minister's public approval. Members of Parliament—or of the Lok Sabha, to be more precise—can restrain the government through discussions at party caucuses or debates in the House. When sufficiently dissatisfied and frustrated, they can bring the government down by calculatedly voting against any legislature measure sponsored by it.

Identical power structure exists in the country's seventeen states where the executive committee is headed by the Chief Minister, who, like the Prime Minister at the Centre, exercises tremendous authority, but only so long as he is able to carry with him the majority in the state legislature.

The Indian constitutional setup differs from the British in the existence of the states, which create an extra tier between the Centre and the local governments. For a country of India's size, a two-tier system would have been inadequate. It would have been almost impossible for a central government located in New Delhi to administer with efficiency and understanding every aspect of life of a people as large and diverse as the Indians.

The constitution, therefore, carefully demarcated the areas of authority between the Central Government and the states. In fact, it prescribed three areas, one exclusively reserved for the Centre, one similarly reserved for the states, and the third where both may operate concurrently. Sources of revenue were divided as meticulously as fields of authority.

The Centre's authority is not so restricted as was proposed in some of the political formulae that were considered before independence and were specifically designed to persuade the Muslim-majority areas not to insist on partition. The Centre has many more areas to administer than defense, foreign affairs and communication, which were initially proposed to be assigned to it. Even if the need to placate the states was no longer so great, it was inevitable in a federal system—described by the constitution as "a union of states"—that the states should be allotted a large measure of autonomy. Equally unavoidable in the situation was occasional confrontation between the Centre and the states, particularly in fields where authority is not clearly assigned. Happily, such areas are not many.

Actually, the Centre has wielded considerably greater power than was probably intended by those who framed the constitution. Nehru's mass popularity and the fact that he held the Prime Ministership for seventeen years lent the Centre authority that a lesser leader in that office would not have been permitted. Few state chief ministers could stand up to Nehru, and they usually accepted the Centre's wishes after expressing disagreement in halting, often timid, language. The Central Government has also acquired much extra, if indirect, authority from the fact that it holds the purse strings. After collecting income-tax levies and lucrative import and excise duties and securing billions of dollars in foreign aid of various kinds, it then disburses a portion of this money to the states for their administrative and development needs. In a country where need for economic development is tremendous, few states can afford to adopt an attitude of continued belligerency toward the Central authority. Even since 1967, when eight of the seventeen states have been administered by parties other than the one which runs the Centre, there have been hardly any situations of direct conflict between the states and the Centre.

This absence of excessive friction between the Centre and the states should be welcome in a country where government, whatever its level, touches nearly every aspect of a citizen's life. Under the British, authority maintained its distance from the public and did little more than maintain law and order and collect some traditional taxes. As was expected, the national government readily discarded this attitude of aloofness. It initiated extensive programs for economic development and social welfare. The first two Five-Year Plans, which broadly covered the Fifties, provided for an investment of over twenty billion dollars, increasing the level of annual investment in the nation's economy threefold during this period. More than half of this expenditure was in what was described as the public sector and covered works ranging from provision of single-teacher schools and small medical dispensaries in remote villages to the construction of Bhakra Dam to irrigate over six million acres of land in northern India. Government also became a considerably bigger tax collector than it had ever been. In 1950–51 the Central Government had raised around 650 million dollars; by 1968–69 its estimated revenue was almost ten times as much.

It was the Centre that conceived the plans and the states that were entrusted with their execution. This fact gave the government at Central and state level tremendous responsibility as well as power. If it built the canals to irrigate an area, it also had to provide the impoverished peasantry with loans to buy better seed and fertilizer. If it set up a large power plant, it also had to allocate foreign exchange for the import of the industrial machinery to consume the electricity. In a country where private capital is limited and where need for rapid economic growth is acknowledged, it is perhaps natural that the government should assume a major role, but the constitutional structure that India had devised for itself was not ideally suited for such a task. The introduction of universal adult franchise in a backward, underdeveloped country imposed special compulsions on the politicians, who tended to promise more than the government could deliver, thereby raising public expectations needlessly. In setting priorities, the government often permitted political expediency to outweigh valid economic considerations. The planning machinery was copied from the Soviet Union, but was required to function in markedly different circumstances. The Planning Commission, presided over by the Prime Minister, had only a limited concept of the problems in a field and was often accused of planning unrealistically. It sometimes set targets well beyond the financial and physical competence of those who were supposed to work for them. The states, required to implement the plans, disregarded priorities and targets, for, unlike the republics in the Soviet Union, they were not subject to authoritarian direction from the Central Government. The bureaucracy proliferated rapidly, but its character was not changed. It functioned in virtually the same style and with the same attitudes as it had under the British as an instrument of law enforcement and revenue collection.

The party system on which India's political structure is based is equally alien. Modeled entirely on parties in Western democracies, it is frequently subjected to avoidable stresses and creates awkward situations because not many in India have yet acquired the European political sophistication, disciplines and values. Elected legislators cross floors and topple governments for selfish personal reasons and go unpunished by the electorate. Parties themselves often act with deplorable lack of political integrity in their search for office.

In India today there are eight political parties that can be described as all-India parties. In addition, there are nearly a dozen local and regional parties with distinct identities. Of these the Congress Party, despite its major split of 1969, is still the largest and could justifiably be regarded as the mother of parties. Several of the existing parties were at one time a part of the Congress Party, while others are led and dominated by those who at various times since independence have left it for personal or ideological reasons.

In the first general election, as many as fourteen parties participated as "national" parties. The number of state parties was as high as fifty-one. Under the election law, a party must secure at least 3 percent of the votes polled to be recognized in the following election as a national party and allotted its own distinctive election symbol. The condition prescribed is anything but rigorous. In the 1967 general election the number of national parties had declined to five, but there were still nearly twenty local parties. Besides, there were many independents in Parliament and in state legislatures. In the Lok Sabha their number had risen from twenty in 1962 to thirty-nine in the 1967 election. Unrestrained by party discipline or even moral compulsions, the independents often indulge in blatant horse-trading and only add to the atmosphere of instability in the legislatures.

In a country as large as India, lacking a common language or a cohesive religious faith, multiplicity of political parties is probably an unavoidable phenomenon. But their proliferation has indeed been helped by the system that India has adopted for itself. In the rules prescribed by the Election Commission, which oversees all elections, there is no ceiling on the number of parties that may claim to be recognized as national parties. This combined with the fact that garnering only three percent of the total votes polled entitles a party to be officially recognized, is an inducement to small groups to maintain their separate identity rather than seek merger with like-minded parties.

2: *The Congress Party*

The split that the Congress Party suffered in 1969 is undoubtedly serious, but it is by no means the first. At various times in its eighty-five-year existence, particularly in the last thirty years or so, many groups and factions have left the Congress. Since 1920, when Gandhi turned it into a mass party working for national independence, the Congress has been the prime training ground for politicians and political parties. The Communists were expelled from it as recently as 1945. The Socialists parted company with it in 1948. The Akali Dal, the principal party of the Sikhs, dropped out before independence. Even parties that never functioned within its fold often drew their leaders from it. The Swatantra Party was founded by Chakravarti Rajagopalachari and a group of other disenchanted Congressmen. G. V. Savarkar, who headed the Hindu Mahasabha for several years, was a former Congress member. Even Jinnah, under whose powerful leadership the Muslim League led to India's partition, had graduated to leadership from the Congress Party.

While the struggle for freedom was on, it was not unnatural that Congress should accommodate widely diverse groups under its wing. It was then not a political party so much as a movement whose goal was to secure the withdrawal of British power, and individuals as well as groups professing divergent ideologies could work for it without coming into conflict. Their presence within a massive organization gave the movement the strength it could not expect to have if they stood apart as separate units of varying size and muscle. Those who left the Congress party before independence did so either in unusual circumstances or because certain sectarian interests had become more important for them than the end of foreign rule. Though formally expelled only in 1945, the Communists had for all practical purposes left the Congress much earlier and of their own volition, because after the Soviet Union's entry into World War II they could no longer pursue the parent party's policy of opposing the war effort. Jinnah left partly in personal frustration and partly because he found the party excessively dominated by the Hindus. The Akali Dal was undoubtedly tempted to proclaim separate identity by the solicitude that the British were expressing for minorities in the years preceding independence.

Despite the fact that it shed several of its constituents along the way, the Congress Party managed to retain its substantial size and amorphous character. Every time a group departed, it left behind it a root that sprouted again. The Akali Dal, for example, did not take away all the Sikhs, nor did the Socialist Party wean away all the leftist elements. Even the confrontation with the Muslim League at a time when the latter's slogan of a separate homeland had tremendous mass appeal did not entirely deplete the Congress ranks of Muslims. In its very amorphousness, the party has been much like Hinduism. One may believe in one God or worship 72,000 gods and goddesses or even be a proclaimed agnostic and yet be a Hindu. A Hindu may worship the goddess of destruction, Kali, or Brahama, the creator. There are Hindus who rigidly practice the caste system; there are others who vigorously denounce it. The Congress Party, similarly, shelters beneath its canopy varying, sometimes conflicting, viewpoints. Among its members and even leaders it has many who are near-Communists in outlook, but there are others who are more conservative than even the Swatantra Party. Many Congressmen sincerely believe in the party's secular ideal, but many others share the narrow sectarian approach of the religious parties. These extreme views, however, form only the outer edges of the party. Essentially, the Congress has been a party of consensus, anxious to move collectively, even if rather slowly, dominated by a large centrist group of no fixed ideology, professing to be more socialist than it really is and disclaiming some of its conservatism, moved by a rather vague desire and an equally vague sense of commitment to help the poor and the underprivileged.

Gandhi believed that in the form and shape in which it had existed during the freedom movement, the Congress Party had "outlived its use." India, he argued, had won political independence, but it was still to "attain social, moral and economic independence," particularly for its rural areas. For this purpose, he suggested, the Congress should disband its present organization and "flower into a Lok Sevak Sangh"—a body dedicated to public service and not exposed to unhealthy competition from political and communal parties. Implicit in Gandhi's proposal was the suggestion that parties with specific political and ideological programs be organized to shoulder the responsibility of governance.

There were other seemingly good reasons for creating a new political organization. During the long fight with the British, the Congress had not merely functioned as a rabble-rouser against alien rule; it had also made numerous declarations outlining what it would do when power passed into Indian hands. Such commitments as replacement of English as the official language, reorganization of states on a linguistic basis and imposition of a ban on the consumption of liquor were made formally several years before independence. These promises did not lack sincerity, but, as the government's subsequent enormous difficulties in fulfilling them indicated, they were often somewhat unrealistic. A party ruling so problem-ridden a country as India undoubtedly was after independence would function much more effectively if it were not constantly being reminded of pledges it had made in a mood of idealism and unreality.

But Nehru and others in the party did not share Gandhi's view, and the party's main council formally turned down the proposal for self-dissolution. The party, it was argued, had a mass organization extending even to distant rural areas, and that would be a valuable instrument in the hands of a government required to undertake major tasks of economic and social reconstruction. Its liquidation at that stage would have created a vacuum that a cluster of new parties could not adequately fill. The Congress was the only party large enough to form a stable government and maintain its influence over the people.

Whatever its other failures and drawbacks—and they were many—the Congress Party did fulfill its promise of providing a stable administration. For the first twenty years it ruled at the Centre as well as in the states. The periods when it lost control of a state to other parties were rare and brief. That it had a well-rooted national organization greatly helped it in offering the country a sustained, stable administration. This is where the Congress scored over the Muslim League, which inherited power in Pakistan. Leaders of the League, able to win its objective of partition through its ability to generate mass fervor among the Muslims, commanded as much public adulation in 1947 as Congress leaders, but they did not have a firm party organization behind them. Whatever organizational setup the League had was confined to areas like Uttar Pradesh, Bihar and Bombay, where Muslims were in the minority and which did not form part of Pakistan. In the areas that comprised Pakistan the League had no party machinery worth the name. Consequently, once mass enthusiasm had abated, the League leaders found it hard to communicate with the Pakistani people and preserve their political hold on them.

The setback that the Congress suffered in the 1967 general election was due at least partly to the weakening of the party organization over the years. If the organizational side or what may be described as the field units had been maintained in a state of reasonable health, the party would not have been reduced to a narrow majority in the Lok Sabha and driven out of power in eight of the seventeen states. With passing years of entrenched power, the party became increasingly complacent and slothful. Instead of functioning as a bridge between the party, the government and the public, its workers devoted much of their energy to securing petty personal advantages from the administrations. Gradually the organization shriveled as would a muscle after prolonged disuse.

The party was aware of the problem, but somehow it could not determine what relationship should exist between its parliamentary and organizational wings. The British system, in which the parliamentary wing completely dominates the other, was not suitable for a party functioning in a country of India's size and illiteracy. Only active political workers could communicate public grievances and needs to the government and explain the latter's policies to the people. Organization could not be reduced to a minor, subservient role as in Britain. At the same time, Congress leaders were averse to the Soviet system, where the government is subordinated to the party. The importance of the organization was realized, but somehow little was done to give it the status it deserved and to make party work, as distinct from legislative responsibilities, satisfying and meaningful. In a parliamentary democracy, it was but natural that the Prime Minister should be the most important leader, but the party president who presided over a vast organization should not have been relegated to the position of a lowly functionary, as most Congress presidents were, with little impact on major policies and decisions.

The Congress could never strike the right balance between the two wings. Maulana Azad, who was Congress president during the difficult pre-independence negotiations with the British government and who was far from keen on a ministerial post, reluctantly joined the government because during the few months he stayed out of it he experienced frustration and a sense of purposelessness. J. B. Kripalani, who took over as the party president in November 1946, resigned a year later without completing his two-year term because he felt he did not enjoy the "confidence of those who are in the Cabinet." His resignation dramatized the issue, but did not lead to a solution.

In 1951, on the eve of the first general election, Nehru combined in his person the offices of Prime Minister and head of the Congress. This arrangement, which lasted for the following four years, only concealed the problem; it did not solve it. With the Prime Minister also heading the organization, there was no conflict at the top, but party workers at the lower levels, on whose shoulders the organization rested, derived no particular satisfaction from it. All the rewards were on the parliamentary side, and consequently there was a stampede for them. The organization, which should have strengthened the legislative wing by providing it a popular base, worked for its overthrow in the hope of capturing ministerial offices for its own leaders. In some states, the party organization openly vilified the party government. Those from the organizational side who managed to occupy ministerial offices seldom went back to party work and left the perch only when they were pushed out by others longing for power. In 1961, Sanjiva Reddy, who had given up the chief ministership of Andhra to become Congress president, suggested that those who had held power for ten years should renounce it to labor as the party's field workers—a proposal that was never seriously considered. Reddy himself soon maneuvered his way back to the government. Even in 1963, when the Kamaraj Plan (*see below*) had generated in the party a mood for renunciation of power, most of those who "volunteered" to relinquish office and work for the party did so sulkily.

The party's decline was slow but typical of any organization that remains in office too long. It lost touch with the people whom it claimed to serve and whose goodwill it needed every five years to return to power. The long years of campaigning against the British had left the older leadership exhausted. The younger leadership emerging in some states lacked their older colleagues' idealism and often pursued power for the sake of power. Various groups with vested interests—landlords, businessmen, even princes—who had previously stood away from it rushed into the Congress. Their entry substantially modified its objectives of establishing a socialist society and added to the distance between the party and the poverty-stricken masses for whom it was committed to work. The rich contributed generously to its election fund and, understandably, insisted on their pound of flesh in return through dilution of the party's dedication to socialism. Their pressure and influence led to the virtual emasculation of the land reforms in most parts of the country. In the cities the government was rendered impotent to deal with the black-marketeer, the hoarder and the tax-dodger, for many of these culprits were either active in the party or contributed generously to its election fund. All this dilution of moral purpose and practice was widely noted, and it added to the common man's anger. While pandering to the interests of certain special groups, the Congress administrations neglected the "bread and butter" problems such as checking inflation, providing adequate housing and keeping administrative corruption within limits. Frustrated and personally neglected as he was, the lower-level party worker neither carried the grievances of the people to higher councils nor protested with any degree of vehemence against the inefficiency and highhandedness of the bureaucracy and the enormous greed of the middleman. Under Congress party rule, prices of essential articles of food and clothing were permitted to rise sharply. Traders created artificial scarcities and went unpunished. The bureaucracy's efficiency declined while its callousness increased.

Many Congress leaders invited upon themselves public wrath through their ostentatious living and vulgar exercise of power. They overlooked the fact that the average Indian attaches tremendous importance to simplicity in the living style of the leader. He is impressed much more by an act of renunciation than of acquisition. Gandhi touched the hearts of the Indian masses because he spoke in their idiom, but much more so because he actually lived in the style of the poorest among them. He wore a loincloth of homespun material, insisted on traveling third-class in the Indian railways and during his visits to New Delhi often lived in a hut in the capital's colony for municipal sweepers. Nehru's own charisma was founded on the widespread belief that he and his family had given all they possessed to the freedom movement. Many years before independence, Gandhi had suggested that a Congress minister should serve on a salary of no more than 500 rupees a month (around $150 at the exchange rate prevailing then). The salaries that ministers in India draw do not conform to the standard prescribed by Gandhi, but are rather low; a Central Government minister is paid 2,500 rupees, or a little over $300, per month. But he enjoys all the other accouterments of high living, such as a spacious bungalow, luxury car and a large retinue of servants at state expense. Nehru was probably the only member of the Central Cabinet who rode in a small, four-cylinder, India-produced car. Other ministers, including most in the states, used large limousines purchased specially for them, even though import of expensive foreign cars was virtually banned. A deputy minister of the Central Government once threatened to resign because the official car assigned to her was of indigenous manufacture.

Such ministerial frippery irked many. Indians would tend to forgive a minister for his administrative inefficiency but not for any ostentation or arrogance or wealth acquired through political influence. Most of the top Congress leaders defeated at the polls in 1967, for example, were those who were believed to have amassed wealth through politics and power through wealth or who exercised power too blatantly. In the confrontation with Mrs. Gandhi in 1969, one of the major drawbacks from which her opponents suffered was the fact that several of them were known to be politicians of Tammany Hall style. (Newspapers openly referred to them as the "Syndicate.") It is a measure of the Indian sense of values that what imperiled Mrs. Gandhi's political career was not her ill-timed decision in 1966 to devalue the currency, or any other action with politically damaging consequence, but the allegation by an opposition M.P. in 1966 that she had failed to surrender to the government a fur that she had allegedly received many years earlier as a gift while accompanying her father on a state visit to the Soviet Union. Fortunately for her, the charge was not substantiated.

As the corrupting consequences of power widened the gulf between the Congress and the people, the former was inclined increasingly to rely on patronage and political deals for the support it needed in elections. This tactic created a vicious circle. The more the party relied on unconventional sources for votes, the greater became the public disenchantment with it, which in turn added to its need to make shortcuts to gain support. Nehru himself was guilty of improper bargaining for votes in several situations. Despite the party's declared secular ideals, Nehru agreed to an electoral alliance with the Muslim League in Kerala because without its support the Congress could not hope to come to power in the 1960 mid-term election there. The party made similar compromises with known Muslim fanatics because they could secure the bulk of their community's votes by appealing to its religious sentiments. Where the caste system was strong, the Congress consciously pandered to it by nominating as its candidates only those who could meet the narrow, exacting demands of the majority caste. With every general election, Nehru seemed to lean more heavily on those among the party leaders whose principal qualification was their ability to "operate" elections or keep opposition in disarray. At times he pretended not to look if "operators" indulged in corruption or administrative highhandedness. The inevitable impact of this attitude on his party was the emergence of provincial bosses or election "managers" who could manipulate sizable accounts in "vote banks." The physical weariness of the Congress leadership was obvious even at independence; its intellectual and moral exhaustion was evident before the first decade had ended.

Whatever the party's failings, it provided the country with over twenty years of political stability without which India, given its problems and the divisive tendencies of its people, would literally have fallen apart. In the 1952 election the Congress won 357 of the 489 Lok Sabha seats and 2,248 of the

3,283 state assembly seats. It lost some of this support in the two following general elections, but retained a commanding majority in Parliament and formed the government in almost all states. That the Centre and the states were run by the same party eliminated much of the tension and centrifugal pressures that customarily would plague a federal system of government of the type India had chosen for itself. The process of economic planning would have been even slower and the agitation over language and states' reorganization would certainly have been much bloodier if the Centre and the states had been under different parties. It is also possible that strong secessionist movements would have developed in different parts of the country.

Even when they acted unscrupulously, most Congress leaders appeared to be restrained by certain unstated limits. Nor was their highhandedness ever total or beyond challenge. And much of their corruption was of a petty nature. Other democratic countries such as the United States, where political institutions are more firmly established, the public better educated and the press more vigilant, reportedly suffer much greater corruption than India has since independence.

The Congress Party could have moved toward authoritarianism, but did not. It had the parliamentary strength to amend the constitution and ensure that it remained in power perpetually, but the thought apparently never crossed the mind of Nehru or any other senior leader. Instead, they consciously worked to strengthen democratic concepts. The party passed a preventive detention law intended for use against subversive elements, but provided for periodic reconsideration and extension of the law by Parliament. Whenever constitutional process collapsed in a state and its administration had to be taken over by the Centre, fresh elections were invariably held within the prescribed time. There was no devious attempt to delay elections even when it was evident, as it was in West Bengal in the beginning of 1969, that the Communists and not the Congress would be returned to power.

It has often been remarked that, notwithstanding its democratic constitution, what India experienced was virtually one-party rule. True enough, but this observation should be tempered by noting that the single-party dominance was unaccompanied by the type of repressiveness and selfish appetite for authority which is usually witnessed in countries under one-party rule. The Congress Party ruled alone for so long because other parties, though free to unseat it, were not strong enough to do so.

3: *On the Left*

If other parties failed to grow into organizations capable of replacing the Congress, it was due to their own limitations and not because the ruling party placed any unfair, unconstitutional obstacles in their way. The Socialists were credited with tremendous potential, but did not go far. India's poverty and illiteracy were supposed to be the breeding ground for Communism, but the influence of the two Communist parties has been confined to West Bengal, Kerala and some small pockets elsewhere. The Jana Sangh, a Hindu populist party, should have done well, but failed to do so despite the revivalist frame of mind prevailing among many Hindus in the years following independence. The Swatantra, the only professedly conservative party, had sizable financial and intellectual resources, but its growth has remained stunted. Several other parties, including some which came to power in one state or another in the 1967 election, do not even claim an all-India status for themselves.

No group has demonstrated so marked a disparity between promise and accomplishment as the Socialists. In 1948, when they left the Congress to establish their own independent identity, they had a moderately well-knit organization, which had functioned with a measure of individuality since 1934, even under the Congress umbrella. Several of the top leaders were nationally known and widely respected. In the 1942 Quit India movement launched against the British by Gandhi, the Socialists had participated much more tenaciously than other wings of the

Congress. Its leaders thus had a reputation for courage and dedication. In Jayaprakash Narayan the Socialists had a leader with Nehru-like charisma. Their ideology, which had a noticeable touch of Gandhian philosophy and no taint of authoritarianism, should have appealed to the Indian masses. Despite all these advantages, Socialists have remained a house divided, with no lasting leadership of any consequence and with only nominal impact on the country's governance. In the first general election they accounted for 10.6 percent of the total vote; fifteen years later, in the fourth general election, the two Socialist groups, the Praja Socialist Party (PSP) and the Samayukt Socialist Party (SSP), polled an aggregate of 8.41 percent.

The Congress Socialist Party (CSP) came into being in 1934 as a constituent of the Congress. Its units had existed in a few states even earlier, but it was in that year that the Socialists chose to organize themselves on a national basis. What prompted organized action on their part was the Congress leaders' growing inclination toward accepting office even under limited reforms that the British had offered. The Socialists believed that Congress' willingness to enter the legislatures and government on the basis of partial autonomy while waiting for complete freedom would only weaken the struggle for independence. They also wished to goad the Congress into thinking in more pronounced socialistic terms. Nehru shared their approach to ideological issues and maintained close links with them. Some of the noted members of the CSP were chosen by him to work on his executive committee when he was elected Congress president. Yet, though he was of them, Nehru somehow was not with them. When the Socialists left the Congress in 1948 under pressure from the right-wing dominated by Sardar Patel, the thought that Nehru might go with them never crossed any mind.

For a period of four years the Communists worked in close cooperation with the CSP, but the leftist unity ended abruptly in 1940 when the former decided to support the British war effort in view of Russia's entry into World War II. Such sudden mergers and equally sudden divisions have been the hallmark of the

Socialist movement ever since the Socialists assumed an independent identity. In 1953 the Socialist Party merged with the Kissan Mazdoor Praja Party to form the Praja Socialist Party. The KMPP could be described as a group of former Congressmen of vaguely socialistic persuasion. Led by Acharya Kripalani, who resigned the Congress presidency in 1947, most KMPP members had left the Congress more in personal frustration than in ideological fervor. In the 1952 election their party had polled 6 percent of the total votes and its merger with the Socialist Party should have created a party of considerable strength, but it did not. In the years that followed, a large section of the PSP broke away under the leadership of Dr. Ram Manohar Lohia and revived the Socialist Party. The Lohia Socialists, as they were generally known, represented the more militant section of the Indian Socialists. They later returned to the PSP to form the Samayukt (United) Socialist Party, but broke away again to retain for themselves the new party title.

These factional quarrels undoubtedly played havoc with the party organization and limited its electoral effectiveness. But the movement also suffered from other, even larger, failings and handicaps. It could not, for example, distinguish itself from the Congress Party in the eyes of the average Indian voter. In what way was it different from and better than the Congress? The Congress, too, professed to work for a socialist society. It had passed formal resolutions stating its commitment, and Nehru's presence at its head convinced most people of the sincerity of its declaration. Over the years, Socialist leaders had moved away from Marxist socialism to an indigenous variety reflecting the impact of Gandhi's thinking. They favored land reforms prescribing a ceiling on personal holdings, emphasized the use of small machines in industrial development and stood for decentralization of administration. These positions reflected a somewhat larger influence of Gandhi than the Congress program did. The Socialists also wished to implement these programs with greater speed than the ruling party. But such distinctions were too subtle for an unsophisticated voter to notice. To him the

Socialists look vaguely like Congress-men who could not stay in the party for personal reasons.

Many Socialist leaders have been troubled in their minds by this seeming similarity between their party and the Congress and have even been drawn to the latter. The Lohia group was determined in its opposition to the Congress—Lohia's personal antipathy to Nehru and later to Mrs. Gandhi was almost pathological—but others among the Socialists frequently considered returning to the Congress or reaching some kind of an understanding with it. They loudly accused the Congress of being reactionary and corrupt, but the question of cooperating with it was always uppermost in their councils. In 1953, Jayaprakash Narayan held prolonged talks with Nehru to discuss with him an invitation to join the Cabinet and the question of Socialist cooperation with the Congress. Narayan presented a fourteen-point program on the basis of which the two could work together. Nehru was in broad agreement with Narayan's suggestions, but the move for collaboration failed because as Prime Minister he was adverse to accepting conditions from someone he wished to include in his government. About the same time, Asoka Mehta, General Secretary of the PSP, propounded the thesis that the "compulsions of a backward economy" necessitated cooperation between Socialists and the Congress. He revived this argument periodically, and even though the party would not follow him on this issue, he himself drifted into the Congress.

The principal weakness of the Socialists has been their leadership. Some of the senior Socialist leaders have displayed a strange Hamlet-like trait and tended to shy away from the rough and tumble of politics. Narayan, whose presence lent the PSP tremendous prestige, renounced active politics and took to organizing voluntary efforts for economic and social uplift in the villages. The loss to the party from that decision can be estimated by the fact that in terms of mass popularity and political stature Narayan was generally regarded as next only to Nehru. (He would have been a formidable contender for the Prime Ministership after Nehru if he had not left the Congress Party.) Kripalani, who had come to the PSP via the KMPP and was probably the only other nationally known personality in the group, resigned the party chairmanship and cut himself adrift from it when he found organizational ties too confining. Mehta thrived as long as he held secondary positions in the party, but seemed to wilt when he rose to the top. A reasonable theoretician, he conspicuously lacked the temperament to be a mass leader. Lohia was an impressive speaker in Hindi and something of a demagogue, but he allowed his hatred for the Congress and Nehru to warp his judgment. He publicly vowed to "destroy" the Congress Party and the parliamentary institutions that it dominated. As member of the Lok Sabha, he consistently took a negative, obstructionist attitude, ranted interminably and tended to throw tantrums and encouraged his followers in Parliament to follow his example. Besides these personal limitations and idiosyncrasies, some Socialist leaders displayed a strange tendency to defect from the party at critical junctures. T. Prakasam, who headed the PSP in Andhra, defected to join the Congress and took a section of the party with him. Pattam Thanu Pillai, the most important PSP leader in Kerala and for long the state's Chief Minister, similarly left the party leaderless in 1961, when he suddenly accepted the Congress government's offer of the governorship of Punjab. Since the Congress and the PSP in Kerala were then engaged in a power struggle, Pillai's defection caused the virtual collapse of the PSP position.

The Communists have more to show for themselves since independence than the Socialists, but not substantially more. After the 1967 general election they formed the government in Kerala and dominated the coalition in West Bengal. At the Centre the two Communist parties won no more than 42 seats in a house of 525. In the previous election, when they were united in one party, they had secured 29. Their gain may thus appear sizable, but obviously they are a long way from power. That Indian Communists have captured power, as they did in Kerala in 1957, through the ballot box is an index more of the catholicity of Indian democracy than of the strength of Indian Communists.

Calcutta's slums and other urban problems and the impact of rather rapid industrialization created circumstances in West Bengal favorable to the spread of Communism. A high incidence of unemployment among the educated had offered similar stimulus to Communism in Kerala. Unless circumstances change radically, the Communists should have more than reasonable chances of dominating the politics in the two states for several years to come. The Congress and other non-Communist parties will have to cooperate with one another to an unusual extent and receive powerful backing from the Centre if they are to keep the Communists out of office in Kerala and West Bengal. If another state goes Communist at the polls, it will probably be Andhra, where Communists have a fairly wide organizational base among the landless labor traditionally exploited by big landlords. But even in Andhra their position in the state legislature is so unimpressive that the prospect of Communist control seems rather remote. In the rest of the country, the Communists have a few pockets of influence. They enjoy support, for example, among the peasant proprietors of the Doaba region of Punjab, colliery labor of Bihar and sugar-mill workers of Uttar Pradesh. The trade unions in Bombay were generally acknowledged to be dominated by the Communists, but in recent years some of that influence has been pre-empted by Shiv Sena, a highly chauvinistic and distinctly anti-Communist, local organization. To achieve even this somewhat modest following the Communists have not relied entirely on the attraction of their political philosophy. They have exploited caste rivalries in Andhra and Kerala, regional suspicions between north and south, and the minority sentiments such as the Muslim feeling of insecurity. They have also been helped by the volatile nature of the Bengali mind (before independence Bengal produced the largest number of political terrorists) and the strange combination in Kerala of a very high rate of literacy (55 percent among males) and extensive unemployment.

The advantage that widespread poverty and illiteracy might offer the Communists has been mitigated by the conservativeness of the Hindu mind. Hindu philosophy is essentially pessimistic, and the average Indian's capacity to suffer is enormous. The believer holds that he suffers for his misdeeds in an earlier life. Things should improve in the next life if he follows the tenets of dharma, the laws of his religion. The hope of a better life after death and the prospects of nirvana in the end not only augment the believer's tolerance for pain but also induce a measure of passivity in his attitude toward his immediate inequities.

Even more than the Hindu mind, what baffles and defeats the Communist dogma is the social structure of India's rural community, a part of the country that has been only lightly touched by Western influences. Family ties are still strong and the community has a hierarchy in which everyone is allotted a niche. The Hindu joint family system offers its members a sense of emotional and economic security, for it distributes the family resources according to the needs of its individual members and not in proportion to their contributions. Beyond the family, the village social structure undoubtedly shelters certain disparateness and injustice, but their impact is softened by a general display of benevolence at the top. The resentments and frustrations on which Communism usually thrives are thus not as extensive in India yet as the country's poverty might normally warrant.

Nor has the social and academic background of most Communist leaders equipped them to understand adequately the working of the rural mind. A large number of senior party leaders were drawn from among urban intellectuals. Several of them had studied abroad, usually in Britain, while many others held high degrees in law, literature or economics from Indian universities. In terms of caste, many belonged to the upper crust of society. E. M. S. Namboodiripad, who has headed the Communist government in Kerala, is a Brahmin and, as such, at the top of the social structure. Jyoti Basu, former Deputy Chief Minister in the West Bengal coalition and the principal leader of the powerful Communist faction in the state, is likewise a Brahmin. Other important names in the Communist Party's four-decade existence in India such as S. A. Dange, P. C. Joshi and

B. T. Ranadive also reflect a high-caste background. Their academic attainments enabled them to understand the theory of Marxist teaching, but in applying it to India they were greatly restricted by their limited knowledge of the conditions prevailing in the country. The tendency was to pay excessive attention to factory labor, which in an industrially underdeveloped country such as India was inevitably small, and virtually ignore the massive section of the underprivileged among the peasants. Also, thanks to their Brahminical, academic training, they were attracted to the written word rather than to action. Each party congress and meeting of the Central Committee produced hundreds of pages of hair-splitting theorizing which was not followed by matching performance. To discuss and argue a problem or a situation excessively but undertake little exertion about it is almost a national trait in India, but this tendency seems particularly marked among the Communists.

For a group of individuals so well educated and trained, the Communist leaders have made some serious tactical errors. Because the Communists formed a part of the mainstream of the freedom movement and professed socialist ideology, the Congress Socialist Party was tempted in 1936 to throw its doors open to them. This, the CSP believed somewhat naïvely, would strengthen Socialist unity. The Communists' gain from the merger was much more than consolidation of the leftist forces. By coming into the CSP they could surface legally, for at the time the British government had declared their own party illegal. What was more, the alliance with the CSP allowed the Communists entry into the councils of the Congress Party, which entitled them to some of the public adulation due to a party fighting for national freedom. Communists who rose to party offices or membership of prestigious provincial and central bodies through CSP support included Sajjad Zaheer, later Secretary of the Communist Party of Pakistan, P. Sundarayya and A. K. Gopalan, both of whom later led the Communists in Parliament, and Dr. Z. A. Ahmend, a prominent M.P. for many years. This association, which was entirely advantageous to the Communist wing, ended four years later after a conflict precipitated by its covetousness. Instead of being satisfied with the more than generous share of offices allocated to its members, the CPI was constantly agitating and even intriguing for more. The intention obviously was to capture the CSP from within, but in seeking their end, the Communists acted hastily and impatiently. It was the sheer blatancy of their intentions that prompted the CSP to expel them from the organization in 1940.

The CPI acted with equal ineptness two years later. When World War II started, the Congress was unwilling to cooperate with the authorities in the war effort. The British action in declaring war on India's behalf without even appearing to consult Indian opinion incensed the leaders. The Congress ministries in the states formed after the 1937 elections tendered their resignation, arguing that a "slave India" could not fight with any enthusiasm for the freedom of other countries. But the Congress protest was marked by a degree of diffidence. Though anxious to exploit the situation to hasten the arrival of freedom, the Congress did not wish to embarrass the Allies. The Working Committee (the party's top executive), in fact, formally passed a resolution condemning fascist aggression in strong terms. For the Communists, however, even more important than national independence was the role of the Soviet Union. Stalin's pact with Hitler in August 1939 left them confused, but only temporarily. Realizing that they must be on the side on which the Soviet Union stood, they soon began condemning the Allies for conducting "an imperialist war." A series of strikes was organized by Communist-dominated trade unions in an effort to impede the war effort. At the same time, the Communists chided the Congress leadership for its reluctance to take advantage of the British predicament and paraded themselves as more patriotic than any other political group.

In the following eighteen months, as the Congress moved from hope to despair and resolved to act against the stubborn British government, the Soviet entry into the war on the side of the Allies moved the Indian Communists in the opposite direction. For them the "imperialist war" was suddenly transformed into a "people's war," and it became the duty of every "progressive, patriotic" Indian to extend his wholehearted cooperation to the government in fighting the war. On August 8, 1942, the Congress resolved to launch mass civil disobedience. Despite the arrest of Gandhi and other top Congress leaders the following morning and repressive measures by the government, a violent Quit India movement shook the country amid a mood of deep anger and resentment against the British for supposedly fighting for freedom in Europe while keeping India enslaved. Up to a point Gandhi's launching of the Quit India movement was precipitated by the prevailing mass restlessness and anger. But while the country simmered with fury and clashed with authority (over 50,000 arrests were made during the 1942 movement), the Communists were exhorting the people to join the army and condemning the underground resistance movement as the work of "fascist fifth columnists." The alienation from Indian political sentiment that the CPI thus earned was to plague it for many years.

The Communists misjudged the public mood again in 1948. At the end of the war, as prospects of Indian independence improved, the CPI stood alone and distrusted. Its role during the war had rendered it a virtual political pariah. In 1947, when Nehru formed the first government of independent India, the CPI tried to end its isolation and join the mainstream by supporting the government. But this phase proved exceedingly short-lived. In February 1948, barely six months after transfer of power, the Second Congress of the CPI, held in Calcutta, theorized that what India had achieved was only "an illusion" and that the final struggle for "real freedom and democracy" must still be launched. To a people whose sense of exultation over their new status was strong enough to deaden even the pain of partition, this reasoning seemed shockingly impertinent.

The "final struggle" was launched later that year and the outcome was a period of lawless activity by Communists in several parts of the country. The then party leader, B. T. Ranadive,

believed India was as ripe for revolution as Russia had been in
1917. The tactics the party adopted to usher in "real democracy," similar to those adopted in Russia thirty years earlier,
were marked by violence and extensive attempts at insurrection.
Workers were exhorted to strike and peasants to snatch the land
from the landlords. A series of acts of sabotage was directed
against public property. The insurrection was most effective in
the Telangana region of South India, which at the time formed
part of the princely state of Hyderabad, the area where Communists had captured the Socialist party machine during the period of leftist unity and entrenched themselves before the Central Government had taken over the state. Here landlords were
deprived of their possessions, police posts frequently attacked,
revenue officials assaulted (even murdered), government property was seized or burned down and communications were dis-
rupted over an extensive area. It took the government several
months to restore normalcy in Telengana, but in other parts of
the country such as Bengal, Madras and Punjab the "uprising"
proved short-lived. Troops had to be sent into certain areas to
quell the lawlessness, but local authority was largely able to
meet the challenge with the help of the armed police. By the
time the "final struggle" petered out, the Communist Party stood
badly scarred and humiliated. Its reputation had been tarnished,
and its organization was in disarray in several parts of the country. This was the price it paid for not realizing that, however
illusory the independence granted by the British, Nehru's was no
Czarist regime in India.

Besides its periodic inability to judge the situation correctly,
the Communist leadership in India has displayed two principal
weaknesses. It has been too noticeably subservient to Moscow
or political authority residing outside India, and it has been too
prone to personal jealousies and rivalries.

The change in the CPI's attitude to World War II in 1941–42
following the German invasion of the Soviet Union not only
blatantly disregarded the Indian situation, but was affected
under direction from abroad. Even after the Soviet entry into the

war, Indian Communists, then under detention for denouncing the war as an "imperialist" war, were unsure for a time whether Russia's involvement changed the situation for them. A month after Hitler's attack on the Soviet Union, the CPI published a pamphlet which stubbornly stuck to the position that Britain was waging an imperialist war and that "we can render really effective aid to the Soviet Union only as a free people." The issue was, however, decided for the party by a letter that its leaders received in jail from Harry Pollitt, Secretary of the British Communist Party. The British party, which then seemed to exercise some kind of overlordship upon the CPI, directed a clear change in the attitude to the war, and the Indian leaders quickly overcame their doubts and accepted the new line dutifully. Similarly, the 1948 "uprising" against the allegedly spurious democracy was clearly inspired by the doubts about the authenticity of Indian independence that the Soviet Union nursed during Stalin's years of power. Again, the CPI adopted an indulgent attitude toward Nehru after 1954–55 because Russian Premier Khrushchev chose to befriend India for reasons of international politics.

Indian Communists' subservience to Moscow has declined in recent years. In fact, among its leaders and the rank and file the party had always had a sizable section which, though dogmatic in its beliefs, chafed under Soviet control. Since the beginning of the Sixties this wing has become more assertive and ultimately caused the major split of 1964.

Almost since its founding, the party was divided into two wings. One was activist in its approach, resented excessive Soviet domination of party affairs, vowed to oppose the Congress Party and believed in the inevitability of class struggle. The other tended to draw its inspiration from Moscow unabashedly, was not wholly averse to cooperating with the ruling party in certain circumstances and believed that power could be attained even through parliamentary processes. These ideological differences were undoubtedly sharpened by acute personal jealousies among the top party leaders. The split, when it came, was influenced by a combination of factors. The famous Khrushchev speech at the Twentieth CPSU Congress attacking Stalin strengthened the activist group's belief that Moscow was scarcely infallible. At the same time, the ideological confrontation between Peking and Moscow created a new Communist Rome toward which the dissident group could look. The Chinese attack on Indian border areas in 1962 tended to divide the CPI into those who joined the rest of India in condemning the Chinese action and those whose ideological predilections got the better of their sense of nationalism. Therefore, when the split came, the two groups derived their identity, at least in the public mind, from the postures they had adopted in 1962 and were loosely described as the "Moscow faction" and the "Peking faction." The final break also brought to the surface much of the personal antagonism that Indian leaders had mutually entertained, and the parting was bitter and unedifying. Typical of the venomous charges was the one, never convincingly substantiated, against S. A. Dange, a veteran party leader who for long headed the party in Parliament; it was said that he had served as an informer for the British Intelligence and that he had large, undisclosed bank balances abroad.

With the rise of what is described as the Naxalbari group, the Communist movement in India appears to be acquiring a triangular character.

The group derives its name from the backward tribal tract in Darjeeling district of West Bengal which in 1967 witnessed a brief but sharp attempt to rouse landless labor into forcibly taking over the lands they had been tilling. The "uprising" was put down, but only when the Central Government sent in its special police force to help the state after several landlords had been murdered. The group has since extended its activities to other parts of West Bengal and even to the neighboring state of Assam. It has also adopted Mao Tse-tung as its ideological mentor and openly practices and preaches violence as a means of bringing about the "revolution." What dimensions this wing will acquire is not yet clear, but it is generally acknowledged to be not merely a passing phenomenon. In the eight months following November 1969, nearly eighty murders were attributed by the police to members of the Naxalbari group. At the other end of the group's activities, schoolchildren in Calcutta were reported to have disfigured Gandhi's pictures and plastered the city's walls with slogans exhorting Indians to follow China's way to Communism.

The Communist Party (Marxist) or the Peking faction, itself accepts Mao's thoughts as a purer form of Communism, but what earns it the contempt and hostility of the Naxalbari group is the fact that it is not averse to bringing about revolution through parliamentary democracy rather than through a violent class struggle. Significantly, by the end of 1970 a sizable section of the militants in the CPM had reportedly been drawn to the new group, which seemed to hold particular fascination for the restless, educated youth of Calcutta city.

4: *On the Right*

If India's poverty and traditions of feudal exploitation are not reflected adequately in the growth of the left-wing parties, its conservativism and susceptibility to religious sentiments have lent only limited strength to the right or sectarian groups. Despite the loss of élan on the part of the Congress Party and other favorable circumstances, the conservative parties—the Bharatiya Jana Sangh and the Swatantra Party are the principal ones —are still a long way from power at the Centre. In the 1967 general election the Jana Sangh won 35 Lok Sabha seats while the Swatantra won 44. This marked a considerable improvement over their performance five years previously, but by itself it did not amount to much in a house of 525.

The Jana Sangh, formed in 1951 on the eve of the first general election, resents being described as a party of the Hindus. It claims to be different from the Hindu Mahasabha, which led a blatantly communal if somewhat anemic life before partition and virtually withered away soon after. Unlike the Mahasabha, the Sangh opens its doors to people of all communities—but only technically. In every election one or two Muslims stand as the Sangh candidates (they are always defeated) and while they prove that the Jana Sangh claim is literally true, they also emphasize that, notwithstanding the claim, it is a purely Hindu political party. Actually, the Jana Sangh's support is even more restricted. It is really the party of the urban Hindus of northern and central India. In the south, which is predominantly Hindu, the party has little support.

Organizationally, the Jana Sangh tends to stand on the shoulders of the Rashtriya Swayamsevak Sangh (RSS), a militant Hindu volunteer body, revivalist in outlook, avowedly anti-Muslim and not above using large-scale organized violence against the minorities. For the Jana Sangh the RSS provides a useful cadre of dedicated, disciplined workers; to the RSS the Jana Sangh offers a welcome political outlet. It is a marriage that both sides disavow, but it has lasted all these years because of its obvious mutual convenience. Also, the thinking of both groups is strikingly similar. Militantly nationalistic, they believe in the superiority of traditional Hindu culture and hope for its acceptance as a way of life in India. They also nurse resentful memories of Muslim domination, accuse the Congress of pandering to the Muslims at home and to Pakistan in foreign policy, and are averse to modern Western thought. The RSS expresses itself by imposing strict discipline on its members, emphasizing the importance of physical culture and fighting the Muslims in the streets. (The RSS has been behind some of the worst communal riots during the past thirty years.). The Jana Sangh demonstrates similar attitudes in the field of politics. If it conducts itself more decorously than the RSS, it is not due to lack of belligerency among its leaders but because it functions in Parliament and the state legislatures, which does not permit one the license of the streets.

The Jana Sangh's excessive preoccupation with the Muslims and Pakistan explains why it offers little appeal to the Hindus of south India. Historically, the southern region escaped the impact of Muslim political domination, and its people have few memories of humiliation at the hands of Muslim invaders. Nor was the Muslim population in the south large enough to constitute a challenge to the Hindus as it did in Punjab, Uttar Pradesh, Delhi and Bihar. In the south, the problem of dominance and the consequent resentment was created not by the Muslims but by a Brahmin elite. The fact that the leadership of the RSS was provided largely by Chitpavan Brahmins of Maharashtra and central India blocked the Jana Sangh from finding a home in that region. The Jana Sangh's vigorous support for Hindi as the official national language in place of English—a posture its leaders softened later, but only belatedly—also made the south and other non-Hindi parts of the country react to it warily. To many it understandably represented a form of north Indian domination that they were unwilling to accept.

The Jana Sangh's major weakness has been its inability to formulate a program of economic action. In fact, the intellectual caliber of its leadership has been pitifully low. Even if the Jana Sangh leaders hold some views on economic problems, these remain buried under a mass of rhetoric on the importance of reinstating Hindu culture, the Congress Party's alleged "communalism" in appeasing Muslims and the need for "reciprocity"—which in reality means a tit-for-tat attitude—in India's relations with Pakistan. Such slogans win popularity and votes for the party in certain areas, but they do not provide the balanced diet that it must have for rapid, healthy growth. Perhaps this excessive reliance on attractive, emotionally appealing slogans is the unavoidable result of the fact that, except for the first two years of its existence, the party has had no leader of national or even regional stature. Dr. Shayama Prasad Mookerjee, who resigned from Nehru's Cabinet in 1950 in protest against the government's weak-kneed policy toward Pakistan, was its first president. Mookerjee was a powerful speaker, a skilled parliamentarian who could stand up to and often humble Nehru in an exchange in the Lok Sabha, and who blended in himself modern

Western thought and a typically Indian way of life. If he had not died in 1953, Mookerjee might have succeeded in giving the Jana Sangh an all-India image and a modern look without unduly limiting its chauvinism. But those who succeeded Mookerjee were lesser-known men with limited, local followings and often cast in the constricting mental mold of the RSS.

The Swatantra, the other major party on the right, has suffered from inadequacies of a different type. Formed in 1959, the Swatantra has precise views on economic issues. Its program is strictly conservative, with an unconcealed aversion to state ownership of industry and to state control of national economy. Its program does not suffer from the vagaries that typify the Indian socialists. Nor does it, like the Congress Party, attempt to mean all things to all people. It does not try to hide its beliefs under sham professions to the contrary. A Swatantra member is not embarrassed by his faith in the principle of private enterprise as a Jana Sangh leader might be of his party's communal character. The party also does not lack leadership or intellectual prowess. In its founder, Chakravarti Rajagopalachari, it has a leader who was foremost during the freedom movement, was the first Indian to be appointed as the constitutional head of state after independence, held several senior positions in Nehru's Cabinet and is widely acknowledged as a man of integrity and high intellectual caliber. The party's top echelons include many others with modern minds and capacity for original thought.

What the Swatantra has lacked is a grass-roots organization of the type the Congress built up over decades under the impetus of the independence movement and the Jana Sangh acquired through a tacit association with the RSS. Ten years after its formation, the party is still without a proper, disciplined cadre of workers. Some of the leaders who joined it brought with them splinters of their respective parent organizations, but somehow these could not be welded together in a relevant structure and over the years have tended to revert to the original bodies.

The structure of its leadership discourages the formation of an extensive lower-level organization or a mass following. The presence at the top of men like Rajagopalachari, M. R. Masani and N. G. Ranga, another former Congress leader from Andhra, gave the Swatantra a general appearance of being a political party in traditional terms, but the bulk of its leaders were of a different type—mostly former princes, retired senior civil servants, some big businessmen or Western-educated professional men. A photograph of the Swatantra leaders taken at its founding and published extensively in the newspapers looked much like pictures of the annual meeting of the Princes' Chamber or of the federation of the leading chambers of commerce. Among the founder members were retired members of the Indian Civil Service (ICS), some junior princes, a few leading Bombay businessmen and even some who had been knighted by the British for their loyalty. Most were far too well dressed, far too rich and far too Westernized for a party which, if it aspired to achieve an all-India character, must deal with illiterate, tradition-bound masses living in rural India. They were obviously not the type who would work in the villages or create any rapport with the masses, and their conservatism further limited the party's political appeal. The Swatantra thus acquired the image not of a modern-minded party which prescribed a right-wing path for the country but of a gathering of individuals anxious to protect certain vested interests and personal privileges.

Its legislative strength has thus been virtually an aggregate of gains that some of its leaders were able to make through personal or family influence. Some of its princely adherents, such as the Maharani of Jaipur, have benefited from the veneration in which their former subjects were traditionally taught to hold the ruler. Like other parties, it has also negatively benefited from the general public disenchantment with the ruling party. At places it has been the refuge of politicians whose desire for power remained unfulfilled in other parties. The strength that such transient leaders brought it usually turned out to be short-lived. In Bihar, for example, the Swatantra claimed a unit of a reasonable size, but then suddenly it was left with virtually no party because a prince and his followers who formed the bulk of the party received better terms from another group. In the 1967 election, significantly, the Swatantra won seats mainly in Orissa, Gujarat, Rajasthan and Madras. Of these, the first three have sizable areas of princely influence, while Madras is the home state of Rajagopalachari.

A merger of the Jana Sangh and Swatantra, seemingly like-minded and organizationally complementary, has often been talked about, but the difficulties in the way are considerable. Though both are right-wing parties, the Jana Sangh is more a populist party than a conservative one and is critical of the Swatantra for being a party of the rich; the Swatantra thinks the Sangh's reputation is tarnished by its communalism. A by-product of the Sangh's chauvinism is its desire to absorb another party, not merge with it; the Swatantra is equally proud of its identity and does not wish to dilute what it regards as its distinctive political role. The two parties may enter into electoral alliances in certain areas to guard against dissipation of their strength in mutual opposition, but they will need to change their outlook and image considerably before a merger becomes feasible.

5: *The Parties in Crisis*

Like the Socialists and the Communists, the Congress suffered a split in the autumn of 1969. In what was essentially a power struggle, the organizational wing headed by the party president parted company with the parliamentary wing led by Mrs. Gandhi. Each faction claims to be the original Congress and describes the other as the renegade section. The dramatic division has been variously described as the polarization of ideological groups within the party, as a rift between the organization and the legislative wing, and even as a clash of generations. None of these labels, however, fits the event perfectly. The split did not separate the Congress Party in Parliament from the party organization. Mrs. Gandhi was left with the bulk of the parliamentary party, but the rival faction won over the allegiance of nearly 60 of the party's 288 members in the Lok Sabha, thereby depriving Mrs. Gandhi's government of the absolute majority. Mrs. Gandhi's faction also captured the party machine in all states except Uttar Pradesh, Mysore and Gujarat. At the same time, the split has not given the two groups a precise ideological personality. Mrs. Gandhi's group had dubbed the rivals as the right wing which constantly obstructed the government in the implementation of socialistic policies. With her, however, remain many Congressmen whose support for socialism is known to be lukewarm. At the same time, personal circumstances rather than ideological considerations have forced several genuine socialists into the camp of the old-guard Congress. At its policy meeting in Bombay soon after the break, the Gandhi group of Congress-men shied away from committing themselves to some of the more radical tenets of socialism. The other group, which held a similar meeting about the same time at Ahmedabad, adopted for itself a fairly left-wing program including land reforms and socialistic control of industry.

The Congress split could lead to any of three possibilities. Perhaps, notwithstanding a certain degree of blurring on the edges, the division has created two groups whose ideologies are sufficiently distinct to begin a process which may finally create two national parties strong enough to form alternative governments. Under such an arrangement, the old-guard Congress, which for the first time in the Lok Sabha fulfilled the minimum-strength requirement and been formally recognized as the official opposition, would serve as a bridge for the Jana Sangh, Swatantra and other conservative elements. The Congress, headed by Mrs. Gandhi, may similarly attract the Socialist groups and perhaps even some of the less committed among the Communists. A second possibility would be for the Congress, led by Mrs. Gandhi, to repair the damage caused by the split and continue to function as a large party of consensus. Mrs. Gandhi, who is probably the only nationally known leader in India now, may acquire some of her father's charisma and secure for the

Congress a position of dominance. Either of these possibilities, it may be argued, is welcome. A two-party system in the traditional democratic system should give the country the stability it needs and strengthen the parliamentary institutions. On the other hand, a vast country comprising diverse political, economic and cultural elements may be served well by a monolithic, if ponderous, political party. The lack of expeditiousness in the working of such a party may be adequately compensated for by the sense of national unity that it ideally fosters.

But the third development is more likely than the two suggested above. The Congress Party—Mrs. Gandhi's faction as well as its rival—may continue to lose ground steadily, though not precipitously. Other parties may pick up that following in small bits. The old-guard faction does not appear to have the vitality to form the nucleus of a rival national party. In the public mind, many of its top names carry a tarnished image as those who practiced power unscrupulously with little regard for the good of the country. (They allegedly amassed wealth and used their offices to perpetuate their power.) The other right-wing parties, moreover, are too proud to lose their identity through a merger with this part of the Congress. At the same time, what is left of the Congress under Mrs. Gandhi no longer has the capacity to heal its wounds and grow new flesh. It also suffers from pronounced personal jealousies. At least two of its principal leaders, Y. B. Chavan and Jagjiwan Ram, are ambitious enough to bid for the Prime Ministership at any time that Mrs. Gandhi's hold on the leadership should falter even slightly. In the foreseeable future, therefore, the country may be ruled by a coalition built around the Congress. Mrs. Gandhi, or whoever heads that party, may be compelled to make diverse electoral alliances with local groups to stay in office. Following the split, she has tended to lean on the Akali Dal, the Dravida Munnetra Kazahgam (DMK), the Praja Socialist Party and some independents, and seeks the goodwill of the Communist groups to ward off any challenge from the opposition. This arrangement may seem like politics of consensus in a modified form, but it conspicuously lacks the merit of national unity. Any administration that has to watch the mood of so many small groups cannot act purposefully. Also, any coalition—formal or otherwise—which gathers under its canopy parties so diverse as, for example, the Akali Dal and the Socialists must experience constant tensions and prospects of a break-up.

Virtually the same situation may prevail in a number of states. Besides the Congress, there are numerous "all-India" parties, but none of them has a national following or even a country-wide organization. Whether it is the Communist Parties which are in a dominant position in two states, or the conservative Swatantra, which has been the largest conservative group in Parliament, their influence and party structure have been limited to small areas, often separated by hundreds of miles. The two states dominated by Communists, for example, are more than a thousand miles apart. In the Parliament dissolved in December 1970 the Communists had seats from only seven of the seventeen states. Even these small and dispersed all-India parties have languished recently. The Swatantra, Jana Sangh and both groups of Socialists lost ground in what was called the mini-general election held at the beginning of 1969.

Local parties, on the other hand, have lately gathered strength. At least three states—Madras, Punjab and Orissa—are being ruled by parties that have neither the capacity nor the desire to extend their operations beyond the boundaries of their home states. Their outlook is inevitably narrow and parochial, and as such groups come to power in other states, independently or in coalition with the Congress, India's sense of unity and its capacity to plan and act on a national basis must suffer. Some of the parties have no programs worthy of the name and are driven primarily by local compulsions and the prejudices of the individuals who lead them. The Akali Dal in Punjab, for example, was long acknowledged as a party dominated by the backward-looking, semiliterate and fanatical among the Sikh clergy. It had no concept of national problems nor any desire to look beyond the interests of the small Sikh community to which it successfully appealed in the name of religion. In July 1970, however, when defections threatened its ministry, it looked for support from the Congress group in Punjab. To woo the Congress, the Akali Dal overnight enunciated for itself an elaborate socialistic program, only to forget it and revert to its parochial outlook as soon as the crisis passed.

LEADERSHIP:
A DWINDLING RESERVE

1: *Abundant Resources*

IT WAS a warm April evening in Gwalior, the princely city in central India. The desert air, normally clean and crisp, was laden with dust churned up by hundreds of rickety buses and bullock carts and tens of thousands of pairs of human feet. It was four months before Indian independence, and what seemed a forbidding mass of humanity had assembled in an open-air enclosure in the hope of hearing Jawaharlal Nehru.

Nehru was late by several hours, but that was a matter of little consequence to those who had spent countless hours walking cross-country in blistering heat or expended a whole week's earnings on a rail or bus journey to Gwalior for a glimpse of the leader. It was not often that they had the opportunity to see a man such as Nehru, and they were prepared to wait. Their love for him was not marred by impatience.

It was long after dusk when Nehru appeared on the stage, looking tired after a day spent in fulfilling similar engagements in other equally dusty surroundings. But an old peasant in the midst of the crowd, as he peered at the leader on the distant dais, murmured in the local dialect something that few leaders in the Western world can expect to hear from even the most devoted of their followers. With one glimpse of Nehru, the peasant remarked, he had achieved the ultimate purpose of his life.

In his speech, Nehru made the first public disclosure that the Congress Party had accepted the country's partition. "We cannot wait endlessly," he told his listeners. "If some parts of the country do not wish to come along with us, let not the rest of the country stay in slavery." The ghost of partition had already caused widespread nervousness and tension. Gandhi had denounced it as evil, and many parts of the country had witnessed extensive demonstrations against it. Yet Nehru's disclosure was greeted not by derision and anger but by a mild applause in which resignation was seemingly mixed with hope.

The peasant's remark on seeing Nehru that night and the audience's ready acceptance of a decision so basic and controversial as India's division typified the enormous power that Indian leaders wielded on the eve of independence. But if they enjoyed tremendous support from and power over the people, what they offered them in terms of political wisdom, dedication and idealism was no less impressive.

At the time of independence, India's leadership resources were rich indeed. Not only the people of India, many of whom were emotionally involved in the freedom movement and as such tended to idolize their leaders, but also others—including some who had watched the liquidation of the British Empire with a lingering sense of sorrow—were impressed by the number and caliber of those who were there to assume responsibility of leading the country to the goals of political and economic achievement that it had set for itself.

At the top of the pagoda-like structure of this leadership was Gandhi, who had dominated the country and the freedom movement for nearly thirty years during which he roused many Indians to acts of personal sacrifice and heroism that they had not realized they were capable of. His public advocacy of Hindu-Muslim unity even after the country's bloody partition on the basis of religion inevitably brought upon him the wrath of the fanatics among the Hindus. At the same time, his own associates and followers found the halter of his dominant personality somewhat chafing and his insistence on moral values in the country's governance impractical and irritating. But he was still a man of remarkable power with the masses and he possessed enormous capacity to goad the new government of India, headed by Nehru, into unpalatable action. He held no formal office in either the party or the government. His was the father figure, and he rebuked the people as well as the government when they acted with what he regarded as pettiness and offered them solace when they felt bruised or bewildered. He had spent weeks preceding independence in trying to put out the fires of communal hatred in East Pakistan and would not be distracted from this task even to visit New Delhi on the day of the transfer of power and bless independent India's new government. Later, despite the fact that he had opposed the creation of Pakistan with vehemence ("over my dead body"), he took the drastic step of going on a fast unto death in an attempt to persuade the government to release to Pakistan a disputed amount of 550 million rupees which he thought India was morally obliged to pay. A few weeks after independence, when the Kashmir dispute erupted and Nehru decided to dispatch the Indian Army to expel the invading tribesmen, he did so only after he had obtained Gandhi's approval to this course of action—an endorsement that he seemed to regard as the principal justification for his controversial step.

Nehru himself presented a remarkable combination of charisma, a deep sense of involvement with India's future and an acute awareness of what was happening in the world. Around him stood a group of leaders who had played notable roles in the freedom movement and who were acknowledged stalwarts. There was Sardar Patel, who, on the eve of independence, had hoped—and not without good reason—to be India's first Prime Minister and who accepted the post of Nehru's deputy only in deference to Gandhi's wishes. He lacked Nehru's rapport with the masses, but he was a man of action who did not suffer from doubts and uncertainties of the kind that often assailed Nehru when on the verge of a decisive step. He knew where all the levers of power were and had his hand on them firmly. Ideologically he was a perfect foil to Nehru's socialism, and administratively he tended to cover up such of Nehru's weaknesses as indecisiveness and lack of a practical approach. He spoke briefly and bluntly and could stare an opponent into submission. During the three years that he was Minister for Home Affairs, Patel's displeasure, even if conveyed indirectly, was enough to unnerve and bring back into line any erring state Chief Minister, however well entrenched and powerful.

Others made notable contributions to this consortium of leadership. Maulana Azad, a distinguished scholar of Arabic and Persian, was president of the Congress Party during some of the most difficult phases of the independence movement. His faith in secularism sustained and stimulated Nehru's endeavor, as Prime Minister, to eradicate religious bigotry in India. Rajendra Prasad, who became Agriculture Minister in the first Cabinet and was later India's first President under the new constitution, brought to the thinking at the top a measure of religious orthodoxy. During his two terms as President, he preserved—in fact, added to—the wide measure of public esteem that he enjoyed. Chakravarti Rajagopalachari is still acknowledged as one of the sharpest minds of south India—a man who visualized the possibility of the country's division at a time when almost everyone else in the Congress dismissed Pakistan as a fanciful and wholly impracticable concept born out of Jinnah's negative mind. Before personal frustration drove him to the opposition some years after independence, C.R., as he is popularly known, was the country's first Indian Governor-General and its Home Minister after Patel's death in 1950. He now carries on his aged shoulders virtually the entire burden of the Swatantra Party, one of the principal opposition groups in India's Parliament.

Just below the national level were several others who dominated their respective states and administered them firmly. Govindvallabh Pant was Chief Minister of Uttar Pradesh until 1956, when Nehru invited him to come to the Centre. Morarji Desai was the Chief Minister of the even bigger and more important state of Bombay. He joined the Central Cabinet in 1956 and was to play a significant and highly controversial role in the struggle for power after Nehru. B. C. Roy not only headed the administration of West Bengal, politically the most sensitive state of India, but was by far its most popular leader. Ravi Shankar Shukla filled a similar role in the relatively more placid region of central India. Not all of them had Gandhi's sense of moral righteousness or Nehru's vision or C.R.'s historical perspective, but they understood their states and were competent practitioners of politics and firm administrators.

Outside the Congress Party—and yet of it—were men like Acharya Narendra Deo, Jayaprakash Narayan, Shayama Prasad Mookerjee and the leader of the Untouchables, Dr. B. R. Ambedkar. Deo and Narayan had parted company with Nehru and the Congress Party in 1948 because they found the party's faith in socialism too diluted for their liking, but their personal and emotional ties with Nehru continued. In political stature, Narayan is probably the tallest in India today, and many believe that if he had not "renounced" politics and the Congress Party he would have succeeded Nehru as Prime Minister. Mookerjee and Ambedkar were for a long while strong pillars of the Central Government. This large gathering of leaders was widened by the Congress Party's willingness—in fact, Nehru's anxiety—to draw into the government even those who had played no notable role in the freedom movement. Most political posts were admittedly filled by party members, but the government did not become the exclusive club of those who had been imprisoned by the British or had publicly professed faith in Gandhism. Even those who had accepted and for long flaunted British titles were invited to share power and office. The first two Finance Ministers, John Mathai and Sir Shunakukham Chetty, were rank outsiders. So was Sir Gopalaswami Ayyangar, who held such important portfolios at the Centre as Home, Railways and Defense. Dr. S.

Radhakrishnan, whose first assignment was as India's ambassador to the Soviet Union and who later became the country's President, had held a knighthood under the British. V. K. Krishna Menon, who had stayed away from the country for over three decades, was encouraged by Nehru to leave the rather low level at which he was taking part in the Labour Party politics in Britain to be India's first High Commissioner to the Court of St. James. Nehru sought to create, particularly at the Centre, a government fully representative of all sections of the Indian people and abounding in talent.

Few Asian or African countries were able to forge so powerful and effective a national consensus immediately on attaining independence. In India the legitimacy of the Congress Party's claim to inherit power from the departing British rulers was never challenged, even by the party's worst critics. The Congress had been a movement rather than a party, and Nehru gave it new vitality by drawing into its fold many who had stood away from it. Rather than accept Gandhi's advice to dissolve the Congress Party as a political instrument and to organize new parties on ideological bases, Nehru's endeavor was to make the party— and to an even larger extent the government—more heterogeneous and representative. His efforts at creating a national consensus were facilitated by the fact that the transfer of power was a peaceful process. There was much bloodshed owing to the country's partition, but this blood was spilled by religious fanatics on both sides of the India-Pakistan border, and not by a colonial power withdrawing against its wishes and intent upon a gory exit. Even before British power was withdrawn from the subcontinent, a Constituent Assembly had been set up to frame independent India's new constitution. The existence of such a body for some months before the transfer of power and the earnestness with which it addressed itself to its assignment visually demonstrated the existence of a national consensus for the emerging nation. After independence and until a new Parliament could be elected in accordance with the new constitution, the Constituent Assembly filled the dual role of a constitution-making body and a national legislature, thus assisting in the transition to a formal democratic government.

2: *The Charisma of Jawaharlal Nehru*

Impressive though they were, these resources in leadership began to be depleted soon after independence. Even before six months of independence had passed, Gandhi was assassinated by a Hindu fanatic incensed by the leader's continued pleas for tolerance and forbearance despite the fact that several million Hindus had been forced to flee from their homes in what had become Pakistan. Patel, many years Nehru's senior and in much feebler health, died of a heart ailment in December 1950. Reasons of health prompted Rajendra Prasad to quit active politics and accept the chairmanship of the Constituent Assembly, followed by two terms as the country's President, and though he lived for nearly fifteen years after independence, the sum total of his political power—or even influence—was negligible. Rajagopalachari drifted into opposition via a period of retirement during which he sulked over Nehru's seeming indifference to him. Maulana Azad lived for nearly a decade after independence, but partition on the basis of religion had created a situation and an atmosphere in India in which, despite the country's avowed secularism, a Muslim leader had to take a back seat. The Maulana, also physically tired by the freedom movement and spiritually saddened by the country's division, retreated into himself and did little more than advise Nehru occasionally on problems of domestic politics.

The Socialists who were within the Congress Party during the freedom movement left it soon after independence in search of a more precise and clearly etched identity for themselves. Shayama Prasad Mookerjee, a forceful speaker and an assertive minister, found Nehru's domination intolerable and his politics too radical, and left the government. With the exit of the Socialists under Narayan and the resignation of Mookerjee, a measure of ideological polarization had undoubtedly taken place, but it touched only the outer fringes of the consensus that Nehru had forged. Many votaries of socialism remained in the Congress Party, hoping that Nehru in power would be a more effective instrument of socialism than a group in the opposition. Nor did Mookerjee's departure from the government lead to a mass exodus of the right-wing elements. What he organized in the Jana Sangh were the small segments of the extreme right-wing that had always been opposed to the secular ideology of Gandhi and Nehru. He did not draw within the folds of the new party any members of the Congress disillusioned with their leaders and in search of new guides. The Congress retained its amorphous character, and the core of the national consensus was intact. Within that party, death, resignations or other circumstances had removed all those who had either the intellectual capacity or the political strength to challenge Nehru in any way. Those who had left the party or were in the opposition previously were torn by personal dissensions and suffered noticeably from ideological doubts and political inexperience. Even though they were united in their opposition to the Congress, the CPI, the Socialists and the Jana Sangh were divided among themselves by strong walls of suspicion and distrust. The Socialists were also bound virtually hand and foot by their ties of personal affection for Nehru, for was it not Nehru who had originally organized and for long inspired the Socialist group within the Congress Party? The cumulative effect of these developments was to place almost unchallenged political power in Nehru's hands.

If a date had to be fixed for the beginning of the period during which Nehru exercised supreme, unchallenged authority, it would be the day Patel died in December 1950. Patel's death threw his group into disarray. As is the fate of nearly all groups or parties led by a powerful, domineering personality, the group had no natural successor to Patel. When he formed the government after the 1952 elections, Nehru unceremoniously dropped all those who were Patel's nominees and filled the vacancies with those whom he liked and trusted. Inside the organization (as distinct from the parliamentary wing) Patel's followers fought an energetic battle against Nehru; but, without a strong personality at their head, their cause was almost hopeless. By 1951 Nehru had established his supremacy over both wings of the party by "accepting" the presidency of the Congress Party in addition to the Prime Ministership. He retained the party's presidency for the following four years.

The office of Congress president had by then lost much of its former importance and glory. After independence, real power inevitably resided in the parliamentary wing of the party and its leader, the Prime Minister. After 1955, when Nehru once again chose to part with the top party post, it was held by secondary leaders and, for one brief term, by Mrs. Indira Gandhi, who, at the time the post was offered to her, was more or less a novice in politics. Congress presidents virtually served at Nehru's pleasure and acted not as his advisers but as his minions. Sanjiva Reddy, who left the Chief Ministership of Andhra to serve a term as the party chief, made no secret of his discontent and his wish to return to ministership. On the eve of leaving the presidency, Reddy publicly remarked that a junior ministership in a state government offered greater satisfaction than presidency of the Congress Party.

Congress presidents were not alone in serving at Nehru's pleasure. Barring B. C. Roy, the masterful Chief Minister of the problem-ridden state of West Bengal (who, older than Nehru, tended to treat him with the affectionate arrogance of an elder), senior ministers at the Centre as well as chief ministers in the states tended to watch Nehru's mood before making any political move. Congress executive meetings and even the weekly meetings of the Central Cabinet were often monologues at which his colleagues heard an account of Nehru's latest foreign trip or thinking on some issue then before the country. Decisions were then taken quickly in accordance with the Prime Minister's wishes. Maulana Azad was among the few persons around Nehru who spoke their minds freely when they wanted to, but the area of his interests was restricted and it was not often that he felt impelled to pit his wisdom—and his wisdom was widely acknowledged—against Nehru's judgment. Pant, who succeeded Azad as deputy leader of the Congress Parliamentary Party, expressed his opinion only when asked and was usually circumspect in his approach. Shastri, who was fairly close to Nehru in the later years, tended to act as his troubleshooter rather than an honest and outspoken adviser. Menon was perhaps the only person who spoke his mind freely not only when asked but also when he felt strongly on a subject. This was possible because his advice was usually confined only to the two interrelated subjects of defense and foreign affairs. As his panicky response to the Chinese attack in 1962 indicates, Nehru did not have a steady grasp on defense issues, while on foreign affairs the two leaders had a noticeable unanimity of approach and a remarkable capacity to influence each other. If Menon threw up what seemed a new idea, it was often something that Nehru had presented to him in a nebulous form earlier and Menon's mind had honed into shape.

An inevitable corollary to this situation was that men in responsible positions exercised authority in direct proportion to the measure of confidence that Nehru reposed in them. Menon was a "stranger" to India in that emotionally and intellectually he was out of tune with the average Indian. Politically, he was a man of no fixed address since he hailed originally from the southern state of Kerala, was elected to Parliament from the city of Bombay and lived permanently in Delhi. He had few supporters in the party. And yet he was able to dominate the Ministries of Defense and External Affairs, browbeat into submission the seniormost among the country's generals, ride hobby-horses in the U.N., needlessly squander the country's limited fund of international goodwill and at times even speak arrogantly to India's sensitive Parliament. T. T. Krishnamachari, who was the most powerful of the seven Finance Ministers India has had since independence, had no political base worth the name. It was only Nehru's trust that enabled him to nationalize the insurance companies and follow other financial policies that disturbed some firmly entrenched political forces. By contrast, Morarji Desai, whose seniority and stature in politics were far superior to that of Krishnamachari's and who was no less assertive as a minister, could not implement certain decisions even when they were taken by the Cabinet collectively or were of vital importance to the economy. After the Chinese border attack of 1962, for example, the government launched measures to discourage hoarding of gold, a widespread and traditionally accepted practice in India, and encourage personal savings, but Desai fought alone and ineffectively to implement them. Even the fact that he had a sizable group of supporters in the Congress parliamentary party did not make up for the absence of Nehru's trust in him. In the border state of Punjab, Pratap Singh Kairon was Chief Minister for nine continuous years, during which he ruled the state with sternness bordering on ruthlessness. There were serious charges of corruption, nepotism and highhandedness against him, but he could not be dislodged, primarily because Nehru's faith in his integrity had not been shaken. By the same token, Rajendra Prasad, a stalwart of the freedom movement who was widely respected in the parliamentary party and the country, had no impact on the government during his twelve years as President, for there was no meeting of the minds between him and Nehru. He frequently wrote notes to Nehru expressing his views on issues before the government and making concrete suggestions, but his labors seldom earned anything more than a routine two-line acknowledgment from the Prime Minister's secretary. On the other hand, his successor, Radhakrishnan, though as much a constitutional figurehead as Prasad, was able to exert considerable influence on the government, thanks to his rapport with Nehru.

Nehru wielded this enormous, unchallenged power not because he was a politician in the Tammany Hall tradition but because of his strange, almost inexplicable charisma. He understood little about party organization or balancing groups and factions. If some people stood behind him in the party, they did so either through personal devotion or in the hope of basking in his reflected glory or, as was the case in the years before Patel's death, because they had fallen out with Patel's men. Nehru never organized any group of followers at any level in either the party or the government. There were persons he liked or trusted more than others and he allowed them a greater measure of proximity to himself, but they functioned as individuals and not as an organized body of political workers who could be used as an instrument of power by Nehru. In fact, he was incapable of organizing a disciplined group. Even members of his Cabinet, most of whom were men of no outstanding caliber and were there at his pleasure, were constantly flouting the routine discipline that a minister must observe. Nehru frequently delivered homilies at Cabinet meetings or sent his colleagues tersely worded notes about such matters as maintenance of secrecy of Cabinet decisions or curbing avoidable travel, but the effect of such caveats was always short-lived. Yet his magical sway over the masses of India never weakened. He could make them endorse official policies they did not understand, vote for candidates they did not care for, and even accept a humiliation of the kind India suffered at the hands of the Chinese in 1962. In 1950, a few months before his death and shortly after he had humbled Nehru in the Congress party elections, Patel saw the large mass of people assembled at a meeting in Nasik and sadly confessed, "I could not have brought them out. They have come to see Jawahar."

The secret of Nehru's charisma has always been hard to explain. He had neither the appearance nor the temperament of the average Indian. In his autobiography, he himself admitted somewhat sorrowfully that he did not seem to belong wholly either to India, where he was born, or to Britain, where he was educated. He did not think the way most Indians would, and had developed a sense of values that did not conform to the traditional pattern of life existing in India. At party gatherings he often felt uncomfortable, at times even revolted, by the way some of his colleagues and associates ate and drank or conducted themselves generally. As a speaker, he was poor. When using English, he could express himself coherently and often coin attractive expressions, but in Hindi he spoke haltingly and tended to meander in thought and be repetitive in language. Gandhi spoke to the masses in terms they understood and often said things they wanted to hear. The economic philosophy built around cottage industries that Gandhi propounded and the religious jargon with which he punctuated his speeches had a powerful appeal for them. But Nehru resorted to no such idiom. He spoke not of the small-scale industries that would bring prosperity to their villages but of the big and remote dams and steelmills that would transform the entire country. Similarly, he never used religious symbols or pandered to the religious susceptibilities of his listeners by repeating traditional ideas on issues like cow protection. If he spoke of Hinduism, it was only to remind the people of its basic tolerance and to rebuke them for their bitterness or hostility toward their Muslim fellow countrymen.

Perhaps a large number of Indians came to see and not to hear Nehru. The three lofty images that many an Indian has traditionally enshrined in his mind are those of the saint, the noble prince and the brave warrior. If Gandhi with his loincloth and his constant reference to dharma and emphasis on truth and nonviolence conformed to the image of a saint, Nehru with his background of family affluence and foreign education, his handsome appearance and sophistication of manner looked the prince. The fact that the palatial family home in Allahabad had been given to the freedom movement and that Nehru had discarded his Western garb to wear the "dhoti" of a peasant made him an authentic monk-prince in the eyes of his countrymen, who regard renunciation as a virtue of the highest merit.

To ascribe Nehru's sway over the masses to his princely appearance or the work of the legend-builders about the family's material sacrifices would be to do Nehru an injustice. Nehru had a strange capacity to communicate with illiterate Indian masses. They sensed the trend of his thinking even when he spoke haltingly, in terms they were not familiar with and of things they could not conceive. Nehru acquired this power essentially because he felt for the people deeply and passionately. He could not hide his revulsion if a senior party colleague ate noisily or indulged in the common Indian habit of spitting out betel-nut, but his smile would be warm and genuine if a poor peasant in a dirty shirt embraced him affectionately after a public meeting. He recoiled only if anyone tried to touch his feet, for that gesture, to his mind, represented the type of self-abasement and acceptance of outside subjugation from which he wanted to free his people. The sincerity of his feelings for the Indian masses drew them to him, and even if they failed to understand the jargon of socialism that he often used or see in concrete terms his vision of India's future, they instinctively trusted him. They gave him, as he recorded it in his will and testament, so much of love and affection "that nothing that I can do can repay even a small fraction of it."

3: *Reality Gap*

In nearly all Nehru's endeavors there was a noticeable gap between the vision and the reality. There were areas of conspicuous success and of disheartening failure. He was a leader of remarkable qualities and tremendous strength, but he suffered from certain obvious weaknesses. Many of his decisions were wise, but he also made some avoidable mistakes and often displayed unusually poor judgment. Nehru's vision and sense of dedication as well as his capacity to move a large mass of people were his principal strengths, but his indecision and vacillation in moments of crisis, his perpetual reluctance to take drastic action and his readiness to compromise with opponents, however just his own stance, needlessly frittered away some of that strength.

The goals that he had set before himself and India were truly stupendous. As his writings and speeches (he wrote millions of words and delivered hundreds of speeches) during his seventeen years of Prime Ministership indicate, Nehru's aim was to strengthen India's political unity, establish democratic institutions and create among the people a taste for democracy, modernize Indian attitudes and values, bring about rapid social change and economic growth and, finally, pull the people out of their traditional attitude of passivity and apathy and rouse them to new expectations. The enormity of the undertaking was fully appreciated only by those who knew from their study of Indian history how divided the country had always been till British power imposed an administrative unity on it, and how foreign the institutions of parliamentary democracy were to Indian soil, how decadent and stagnant India's economy was at the time of independence, and how deep-rooted the philosophy of karma had been in Indian life attitudes.

Not many Asian and African countries that achieved freedom during the past two decades have had in a single leader so much charisma and so deep a faith in the country's future as India had in Nehru. Charisma without dedication to national good leads to empty demagoguery or, worse, to misuse of power and to dictatorship. Similarly, earnestness without a mass following leads, particularly in a backward country, to nothing better than pipe dreams and frustration. Nehru possessed both requisites and, whatever the net balance of his success or failure as a leader, it is a measure of his greatness that he did not allow his personal power—almost absolute as it was—to weaken his sense of purpose or corrupt him.

There were other, more concrete, tools that Nehru found handy. First, there was the Congress Party, a massive organization with a membership of millions and links and affiliations reaching the remotest of Indian villages. In later years of Nehru's Prime Ministership, it came to acquire a paunchy look symptomatic of partaking of power excessively and for too long, but at the time he was setting national goals it was a valuable vehicle of political action and remained so for many years.

The bureaucracy was another useful tool that Indian leaders inherited from the British. At the time the British Raj ended, the armed forces had been Indianized to the extent that several Indians had risen to the rank of brigadier general, while on the civil side many posts of Secretary to the Government (the most senior permanent civil servant in a ministry) were held by Indians. Britain had run a tightly administered empire in India and, unlike colonial powers in Africa and other parts of Asia, had entrusted many responsible positions to Indian administrators. Apart from local and provincial administrations manned almost entirely by Indians, there was the Indian Civil Service, a national cadre of top bureaucrats; they numbered 1,157 at the time of independence, nearly 50 percent were Indians. Thus, the leaders of the new nation did not have to face the type of administrative vacuum that existed when, for example, Belgium withdrew from the Congo or the kind of dependence on foreign civil servants and advisers that Jomo Kenyatta found unavoidable for many years after Britain granted independence to Kenya.

If the instruments of government were there, were they geared to a viable political philosophy? Nehru's ideological beliefs were always somewhat fuzzy. In his time, he was denounced as both a crypto-Communist and "a running dog of imperialism." The truth lay somewhere between the two extremes. As he himself once acknowledged in a press interview, he considered "communism in theory to be a revolutionary and scientific doctrine conforming to the laws of historical development and the social and economic urges of our time," but he also did not "like the rigid dogmas of communism and its unnecessarily violent and intolerant attitude." He admired the Soviet revolution and what it meant in terms of ending social injustice, but he was also disgusted by the cruelty of the Stalinist era. He accepted the Marxist theory of the social and economic emancipation of the people, but he doubted the inevitability of class conflict and certainly did not accept the theory of the dictatorship of the proletariat or the unavoidability of violence in creating a classless society. Essentially he wished to bring about a synthesis of the good features of the socialist and democratic systems. His endeavor, as he once mused shortly before his death in 1964, was to evolve "a new way to socialism by consent and cooperation."

In evolving this approach, Nehru was guided not only by his temperament but also by his surroundings and circumstances. Just about the time he was being exposed to Marxist literature as a student in Britain, he was also acquiring a degree of admiration for British democracy and parliamentary institutions, giving his socialism a Fabian flavor. Later, circumstances of the Indian freedom movement made him a lieutenant of Gandhi, who represented in his appearance as well as his actions the stark realities of the poverty of the Indian masses.

The political program that grew in Nehru seemed, consciously or otherwise, uniquely adapted to the problems and needs of India. He was open to pressures and influences and had a marked tendency to compromise when challenged—an attitude that led to certain contradictions and anomalies—but by and large his approach to economic issues was consistent and reasonably coherent. It appears confusing only when one tries to measure it by standard Western political concepts, which tend to overlook many of the special circumstances of a country like India. Socialism was the goal that Nehru set before the country, but he did not rule out a meaningful role for private capital. The infrastructure, he felt, had to be developed through state ownership in a country of India's size and poverty. No private industrial concern, for example, had the managerial skill, capital or technical resources to run the railways or even set up a 2.5-million-ton steel plant or a big aircraft factory. For similar reasons, and only partly for reasons of ideology, the basic industries were also placed within the sphere of state ownership. But there was no need, Nehru apparently felt, to implement socialism in a copy-book style by nationalizing private capital. The capitalists could make a contribution to the country's development, and, however meager that contribution, it should not be spurned in a country where resources were exceedingly limited and the need for development was enormous. In any case, to nationalize much of the existing capitalist structure, such as outdated sugar factories and textile mills, would have amounted to acquisition of virtual junk. (Some of the operational problems of Indian Airlines, the nationalized airway for domestic traffic, can be traced to the personnel and equipment that it had to acquire when the government nationalized a group of privately owned airlines in the early phase of its socialist fervor).

India, therefore, aimed at achieving a "socialistic" (not socialist) society and developed the concept of "mixed economy" in which the capitalists had a sizable role to play. Whether capitalists were given too large or too small a slice of economic power depended upon the angle from which one viewed the picture. Broadly, however, efforts to protect the interests of the workers took the form of labor legislation recognizing collective bargaining, trade-unionism and the workers' right to strike. At the same time, the power and ambitions of the capitalists were intended to be kept within bounds through rigorous official price controls and regulations relating to the granting of licenses for import of raw materials and machinery. Needless to say, a formula so full of checks and balances did not always work smoothly or to the satisfaction of everyone concerned, but it reflected the clear stamp of Nehru's mind and the catholicity of his political beliefs as well as the narrowness of some of his personal prejudices.

As a leader, the major fault in Nehru's style was his propensity to try to attend to too many things, many of which did not need attention at his level. Consequently, many important issues requiring his support languished. He tried to do too much over too wide an area and in too short a period. Some of the tasks he assigned himself, such as creation of national solidarity, establishment of democratic institutions in ruggedly inhospitable soil, and moving a backward, illiterate mass of people, incapable even of self-pity, toward modern economic planning and action, were too large to be achieved in a single life span. But, additionally, he tended to fritter away his energies on paltry undertakings. Yet if he agreed to serve on the committee entrusted with the landscaping of the Buddha garden in Delhi or devoted some of his time designing the close-collar official formal wear (it later briefly set the fashion for the "Nehru jacket") and setting of the country's national anthem to music, it was essentially because he was genuinely interested in these tasks. Combined with it was a sense of impatience and a desire to do many things in the short time he had. He took over the country's Prime Ministership when he was approaching fifty-eight, a fairly advanced age by Indian standards. Probably he felt a sense of urgency as he surveyed the enormity of what needed to be done. The combined effect of this compulsive hurry to accomplish much and seemingly limitless range of interests was to make him flit from issue to issue and to replace concrete action and achievement with slogans. As early as 1950, Nehru first talked of the urgent need for self-sufficiency in food, but before any concrete results had been achieved or even seemed probable, he had moved on to other issues and problems. He returned to the food issue, in 1957, but again briefly and without ensuring that this realization of the gravity of the problem had been translated into concrete action at various administrative levels. At other times he pushed campaigns ranging from growing more trees to slum clearance in various Indian cities, but his interest in these undertakings sustained itself only as long as his attention was not taken up by other subjects.

That Nehru moved from idea to idea without building a sound base of administrative action for them also suggests the inadequacy of his colleagues and those working under him. His greatness and a degree of intolerance of his colleagues disheartened those who wished to function in the government with a measure of independence. These qualities drew to him mediocre careerists, politicians with no political base worth the name, and sycophants. Men who chose to work with him often lacked either the will or the capacity to implement what he would suggest. Strong, assertive men like Morarji Desai, S. K. Patil and even Y. B. Chavan, whom he brought into the Central Cabinet, enjoyed little of his confidence, and their effectiveness was consequently limited. There were others who, perhaps deliberately, sabotaged his concepts and plans through studied inaction. A curious phenomenon of the Nehru era was that though few opposed him openly, those who differed with him for personal or ideological reasons placed subtle—and at times not so subtle—obstacles in his way. He passionately believed in reforming India's medieval land system and transferring ownership of land from absentee landlords and other such feudal elements to the cultivators themselves. His home state of Uttar Pradesh was the first to pass massive land legislation to that end. In the years following independence he urged various state governments—agriculture and land reforms are a state subject under the Indian constitution—to pass new land laws, but while most states went through the motions of introducing reforms, they left enough legal lacunae and loopholes to deprive the peasant of many of the benefits that were intended to reach him.

On the sensitive question of official language, Nehru promised the southern states that Hindi would not be imposed on them, but the assurance, though solemnly offered in Parliament, was never formally incorporated in the Official Language Bill passed later. Pant, then Home Minister and a strong Hindi protagonist, did not have his heart in the Prime Minister's approach to the language question. If what Nehru had suggested had been implemented, Madras and Uttar Pradesh might have been spared the bloody language riots they witnessed in January 1965.

His unwillingness—or inability—to back his decisions and ideas with firm action was one of the several weaknesses, some of judgment and some of compassion, that seriously restricted his area of achievement. If he had wanted to, he could have implemented his promise to retain English as an "associate" official language despite Pant's somewhat passive opposition. His daughter, Mrs. Indira Gandhi, though lacking a towering personality and facing many more problems and difficulties, was able to put the promised guarantee through Parliament in 1968. One important occasion when he displayed an unusual tenacity of purpose and unwillingness to surrender to opposition concerned the controversial question of modernizing the Hindu social law. Many of his supporters were too orthodox at heart to accept such radical changes in ancient laws as granting equal property rights to women and providing for divorce in Hindu marriage. Opposition also came from such lofty quarters as the President of India, Dr. Rajendra Prasad. But, curiously, Nehru persisted, and though it took him almost five years, he saw to it that the bill introducing some basic changes in the Hindu law was placed on the statute book.

But such unbending perseverance was exceptional. Normally, he was prone to give in to opposition or seek avenues of compromise. From 1953, when the Telugu-speaking people demanded a separate state for themselves, to 1960, when the bilingual state of Bombay was split into Maharashtra and Gujarat, India's reorganization on the basis of language was a sad story of Nehru yielding to pressures, making compromises and being moved by political expediency. Some of the compromises he made were aimed at such limited political gains that they shocked many in the country. After having denounced the Muslim League for years for its narrow, communal outlook, for example, he accepted an electoral alliance with it in Kerala in 1960 in the hope of defeating the Communist Party. In 1956, when he found the Congress Party faced with doubtful prospects in Punjab on the eve of the general elections Nehru similarly agreed to do business with the Akali Dal, a regional party of the Sikhs, which he had severely criticized in the past for its sectarian politics.

Perhaps Nehru accepted these compromises because he hardly understood the intricacies of state politics. Each state had its own pattern of factionalism, pulls and pressures based on personalities, caste and economics. Unlike Lal Bahadur Shastri, who succeeded him as Prime Minister, Nehru had no head for such details. Even before independence, what largely occupied his mind were international issues and certain broad ideological problems. How the Hindu Jats of Punjab were pitched against the Sikh Jats of another part of the state, or how Bhumiars and Rajputs formed the pattern of power in Bihar and who the persons were behind such elements, did not seem to interest Nehru. Significantly, he did not discern the revolt in Madras against

Brahmin domination until quite late.

His insufficient acquaintance with the forces and individuals involved in state politics made it necessary for him to rely on powerful state satraps, not all of whom exercised authority with a pronounced sense of propriety. At times, instead of backing a state leader who could offer the state honest, purposeful administration and could be relied upon to implement the party's accepted policy, Nehru chose to support or at least passively accept a rival candidate who could rule with a firm, if not very clean, hand and could be relied upon to keep factional bickerings within the Congress Party under check. Despite personal distrust of him, he allowed Atulya Ghosh to dominate the party in West Bengal. Apart from the appearance of youthfulness and initiative that Biju Patnaik presented, what endeared him to Nehru was the fact that in Orissa, which had seen much political instability, he was able to win the elections and to keep the party well shepherded. The Prime Minister similarly shielded Pratap Singh Kairon in Punjab and accepted Bakshi Ghulam Mohammed as the Kashmir Premier.

Himself a man of unblemished honesty and integrity, Nehru took no action against men in authority in his own cabinet or in the state even if he knew that allegations of nepotism and corruption against them were not without basis. His trusted friends reported to him how Bakshi Ghulam Mohammed's family had enriched itself during his term in office, but Nehru allowed him to rule Kashmir for ten years and took little notice of his alleged highhandedness. Kairon, who was Chief Minister of Punjab for almost a decade, was similarly accused of gross nepotism and of having helped his family amass a fortune, but for years Nehru would not accept the demand for a judicial probe of the allegations. Two other chief ministers had built impressive fortunes rapidly, but there was no inquiry into their methods of self-aggrandizement. Several ministers in his own Cabinet had invited widespread allegations of corruption, and Nehru himself was known to entertain similar suspicions against them. But he chose not to exclude them from the government.

4: *Measuring Greatness*

It is not easy to strike a clear balance sheet on what Nehru achieved. Possessed of a complex mind, he acted in ways that touched the lives of the people in a subtle, often intangible, manner. It may be possible to begin to assess his performance only in terms of certain specific goals that he had seemingly set for himself.

Even before he died, it was becoming apparent that the secularism in which he so earnestly believed had not taken firm root in India. He seldom missed an opportunity, whatever the forum or the occasion, to urge the people to forget their past of religious strife and bitterness and weld themselves into a nation in which an individual's caste and religion were his personal affair and did not influence his politics. Despite failing health, he increased his efforts for communal amity after the Hindu-Muslim riots in Jabbalpore in 1961, but more bloody clashes elsewhere in the country in the years following suggested the hopelessness of the task. Since his death some riots, such as those in Nagpur in 1968, in Ahmedabad in 1969 and in Bhiwandi in 1970, displayed unprecedented levels of venom between the majority community and the Muslims, the principal minority. It clashes between the two are not so frequent and extensive as shortly before partition, it is mainly because since the creation of Pakistan the two communities have been unevenly matched. Otherwise there is little to suggest that Hindus and Muslims have moved even a short distance toward amity and an understanding of the kind Nehru so fervently sought.

India's political unity, another article of faith with Nehru, is also faced with chronic challenges, though not so serious as those confronting secularism. His personality and charisma lent the country an unusual sense of unity, which, as was bound to happen, has weakened perceptibly with his exit from the scene. Language continues to be a major divisive issue. Acceptance of

Hindi as the national official language in place of English is still largely nominal in the non-Hindi-speaking areas. State governments wrangle among themselves over petty issues. Several of them have tended to virtually debar people from other parts of the country from securing employment and business opportunities and have discouraged the exchange of students, teachers and administrators with other regions. Territorially, there seems scant prospect in the foreseeable future of China's withdrawing from nearly 40,000 square miles of territory that India regards as its own. At the same time, a movement inspired, if not actually helped, by Peking has grown in West Bengal and has the potentiality of developing into a Vietcong-style bid to take over what is one of the most important parts of India in terms of industrial development.

In instilling a taste for democracy, Nehru's efforts appear to have attained greater success. It was obvious that India could achieve decidedly more impressive economic results if it accepted a totalitarian form of government. But Nehru's devotion to democracy was deep enough to forbid any cutting of ideological corners in the struggle toward progress. He scrupulously adhered not only to the spirit but also to the forms of democratic procedures. He made certain that Parliament and the state legislatures functioned independently and did not become handmaidens of the executive. Elections were held regularly, and the Indian press enjoyed a degree of freedom not available to the press in any Asian country except perhaps Japan.

When the Constituent Assembly approved of universal adult franchise, many in India, accustomed to voting rights determined on the basis of property and educational qualifications under the British, believed that the Assembly had hastened the process of democracy unduly, perhaps dangerously. How could an illiterate person—and over 80 percent of Indians were illiterate at the time—be expected to use the franchise judiciously? Nehru realized the hazard involved, but, as he explained to a press conference at the time, "the right has to be given now or maybe it will never be given." He was averse to the creation of a privileged class with the exclusive right to vote, for such a class would be reluctant to share its power with others and would tend to obstruct the widening of the franchise.

The voters themselves have largely allayed such fears and concerns. They have been influenced by local predilections and narrow factors like caste, community and language, but by and large they have not been dumb cattle driven by sinister elements. In fact, they have shown themselves capable of a measure of independence that voters in more advanced countries do not always demonstrate. The 1967 general election saw the defeat of powerful leaders such as Kumaraswami Kamaraj, the then Congress President; S. K. Patil, acknowledged strong man of the Bombay city congress; Atulya Ghosh, "boss" of the West Bengal Congress; and several state Chief Ministers. Their humiliation shows, on the one hand, the fairness of the elections in India and, on the other, the voter's capacity to cast his vote freely and without being overawed by established authority.

Defections in legislatures and frequent changes in government in some states since 1967 have caused some criticism of the form in which democracy is being practiced. The structure will undoubtedly be modified, but the desire for democracy appears not to have weakened. Significantly, in 1970, when Indians yearned for a strong leader, they usually were thinking of one who might function within a democratically elected framework and not with totalitarian power behind him.

If it created a feeling of continuity when power was transfered from British to Indian hands, Nehru's leadership also created a void in his wake. He has often been blamed for not having trained a cadre of leaders in the states and at the Centre to succeed him, but this criticism is not wholly valid. He frequently asserted that it was not for him to nominate his successor—that the party and the people should choose their leader. That a person is specifically nominated as the successor to power or placed in a position to succeed does not always ensure the inheritance of leadership, or that the beneficiary, having inherited, will be able to retain it for long. Despite all the grooming and build-up in the public eye that Anthony Eden had received, he could not survive the first major crisis his government faced. The leader, Nehru realized, emerged as a result of certain complex political forces and not through a simple process of nomination by the outgoing leader. He would, therefore, always reject tersely any suggestion that he indicate his preference for a successor. At the same time, however, it is undeniable that through various means he tried to tamper with and give some direction to the political forces that would decide who the next Prime Minister would be.

The first attempt to influence, though perhaps negatively, the pattern of leadership after him came in 1961, when Nehru downgraded, deliberately and without convincing reasons, the post of deputy leader of the Congress Parliamentary Party. Till then, whoever occupied the second position in the Cabinet, whether he was formally designated as Deputy Prime Minister or not, was usually chosen as deputy leader of the party. On the Prime Minister's death, the deputy leader would automatically succeed him as head of the government and leader of the party, though only in a temporary capacity. For confirmation, he had to be formally elected by the party as its new leader. The deputy leadership thus did not specify the line of succession, but the position carried prestige and certainly improved an aspirant's prospects of being chosen the leader. In the first fourteen years after independence, the position had been held by Patel, Maulana Azad and Pant. Patel served due to his own strength in the party and the other two because they enjoyed Nehru's trust and confidence. On Pant's death in 1961, Morarji Desai automatically moved up to the second position in the Cabinet and would normally have been entitled to be chosen deputy leader in the party, too. Even though he was not widely popular with party members, his seniority in the party and claim to deputy leadership were virtually unchallenged. But though he had come to the Central Cabinet at Nehru's invitation and had already been there for five years, first as Minister of Commerce and later as Minister for Finance, Desai had not endeared himself to Nehru. Desai's markedly right-wing politics, his alleged proximity to big business and his rigid approach in administrative matters had created a gulf between the two. His personal fads—he is a staunch "prohibitionist" and would not take vaccination and cholera injections even when traveling abroad—also irked Nehru. It was this known lack of warmth on Nehru's part for Desai rather than any inadequacy of support for him in the party that brought about a formal challenge to the move for his election as deputy leader. It is not unlikely that some close to the Prime Minister encouraged this challenge and creation of a situation in which Nehru had to be called upon to save the party's unity. Nehru's advice, accepted by the party with the expected alacrity, was that there be two deputy leaders and that they need not be ministers. He also deferred the election for almost a year, and when it was held, he ensured that the posts were filled by people of no political consequence. Thus Desai's claim to succession suffered a severe setback.

A further blurring of the line of succession occurred in 1963 through what came to be known as the Kamaraj Plan. Under this plan twelve senior members of the government at the Centre and in the states resigned "voluntarily" to devote their time and energies to rehabilitating the Congress Party, which, it was argued, was increasingly drifting away from the people, showing signs of having been corrupted by power and badly in need of rejuvenation. Desai, denied his chance of becoming deputy leader earlier, was among those who were "drafted" for party work under the Kamaraj Plan. He was thus deprived also of his second position in the government.

The origin of the plan was rather humble and its aims were not so ambitious. The Madras Chief Minister, Kumaraswami Kamaraj, who gave his name to the plan, was worried about the increasing disenchantment of the people in his state with the Congress Party. The challenge from the DMK, a local right-wing party with secessionist overtones to its program, was proving formidable. In a private talk with Nehru during a party meeting in Hyderabad, Kamaraj expressed his desire to give up

the chief ministership and offer his undivided attention to burnishing the party image in Madras. Nehru was distinctly unenthusiastic. Patnaik, the Orissa Chief Minister, had his own set of
personal and political troubles and was seemingly anxious to
find an opportunity to step down from office. He took to Kamaraj's idea enthusiastically, enlarged its scope to cover other
states, and, during a visit to Kashmir, where Nehru was having a
brief summer holiday, he urged the Prime Minister to accept the
idea. If Nehru had any reservations about the usefulness of such
a course of action, they were removed by the support that Indira
Gandhi and G. L. Nanda, then Minister for Labor, gave to the
plan.

Desai was wary of the plan. He suspected from the very start
that it was aimed at eliminating him. He also doubted that it was
an effective way of revitalizing the party and said so in a letter
to Nehru. By then, however, the plan had caught the imagination of the public and the party rank and file. In fact, their fervor
was so great that any minister refusing to submit his resignation
would have been marked out as one who clung to power for
selfish reasons. Consequently, there was an avalanche of resignations by people professing anxiety to renounce office to be
able to serve the party. The atmosphere in the party and the
country was such that, despite his reservations and suspicions,
Desai had no choice but to sullenly hand in his resignation. As
was foreseen from the very start, the task of deciding whose
resignation might be accepted and who might be chosen to work
for the party was left to Nehru. Those whom he chose for this
act of renunciation included, besides Desai, Central Ministers
such as Lal Bahadur Shastri, Jagjivan Ram and S. K. Patil and
some well-entrenched state Chief Ministers who, unlike Kamaraj
and Patnaik, had no desire to give up power.

By supporting and implementing the Kamaraj Plan as he did,
Nehru invited upon himself serious allegations of playing under-
hand politics. By removing ministers of the seniority and stature
of Desai and Shastri, he allegedly paved the way for his daughter's rise to Prime Ministership. Some accuse him of curbing

Desai's prospects of succeeding him and promoting Shastri's chances. The most charitable among the critics suggest the plan was a Machiavellian way of getting rid of unwanted Cabinet colleagues or Chief Ministers who were being uncooperative in the states.

Nehru himself angrily denied these charges and what he described as the "most fantastic kind of motive-hunting." He argued that if he had wanted to discard any members of his government, his acknowledged popularity with the people would have enabled him to eliminate any minister, however senior. Why, he asked, should he have to resort to a ruse to accomplish such a task?

Nehru admittedly had the mass support and the strength to act against any colleague he did not wish to retain, but, as his entire career indicates, he lacked the temperament to wield an unsheathed knife. In his long years in office he had never expelled a colleague, however unwelcome the latter might have become. Those who left the Cabinet either did so by their own choice or were pushed out by circumstances. In 1962 he could not persuade Hafiz Ibrahim, Minister for Irrigation and Power, whose advancing years had rendered his continuance in office untenable, to move to the sinecure of a state governorship. Only a few weeks before the Kamaraj Plan was implemented, he had asked Patil to give up Food and Agriculture and take the Railways Portfolio, but the latter protested against the shift and the Prime Minister let him stay where he was.

To suggest, as some have, that Nehru devised the plan to clear the way for his daughter's rise to power is, to say the least, far-fetched. In 1961, while discussing the issue of the party's deputy leadership, Nehru had once remarked that the next leader of the party might not emerge from within the parliamentary party and might be someone from outside. This remark, which then roused no suspicion of any kind and was taken in its rhetorical sense, was later regarded as an indication of his "secret" plan to install Mrs. Gandhi as Prime Minister. Whatever his other faults, Nehru was incapable of planning her rise to power with such deviousness and a master chess-player's capacity to anticipate a maze of intervening moves. As he himself admitted, he did not rule out her playing an important role. He allowed her to become Congress president in 1959 but did not press her to accept a second term in office, tenure that would have enhanced her political stature. A few months before his death, nearly a dozen state Chief Ministers had jointly written to Nehru urging him to include Mrs. Gandhi in the Cabinet as Foreign Minister, but he did not agree. He had just suffered a paralytic stroke which, though minor, was a clear warning of the hastening end, and if he had been planning for three years to install Mrs. Gandhi as his successor, he would have accepted the Chief Minister's plea. The purpose of the Kamaraj Plan apparently was not to clear Mrs. Gandhi's way to Prime Ministership, though if its implementation improved her prospects, Nehru probably did not mind.

A mass of circumstantial evidence, however, does indicate some kind of design, perhaps limited in scope, behind the Kamaraj Plan. Perhaps it would be more accurate to say that, though it was designed to strengthen the party, Nehru also used it to resolve some of his difficulties that otherwise would have needed harsh, unpleasant action. Even if the plan was not directed specifically against Desai, it is undeniable that the list of those whose resignations were accepted reflected a distinct pattern. By excluding Desai and Patil, both of whom represented right-wing forces, Nehru was able to achieve the ideological cohesion that his Cabinet had always lacked. By choosing Jagjivan Ram for party work, he dropped a minister whom he had wanted to exclude a year earlier but could not. Shastri was his trusted troubleshooter, and apparently his exclusion from the Cabinet was intended to ward off the charge of partisanship in drawing up the list. The exclusion from the government of the Ministers of Education and Information and Broadcasting under the Kamaraj Plan was seemingly intended to remove some of the political deadwood that the Cabinet had accumulated over the years. In choosing the state leaders for the renunciation of office,

Nehru appeared to be guided by considerations other than their capacity or desire to strengthen the party organization. Besides Kamaraj and Patnaik, the original authors of the concept, there was Bakshi Ghulam Mohammed, whose highhandedness and alleged corruption in Kashmir had begun to cause much embarrassment at home and abroad, and C. B. Gupta, the masterful Chief Minister of Uttar Pradesh, who headed the anti-Nehru faction in the Prime Minister's home state. The other two Chief Ministers whose resignations he accepted were similarly known to be well outside the circle of Nehru's trusted men.

Besides the composition of the list, there were other reasons to suspect a political design behind the plan. After renouncing office for the specific purpose of working for the party, none of the twelve except Kamaraj, who became Congress president, was assigned any special duties. They sat stonily in Parliament or sulked and conspired in the states. Shastri returned to the Cabinet within four months, thereby strengthening the belief that earlier he had only been a decoy. After the twelve had left office, the plan virtually came to an end. A second list of leaders drafted for party work was supposed to emerge, but never did.

Whatever the motivation behind the plan, its impact on the succession issue has been exaggerated. Even if Desai had been in office when Nehru died in May 1964, it is doubtful that he would have served as acting Prime Minister for more than a few days. The line-up of the political forces was such that neither Desai nor Mrs. Gandhi could seriously have hoped to be chosen leader. Nor could the choice for leader—Kamaraj Plan or no Kamaraj Plan—have been anyone other than Shastri.

It was not the Kamaraj Plan but his personality and temperament that blocked Desai's rise to the top. Support for him within the party, though sizable, was not large enough to bring him to power. Also, much of this support was somewhat negative in character, inasmuch as it came from those who were compelled to stand behind Desai due to their failure to find a place in Nehru's camp. Besides his home state of Gujarat, the principal support for Desai came from the Gupta group in Uttar Pradesh, which for reasons of local factional politics was opposed to Nehru. Another prominent Desai supporter, K. Hanumanthaiya, former Chief Minister of Mysore, had similarly fallen out with Nehru for personal reasons, and Bakshi Ghulam Mohammed edged closer to Desai only after Nehru accepted, to the Kashmir Premier's utter astonishment and deep distress, his resignation under the Kamaraj Plan.

Not all those who were opposed to Desai had ideological differences with him. Some of his leading opponents at the time the succession issue arose were as right-wing in political outlook as he himself was. In fact, the bulk of the Congress Party members were rather orthodox in approach and should have been behind Desai, but his arrogant behavior and holier-than-thou attitude offended them. Like Patel, strong and assertive and brusque in manner, he singularly lacked both the capacity to see the other person's point of view and Patel's ability to inspire confidence and win loyalty.

The "caucus," as Desai angrily described the group of leaders who barred his election as leader on Nehru's death, was moved not so much by the abrasiveness of his manner as by his inability to share power with others. In Nehru they had had a supreme leader who was not beholden to them for his position and whom they could not manage. If Desai were to succeed him as Prime Minister, the situation would, from their point of view, be even worse. Without Nehru's stature and unchallenged claim to leadership, it was feared Desai would tend to hold the levers of power firmly and exercise power almost selfishly.

The principal role in the "caucus" was played by a group of five leaders who later came to be identified by the public and a section of the Indian press as the "syndicate." Headed by Kamaraj, the syndicate included Atulya Ghosh and S. K. Patil, acknowledged bosses of the Congress in West Bengal and Bombay city respectively, and Reddy and Nijalingappa, who were then Chief Ministers of Andhra and Mysore. The five were drawn to one another gradually by a measure of like-mindedness on political issues and a certain similarity in temperament. All were regional leaders of some eminence and strength, enjoyed wielding political power, belonged to the non-Hindi parts of India and were stern party organizers in the style of Mayor Richard Daley of Chicago. None of them stood any chance of becoming Prime Minister himself. While they had been in touch with one another for almost two years before Nehru's death, they agreed on a precise political objective only in October 1963, when four of them assembled for parleys at Tirupathi in Andhra. Patil, who could not be present, reportedly kept in touch by telephone. The program of action involved keeping Desai as far from power as possible and working for the acceptance as Nehru's successor of one who would be least likely to divide the party and, presumably, be amenable to the syndicate's wishes. Their first concrete move was to prevent Desai from becoming Congress president, a post that had fallen vacant and that Desai was anxious to secure. This objective was achieved by persuading Kamaraj—with Nehru's tacit approval, of course —to accept the job after Shastri had declined it.

In the struggle for succession that followed Nehru's death, the syndicate did mobilize support for Shastri (a fact that gave the new Prime Minister an unfortunate image of a political marionette), but its strength and influence appeared to be much greater than they actually were. It seemed to be dominating the situation because it was in harmony with the majority will of the parliamentary party and the leaders in the states. The bulk of the party and leadership was genuinely opposed to Desai and in favor of Shastri. The syndicate merely expressed that broad consensus in an organized, articulate manner. It did not, as Desai bitterly complained, stage-manage Shastri's election as leader. It could not have done so if support for Shastri's candidacy had not been widespread. It is a measure of the syndicate's limited influence that it almost certainly could not have, should it have so wished, sponsored any of its own members for Prime Ministership.

Even if Shastri seemed to stand on the syndicate's shoulders at the time, he was really the only effective candidate in the field.

If Desai had had any hope of success, he would not have accepted Kamaraj's assessment that the party preferred Shastri; rather, he would have insisted on a regular ballot, as he did nineteen months later when the question of succession arose again following Shastri's sudden death in Tashkent. Unlike Desai, who made no secret of his ambition, Shastri was markedly reticent. In the days that followed Nehru's death, he did not suggest by word or action that he was eager to be Prime Minister. This is not to say that he was devoid of ambition. But his personal values would not allow him to resort to questionable means to advance his own cause or undercut a rival or even make promises in return for support. Still, he was aware of the strength of his position in the impending struggle for power, and in a gentle, unobtrusive and totally characteristic manner he sought to buttress it further. He maintained cordial relations with the syndicate, even though at least three of its members—Atulya Ghosh, S. K. Patil and Sanjiva Reddy—were anathema to Nehru. In the months before Nehru's death, Shastri never missed an opportunity of displaying personal courtesy to them and generally strengthening his bridges with them. He undoubtedly did not make any promises about sharing power with its members, but if they hoped that on being chosen Prime Minister he would be their man or amenable to their influence, he did nothing to disabuse them of this belief. As he publicly admitted once, Nehru did not wish to include his name among those who were quitting the government under the Kamaraj Plan, but Shastri insisted that he, too, be allowed to resign. Renouncing office when everyone knew he did not have to quit brought him public acclaim. Yet four months later, when Nehru suffered a stroke and his end seemed near, Shastri did not oppose Kamaraj's suggestion that he return to the government, seemingly because he knew that that would bring him to the center of power again. On winning the party leadership, Shastri magnanimously invited Desai to join the Cabinet, but offered him not the second but the third position in it. G. L. Nanda, who, as number two in the Nehru Cabinet, had acted as Prime Minister for nine days while the process of electing the new leader was being completed, argued that as an "ex-Prime Minister" he was entitled to a position in Shastri's Cabinet no lower than the second. This argument had no constitutional validity. Nor did Shastri have any personal obligation to Nanda, who in the months before Nehru's death had vehemently opposed a move for Shastri to be designated as Deputy Prime Minister and thereby marked as the intended successor. Yet when Desai would not join the Cabinet except as number two, Shastri politely told him that he could not ignore Nanda's claim to that position. Anyone who was aware of Desai's strong sense of pride would have known, even before the offer was made to him, that he would not agree to being placed below Nanda.

Another person who might have posed a challenge to his position as Nehru's successor was Mrs. Gandhi, and Shastri dealt with her, too, with remarkable shrewdness. He gave her a place in his Cabinet as Minister for Information and Broadcasting, a portfolio which in terms of political influence is of little importance. It was then suggested in the press that the Prime Minister would have liked her to accept a more prestigious charge such as Foreign Affairs but that, overwhelmed by her father's death and conscious of the inadequacy of her administrative experience, Mrs. Gandhi had preferred something less onerous. In reality, Mrs. Gandhi had always set her heart on being Foreign Minister, but she was offered only Broadcasting. Within a month of becoming Prime Minister, Shastri suffered a mild heart attack which ruled out his visit to London to attend the Commonwealth Prime Ministers' conference. He chose Mrs. Gandhi to represent India at the meeting, but not alone. Along with her he sent T. T. Krishnamachari, a strong and assertive personality whose presence inevitably reduced her to an insignificant minor role. While she was away in Britain, Shastri quietly handed over the Foreign Affairs Portfolio, which he had held himself till then, to Swaran Singh, who had spent many years in the Central Cabinet and was personally trustworthy and politically innocuous. With that allotment ended any hope that Mrs. Gandhi might have entertained of receiving Foreign Affairs or any other important portfolio in Shastri's government.

His handling of Desai and Mrs. Gandhi reflected a certain political deviousness or an endeavor on Shastri's part to work around a situation rather than face it squarely—a departure from his usual style, probably the result of nervousness and a sense of inferiority from which he seemed to suffer during the first year or so of his Prime Ministership. Soft-spoken and gentle of manner, he could not display anger and hostility toward even the lowliest of his subordinates. Even when someone had offered strong provocation and earned a reprimand, Shastri's rebuke would display more sorrow than anger. But he did not shirk difficult situations or hesitate to make harsh decisions except in the first few months of his Prime Ministership, when he deservedly earned the charge that his administration was a "prisoner of indecision."

As India's Home Minister for over two years, he made some major controversial decisions and courageously faced several awkward situations. Within a month of his appointment as Home Minister he resolved the language dispute in Assam. The dispute represented Assam's revolt against cultural and political domination of adjoining West Bengal. It had earlier led to a massacre of the Bengali-speaking residents of the state, and Shastri's predecessor, Pant, had conspicuously failed to settle it. In Punjab, the popular leader of the Sikh community, Master Tara Singh, embarked on a fast unto death to coerce the government into dividing the state on a communal basis, and although it was feared that his death might lead to extensive rioting in a sensitive border state, Shastri refused to be bullied into conceding the demand. Ultimately, it was Tara Singh who, after abstaining for over fifty days, broke the fast. Shastri was convinced that the allegations of corruption and nepotism against Punjab's Chief Minister, Kairon, were not without substance, but on his failure to persuade Nehru to have the charges examined by a judge, he quietly decided not to visit Punjab as long as it was being administered by a supposedly corrupt leader. Shastri's role in ending an unpopular regime in Kashmir was even more significant. Nehru had accepted Bakshi Ghulam Mohammed's resignation under the Kamaraj Plan, but the Bakshi's hold on power continued. Bakshi had installed an unknown legislator, Shamasuddin, as Premier and ruled the state in his name. It was left to Shastri some months later to put enough pressure on Bakshi Ghulam Mohammed to ensure that Shamasuddin made way for Bakshi's principal rival, G. M. Sadiq, who offered prospects of a clean administration.

5: *The Overwhelming Burden of Lal Bahadur Shastri*

Deprived of the protective umbrella of Nehru's trust and support, Shastri as Prime Minister felt exposed and vulnerable. Without his predecessor's charisma and family background or Desai's self-assurance, he was nervous and unsure of himself. The size of the country he was asked to rule and the dimensions of its problems seemed to overwhelm him. This feeling of inadequacy was deepened by the stature of the person he was succeeding, his relative inexperience in international affairs and the heart attack he suffered on the eighteenth day of his appointment as Prime Minister. He was so sensitive about his ailment and its impact on the public mind as far as his competence to lead the country was concerned that the fact of his heart condition was never officially admitted.

With Nehru's death also came the divisive, centrifugal political tendencies which, as the study of the country's history would show, are inherent in the Indian character. Whenever an acknowledged leader passes away, power tends to shift away from the center, and regional provincial satraps make a bid to carve out their own autonomous areas of authority. Physically puny— he was barely five feet three inches tall—and victim of a serious ailment, Shastri seemed to present a spectacle of ineffectual leadership and an excellent opportunity for some politicians to grab a slice of power for themselves. If he urged certain states to part with some of their surplus food production to meet the urgent needs of the deficit states, his pleas were unheeded. The deficit states loudly blamed the Centre for its failure to arrange additional food supplies, but ignored all suggestions for such disciplines in consumption as enforcement of rationing and eradication of malpractices in distribution of the supplies they had. Food merchants blatantly indulged in hoarding and price manipulation, practices the government seemed helpless to prevent. Discipline in the party, never particularly strong, suffered further deterioration. In Kerala, where the Congress Party was constantly faced with a serious challenge from the Communists, Congress legislators worked for the defeat of their own ministry. In Uttar Pradesh there was a fierce factional fight. When the All-India Congress Committee, the party's national council, met in Delhi three months after Nehru's death, it hurled charges at the leaders and used language that would have shamed a group of rowdy students. Even the Cabinet displayed a noticeable lack of discipline as individual ministers went off in several directions without any guidance from the top. The government took steps to check corruption and unearth untaxed wealth, but in implementing them the Home and Finance Ministers seemed to be acting at cross-purposes. Junior members of the government spoke indiscreetly in public and brought avoidable criticism upon the administration. It was a measure of Shastri's ineffectualness during the first few months of his Prime Ministership that, in a routine matter relating to the retirement benefits of a senior civil servant, he could not persuade the Finance Minister to accept his viewpoint. In the summer of 1964, therefore, when Nehru's sister, Vijayalakshmi Pandit, charged in Parliament that the government was "a prisoner of indecision," Shastri was deeply distressed, not merely because the accusation came from a senior member of the party, but also because essentially it was true.

Apart from his inexperience and mildness of temperament, what contributed to his vacillation as Prime Minister was his lack of a precise ideological viewpoint. For all his readiness to

compromise, Nehru had a distinct penchant for socialism. Desai's political moorings were known to be clearly of a right-wing
character. Shastri's political beliefs, however, defied classifica-
tion in popular terms. He had neither any strong socialistic commitments nor any links with big business. He could be described
as a centrist or a pragmatist. A pragmatist, particularly one who
is meek and unassertive as Shastri was, invites pressure from
both sides, and this countervailing of authority was precisely
what occurred. The right wing within the Congress Party and
outside urged that a "realistic" and result-oriented policy be
adopted, which, of course, was a euphemistic way of suggesting
that private enterprise be allotted a larger share in economic
development than it had had under Nehru. Within three months
of Shastri's assuming leadership, however, the Socialists held a
conference in Delhi to consider how to preserve the socialistic
character of the government, and at it Indira Gandhi thundered
that Nehru's policies were being betrayed. With rival groups trying to pull the Prime Minister toward them, alternatively bullying and cajoling him, Shastri's image acquired a further indeco-
rous look and his self-confidence declined. Shastri himself was
so bewildered and distressed by these attacks and pressures that
in a private chat with a newsman early in January 1965 he wondered whether he had been right to offer himself for the Prime
Ministership and whether he had the capacity to carry the burden that the office involved.

Curiously, it was around that time that a hesitant, vacillating
Shastri began to give place to a leader who knew his mind, who
imposed his will on his colleagues and who gave the government precise directions when confronted with awkward or hazardous situations. Perhaps the first indication that Shastri had
had enough of being buffeted about emerged a year before his
death in the way he handled the resignation from the government of two of his ministers. Serious disturbances had broken
out in Madras and some other parts of south India over the
replacement of English by Hindi as the official language of inter-
state communication for the country. The two ministers, both of

whom belonged to Madras, resigned to mark their disagreement with the Cabinet's policy, and, much though he valued them as colleagues, Shastri was inclined to accept their resignations. He felt that, by offering their resignations at a juncture when the government was faced with a serious challenge and needed all the unity it could muster, the two had tried to swim to the shore in a storm. President Radhakrishnan as well as Kamaraj urged Shastri not to accept the resignations, for the Madras ministers' exit at that stage would be interpreted to mean that the Central Government headed by a north Indian was refusing to respond to the sentiments of the south. Shastri, however, insisted that in the interest of national unity, the two ministers must withdraw their resignations of their own accord; he would not urge them to stay. After two days of confrontation, the Prime Minister had his way.

Shastri could still not dominate Parliament or even rebuke an ill-mannered newsman at a press conference, but it was obvious that the government was no longer the prisoner of indecision. When Pakistan attacked a marshy border tract in the southwestern area of Kutch and occupied a strip of Indian territory, Shastri stated in Parliament that "if Pakistan continues to discard reason and persists in its aggressive activities, our army will defend the country, and it will decide its own strategy and the deployment of its manpower and equipment in the manner which seems best." This was a clear warning that instead of fighting on a ground of Pakistan's choosing and fighting a defensive battle, India would not hesitate to open a strategically advantageous second front. He followed this announcement in Parliament with an order to the Chief of Army Staff, General J. N. Chaudhuri, to proceed on that basis. Later, when Britain's diplomatic intervention brought about a cease-fire in Kutch, he agreed, contrary to the advice of some of his senior Cabinet colleagues, to refer the dispute to international arbitration. This was a daring step, inasmuch as it exposed India to a Pakistani demand that the principle of arbitration be extended to Kashmir also.

Before he took the major decision in September 1965 to retal-

iate against the Pakistani invasion of Kashmir by ordering the
Indian Army to move into West Pakistan and attack the important city of Lahore, Shastri had offered other indications of independence and confidence as a leader. His government was
among the first in the world to criticize the U.S. action in bomb-
ing North Vietnam. Later, when, irked by the Indian posture,
President Lyndon B. Johnson "postponed" Shastri's state visit
to Washington, the Indian Prime Minister promptly "canceled"
it altogether.

In taking the dramatic step to send the army across the Indo-
Pakistan border, Shastri was undoubtedly helped by the fact that
he was surrounded by like-minded colleagues. Home Minister
Nanda, Defense Minister Chavan and Indira Gandhi, all of
whom were members of the select Emergency Committee of the
Cabinet, held the view that the Pakistani challenge must be met
boldly. At the same time, as those who watched the process of
decision-making would testify, it was not the case of a reluctant
leader being pushed by assertive, chauvinistic colleagues or res-
tive military leaders into drastic action against his wishes. He
was constantly consulting them, but there was little doubt that it
was he who was calling the turns.

His final decision, taken only a few hours before his sudden
death following a heart attack in Tashkent, was perhaps the
most courageous.

During the twenty-two-day war, while it had lost some of the
territory to Pakistan and gained some of the Pakistani territory,
India's principal achievement was the capture in Kashmir of
Haji Pir, a strategic pass, and certain other points beyond the
cease-fire line. While they brought little additional territory, the
occupation of these points enabled India to seal virtually all
routes of invasion and infiltration into the Indian part of Kashmir. The way in which several thousand armed personnel from
Pakistan were able to enter Kashmir surreptitiously in August
1965 and all but occupy Srinagar, the state's capital, would not
have been possible if India had occupied Haji Pir and dominated
the heights at Kargil and Uri. Even before accepting the Soviet
invitation to meet Ayub Khan in Tashkent, Shastri had publicly

declared that these strategic gains would not be surrendered. He repeated this assurance to Parliament after the Soviet invitation and again on the eve of his departure for Tashkent.

At Tashkent he found Ayub Khan adamant about Indian withdrawal from Haji Pir and other important points on the Pakistani side of the cease-fire line, and Soviet Premier Kosygin agreed that troops must be withdrawn from all areas and that no exceptions could be made. There were also clear hints from Kosygin that if Indian refusal to cooperate led to the failure of his peace initiative, India could not rely on Soviet support on Kashmir in the Security Council—and that arms assistance, too, might suffer a setback. These positions presented Shastri with the biggest decision of his political career. Should he stand by the posture he had struck before coming to Tashkent—an attitude that seemed eminently valid to the people of India—or face unpopularity at home in the hope of making a beginning of peace with Pakistan?

Shastri agreed to withdraw troops from Haji Pir and surrender other valuable gains in Kashmir. If he had stubbornly refused to do so and let the conference fail, he would have returned home to ride an extensive wave of personal popularity. The temptation to do so must have been tremendous. It was only during the previous few weeks that he had attained national stature as a leader. His firm handling of the challenge from Pakistan had won him great acclaim. For the first time in his life, his puny figure, instead of inviting derisive laughter, drew admiration. On the eve of traveling to Tashkent, he had addressed a public meeting in Bombay and several hundred thousand had turned out to hear him. Even Nehru had not drawn such crowds in the last years of his life. In Parliament one sensed new respect for him among those who previously had interrupted his speeches with jeering remarks. His rejection of the Pakistani demand and Soviet pressure would have added to his popularity and established him as a strong and unbending leader. By compromising with Ayub in Tashkent, he would jeopardize all that.

But, as he indicated in an off-the-record chat with a small

group of Indian newsmen at Tashkent three days before the agreement was signed, Shastri also realized that if troops were not pulled back soon, fighting between the two countries would flare up again. The new cease-fire line was marked by no natural barriers, and at most places the two armies had no more than a few yards and their sense of discipline to restrain them. Their hearts, moreover, were full of bitterness caused by past memories of communal killings and the heavy casualties in the latest war. If the Tashkent conference failed to bring about a troop pull-back, the resumption of war in weeks was a near-certainty, and that, Shastri felt, would spell disaster for both countries. He denied that Kosygin was exerting any pressure on him and chided a reporter for suggesting in a dispatch that the Soviet leaders were "twisting his arm." But at Tashkent, and more candidly later in Delhi, some of his Cabinet colleagues and official advisers admitted that the Soviet warning was polite but clear and that Shastri was worried because Moscow's annoyance could have serious repercussions for a country which had an awkward issue in the Security Council and which depended heavily on Russia for some of its important defense equipment, including medium and heavy tanks and MIG fighter aircraft.

That Shastri was nervous about the impact of his decision on the public mind at home was undeniable. During a briefing that he gave some Indian journalists immediately after signing the agreement, a reporter was blunt enough to tell the Prime Minister that he had made a bad bargain. He urged them to interpret his action with understanding and sympathy and thus help him overcome the difficulties that he knew would await him at home. The reaction in India was adverse—a mixture of anger and disappointment—even before the newsmen's dispatches could make an impact. If he had not died that night, Shastri would certainly have been greeted by a black-flag demonstration on reaching home. But it is equally certain that he would have been able to ride out the storm. His Cabinet colleagues would have stood by him. He had taken a large delegation with him to Tashkent, and Chavan and Swaran Singh, the Ministers for Defense and

Foreign Affairs, who were at Tashkent, had unreservedly endorsed his decision before he signed the agreement. Others who mattered in the government or the party would have done the same. He would have encountered some awkward moments in Parliament and public demonstrations would have lasted a few days, but ultimately the country would almost certainly have seen the logic behind his action and supported him. The people forgave Nehru when his government lost territory in defeat; they would not have been harsher with Shastri when he conceded some territory from a position of strength. The demonstrations against and criticism of the Tashkent agreement would have added to Shastri's self-confidence and his capacity for leadership.

Apart from his stewardship in the war with Pakistan, which enabled India to regain the self-esteem it had lost in 1962 following the Chinese attack, there is little other evidence of Shastri's achievement as Prime Minister. He was in office for only nineteen months, and much of this time was spent in overcoming the temperamental and political handicaps from which he suffered. Shortly before his death he had sorted out his political problems and established himself as the pre-eminent leader. The syndicate which had seemingly brought him to power was no longer a factor to reckon with. It is a measure of the change in the situation that in May 1965, when the question arose of Kamaraj's re-election as Congress president for another term, he had to look to Shastri to prod an unwilling party. In the Cabinet none challenged his authority and there were no rivals for the Prime Ministership. Desai had resigned himself to waiting for the next general election, which was not due till 1967, and most impartial observers did not give him much chance of success even then against Shastri.

Shastri died when he was just beginning a period of meaningful leadership. If he suffered from faults such as diffidence and inability to speak or act decisively, he also had many virtues needed in a leader of a country such as India. He was singularly free from prejudice, religious or regional. He himself and his family were devout Hindus, but, like his predecessor in office, he could feel sincerely for the Muslims and other minorities and had genuine faith in the ideal of secularism. He did not inspire awe, but he won trust and confidence easily. The masses were not drawn to him as they were to Nehru, but they felt at home with him and found him speaking the idiom they spoke. He did not understand the intricacies of international politics, but he knew his own country, its people and their sentiments better than any other leader after Gandhi. A senior foreign diplomat who had personally known all three Prime Ministers of India once remarked that Shastri was the only "truly Indian" Prime Minister the country has had. He met scores of people daily and his house was open to the lowliest of people. He was often un-punctual in his appointments and disorganized in his routine affairs. Letters remained unanswered—at times unopened—for long periods, but it was largely because he was trying to main-tain at a personal level a degree of contact that was physically impossible. He lacked Nehru's vision or his capacity to analyze a situation, but he made up for it by choosing a group of trusted advisers and giving some of his senior colleagues a sense of in-volvement in the administration. He listened patiently and ex-tensively and subjected the advice he received to the test of his sound common sense. His lack of ideological commitments, a weakness in the beginning of his Prime Ministership, would have proved his strength after he had found his feet. He would have followed more pragmatic policies and freed thinking at the top from textbook socialist jargon and clichés. The signs of an ap-proaching recession and other weaknesses in the economic situa-tion were visible to Shastri in the latter half of 1965, and he was getting ready to make some basic changes in approach to match economic plans with the country's resources. He would probably have reduced the element of socialism and state ownership in the development plans, but he would have done so without giving capitalists undue political influence in the running of the gov-ernment and making of policy. It is significant that although he did not have Nehru's marked suspicion of capitalists, none of the several leading industrial houses was able to establish any links with Shastri or acquire even in a slight measure any additional influence in the government during his term in office. As always and as to everyone, Shastri extended much cordiality to big business, but scrupulously maintained his distance from it.

6: *Nehru's Daughter*

After Shastri died at Tashkent, the battle of succession that followed was much fiercer than after Nehru's death—perhaps, because Shastri's end came so suddenly. A triumphant leader who had gone abroad on an important mission was brought back to Delhi in a wooden casket.

The search for a candidate for Prime Minister started even before Shastri's body arrived in Delhi. As on the earlier occasion, Desai unabashedly announced that he was a claimant. Nanda, who was the second man in the Shastri Cabinet, was sworn in as Acting Prime Minister for the second time, advanced his claim equally unabashedly. There were others who were "available" though they did not assert themselves unduly. Two days after Shastri's death the leading Indian newspapers mentioned as many as five names, with Indira Gandhi rather low down on the list. A day later there was a move, short-lived but indicative of the confusion in regard to the search for a suitable candidate, to sponsor Kamaraj himself for the Prime Ministership.

Ultimately, it was Desai's determined bid for leadership that ended the confusion and gave the search precise direction. The real objective of the various party leaders was as much to keep Desai out of power as to find a worthy leader for the country. The quest, therefore, was to find someone acceptable to the country and yet absolutely sure of defeating Desai. This ruled out Nanda, who, despite his long stay in the Cabinet and his proximity to Nehru and Shastri, had no base worthy of the name in the party. Kamaraj himself was realistic enough to realize that his candidacy would have the effect of uniting the large block of votes from the Hindi-speaking states behind Desai. The choice, therefore, narrowed to Indira Gandhi, who, as Nehru's daughter, inspired an element of popular acceptability and who, though she hailed from the Hindi-speaking state of Uttar Pradesh, was not associated with the kind of Hindi bigotry and assertiveness that could irk people in the non-Hindi-speaking regions. She was willing to accept the responsibility, and in an unprecedented move intended to overawe Desai, the Chief Ministers of ten states publicly pledged their support to her. The Chief Ministers' public pronouncement ensured Indira Gandhi's election and made Nanda renounce his ambition, though with ill grace, but it did not succeed in making Desai withdraw from the fight. In 1964 Shastri had been chosen unanimously, but Indira Gandhi had to fight an election. She won with an impressive margin of 186 votes in a 526-member Parliamentary party.

That her name was late in being mentioned and that she did not advance her claim with the brashness of her rivals did not mean that Mrs. Gandhi was drafted into high office and that she personally lacked the necessary ambition. According to one of her close associates, the question of her succeeding Shastri was seriously discussed by a small group of her friends within an hour or two of Shastri's death. The meeting took place in Indira Gandhi's house in the early hours of the morning, and, while she was not averse to the idea, she shrewdly ruled that the move should not be brazen-faced and that her candidacy should, if possible, be sponsored by people other than those marked out as her supporters. When the request came from Kamaraj for her to offer herself for the post, she accepted as if she were responding to a call of duty.

This kind of shrewdness in party matters, particularly those which affect her own interests and position, is one of the principal assets of Mrs. Gandhi as a leader. She has an uncanny sense about people's foibles and predilections and a remarkable capacity to exploit them to her advantage. In the five years that she has been Prime Minister she has faced many challenges and, even without the stature of her father, has dealt with them deftly and effectively. If Nehru used Krishna Menon to browbeat Desai and his right-wing supporters, Indira Gandhi has played Kamaraj, Desai and Chavan, another leader who has grown to a position of some power in the party, against one another.

Her capacity to detect and exploit the points of political vulnerability among her rivals is only one of the factors responsible for the stability of her leadership. A more positive asset is the family name, which brings her some of her father's charisma with the Indian masses. Like her father, she is an indifferent speaker, but crowds come not to hear her but to see her. She is also the only one among the top leaders who is not associated in the public mind with any particular region. Her ancestral home is in Allahabad and she speaks Hindi, but few in the country would think of her as a north Indian. There is an air of statelessness about her that is a valuable asset for the leader of a country so far-flung and culturally diverse.

Mrs. Gandhi has, however, not inherited her father's indecision and tendency to seek compromises. Her only noteworthy political experience before she joined the government in Shastri's Cabinet was her one-year term as Congress president in 1959. It was during that period and on the specific advice of the party that the Central Government took two major and controversial steps. It dismissed the Communist ministry in the southern state of Kerala for resorting to unconstitutional means to spread Communism, and it divided the bilingual state of Bombay into Maharashtra and Gujarat. Much blood had been spilled in Bombay in support of separate states, but in 1956, while the rest of the country was reorganized into linguistic states, the Centre had stubbornly maintained two states, Bombay and Punjab, as bilingual. The fires of separatism had, however, remained smoldering all this time, and, displaying a measure of political sensitivity lacking in others at the top, Mrs. Gandhi urged the government to reopen the issue and used her influence as the party president to secure the state's division.

She undid the linguistic unity of Punjab within weeks of becoming Prime Minister in 1966. A decision of even greater magnitude that she took soon after assuming office was to devalue the Indian currency. Many were skeptical of the wisdom of that decision, but once she accepted her advisers' view that the rupee should be devalued, she went ahead with the harsh undertaking, undeterred by the fact that a general election was due in a few months and that devaluation was likely to be exploited by her opponents.

If she does not suffer from her father's vacillation, she also lacks his vision and his ideological moorings. She is committed to her father's socialistic policies and has frequently reiterated her intention and determination to stand by them, but her commitment to them is more an act of emotional loyalty to someone she loved than culmination of a process of intellectual search for what is good for the country. This inevitably shackles her thinking and rules out changes in policy to suit the changing conditions at home and abroad. When she acts, she tends to act dramatically, though not always wisely. In fact, many detect an element of impulsiveness in some of her actions and a desire to play to the gallery. Her decision to divide Punjab into two states was taken suddenly and contrary to the wishes of some of the senior Cabinet members. The matter had been hanging fire for some years, and Nehru had opposed it vehemently because division would create small and economically weak units in a sensitive border area exposed to Pakistani pressure as well as blandishments. A committee of four leaders over which Mrs. Gandhi presided before she became Prime Minister saw no reason to revise the earlier decision on Punjab, and during its protracted deliberations she herself gave no indication that she thought differently. Yet, when the moment of decision came, the Prime Minister took, with seeming impulsiveness, such a categorical stand in favor of bifurcation that others had to go along sorrowfully. Many of the fears that the opponents of division had visualized were proved right, and, apart from weakening the economy of the region, the two states have shown much political instability and have bickered constantly over petty matters.

Devaluation of the rupee was even more dramatic and perhaps equally hasty. As subsequent events were to show, it was taken without adequate study of its effects and without finalizing the administrative measures which must be taken immediately after the devaluation announcement.

Owing to the absence of a well-considered approach to basic political questions and perhaps an inadequacy of experience, Mrs. Gandhi has tended to lean too heavily on a few individuals and often has overreacted to minor situations. She is constantly anxious to give the impression of total independence of big powers. After her return from a state visit to Washington, where she received a warm—in fact, effusive—welcome, her opponents in the party started a whispering campaign suggesting that she had established new bridges with the West and that India's policy of nonalignment was on the verge of being abandoned. Instead of ignoring it or taking note of it only to the extent to which it deserved her attention, the Prime Minister bent over backward in the following months to demonstrate that the understanding between India and the Soviet Union had not been weakened.

In domestic matters, a few impulsive decisions apart, Mrs. Gandhi has been singularly inactive. In her first four years in office she did very little to tackle any of the basic problems of the country. Her Prime Ministership was marked by ambivalence, procrastinations and a tendency to live on slogans and promises. On the crucial questions of poverty, unemployment, economic planning and population control there was almost no action. She and her government were unable to decide what ideology to follow and what concrete steps to take in combating communal riots and other forms of challenge to peace and order, growing economic stagnation and increasing public dissatisfaction with the government. The administration appeared to be static, a condition that a backward country such as India cannot afford to tolerate for long. By the middle of 1969 even some of her close associates were growing disenchanted with her leadership and seriously predicting her downfall due to her lack of performance. But later that year Mrs. Gandhi suddenly assumed the party leadership in a purposeful manner and displayed enormous physical and mental energy when a power struggle developed within the party. She personally masterminded the strategy in meeting the threat to her position as the leader and, in the conflict with the party's old guard, acted with unexpected daring. She openly challenged her opponents' choice for the country's President and caused his defeat and brusquely dismissed Morarji Desai, supposedly linked with her opponents, from the Cabinet. She also ordered the nationalization of all major Indian banks and announced her resolve to withdraw the special privileges granted to princes two decades earlier. Both measures refurbished her image as a leader capable of stern, socialistic action and won her much popularity with the masses.

This sudden change in her attitude suggests that her instincts for survival are remarkably strong. She is blessed with shrewdness in discerning threats to her, and with adroitness, bordering on ruthlessness, in facing them. Those whom she vanquished in the party confrontation left it, thereby reducing the Congress Party she headed to a minority in the Lok Sabha and leaving her more vulnerable to threats from outside the party.

Since the beginning of her term as Prime Minister but much more noticeably since the autumn of 1969, Mrs. Gandhi has been trying to win for herself the position of a national leader in the style of her father. She has made little attempt to build a regional political base for herself. This effort may win her an all-India image, but whether it would give her the supreme authority that Nehru enjoyed is doubtful. The circumstances that gave Nehru his power have changed radically and, consequently, so has the pattern of leadership and power.

In the early years of independence, the leadership in India was almost entirely middle-class and urban in its background. Rural areas had only a minimal share of it. This middle-class urban elite enjoyed unfettered influence because other special interests either did not exist then or were disorganized. At the top of this group of leaders were men with a broad, national outlook who thought in terms unaffected by regionalism and parochialism. The enormous public trust they had earned for their role in the independence movement enabled them to create, after independence, a strong center to which the regions and the states looked for guidance and authority. The real fount of political power was Nehru's charisma and the respect that other veteran leaders received from the masses. They did not depend on the party machine in the states or on any influential special interests for support. If Nehru ran the government in the manner of a national consensus, it was because he preferred to do so and not because the limitations of his power compelled him to make compromises.

As pre-independence idealism and post-independence euphoria began to evaporate, the compulsions of electoral politics and desire for power began to shape a new pattern of leadership. Power has begun to move from the Centre to the states, where local and regional interests have started asserting themselves. Special caste or economic groups have begun to organize, aware now of the advantage of collective action. The compensations they demand in return for their support may be more readily dispensed by a state Chief Minister than by Central leaders. The latter often have to depend on the state Chief Ministers for their own election to Parliament. Thus the state leaders have acquired a sizable reserve of the new currency of power. This shift had begun to be visible even before Nehru's authority started declining. In 1952, for example, he chose his Cabinet entirely on his own; after the second general election he pointedly consulted some of the important state Chief Ministers, but the final decision was his; in the last Cabinet that he chose in 1962, he included some ministers primarily because they had strong backing from one Chief Minister or another.

The increase in the power of the state Chief Ministers and other regional bosses has been more rapid since Nehru's death. Members of Parliament depended on the state leaders for assembling the party ticket and winning the election, and consequently tended to look up to them for direction in all important situations even at the Centre. The crucial role of state leaders in resolving the tussle between Mrs. Gandhi and Desai over the Prime Ministership in January 1966 is a key case in point. Mrs. Gandhi or any other future Prime Minister will have to be endowed with extraordinary charisma and helped by highly unusual circumstances to be able to reverse the flow of power.

VALUES AND ATTITUDES

1: *Echoes of the Raj*

A BRITISH JOURNALIST derisively remarked not long ago that India was the only place where true Englishmen could still be found. In so saying, he obviously had in mind the class of West-oriented Indians who flaunted their connections with Oxford and Cambridge, spoke English with a pronounced British accent (at times somewhat exaggerated for greater effect), quoted Shakespeare often and accurately, dressed for dinner, regularly subscribed to the air edition of *The Times* of London, and avidly read, if nothing else in it, the Court Circular. They were more familiar with the geography of London than of their own city and played bridge with considerable competence. In the days of the Raj, effective power was held by the British, but as "natives" who could speak the language of the rulers and had attuned themselves to the latter's thinking, they wielded a measure of influence and enjoyed prestige within the rather narrow, exclusive corridors of power of the time. In its various manifestations—the senior civil servant in New Delhi and provincial capitals, the junior executive in the managing agencies in Calcutta's Clive Street (now renamed Subhas Bose Road) and the Parsi industrialist in Bombay—this group constituted the principal section of the Indian elite before independence.

Two decades after the end of the Empire, many of these "Englishmen" are still there, but changing circumstances and the emergence of new powers that it inadequately understands and holds in ill-concealed contempt have robbed it of much of its plumage and given it a somewhat ragged, pathetic look. Some have made limited compromises with the new forces. Others, such as the civil servants, have altered their tactics, though not their outlook. The rest, however, are stolidly refusing to notice the changes swirling around them and to alter their way of life or their set of values.

In their behavior and outlook, they have little affinity with today's Britain, which, with its labor unrest, racial problem and devalued pound, is only slightly less an anathema to them than the leaders in New Delhi with their policy of prohibition and socialist planning. The bulk of them drew their inspiration from Victoria's England, and they try valiantly to remain within that time dimension. They still like to dress for dinner at the slightest excuse, and the meal must consist of Irish stew, roast meat, baked chicken pie or other dishes that Englishmen supposedly relish. The dinner must be preceded by the ritualistic two small drinks of Scotch whiskey and soda served by uniformed servants, whom they address as "Abdar" (or "bearer") in the style of the British in India. Like the British of the bygone days, they eat Indian curry and rice for Sunday lunch and faithfully observe the colonial Englishman's taboo against drinking whiskey before sundown. On Sunday afternoons they may drink themselves into an alcoholic stupor, but it must be on beer or gin and never on whiskey. Their wives are addressed by the servants as "Memsahib," and the height of their social and professional ambition is to be allotted one of the company-maintained residences that were once occupied by their British predecessors. Like the British, who relieved the tedium of their colonial existence by indulging in amateur dramatics, the young among this class of Indians are avidly interested in the theater. The plays they choose to present are invariably the works of Shakespeare, Marlowe and Ibsen. Occasionally they may pick up a modern play favorably reviewed by *Punch,* but they are disdainful, often unaware, of the achievements of the Indian theater. Indian films have no attraction for them ("Oh, those love songs and that overacting," they moan), but they do not mind watching an inane Hollywood comedy or even a trashy Western.

Time, of course, has not stood entirely still for them. Despite their efforts to perpetuate the colonial era, there are irritating reminders that things around them are not what they used to be. Their clubs are being invaded by the new breed of Indian businessman lacking the caste distinctions honored by the managing agencies that controlled the jute, tea and coal trades from plush offices in Clive Street. With extensive industrialization since independence, the pattern of the Indian economy has deprived those who operate from Clive Street of their traditional superiority. Previously, factory owners and retailers were spurned as "traders" (as distinguished from the "merchants"), but now their role in the country is too big for them to be kept out of the Calcutta Club or New Delhi's Gymkhana Club (appropriately called the Imperial Delhi Gymkhana before independence) or Bombay's Cricket Club of India.

There are other sharper and more distressing reminders that the world has changed. A part of the course of the Golf Club in Calcutta has been occupied by Bengali refugees from East Pakistan. They have been squatting on it for years and have even built small, ugly huts on the club property. Over the years the members of the club had learned to ignore the unsightly structures and their ill-clad occupants, but since the Communists came to power in West Bengal the squatters have chosen to add insult to injury. As the club members play through, properly attired in gleaming white clothes and followed by respectful caddies, they are often pelted with stones by the refugees.

For those who are still living in Kipling's India and tenaciously grasping the attitudes and values of the period, the installation of a Communist-dominated government in West Bengal was probably the ultimate affront from the "natives." In the past, labor relations made only limited demands on their time and judgment. Whenever there was unrest among the workers, it was handled by the personnel officer, who was usually a relatively junior member of the company's administration. He shielded the senior officials from such embarrassments as a face-to-face meeting with the workers' representatives. If he could not handle the labor union, the firm could always take the matter up to the suitable authority in the state government, who, because he played golf on Sundays or belonged to the right cocktail circuit, was almost always prepared to see the employers' point of view with sympathy. Now, with the Communists forming the dominant political force in the state, the workers demand to deal directly with top management, and should the matter be referred to government arbitration, the official concerned, conscious of the beady-eyed ministerial observation, cannot afford to have his social obligations to management reflected in his verdicts. Many a top business executive has, therefore, recently undergone the excruciating experience of facing a union leader across his table and even sharing a cup of tea with him.

For this sector of the onetime elite there is no future but extinction. Its refusal to change with the times is increasingly depriving it of influence. It has survived for so long after independence because a vast, backward, divided country such as India must take time to regear for the process of change. Now that that process has started, Indians who have traditionally lived as mock English country squires are rapidly becoming socially anachronistic and politically irrelevant. Their refusal to think in any terms but English virtually constitutes a death wish on their part. The Communist rise to power in West Bengal could have been foreseen by anyone who had occasion to pass through the area's extensive slums and see the filth and squalor, yet most of the elite, passing through the slums daily without bothering to wonder what they portended, professed surprise at the Communist takeover. As they enter the gates in the big wall surrounding their firms' residential estate on the sloping banks of the Hooghly, they conveniently dismiss from their minds the "bustees" and the slums on the other side.

2: *A Demotion for the Civil Service*

Another sector of the West-oriented elite, the senior civil servants, have shown relatively greater adaptability and resilience. Their values are still British, but after an initial period of confrontation with the politicians, they have realized the untenability of their pre-independence power and prestige. Under the British, the civil servant formed a part of what was popularly described as the "steel frame" of the British power. He served the rulers loyally and in return was rewarded with a high salary, and numerous benefits and all the accouterments of authority. His mental make-up, social background and professional training made him even less amenable to change than the man who worked in the commercial offices of Clive Street. After independence, he started as foolishly as his cultural counterpart in commerce. He showed contempt for the politician for not knowing English as well as he did, for his ignorance of the administrative procedures, for dressing himself in an ordinary shirt and dhoti, but essentially for being so different in attitude and outlook from the British rulers whom the civil servant had learned to serve.

The civil servants' attempt to browbeat the politicians who assumed authority in independent India failed almost as soon as it was launched. The political leaders who took over as Central Ministers and state Chief Ministers were in a triumphant mood. What they lacked in administrative experience and knowledge they made up in self-confidence and public support. They were ready to take on the civil servants, most of whom, according to public thinking, had served as willing tools of a foreign power and deserved to be dispensed with in the new setup. In the early years of independence, the government in New Delhi and in most states was dominated by powerful personalities who could not be overawed by civil servants, however competent and assertive. Those among the officials who would not let the new ruling class put a ring through their nose allowed themselves to be corrupted through promises of appointment beyond the age of retirement and such bureaucratic plums as the posts of ambassador and state governor.

The rise in the cost of living and a general scaling down of official salaries and allowances after independence also affected the attitude of the civil service. In clubs and other places of social contact which they previously dominated, the civil servants have been reduced to the status of poor relations. In the days of the Raj, a senior civil servant would see nothing wrong in keeping a leading businessman waiting in the veranda of his house for an hour before granting him a brief audience, and if he allowed himself to accept a gift of fruit and sweets from the latter on a festive occasion, he did so as a personal favor. The situation has changed radically now. The businessman has grown richer through the enormous expansion in commerce and industry since independence and has acquired direct contact with those who wield power. Consequently, he no longer needs to call on the civil servant at his house, but meets him, if necessary, in the club bar, where the bureaucrat gladly, almost gratefully, accepts his hospitality.

There is an element of poetic justice in the decline of the power and prestige of the senior bureaucrat. His salary has been reduced. At the highest rung of the official ladder, a member of the Indian Administrative Service, a cadre organized after independence, is paid 500 rupees less than his counterpart belonging to the Indian Civil Service, created by the British, still receives. Even the ICS members, whose salaries and allowances were guaranteed by the departing foreign rulers, have been compelled by inflation to count their pennies. The social and political scales have shifted in such a way that the former posture of arrogance has become futile, even ludicrous. The senior bureaucrat—there are, of course, exceptions—makes the social rounds almost unashamedly consuming drinks and accepting other forms of hospitality that he has no intention of returning. The scarcity and high prices of imported liquor have long ended any qualms of conscience that he might have felt about one-sided hospitality. Some years ago Nehru was compelled to administer a general rebuke when he learned that some of the topmost bureaucrats eagerly accepted invitations from Third Secretaries and junior attachés of foreign missions. Contact men and lobbyists for various commercial houses have exploited this weakness of the civil servant extensively and with almost blatant vulgarity. At the same time, the politicians have treated him with scant consideration and shifted him about, promoted him or demoted him in accordance with their whims and political requirements. If he is not amenable to their wishes, he may be stripped of authority overnight and compelled to take an unsought long leave. Often politicians have used him and then discarded him without regret.

The senior civil servant admittedly has many more openings now than he had under the British. Many a bureaucrat has achieved a degree of eminence that he could not have hoped for before independence. He may be appointed as a state governor or an ambassador or nominated to head some large industrial concern in the public sector. But often he has to sell his soul to gain this kind of distinction. He dances to the tune of the state Chief Minister in order to be assigned to the Centre. In New Delhi he has to join a virtual rat race if he wishes to get anywhere. He watches fellow civil servants suspiciously for any signs of an intrigue against him and tries to worm his way into the affections of his minister. He puts in long hours and stays late in his office not because he has work to do but because the minister might send for him and, not finding him, might consider him a shirker. In taking decisions, he subordinates his judgment to that of his minister and is anxious to pander to his political needs in the hope of winning his personal goodwill, which may result in a brief extension in service after retirement or a diplomatic post abroad. At the same time he also assiduously culti-

vates the bosses in some of the big commercial houses by fawn-
ing on them and granting their concerns special consideration in
their dealings with his ministry. He may permit them to expand
their capacity or allot them a lucrative export license. Such a
favor is his insurance against possible fickle-mindedness on the
part of the minister, for if he is unable to continue in government employment or be appointed an ambassador or chairman
of one of the various state-owned corporations, he may still, in
repayment of the services rendered from the other side of the
fence, be offered a well-paid berth in industry. All this is indeed
a far cry from the times when even as a District Collector, a not
overly exalted position in the official hierarchy, he lived in
splendor and wielded authority which prompted the people then
to describe him as a virtual Rajah (princely ruler).

But this does not mean that the top bureaucracy has been
reduced to a state of impotence and humility. Among the country's new elite groups, it has yielded the top position to the
elected legislator and the entrepreneur, but through superior
knowledge of the working of the administration and command
over the English language and by making some compromises,
the bureaucracy has retained a measure of power. Much of this
power is comprised of its ability to obstruct and thwart through
deft manipulation of the levers of the administrative machine
and clever interpretation of rules and regulations.

3: *The Press: Muted Voice*

To some extent, even India's press—or a sizable section of
it—has tended to act as a handmaiden to the politician in power
or big business or to both.

Since independence, the press in India has grown in size and
attained a hitherto unknown measure of prosperity. But, like
the bureaucrat, it has lost some of its independence of spirit and
declined in public esteem. Journalism in India is no longer the
profession of a handful of dedicated craftsmen, fiercely inde-

pendent and capable of tremendous sacrifices to preserve their intellectual integrity. The profession is dominated now by journalists whose competence is beyond doubt but who are in it largely for the financial rewards. The increase in literacy and the manifold growth of national economy have brought many newspapers larger revenues in advertising and circulation and consequently a sudden boost in wages for journalists. Some of the principal newspapers pay fresh young recruits to their editorial staff more than the entrant to the coveted Indian Administrative Service would receive. Their editors and senior writers get as much as, often more than, the most senior civil servants are paid. These financial benefits subtly circumscribe newsmen's capacity to write and edit independently, for opportunities for alternative and equally rewarding employment are limited.

Yet the financial aspirations have been a relatively small factor in bringing about the change in the character of the Indian press. More responsible is the pattern of newspaper ownership developed since independence. In 1969 more than 10,000 newspapers and periodicals were being published in India in 49 different languages and commanded a circulation of 26 million —a relatively small circulation, owing to widespread illiteracy and poverty and the vastness of distances. Of the 10,000 newspapers, nearly a quarter were part of newspaper chains owned by various business houses. In the daily field, the chains claimed as much as 70 percent of the total national circulation.

The Indian press, in a democratic, free society, was expected to function as an outspoken guardian of the rights and privileges of the people. But in the performance of this duty it has been hampered not by an intolerant administration but by its affiliation with various political groups or business houses. Happily, attempts by the government to curtail its liberty or browbeat it into submission have been singularly rare and ineffective. But in the new pattern of ownership, many a leading newspaper found itself part of a large and varied industrial portfolio. In a business house it could be stabled with such diverse companions as a fertilizer factory, a steel plant, a shipping company, a jute mill or a string of petrol stations. Since the profits it brings its owner are relatively low, it is often expected to yield political dividends. When the owner has such wide-ranging interests, the newspaper is required to—and at times its editor assumes that it is required to—act as the vocal watchdog of those interests. This inevitably limits its freedom of expression and its credibility with its readers.

Many other newspapers, though not owned by business houses, are constrained by their links with political leaders and parties. Political parties run as many as eighty newspapers. Several papers, though not actually owned by any political party, blatantly serve the interests of certain politicians. The English newspapers published in Delhi typify the pattern. Of the seven dailies, four are controlled by business houses, one belongs to the Jana Sangh, another is known to receive its direction from and is committed in its loyalty to Mrs. Indira Gandhi, and the seventh, though not formally owned by the Communist Party, virtually acts as its spokesman.

4: *The New Elite*

This decline in the importance of the role of the senior civil servant and the journalist was perhaps unavoidable. Changed circumstances must effect the character of the "chosen" classes. In a democratic, developing society such as India is today, the elected legislators and the entrepreneurs must inevitably occupy a pre-eminent position. The new elite groups exercise their influence and authority effectively, but without the trappings of power that typified their colonial predecessors. They are conscious of their power and appear to enjoy it, but they are not cut out in the image of the Rajah. The legislators at the Centre and in the states include a sprinkling of princes, big landlords, rich businessmen and retired civil servants, but the majority are men of modest means, many perilously close to the poverty line. Many of them are also of limited education—people to whom the sophisticated jargon of modern economic planning conveys precious little. But their role in India's new power structure is not dependent on their material worth or their familiarity with the modern political and economic idiom. Nor should their apparent passivity prompt one to dismiss them as unavoidable frills of democracy in a poor, underdeveloped country. A former prince or a nominee of an industrial house may win the election because he campaigns more effectively, but he still lacks the professional politician's talent for communication with the masses. The latter's capacity to act as an agent between the people and the government gives him importance that his more affluent and better educated colleague cannot claim.

Most of the time, a professional politician is quite content to be driven by his leaders. He does not require much persuasion to go along with what the government is proposing, or, if he belongs to the opposition, to support the party line. But all the time he keeps his eyes open for anything that may concern him personally or his constituents and supporters. The attitude of submissiveness that the legislator adopts fosters a rather misleading idea of his role in politics and the processes of decision-making. Beneath this seeming passivity there is usually an acute awareness of his own and his supporters' interests and a capacity to exercise his power uncompromisingly in their defense should they be threatened. There were many occasions during the past two decades when the legislators firmly refused to take the path suggested by their leaders and in fact compelled the latter to follow them. To mention only a few such instances, the Congress M.P.s would not be mollified by all that Nehru said in Krishna Menon's defense in 1962 and made sure of his exit from the government. A powerful and assertive Finance Minister such as T. T. Krishnamachari could not get his plan for the nationalization of banks through, and Nehru's pet economic project for the introduction of cooperative farming languished through lack of legislative support. In 1969 Morarji Desai's attempt to levy a small indirect tax on agricultural incomes caused him serious trouble in his own party in Parliament.

The relationship between the legislators and the growing class of Indian entrepreneurs is based on mutual understanding and cordiality. They need each other and use each other's muscle on a basis of give and take. Most M.P.s and state legislators would appear horrified at any suggestion of the existence of links between them and an industrialist, but the number of those who could make such denials with any degree of honesty would be rather small. Elections are an expensive business and those belonging to the class of professional politicians do not always have the necessary resources to run for office every five years. The modesty of their means, more than any ideological affinity, pushes them toward big business. The need for money is a compulsion that even Communists and Socialists seldom manage to overcome, and business houses of Calcutta and Bombay are known to extend financial support to the left and the right in the legislatures with unbelievable impartiality. In return, their beneficiaries watch their interests when new laws are being passed, warn them of any probe that a legislative committee might choose to undertake into alleged violations by them and, if necessary, put in a word with the right minister at the right moment on their behalf. The leftists are more circumspect about their association with the business elite and repay their obligations negatively by not fomenting labor unrest and by generally keeping the workers in the favored industrial establishments on a tight leash.

Wherever land reforms have been effective enough to dislodge the traditional absentee landlord or where introduction of irrigation facilities, fertilizers and "miracle" seeds has brought prosperity to rural areas, a new class of leaders is slowly coming into being. Soon the rural elite will have its own team of professional politicians or come to an arrangement with the existing lot.

The politicians have looked at the rural areas with particular fondness even before the outlying regions acquired their present economic power. Because almost 80 percent of India lives in the villages, the provision of adult franchise in the Indian constitution had made it imperative for the legislators to woo the rural population at least every five years when elections approached. There was much expression of sympathy for this group of Indians, but by the large they were taken for granted. Many peasants were themselves elected to legislative bodies, but the influence they exercised was limited. Owing to their economic and educational backwardness and their failure to act in an organized manner, the rural areas previously received only what may be described as crumbs of political power and economic development. Now, with increasing education and prosperity, the rural people are not content with what they have been customarily offered. In Punjab, where agricultural prosperity came earlier and in larger measure than in most other parts of India, the rural leadership has dominated the political scene since 1955. The rural areas in Andhra, Gujarat and Madras have since displayed similar assertiveness, and the vehement opposition that the proposal for the levy of an indirect tax on agricultural incomes encountered in 1969 suggests that an aggressive farm lobby has come into being at the Centre.

The fact that the political structure in India is democratic in character and that power is shared by diverse elements—professional politicians, urban industrialists, well-to-do peasantry and Anglicized bureaucracy—has had a negative twofold effect on India's administration. There is seemingly more corruption and it is accepted with less protest than in the past. And discipline and sense of moral duty among the public services have declined noticeably.

5: *The Varieties of Corruption*

Under the British, corruption and nepotism wove a strange, contradictory pattern. Certain sections of the administration such as police, irrigation and public works and revenue were notoriously corrupt, while many other departments were singularly free from corruption. At lower levels of administration, acceptance of routine benefits, particularly if they were offered without undue resentment, was scarcely considered corruption. If a policeman visited a village in response to a call, it was assumed that he would be fed and housed by the community. But a senior officer on a tour was not to accept food or services, not even a bundle of grass for his horse, without payment. There were stern rules of conduct forbidding acceptance of even small gifts by a responsible officer. Young probationers to the Indian Civil Service were constantly reminded of the rules and rebuked, sometimes reprimanded, if they were found to have accepted, even unwittingly, a gift as trivial as a small melon or a glass of buttermilk. At the same time, many of those who prescribed such rigid standards of official integrity would see nothing improper in a high-ranking British officer collecting, toward the end of his career, a heap of costly presents from those whom he had helped or befriended. Many a viceroy or governor, for example, is known to have undertaken a farewell tour of his domain in the final months of his term and collected fabulous gifts from princes and rich landlords. If the departing dignitary did not care to soil his own hands by taking presents, he often looked the other way as his wife or daughter graciously accepted pearl necklaces or other costly jewelry from the native gentry as reminders of loyalty and affection.

The British similarly observed dual standards in regard to nepotism. An Indian district official would not be posted anywhere near his home town lest he favor his kith and kin with lowly jobs and in routine administrative matters; yet certain classes of people whose goodwill the foreign rulers needed for political reasons were permitted to practice blatant nepotism. The Muslim feudal elements of northern India, whose loyalty to the British counterbalanced the hostility of the urban Hindus, were able, for example, to have government rules and regulations ignored to secure jobs for which they were not qualified and rewards to which they were normally not entitled.

The situation has changed significantly since the British left. The Britons who exercised authority in India were few in number, represented an autocratic regime and were not exposed to the kind of family and caste pressures which their Indian successors have to suffer constantly. The area over which their administration touched the lives of the people was also limited. Theirs was a "law-and-order" regime administering a country with a stagnant agricultural economy. The scope for corruption as well as temptations was limited. The British could, therefore, evolve an impersonal law and enforce it by and large impersonally. They could also afford to adopt a sanctimonious attitude on the subject.

Indians, on the other hand, have traditionally looked at corruption with resignation. Until very recently, the Indian society was largely feudal in character, and a measure of highhandedness and corruption has always been inherent in it. Over the centuries, the local despots and others who acted as their agents have always extracted money, gifts and services from the public and favored their friends and relations. Corruption and nepotism have usually gone hand in hand with power, and a certain amount of such waywardness is accepted without protest. Resentment is felt and expressed only when highhandedness or corruption is excessive. In the Indian set of common values, it is generally assumed that those who exercise authority or happen to be close to those who do so must be entitled to a privileged position, and that up to a point their indiscretions must be overlooked. Once when a newsman pointed out to a state Chief Minister how the latter's son had forcibly occupied accommodations reserved for someone else, he offered no apology for his son's misbehavior. Instead, he was surprised that anyone should consider the incident worthy of complaint. "I am the state's Chief Minister. Is not my son entitled to special consideration?" he asked the complainant in genuine amazement. He similarly considered it nothing if his wife telephoned the Chief Secretary to the state government to put in a word for someone's promotion or transfer or the granting of a lucrative permit to a relation. In India, even at relatively lower levels of power, one blithely uses one's influence and position for such petty privileges as getting the police summons for a traffic offense canceled and securing additional food rations.

The damage that public tolerance of corruption and nepotism caused under the British was limited. The economy was primitive, and only a small segment of the population came in contact with authority. Official graft, therefore, touched their lives rarely and briefly. In independent India, however, the government and its numerous agencies disburse vast funds and patronage and its decisions affect the citizen's life intimately. The Central budget for 1969 was many times as large as the budget in 1946, when, on the eve of independence, India was much larger in size and had extensive wartime problems still to cope with. In 1969 the Centre, states and state-controlled corporations had over nine million on their payrolls, while another million or more were in the armed services. The government's activities range from distribution of subsidized seeds and fertilizers in the villages to the management of India's only domestic airline. When the administration assumes so large a size and so intensive a role, graft, even if practiced at the traditional level, adds up to enormous amounts.

In fact, corruption is not limited to the traditional scale. It is not, for example, confined only to police and a few other departments of government. The Parliamentary Committee on the Prevention of Corruption, which conducted a probe in 1962, reported that it "heard from all sides that corruption has, in recent years, spread even to those levels of administration from which it was conspicuously absent in the past." Nor is graft restricted to the junior, low-paid employees. It has traveled noticeably to the higher levels of administration—a point the Committee on Corruption made with marked circumspection. "We wish we could confidently and without reservation assert that at the political level, Ministers, Legislators, party officials were free from this malady," said the report. Finally, corruption no longer means that one gets special treatment, for now one is required to pay extra even for routine services and facilities that were previously freely available. Unless personal position or influence can take the place of money, one has to pay a premium for a railway ticket or a seat on a domestic plane flight. The reservations for certain railway routes can be made ten days in advance, but within minutes of the opening of the booking all seats are customarily declared sold out. In air travel, after one has paid 20 to 25 percent extra to get a seat on a plane that is "fully booked," it would not be unusual to find more than half the plane empty. In other areas of administration, "speed money" is now virtually acknowledged as a fact of life. Bribery is no longer considered a means of overcoming inefficiency in a government department; inefficiency is often deliberately created to prompt bribery.

Corruption at higher administrative and political levels is of considerably greater magnitude, though, for obvious reasons, rather less blatant. It is no longer a case, as it was before independence, of some greedy governor or top executive making a brief killing on the eve of his exit from the country. Nor are the victims of high-level avarice wealthy rulers who could be bled without serious strain even on an honest conscience. The new rulers exchange money, favors and services in a pattern that has steadily become more elaborate over the years. The politicians, businessmen and high-ranking civil servants who now constitute the country's top leadership understand one another's needs and pander to them with a remarkable sense of mutual accommodation. The politician needs money to fight elections and he needs jobs and administrative favors for constituents and supporters. He gets the former from the businessman and the latter from the civil servant. As reward for his cooperation, the senior bureaucrat may be rewarded in diverse ways. He may be promoted to a higher post before his time or be given a relatively more prestigious assignment or allowed to work beyond retirement age.* The businessman is anxious to influence legislative policy and its execution by the executive branch. His friends in the legislature whose election he might help covertly—and when necessary, overtly—exert appropriate pressure on the government in de-

* Most civil servants have a strange dread of retirement and the loss of imposing official residence, servants and other trappings of office. Many are also unable to cope with the problem of occupying their time interestingly.

fense of his interests. In order to secure this advantage, he makes sizable contributions to the election funds of various political parties and, in addition, gives generously to individual politicians. On the payroll of the firms he controls there is always room for the sons and relations of powerful legislators and accommodating bureaucrats. In New Delhi and state capitals he posts contact men who entertain officials lavishly and at times even cater to their personal weaknesses and fancies. (The vulgarity and ostentation of the typical evening party held in New Delhi by a business house's representative is appalling, but, considering the large turnout of Secretaries to the Government and other senior officials, they are apparently successful.) It was probably the activity of the contact men that prompted the committee on corruption to remark that "the tendency to subvert integrity in public services, instead of being isolated and aberrative, is growing into an organized well-planned racket."

It is a measure of the success of this tripartite understanding that certain important policies to which the government is publicly committed but which would have affected the interests of certain business houses have remained unimplemented for years. At times, executive decisions have been taken suddenly and inexplicably that have enabled certain industries to reap additional large profits quickly. Some years ago, for example, the price of sugar cane, traditionally controlled by the government, was lowered briefly and with no seeming justification, bringing large, unmerited profits to the industry. It was not considered a coincidence that this arrangement was made on the eve of a general election. In 1965, when India was faced with a serious shortage of food, authority was unable to proceed effectively against merchants hoarding food grains because of the political influence that the offenders enjoyed by virtue of generous contributions to parties and politicians. The government has similarly been powerless in dealing with tax-dodgers who have salted away vast untaxed fortunes. The number of such hidden fortunes was so great—they are estimated in the range of hundreds of millions of dollars—and they were being surreptitiously used in business transactions on such an extensive scale that many economists justifiably described them as "parallel currency."

Since independence, at least four Central ministers—two of them held the Finance Portfolio—and four state Chief Ministers have come under a cloud for alleged corruption. Their exit and the public outcry that preceded it, however, is not typical of the public attitude to corruption in high places. A small section of the intelligentsia which has been influenced by Western liberal thought on the integrity of public services occasionally protests against seeming acts of impropriety in politics and the administration, but the average Indian accepts political corruption nonchalantly. Nor was the downfall of the ministers and Chief Ministers the result of the public outcry against them or of any exposures in the press. Most of the ousted ministers came to grief because their exercise of power had assumed tyrannical proportions or they had alienated some influential elements in Parliament or they fell unsuspecting victims of rivalry between powerful business houses. There were disclosures in Parliament of alleged acts of indiscretion and impropriety on their part, but those who led the attack on them were seldom motivated by any concern for integrity in public services.

It is doubtful that allegations of corruption in the grant of mining leases would have been leveled against Oil and Mines Minister K. D. Malaviya if his strong left-wing views and aggressive measures to curb profits of private oil companies had not antagonized entrenched conservative elements. Pratap Singh Kairon and Bakshi Ghulam Mohammed had to go because their nepotism had become too blatant and was accompanied by highhandedness in dealing with their critics in the party. T. T. Krishnamachari had to leave the Finance Portfolio in 1965 primarily because his arrogance and stubbornness in even petty, routine matters had made many in Parliament his enemies and exasperated even the Prime Minister. Significantly, several other state Chief Ministers and Central ministers whose reputation for graft is widely known have escaped similar censure.

The Federation of Indian Chambers of Commerce and Industry, the principal association of India's big business, was apparently so disdainful of the public talk about corruption that it declined to testify before the Committee on the Prevention of Corruption. With such acceptance of corruption at the top, it is not surprising that families arranging a marriage should unabashedly discuss, as they often do, the prospective bridegroom's income from bribes.

Similar indulgence is now also extended to slack discipline and inadequate, shoddy work. In India, poor performance is seldom punished and meritorious work seldom rewarded. With the replacement of an autocratic foreign regime by paternalistic, democratic, labor-oriented authority, the employee has lost the fear of his superior, but has acquired no new incentives. Every morning, long past the time for the opening of government offices, thousands of junior employees can be seen cycling leisurely to work; in the afternoon, thousands are on their way home long before official closing time. The lunch hour starts early and ends late. Even Nehru's charisma failed to spark a sense of national commitment in the average Indian.

The junior government employee or the millworker, conscious of the power that his vote and the union to which he belongs give him, suffers from no moral compulsion to put in a full day's work. His conscience seldom intervenes. If it does, it is quickly stilled by reminders of the high cost of living and the enormity of the profits that the upper classes allegedly make. A clerk will take an hour to deal with a document that should take him no more than a few minutes. A messenger may take half a day to deliver a file from one part of the building to another. Two clerks in a post office will gossip interminably with each other while long lines of customers wait stoically for their attention. The young secretary or the woman program assistant in All-India Radio may spend much of her time in the office making flirtatious telephone calls, writing personal letters or reading a popular magazine. This is the tyranny of the underprivileged, against which there is no redress in democratic India. Their jobs are secure since unions are strong and rules governing disciplinary action hopelessly cumbersome. The conscionable among the managers have learned the futility of prodding a subordinate into more energetic action or trying to dismiss him for his refusal to be pushed. The worker thus has no sense of fear to goad him. At the same time, the rewards that a backward economy have to offer him for good work are not worth the extra effort involved. Public administration has become virtually an enlargement of the system of a joint Hindu family in which the facilities a member receives are unrelated to the contribution he may make to its finances. A son whose industry keeps the family business flourishing will occupy the same kind of accommodation and be served the same food as the son who is a scoundrel and a waster. The joint family does not reject a parasite, nor does the government.

It is perhaps an unavoidable corollary to administrative casualness that slogans should take the place of meaningful action. The important thing is not to work hard but to appear to do so. What matters is the ritual and not the spirit or the deed behind it.

India's land, for example, is sun-baked and parched because previous generations have squandered its forest wealth. The importance of afforestation is widely realized, but the official tree-planting campaign is nothing more than a political ritual. Every year at the beginning of the rainy season, ministers plant saplings under the benign view of their political supporters and the press, but after the monsoon most plants die because there is no one to water them or protect them from hungry stray cattle. Similarly, there is a special week each year to promote courtesy (Indian administration is among the most discourteous in the world) and another to encourage cleanliness (Indians can tolerate unspeakably unhygienic conditions), but they are occasions only for ministerial platitudes, photographs and publicity. Official rudeness and unhelpfulness prevail and smelly, choked, open drains go untended even during the observance. Following the Chinese attack on Indian territory, there was much public talk of the need for austerity in domestic consumption to conserve resources for national security. It was decided that austerity must start at the top and be reflected in official hospitality; all that actually happened was that a "banquet" was described more austerely as a "dinner" on official invitation cards. The scale and style of hospitality was scarcely changed. In 1966, Prime Minister Shastri urged everyone to miss a meal every week to conserve scarce food grains. Restaurants stopped serving the midday meal on the suggested day, and there were again many public vows to cut consumption. But the resolve was forgotten long before the drought, which had caused the crisis, relented. The average Indian's social conscience is weak. Apparently, the family and the caste or the community make such exacting demands on his loyalty and affections that he is left with little inclination to concern himself with issues and problems concerning the areas beyond. National problems, therefore, arouse his enthusiasm only mildly and temporarily. He cannot generate a durable sense of compulsion to forgo a meal if famine has struck an area hundreds of miles away, nor will he water a sapling that will not offer shade to his own small courtyard.

6: *Caste and Contradictions*

The Indian mind seemingly has a strange capacity to function in different and even contradictory compartments. If the narrowness of an Indian's loyalties makes his actions appear selfish, the existence of numerous sets of norms and values makes him look something of a humbug. He works himself into a state of tremendous rage over legislative delay in passing a law against cow slaughter and refers to the cow as "the mother," but he would let his own cow starve when it has grown too old to yield milk. A Hindu may bathe daily, as the scriptures expect him to, but after bathing he will unhesitatingly wear clothes that have not been washed for days. The wife of a wealthy businessman lives in opulence and her girth reflects overconsumption, but once a week she will discard her jewels and wear a simple cotton sari for a visit to the temple because poverty is a holy state. The grocer will mix ground bones into sugar, sell colored sawdust as tea and papaya seeds as pepper, and the chemist will dispense water in penicillin capsules, but the fact that their greed may cost lives would not seem to them to conflict with their daily ritual of feeding the orphans. One is business, the other charity, and there is no need to mix the two.

There are other, less objectionable ways in which the conflicting elements and attitudes can coexist in a single mind. Senior ministers functioning under a Western system of parliamentary democracy and committed to modern concepts of socialist planning have a pathetic reliance on astrologers and soothsayers. In March 1969 the newly appointed Chief Minister of Madhya Pradesh insisted on being sworn in at a particular moment that his astrologer had described as auspicious. (That his ministry was overthrown three days later did not lessen his faith in astrology.) Even a nuclear scientist would not hesitate to seek, with astrological guidance, the moment of maximum divine blessing for the launching of a new reactor. The retired railway official who amassed a fortune through presumably corrupt means may spend the afternoon playing golf, but while he is being driven from Delhi's plush golf links to a diplomatic cocktail party in his Mercedes he must recite the holy scriptures, and he will not step out of the car until the recitation is completed.

Beneath this medley of double-think, superstition and humbuggery, however, there are signs that Indians are acquiring a new, modern set of values. Perhaps chanting of Vedic hymns at the opening of a modern irrigation dam and ministers' reliance on astrologers are unavoidable manifestations of the transition from the old to the new. Many in India see the validity of modern concepts and ideas, but are reluctant to discard what they are traditionally expected to believe in and what gave emotional sustenance to their parents and grandparents. They therefore appear to face in two directions at the same time.

Even villages, often linked with the outside world by a rutty road and a solitary radio set in the community center, show

signs of trying to break away from the past and discard attitudes
that have perpetuated poverty and stagnation for generations.
For the first time in centuries, the Indian countryside is acquiring a taste for material well-being. The slogan of planned economic development that Nehru raised and his undivided emphasis on the importance of life without poverty have given the rural
areas new hopes. Hopes are being fulfilled too slowly and only
partially—a rate of progress that creates frustration and anger.
But the important thing for a tradition-ridden society is to learn
to look in a new direction, hope for a better life now rather than
in the hereafter and develop a capacity for anger. This change
seemingly has occurred in some parts of India and is beginning
in others.

In 1943, when famine struck Bengal, as many as three million
were believed to have died of starvation. The hungry would lie
down passively on the pavements of Calcutta to die. The tragic
episode was marked by apathy and sorrow over human fate, not
rage over the iniquitous situation in which hoarders and profi-
teers were allowed to create an artificial scarcity. They died un-
protestingly because they felt they were fated to live in abject
poverty, and death might mark the beginning of a new and better life for them. It is doubtful that the people would have accepted the situation so resignedly if in 1966, when Bihar suffered
a severe famine, the government had allowed matters to deteriorate to anything even remotely like what happened in Bengal.
The government at the Centre and in Bihar would almost certainly have fallen as a price for official negligence.

The fever of rising expectations has affected many parts of
rural India. Foreign and Indian authors have traditionally written sorrowfully of the Indian peasant's refusal to be shaken out
of mental lethargy and to experiment with new ideas or better
implements and of his stoic acceptance of his mud-hut existence.
There is a touch of hopelessness about their assessment of his
aspirations and capacities.

Since the beginning of the Sixties, the situation has altered. A
majority of Indian villagers are still illiterate, but they are no

longer content with producing only the two bags of paddy required to meet their own needs. Nor are they averse to trying out new implements and improved methods of cultivation. Large parts of Uttar Pradesh, Bihar, Orissa and Madhya Pradesh have still to respond to change and new ideas, but farmers in Punjab, Haryana, Andhra, Gujarat, Maharashtra, Madras and Mysore have displayed remarkable initiative in adopting modern techniques and an unsuspected desire for material well-being. The same farmers who only a few years ago scratched the surface of their holding with an old-fashioned, bullock-drawn plow and accepted their poverty as an act of God against which they could do nothing have now come to regard tractors, chemical fertilizers and "miracle" seeds as the routine wherewithal of their profession. Unable to read and write themselves, they are sending not only their sons but also their daughters to school and even to college.

Even the caste system, which has preserved its basic form since its origin in the time of the Aryans some four thousand years ago, shows signs of change under the impact of modern circumstances and concepts. But, as with most deep-rooted institutions of this nature, its state of change presents some contradictory views. In some respects it appears to be getting stronger and more pervasive, but, at the same time, the rigid caste barriers that divide the Hindu society seem to be breaking down.

The pattern of life in India has changed enormously since the Vedic hymns propounded the concept of a society divided horizontally into four principal castes for whose members professional responsibilities as well as social privileges were specified. If until recently the caste system prevailed in virtually its original form, it was partly because of the average Hindu's penchant for tradition but primarily because the society in India retained, until almost the beginning of World War II, the agrarian character that it had inherited from the Aryan invaders and for which the caste system was devised.

Exceptions there have always been, but by and large the

Brahmins, who formed the top of the caste pyramid, were the custodians of the places of worship as well as of learning. The Khashatriyas, who came next in the hierarchy, were the warriors and also owned land and provided political leadership. The Vaishyas, the third caste, engaged in business and commerce; and, lastly, the Sudras, or serfs, comprised landless laborers, sharecroppers and those who performed such menial duties as scavenging, removing dead animals and making shoes. The lowliest among the Sudras were the "unclean" ones or the "Untouchables." Within this four-tier structure have grown, in time, innumerable other subdivisions, creating a complicated maze of castes and subcastes. An Aiyer, for example, is a Brahmin and so is an Ayyangar, but somehow the former is superior and will not contemplate a matrimonial alliance with an Ayyangar family.

Over the centuries the system has served its purpose in providing some kind of hierarchy and order in the Hindu society. The division, though patently unjust, helped create a certain degree of social stability among the Hindus, for belonging to a caste gave one a sense of collective security. Some social scientists seriously argue that if India escaped violent revolution, it was largely because "each caste group is a little oasis of security in the prevailing uncertainty."

Despite its supposed merits, Gandhi, himself a devout and a traditionalist Hindu, raised his voice against the iniquity of the system. He vehemently denounced the practice of untouchability, which forbade the Sudras to enter the temples or even to draw water from the same well that the upper-caste Hindus used. He discarded the term "Untouchables" and called the Sudras "Harijans," or the children of God. If he had his way, he once remarked, he would see that the first head of state of independent India would be a Harijan girl.

India's first President was not a Harijan, but under Gandhi's influence the Congress Party tried earnestly for the uplift of the lower-caste members of the society. In selecting candidates for Parliament and state assemblies, the party gave the Sudras (who constitute over 20 percent of India's population) special weight. The party also insisted on the appointment of a Harijan minister in all cabinets at the Centre and in the states. For a number of years, Harijans were also given special consideration in recruitment to the services. The constitution formally disallowed discrimination on account of caste, and the practice of untouchability was termed an offense punishable with imprisonment. Obviously, it will take longer than two or three decades to undo injustice to the low-caste Hindus perpetrated for thousands of years, but they can at least experience the satisfaction of having some political power, even though it be much less than their numbers should entitle them to. Jagjiwan Ram, Defense Minister in Mrs. Gandhi's Cabinet, is an Untouchable, and so is D. Sanjivvaya, the Minister for Labor Employment and Rehabilitation. In the states, some have risen to be Chief Ministers.

Even more than the educated high-caste Hindus' sense of guilt over the society's past unfairness to the Sudras, what has undercut the caste system is the impact of industrialization, the movement of the population from rural to urban areas, and the spread of education. Besides, the fact that Indian agriculture is ceasing to be as stagnant as it had been for centuries has tended to weaken the system's inequality and divisiveness. Millions who move every year from the village to the city in search of jobs in the country's expanding industries manage to escape from the possessiveness of their caste. In the big-city slums they lose their individual identity, but they are also freed from the tyranny of caste. If in the city the fact that they belong to a particular caste no longer offers new migrants the sense of security and emotional solace that it did in the village, neither does it condemn them to a lowly position for reasons of birth. In the rural areas, too, the winds of change have been felt recently. Thousands of those who return to their rural homes after serving in the armed forces, where their caste placed them at no special disadvantage, refuse to revert to their earlier subservient position. Prosperity, combined with the land-reform laws, has enabled some landless laborers to buy land of their own and thereby cross the economic barrier that caste had erected.

These indications, though heartening, as yet relate to only a small segment of the social order. Nearly 80 percent of India's population is still living in rural areas, where tradition, particularly one sanctified by religion as the caste system is, means much. Those in the cities who have developed a Western liberal outlook on the issue are not numerous, and even their rejection of the system is not complete. Many a thoroughly Westernized, highly educated senior bureaucrat or executive in a commercial organization would, for example, hesitate to employ an Untouchable as his cook. The possibility of a high-caste Hindu marrying into a Harijan family, however prosperous and educated the latter might be, is of course too much to contemplate as yet.

In certain ways the tentacles of the caste system seem to be getting stronger and reaching farther than before. Previously, caste ties bound only small groups of people. When he contemplated his caste, a person normally felt a sense of parochial loyalty to its members living in his own village or in the few square miles around it. Now, improved communications have widened his horizon and made him think of his caste as a considerably larger community. He feels the bond of caste not only with people in the neighboring village but also with those living in the adjoining state and even beyond. Caste bodies have lately attempted to organize their members over large areas and influence their thinking and actions.

Universal adult franchise and promise of political power have encouraged the growth of such large caste organizations. Members of a particular caste, it is realized, may get a sizable share of political power by bargaining with other caste groups. The pull of caste is still strong, and politicians—including many of those who publicly condemn the caste system—have actively pandered to it in the hope of getting votes and power.

This phenomenon is perhaps typical of the transition from a caste-ridden people to a society in which birth does not determine an individual's position. In time, economic and ideological factors may displace caste considerations. When Sudras or Brahmins organize themselves into separate groups to win elections, they are using the system in a way the original Aryan settlers did not intend. This change in purpose really means the creation of a new system while retaining the outer shell of an earlier one. In any case, when caste groups negotiate among themselves over the sharing of power, they do so with a sense of equality that negates the basic assumption of caste.

VI

DEMOCRACY'S SOLDIERS

1: *A Distaste for Politics*

THE INDIAN ARMY is perhaps the only organized body of armed
men in Asia that has respected democratic institutions, accepted
civilian control and leadership and never coveted political
power. During the past two and a half decades, democratic regimes in most newly independent Asian countries have either
been the victims of an army coup—or at least been threatened
with one—or have had to share power in one form or another
with the armed forces. But India has been spared even a minor,
abortive attempt at military control of the kind Ceylon experienced in 1964.

The Indian Army's lack of political ambition is not the only
puzzling aspect of its role. Its performance in the field and its
effectiveness as a shield as well as a sword have seen some remarkable fluctuations. Immediately after the country's independence and though fighting a limited, defensive battle in
Kashmir, it pushed the raiders and the Pakistan Army out of
many difficult, well-defended, strategic points, and in 1949,
when the cease-fire was enforced, it was generally acknowledged

to be poised to recapture much of the area that remained under Pakistani control. Yet the same army fought fitfully and indecisively against the Naga rebels in the country's eastern region. In 1962 the army suffered utter defeat at the hands of the Chinese, who fought a conventional war with equipment not markedly superior to what India possessed. But three years later, when pitched against Pakistan's admittedly superior armor, it gave a creditable account of itself and crippled a sizable portion of its opponent's sophisticated SEATO weapons. In the conflict with China, many of its officers invited the derision of the men they commanded by their lack of valor and qualities of leadership, but in the war against Pakistan, as many foreign observers testify and as their high death toll suggests, the officers fought with bravery bordering on recklessness and exposed themselves to hazards well beyond the call of duty.

The ease with which the Indian armed forces have changed from a colonial force committed to the defense of the interests of a foreign imperialist power to the strong arm of a proud, sovereign nation is also remarkable. In 1942, when India was in deep political turmoil following Mahatma Gandhi's Quit India movement and when all top national leaders had been imprisoned, the armed forces stood loyally by the British rulers, unaffected by national fervor. But soon afterward, when the country achieved independence, the same force earned the confidence of the new political leadership despite the small section of the army that had collaborated with the Japanese during World War II with the seemingly laudable and sincere intention of fighting for India's liberation from foreign rule.

Some of these apparent paradoxes about the role of the Indian Army may be resolved if one studies its class composition, the economic factors influencing its members, and the rigid discipline which the British imposed on it and which by and large continues to be enforced.

The numerical strength of the Indian Army is now around one million. Though not as well equipped, it is larger than the armies of Taiwan and South Korea. It has risen to its present dimensions since independence. In fact, much of its growth has taken place since the Chinese attack on Indian borders in 1962. Under the British, it was a relatively small force. In these days of massive armed forces and stockpiling of arms, it seems strange that the task of keeping a country of India's size subjugated and orderly and defending the Empire and other British interests in the region against a possible threat from Russia should have been entrusted to an army no bigger than 200,000.

British political interests made it imperative that the recruitment of such an army be selective, and the size of the Army in that era made selectiveness possible. The British drew recruits largely from what they described as "martial classes." The "martial classes" theory assumes—up to a point, correctly— that, due to certain racial and historical reasons, certain sections of the people make better soldiers than others. The Sikhs from the northern state of Punjab, the Rajputs from Rajasthan and the Marathas from the eastern region were involved in powerful political conflicts and prolonged military operations in recent centuries and had acquired a martial tradition and a rugged approach to life. Thus, they should, it was argued, make better soldiers than those involved for generations in, for example, commerce and trade. In implementing this theory, however, other political considerations were taken into account. The army was drawn largely from communities that, apart from possessing a martial background, were culturally backward and politically less sensitive (Ahirs, Jats, Dogras) or that were to be turned into privileged minorities (the Sikhs and the Punjabi Muslims). Hindus, who formed the majority community and were the leaders of the freedom movement, were generally debunked as poor soldiers, as were the people of South India and Bengal, who had higher standards of education and political awareness. At the officer level, the recruitment was in very small numbers —in 1939 there were only 508 Indian officers—and they were literally hand-picked from among the families of big landlords who were traditionally loyal to the government of the day and from a small section of highly Westernized Indians who in their own way formed a privileged class. Thus, the British were able to raise an Indian Army on whose support and loyalty they could rely almost completely.

Certain economic factors and the discipline that the British enforced augmented the army's loyalty to the foreign rulers. For most of those who joined the army then, soldiering was an economic necessity, and this is still true today. More than two decades after independence, when a soldier faces the Pakistan Army's sniping across the cease-fire line in Kashmir or maintains a lonely vigil on a 14,000-foot-high post on the border with China, he is motivated as much, if not more, by the need to keep a job as by a sense of patriotism. The soldier—or the "jawan," as he is called in army terminology—draws a basic salary of less than sixteen dollars a month. Before independence he drew even less and was perhaps the worst-paid soldier in the world. And yet he came forward eagerly to fight not only in India but also in war theaters thousands of miles away. He had little option in the matter because a stagnant rural economy, a tired and neglected land which yielded very little, and an antiquated system of land ownership which reduced individual holdings to an unworkable size, made the search for alternative opportunities imperative. Often it was the money sent by the soldier that kept the family fires burning in the village home. Neither the British nor the present government of the country found it necessary to introduce compulsory recruitment during any of the several emergencies that India had to face. The economic realities of the situation offered the necessary compulsion.

Discipline in the Indian Army was always rigid, perhaps more rigid than that the British imposed on their own soldiers. The jawan was turned almost into a fighting machine that obeyed orders and asked no questions. In the kind of jargon now commonly used, the most accurate way to describe his training would be to say he was "brainwashed" into loyalty and obedience. He was to fight not because he was involved in a cause but because his superiors ordered him to do so. Cultivation of such an attitude and of obedience as a reflex action was facilitated by the personal care and consideration that the British officers and later their Indian successors customarily offered to the men under their command. Even in 1962, when in the brief war with China the Indian defenses and army morale in the northeastern sector collapsed totally, many an officer placed the security of his men above his own. In the final phase of the battle, at a time when the Chinese had crossed the Himalayan barricade and had reached the foothills, the commander of the sector, Lieutenant General B. M. Kaul, spent much of his time in an area two hundred miles away from the main battlefield, picking up in his helicopter retreating Indian soldiers who had got separated from the main columns. It was foolish on the part of the commander to be engaged in a routine mercy mission when his job was to supervise operations to prevent Chinese entry into the plains of Assam, but the gesture was not devoid of nobility and typified the relationship between officers and men that has traditionally existed in the Indian Army.

Under the British, the Indian armed forces lived in a politically sterilized atmosphere. An army cantonment, even when adjacent to a city, has been separated from it by an invisible wall. Even if the civil administrative headquarters happened to be situated in the cantonment, the district collector had almost no jurisdiction over it. The cantonment was administered by an appointed board which firmly disallowed any activity that even remotely smacked of politics. The army had its own cinemas, shopping centers, playing fields and clubs.

From almost the day he joined the training academy, an Indian officer was encouraged to fit himself into a standard personality. He was a jolly good fellow who liked his drink and sport, read thrillers and kept away from civilians as far as possible because he regarded them as an inferior, vulgar species. His reading material was carefully if unobtrusively censored. The mess library abounded in fiction, books on shooting and hunting, and war histories written by European experts. It is doubtful if before independence any army mess library dared expose its members to such "subversive material" as Nehru's autobiography or the novels and poems of Dr. Rabindranath Tagore. Tagore had won the Nobel Prize for literature, but the fact that in nationalistic fervor he had rejected a British-awarded knighthood was enough to put him on the blacklist as far as army reading was concerned. Newspapers were chosen equally carefully. It was always the British-owned newspapers, which extolled the virtues of the Raj, that were considered suitable reading for an officer, be he British or Indian. The nationalist newspapers were barred. The army would buy *The Statesman* in Delhi and not its nationalist rival, the *Hindustan Times*. In the Bombay area the services would inevitably patronize *The Times of India* and not the *Bombay Chronicle*. In Lucknow it was always the loyalist *Pioneer* and not Nehru's *National Herald*.

Nehru wisely continued the practice of keeping members of the armed forces as aloof from politics as possible. It was no longer possible or necessary to be censorious about what they read and how they associated with civilians, but active association with politics or politicians was clearly discouraged. Nehru had pronounced ideas on the question of the supremacy of the civil authority over the military and frequently expressed them in Parliament. The soldier, he felt, had an important task to perform, but it did not include taking political decisions. This position was demonstrated convincingly by his attitude toward the Indian National Army. The INA was a small force raised during World War II from among the Indian Army personnel taken prisoners by the Japanese. Most of its members—officers as well as men—were prompted into collaborating with the Japanese by their anxiety to liberate India from British domination rather than a desire to free themselves from the rigors of a war prison. Even though they failed miserably in their task and were at no stage much better than Japanese puppets, they won tremendous public acclaim in the country after the Allied victory when some of their principal leaders were tried by a British military court. The Congress Party, then in the final stages of its agitation for freedom, stood solidly behind the INA and turned its officers into national heroes. Nehru joined the panel of lawyers chosen to defend them. But a year later, when he himself assumed authority, he was distinctly cool toward the INA, and its members were never rehabilitated in the Indian Army. They were treated as political sufferers and given some assistance in finding a niche in life, but their request for return to the army was firmly rejected, for granting it would have meant condoning unsoldierlike behavior on the part of men who were subject to army discipline. In forming themselves into a new force under the umbrella of the Japanese, they had taken a political decision beyond their responsibilities and competence as soldiers. That they were motivated by genuine patriotism did not mitigate the impropriety of their action in the government's eyes.

More than twenty years after the British left India, the armed forces are still separated from the rest of the country by an invisible wall. It is not as high as it used to be and has several large apertures in it, but it is still there. It is a measure of the soldiers' isolation from politics that in 1960, when a number of senior generals felt aggrieved over their allegedly unjust supercession under orders of the then Defense Minister, Krishna Menon, they could not establish contact with even the sympathetic members of Parliament for redress of their grievances. Almost no senior officer knew any M.P. well enough to speak to him in confidence. In the opposition as well as in the Congress Party there were M.P.s who, for reasons of personal antipathy to Krishna Menon or genuine concern over reports of discontent among senior army officers, were anxious to debate the issue. But when Parliament took up the subject, the Defense Ministry escaped almost unscathed because, as was obvious from the vagueness of the critics' speeches, there was no line of communication between the disgruntled officers and the politicians.

Until 1932, when the arrangement was terminated, Indians who received what was then called the King's Commission in the Army were sent to Sandhurst in Britain for training. (Those who joined the army subsequently were called Indian Commissioned Officers and were trained in India.) Because of their training abroad and later association with their British superiors, many of the King's Commissioned Officers acquired the somewhat British attitude of willing acceptance of the supremacy of civilian authority. They tended to speak of politics and its practitioners patronizingly, almost superciliously, but they seldom entertained any serious thought of challenging the politician. The feeling that they, as soldiers, were not required to take political decisions was fairly deeply ingrained in them. A former Indian Army Chief, himself a Sandhurst trainee, once remarked that India would experience no military coup as long as its army was headed by a King's Commissioned Officer. This, of course, was an obvious exaggeration or an oversimplification of the point. Mohammed Ayub Khan, who staged the coup in Pakistan in 1958, and some of his close associates in the undertaking were all Sandhurst-trained officers and had at one time willingly accepted civilian dominance.

Ayub was able to act effectively because political leaders in Pakistan were divided and generally discredited. After Liaqat Ali's assassination, for years no one seemed to be in control. Prime Ministers changed rapidly and ruled ineffectively. Several of them were men of limited competence and doubtful integrity. Even Iskendar Mirza, President of Pakistan at the time of the coup and reputed to be a strong man, lacked a proper political base. Ayub, strong and assertive, a shrewd judge of men, understood the basic rules of the game of power and was capable of correctly discerning the sources of political strength. At the time he staged the coup he had a sizable section of the Pakistan army leadership standing loyally behind him. The political leaders, on the other hand, quarreled among themselves incessantly. Their authority as well as their respective political bases had eroded markedly in the years preceding the coup, and their exit brought the public relief, not sorrow.

In India the situation has been quite different. Political leadership has been in firm control from the day the country became independent, and the large degree of public support that it commanded was always convincingly evident. Nehru's awe-inspiring personality and his tremendous popularity with the Indian masses was probably the biggest single hurdle in the way of any military leader contemplating a coup. His two successors as Prime Minister did not command the same degree of public affection and support, but they were not as inconsequential and discredited as those whom Ayub overthrew. Army leadership was weak and at times, particularly during Krishna Menon's six-year term as Defense Minister, sharply divided. Of the eight Indian Chiefs of Army Staff that the country has had since independence, at least five were not of the dictatorial timber. They could not have staged a coup even if the politicians were in a state of disarray and public disfavor. Several of them had reached the top not because of any personal qualities as leaders or as soldiers but because the rule of seniority was given excessive consideration in determining promotions. Also, most of them entertained sharp but petty personal jealousy of their colleagues—a failing that Krishna Menon exploited ruthlessly. If he was able to treat them discourteously and run one of Asia's largest armies the way he would not have been allowed to run the St. Pancras Borough Council, it was largely because the senior generals, instead of putting up a united front against high-handedness and unwarranted political interference, delighted in one another's discomfiture at the hands of the politicians.

Personal pettiness apart, a certain degree of divisiveness is inherent in the composition of the Indian armed forces. Following the abandonment of the British concept of "martial and non-martial classes," almost every section of the Indian people is represented in the defense services. The armed personnel not only hail from different regions and speak diverse languages, but they also profess faiths as divergent as Hinduism and Islam or Christianity and Zoroastrianism. Even in the last two decades the army has drawn its chiefs from the southwestern region of Coorg, the eastern state of West Bengal, the northern state of Punjab and the southern state of Madras. The present chief of the air force is a Hindu from Uttar Pradesh. His predecessor was a Sikh who was preceded by a Parsi from Bombay who succeeded a Hindu from West Bengal. This heterogeneous character of the armed services, combined with the enormous size of the country (India is divided into four commands with headquarters separated by hundreds of miles), makes almost impossible the unity of purpose and surreptitiousness of action that a successful coup requires. In this respect, again India differs from Pakistan. Divided into two cultural units, Pakistan lacks even the territorial contiguity that India has, but in 1958, when Ayub took power, these diversities and geographical divisions were not reflected in its army. The army leadership itself was comprised largely of Punjabi Muslims and the Pathans, who, apart from belonging to a common faith, come from adjoining areas, have no major linguistic barrier between them and have much in common culturally. East Pakistan, separated from the dominant western wing by over a thousand miles of Indian territory and a different language and outlook on life, had no place of any consequence in the army then.

This does not mean that a military coup is completely ruled out in India. Towering all-India leadership of the kind that Nehru represented is no longer there. It is not unthinkable that a situation similar to the one in Pakistan, which paved the way for military dictatorship, could develop in India. Apart from a decline in the popularity of the Indian politician, the economic situation has deteriorated, corruption—particularly of the variety that affects the life of the ordinary citizen—has increased steadily in recent years, the euphoria of the early years of independence is dissipating rapidly, and hope is giving place to bitterness and cynicism. The climate is thus worsening for democratic institutions. This fact is reflected in the private talk of some of the senior military officers who only a few years ago firmly dismissed any prospect or possibility of an army takeover; now they tend to speak of the shortcomings of the present system and "the army's responsibility to the public to ensure an orderly society." They admit, however, that matters would have to deteriorate markedly and over a long period before a military dictatorship could become a serious possibility in India.

This is, of course, a look into the distant, misty future, but the fear of an army coup has long haunted Indian leaders. In the inner councils of top leadership, the possibility of a coup was sometimes visualized and discussed even before Nehru's death. Politicians, notably those who drew their inspiration from or were close to Krishna Menon, often cast a suspicious eye on the late General K. S. Thimmayya in this respect. Thimmayya, who was Army Chief for four years, was a colorful personality with an impressive service record, an easy, affable manner and a knack of winning the loyalty and affection of his subordinates. He was already the Army Chief when Krishna Menon was appointed Defense Minister in 1957. Initially their relations were cordial, but soon began to sour, primarily because Thimmayya resented what was euphemistically described as Menon's "unorthodox method of running the Ministry." Menon was often brusque, sometimes positively rude, in his behavior and thought nothing of bypassing Thimmayya and dealing directly with his subordinates. At a later stage Menon's style drove Thimmayya to the drastic and unprecedented step of offering his resignation —which he naïvely allowed Nehru to talk him into withdrawing —but long before that a seemingly planned whispering campaign had been afoot in New Delhi insinuating that Thimmayya was contemplating a coup. On the face of it a campaign of this kind is utterly absurd, for anyone planning a major operation of this nature would not allow his intentions to become the subject of speculation on the city's extensive cocktail circuit for weeks and months. Actually, it was not merely a whispering campaign kept alive by petty, mischievous minds. Allegedly prodded by the Menon group, the intelligence authorities had warned Nehru of the possibility of a coup and had even mentioned a particular day for which it was planned. Thimmayya knew of the intelligence report, but did nothing to deny it, for he realized that a protest on his part would not remove the suspicion against him and would, in fact, allow his enemies to suggest that a leakage of the intelligence report had led to a postponement of the operation. It was only on the day that the coup was supposed to take place and after the best part of it was over without any sign of the predicted seizure of power that Thimmayya requested a meeting with Nehru. When he met him in his office in the External Affairs Ministry that evening he talked to Nehru in a manner that few had dared talk to him during his seventeen years as Prime Minister. He claimed to have told Nehru in blunt, angry words how by relying on advisers like Menon he was ruining a fine fighting force.

The politicians' fears of a military coup were roused again, but briefly, the day Nehru died. Perhaps the passing of the great leader deepened the sense of insecurity of some of the top political leaders and made them acutely conscious of the enormity of the task of filling the gap at the top. When they were in such a frame of mind, even the routine action of the then Chief of Army Staff, General J. N. Chaudhuri, in moving two regiments from Agra, 120 miles away, to Delhi caused noticeable tremors of anxiety that lasted till Shastri assumed the Congress Party leadership and the Prime Ministership several days later. The fact that the troop movement was of negligible proportions and a standard precautionary step against any outbreak of lawlessness—and that Chaudhri's action was within the knowledge of the President of India—did little to allay the politicians' fear of a military coup.

All those who have known Thimmayya and Chaudhri personally would readily testify that suspicions of dictatorial ambitions on their part were unjustified. They were both competent generals capable of a measure of brilliance in planning the strategy for a battle but for temperamental reasons equally incapable of plotting a coup. Thimmayya was fond of gay life, talked openly, often indiscreetly, had little interest in or understanding of politics and could not have organized a secret attempt to usurp power even if he had wanted to. If he had ever had any plans for the overthrow of civil authority, furthermore, he would not have tried to end his frustrations as the Army Chief and personal annoyance with Menon by such tame means as the submission of his resignation. By comparison, Chaudhri is a deeper and more ambitious person with greater perception of the factors and forces that constitute political power, but he lacks Thimmayya's warmheartedness and magnetism. Nor had he ever acquired abiding loyalties over a wide area that are an essential prerequisite for anyone thinking in terms of a surreptitious acquisition of authority in a country of India's dimensions.

If ever there was a time when an ambitious soldier could have struck against civil authority with the approval and support of the bulk of the fighting forces, it was in the winter of 1962, when the Chinese inflicted deep humiliation on India and its army. Writing anonymously as the military correspondent of *The Statesman* as far back as 1958, Chaudhri visualized a "situation where the armed forces feel themselves aggrieved and decide to take over control of the country. . . . Military grievances usually stem from an infructuous campaign waged with bad equipment, unnecessary casualties and a civil government showing little comprehension of the soldier's problems." Chaudhri's remark was part of an academic exercise, but what happened when the Chinese invaded the border areas in Ladakh and North East Frontier Agency completely fulfilled the conditions he had mentioned.

2: *The Chinese Encroachment*

Much has been written or said about the India-China conflict, but the episode still has many areas of darkness and some pertinent questions remain unanswered. The fact that in the area across the McMahon Line in the northeastern sector the Indian Army suffered a decisive defeat is widely known and even acknowledged officially, but, for the rest, much of what goes for truth is often the personal predilections and prejudices of the writer, some broad assumptions and some intelligent guesses. A couple of accounts by men who were personally involved in the situation suffer from an obvious attempt to doctor facts, with the intention of shifting blame from themselves to others. Why the

Chinese decided to launch the massive attack and why they chose to withdraw unilaterally from Indian territory that they had occupied can, for obvious reasons, only be surmised, but there are other questions to which convincing answers should be available on the Indian side. Did India do anything which might have been considered provocation by Peking? Is it true— as is alleged by Menon's critics, but vehemently denied by Nehru himself—that Indian soldiers were sent into battle at Himalayan heights of 12,000 feet and above without proper shoes and blankets? What was the role of Nehru's civilian advisers, and what prompted him to make his famous and undoubtedly provocative statement that the "army had been ordered to evict the Chinese" from the Thagla Ridge area? Did the army generals warn Nehru of the hazards involved in taking on the Chinese at that time? And, finally, what was Menon's responsibility in the matter?

The only probe into the causes of the debacle was conducted by Lieutenant General T. B. Henderson-Brooks. The terms of reference of the inquiry were somewhat limited in scope, and a serving officer who had many superiors in the army and government was not ideally suited for the task, but even this probe unearthed some disturbing facts. The Henderson-Brooks report is still a classified document. A brief "summary" that the government presented to Parliament was marked by its inadequacy and was seemingly a calculated attempt to hide the report's grave and damaging conclusions from the public eye.

The original report and certain other official documents that have a bearing on the events of 1962 reveal the shocking extent to which national security had been undermined by Menon's unorthodox methods in running his ministry, his tendency to play favorites, and, for all that, Nehru's deep confidence in him. They also present a sad story of the ineptitude of some generals, of utterly faulty judgment on the part of the political leaders and their civilian advisers in assessing the Chinese mood and intentions, and of the way a Prime Minister can be kept in ignorance of the state of unpreparedness of the country's armed forces. After the failure, Menon as well as the Chief of Army Staff,

General P. N. Thapar, and Lieutenant General B. M. Kaul, who conducted the operation in the eastern sector, resigned.

On Menon must rest the major share of the blame for reducing the army to the condition in which it found itself in 1962, but a slow process of deterioration in its efficiency had started even before he took over as Defense Minister. In fact, the decline began soon after independence. In 1947, when the British left the subcontinent, the army was a trim fighting force that had won honors in several theatres of World War II. Its partition into two armies had affected its competence, but only marginally. By standards prevailing then, the army was well equipped and possessed a sizable stock of arms and ammunition. Most of the ordnance factories that the British set up during the war came to India's share. The British and their allies also left large quantities of war surplus arms and equipment in India and Pakistan. Unlike Belgium and some other colonial powers that relegated the natives to lowly positions in the administration and armed forces, Britain had enabled Indians to attain fairly high ranks in the army hierarchy, so the leadership gap at the top following the withdrawal of British officers was of no serious consequence.

This gap, however, grew larger than it need have been because the government relied excessively on the rule of seniority in army promotions. For several years the army was headed by officers who gave no convincing evidence of purposefulness and initiative and who seemed merely anxious to serve their term at the top in personal tranquillity. The weakness and lack of drive on the part of the professional soldiers were compounded by the fact that until Menon took over as Defense Minister, the Defense Portfolio was held by people who had little conception of the role and needs of the armed forces and who conspicuously lacked political strength and physical stamina. Of Menon's predecessors—Baldev Singh, Kailash Nath Katju, Gopalaswami Ayyangar and Mahavir Tyagi—none had any impact on the ministry, and all more or less allowed their secretaries and advisers to run it on their behalf. Owing either to temperamental differences or failure to understand their respective roles, the military wing was frequently involved in avoidable controversy with the bureaucracy in the ministry. At one stage, so bitter were their personal relations that the Chief of Army Staff and the Defense Secretary, the highest civil servant, would not even speak to each other.

In these circumstances, it was inevitable that the Ministry of Finance should exercise a much more rigid check on defense spending than it might otherwise have done. There is evidence to suggest that during this period the Finance Ministry not only decided how much was to be spent on modernization of the armed services but also prescribed what kinds of arms and equipment were to be purchased. At about the same time, Britain, the traditional supplier of India's defense requirements, developed a marked reluctance—apparently for reasons of international politics—to furnish even what the Finance Ministry's penny-pinching attitude allowed India to buy.

The policy of indigenous defense production which Menon sponsored was the obvious and logical course of action for India to adopt, but, like much else that Menon did, the execution of this policy suffered from his personal prejudices and his penchant for favorites and sycophants. His view that India should produce its own automatic rifles, tanks, jeeps, ammunition and even fighter aircraft was basically sound, but making the country self-reliant in an essential field was probably not the only purpose behind it. The Industry Ministry supervised the functioning of a number of state-owned industrial units and generally coordinated industrial policy covering private as well as public sectors. But, curiously, it was allowed no role in developing defense production, which was kept directly under the Defense Ministry. The latter soon had a sizable industrial empire of its own for production of equipment ranging from semi-automatic rifles and three-ton trucks to tanks and supersonic aircraft—an empire that Menon chose to control through men whose principal qualification was often their capacity to worm their way into his confidence through flattery and by pandering to his whims and fancies. Menon's prejudices within the ministry and sometimes outside the government were often clearly reflected in the growth of defense production. The government, for example, would set up a unit of its own to produce an item even if capacity for its production already existed in the private sector or if a privately owned factory could be expanded less expensively to meet the defense needs. Instead of awarding the contract for producing trucks to Tata-Mercedes, which already had considerable experience in the line, the government set up its own factory at Jabbalpore at much additional cost in money, foreign exchange and time, essentially because Menon had a personal prejudice against the Tatas. Even the choice of foreign collaborators was sometimes ruled by Menon's irrational preferences. If the Soviet Union and the United States stood in competition with each other in offering cooperation, Menon preferred the former, which, considering his ideological inclinations, was natural, but should a British firm challenge even a Soviet offer, it usually won the Defense Minister's support. British collaboration, for example, was accepted in the manufacture of tanks at Avadi and the establishment of the Avro aircraft factory at Kanpur even when rivals offered relatively better terms.

Menon could never suffer fools, but his capacity to suffer his own favorites was almost inexhaustible. Long before the Chinese attack revealed the failure in defense production, the mismanagement in this field was obvious to many in Parliament and the press, but the government firmly refused to act. Indian soldiers faced the Chinese, who carried automatic weapons, with manually operated rifles of World War II vintage while the government factory at Ishapur, which produced semi-automatic rifles, was eighteen months behind schedule. The Avro aircraft project was suffering from delays and indecisiveness in choosing an engine. The older ordnance factories were also the victims of poor administration and lack of proper production plans. When the army was badly in need of vital equipment and material, some of the factories stood idle or were engaged in the manufacture of such unessential articles as coffee percolators. Menon either overlooked the failure of his nominees who ran the various units or permitted them to delude him into believing that everything was working according to plan. As subsequent events disclosed, phony reports and padded production figures were often submitted to the government about the targets achieved in defense production. Menon, who accepted such reports, in turn talked Nehru into believing that great strides had been made in making India self-sufficient in its defense needs. Only a few weeks before the conflict with the Chinese, when Thapar told Nehru of the unpreparedness of the army and of the hazards of engaging the Chinese in a battle at that juncture, the Prime Minister would not believe him. Nehru told Thapar that he was aware of how ill-equipped the Army had been, but he had reasons to believe that much of this defect had been repaired through indigenous production.

Whatever his other mistakes and inadequacies as the Army Chief, Thapar had no illusions about India's military preparedness. He drew the government's attention to the army's weaknesses in a series of letters that he addressed to the Defense Committee, over which Menon himself presided. In his sixth letter, dated June 30, 1962, he pointed out that the "Indian Army, if attacked by Pakistan or China, will be unable to defend itself for long due to its deficient equipment as also a serious paucity of reserves." He pointed out that the strength of the army had been raised by 100,000 men in the previous three years, but that "weapons, equipment and ammunition available to us are so meager that we are finding it impossible to equip the new raisings." He estimated the deficiency in rifles alone at 60,000 and remarked that it would take five years to meet the requirement through indigenous production. The radar equipment, he pointed out with similar frankness, was so old and inadequate that an enemy plane could easily reach Delhi without being detected. The replacement of the pre-1948 transport vehicles was estimated to require eight to ten years.

If the army's equipment was scarce and shabby, its leadership was not in much better state. Menon's six years as Defense Minister had divided the top officers of the three services into two groups. One, much larger than the other, comprised officers embittered by his arrogance or demoralized by his officiousness, and the second included those who had somehow won his favor and consequently wielded influence and authority far in excess of their rank or competence. Menon had little time for those who thought independently and would not tailor their views or assessments to suit Menon's thinking. It was part of his unorthodox method of work to humiliate high-ranking officers publicly. His jibes about them were often cheap and always wounding. He would, for example, often describe one general as "a toothless old woman." At a production conference at which the three service chiefs were present, he remarked to a group of listeners that "seventy-five percent of our difficulties are due to our Chiefs of Staff. I am not saying that they cannot make up their minds, for they do not have a mind to make up." He would deal directly with relatively junior officers, and when the top generals protested, he would take no notice.

Insults and disregard for normal procedure apart, there were other ways for Menon to demonstrate his strength and insist on strict obedience to his wishes. During his term of office, inquiries were instituted against several generals for alleged remarks at army mess parties criticizing or ridiculing the politicians. Thimmayya was the victim of such an inquiry because at a farewell function on the eve of his retirement as the Chief of Army Staff he spoke brashly about the politicians' lack of understanding of the army's problems. Lieutenant General S. P. P. Thorat attracted a similar probe on his retirement from service. These inquiries usually came to nothing, but they caused a measure of harassment and even demoralization because they continued for months and sometimes their findings were not disclosed for long periods after their conclusion. General S. H. F. J. Manekshaw, the present Chief of the Army, was, for example, exonerated by an inquiry board in 1961, but the verdict was not formally announced for over a year and during that period his promotion was kept suspended.

Lieutenant General B. M. Kaul, who later resigned from the

army after his ignominious failure in the battle against the Chinese, suffered from no such harassment. He, in fact, belonged to the small group of officers who were—and, what is more important, were generally known to be—Menon's confidants and who used their proximity to the minister to build for themselves a position of remarkable power. Kaul was shrewd, suave, ambitious and possessed a remarkable and un-soldierlike capacity for playing politics. What bound Menon and Kaul together is not clear, for in temperament as in appearance no two people could have been more dissimilar. What ended their show was not any lack of personal accord or any deterioration in their teamwork but their mistaken assessment of each other's skill and prowess. Even after his downfall, when circumstances had markedly aggravated his customary bitterness and venom, Menon continued to describe Kaul in private conversations as "a brave soldier" who had been mistreated "by scheming men around him." Menon, of course, was among the very few people who assessed Kaul's capabilities that way, for even the General's friends would hesitate to attribute to him qualities of dauntlessness and courage in battle. Till he was confronted with the Chinese on the McMahon Line, his long career in the army had offered him no opportunity to show his skill as a soldier. In fact, in the history of the Indian Army few have risen so high with so little exposure to battle conditions as Kaul. What were often described as qualities of dash and leadership on his part were nothing more than a talent for gimmickry. In 1961–62, however, very few detected his limitations or understood his style of work, and even fewer, in Parliament or the press, spoke of him critically. That Kaul was a future Army Chief was obvious, but some, particularly foreign observers, visualized an even greater position for him. In his book *After Nehru, Who?* Welles Hangen, for example, listed Kaul among the eight most likely contenders for supreme power after Nehru's death. The foreigners, with their belief, often unconscious, in the inevitability of a military takeover in India, tended to exaggerate Kaul's future, but even many Indians regarded him as a man of destiny. Every time one visited Kaul's house one could not help feeling that a great deal of power resided there. Top military brass, some of higher rank than Kaul himself, would wait patiently in the long veranda of his New Delhi house or in an anteroom adjoining his office for an opportunity to have a word with him. It was a measure of his personal importance and power that the day he was leaving Delhi to return to his NEFA post after a brief "illness," among those who called on him at his house to offer him personal greetings was General Thapar, then Chief of the Army Staff and several places Kaul's senior and superior. Under normal rules of protocol—which, incidentally, are more rigidly observed in the Indian armed forces than in the United States Army—Kaul should have gone to Thapar to get the boss's good wishes.

Like Menon and Kaul, Thapar resigned when the advance of the Chinese army into Indian territory could not be stemmed, but the political compulsion for him to quit was not so great as in the case of the other two. He could have retained his post if he had wanted to, for all those letters that he had addressed to Menon about the unpreparedness of the army showed that there had been no negligence or even faulty judgment on his part. He resigned primarily because he thought that, as head of the army, he must accept responsibility for what had happened. He could have shifted blame onto Kaul and a couple of other generals associated with the NEFA operations, but refused to do so. Yet his downfall was basically the result not of an excessive sense of honor but of weakness and unassertiveness. In a way he seemed to fall between two stools. Menon had chosen him for the post of Army Chief because of his reputed mediocrity and weakness, and in the apparent hope of using him as a mere instrument of his own wishes. But within months of his appointment it was obvious that he would not be the doormat that Menon had expected him to be. Later, when his relations with the minister became strained, Thapar tried to minimize his hostility through halfhearted acquiescence in doing Menon's bidding, instead of sitting out his time away from the small circle of Menon's trust and goodwill, as his predecessor had done and as several other senior generals were doing at the very moment. Thapar was aware of Kaul's lack of battle experience and yet he assented to his appointment to the crucial border post, to please Menon. He addressed blunt letters to the Defense Ministry about the army's poor equipment, but did not insist that the issue be discussed by the Defense Subcommittee of the Cabinet. At a meeting in Menon's room on September 22, 1962, at which it was decided to "evict" the Chinese from the Indian territory they had occupied in the NEFA, Thapar spoke clearly of the army's inability to fulfill the assignment and visualized the possibility of massive Chinese retaliation in NEFA or Ladakh in the northwestern sector, but he did not make an issue of it. All he ultimately demanded was that the orders for the eviction of the Chinese be given to him "in writing." If instead of reacting like a junior civilian bureaucrat and being satisfied with written orders, Thapar had insisted on a meeting with the Prime Minister and, in the event of Nehru's refusal to change the order, had tendered his resignation, India would probably have been spared the defeat it suffered four weeks later and many lives lost in battle might have been saved.

The decision to take on the Chinese was the culmination of a period of well over a year that reflected markedly faulty judgment on the part of Nehru, Menon and some of their principal civilian advisers such as M. J. Desai, the Foreign Secretary, S. S. Khera, the Cabinet Secretary, and B. N. Mullick, head of the Central Bureau of Intelligence.

Conflict with Pakistan over Kashmir within weeks of the subcontinent's independence had prompted Indian leaders to believe that the real danger to the country's security came from Pakistan, not China. Pakistan's alliance with the United States and continued belligerence over Kashmir deepened this belief and dulled the suspicions, if any, that the Indian leaders might have held about the Chinese intentions. Under Menon's stewardship, thanks to his pathological distrust of Pakistan and the United States, the army's "primary role" was unambiguously determined as defense against Pakistan. The purchase of equipment as well as the various training programs were oriented toward containing Pakistani aggression in Kashmir or the plains of Punjab. The size of the tanks that India manufactured or purchased from Britain and the Soviet Union reflected this approach. The forty-eight-ton tanks it acquired were meant for the flat lands between India and Pakistan, not the mountainous terrains of NEFA, Ladakh or Bara Hoti, from where the Chinese threat could emerge. All tactical exercises were similarly designed to cope with situations arising from a conflict with Pakistan. India did not have a single mountain division, and little research had been done in the problems of high-altitude warfare. Even after the Chinese occupation of Tibet in 1951, the possibility of a threat from China was not visualized. A paper prepared by the three service chiefs suggesting that Tibet's disappearance as a buffer had materially altered the situation received scant attention from the government.

The government realized the danger from China not much sooner than the public, which had at its disposal only some small crumbs of information about what the Chinese were doing on the border. Even when the Chinese hostility had become obvious, the government, and particularly Menon, tried to play it down. Only three months before the border conflict and after the two countries had had a series of fruitless talks at the highest level to resolve their differences and had exchanged some sharply worded notes and much gunfire, Menon endeavored constantly to minimize the threat from Peking. Typical of his attitude was his action in softening the press statement that the government had issued on July 10, 1962, when several hundred Chinese soldiers entered the Galwan Valley in Ladakh for the first time and encircled a small Indian post held by twenty-nine men. Both Nehru and Menon were away from New Delhi when the news of the Chinese entry into an area deep in Indian territory was received. Besides publicizing the fact of the encirclement of the Indian post, the Foreign Office considered the development grave enough to justify summoning the Chinese Ambassador late in the night to receive a stern note of protest. But the following day, after Nehru and Menon had returned to the capital, the Chinese provocation had become—in the words of the official spokesman—"one of a series of incidents aimed at harassing Indian posts and patrols." There was no reference to the implications of the Chinese penetration into an area that previously they had not reached. Nehru publicly described the action of his own government as being "pitched on a high key," and Menon privately rebuked officials for having issued an "alarmist" statement to the press. The official spokesman amended his earlier statement about the Chinese action by saying that the post had been "approached," not "encircled." Menon was able to make the spokesman play this somewhat pointless verbal game because the Chinese stood on "only three sides" of the post. What was not disclosed to the press then was the fact that the fourth side comprised a sharp fall of more than a thousand feet and that to approach the post from that direction was physically impossible.

This studied nonchalance, however, concealed a degree of worry, perhaps nervousness, on the part of the government. The press and Parliament had become aware of the threat from China and were on the verge of discovering how the government, by its excessive reliance on Chinese goodwill, had neglected the country's northern defenses. On the other hand, Peking was taking advantage of the "unadministered" character of the India-China border and steadily occupying the areas that it claimed. Out of this twin concern was born the "Forward Policy," whose formulation suffered from a defective reading of the Chinese intentions and whose implementation revealed criminal ineptness on the part of the army headquarters.

It was in September 1961 that the Indian government became convinced of the need for military action to check the Chinese advance into its territory. What was seemingly the last straw was the discovery of a Chinese post seventeen miles southeast of Daulat Beg Oulde in Ladakh, a point well beyond the area that Peking had previously occupied. The Chinese not only established the post, but also tried to capture an Indian patrol which came into its vicinity. At a high-level secret meeting summoned to discuss the development, Kaul, in his capacity as the Chief of General Staff of the Army Headquarters, submitted a minute stating that "one of the most effective methods of stemming the Chinese policy of gradually moving westward across our borders would be to give them an occasional knock in chance encounters in our own territory. . . . For instance, if we found one of their patrols in a setting tactically favorable to us, it would be worth our while to engage them in a short offensive action." The Director of the Central Bureau of Intelligence, Mullick, was then asked to consider the disparate pieces of intelligence that the government possessed and submit his assessment. Mullick adopted a line very similar to what Kaul had suggested. The Chinese, he said, "would like to come right up to their claim line of 1960 wherever we are not in occupation." Stating the point conversely, the paper pointed out that "where even a dozen of our men are there, the Chinese have kept away." It further argued that "the Army must fill the vacuum which still exists or otherwise the Chinese are bound to move in within a few months." Galwan Valley and areas north and south of Pangong Lake were specifically mentioned as the places where absence of evidence of prior occupation by the Indians would invite Chinese penetration. On the eastern border, establishment of posts was recommended along the McMahon Line, which India regarded as its frontier with Tibet.

Assessing the Chinese mood, the Intelligence Bureau reported in that paper that "a show of strength on our part is unlikely to invite any major reaction on the part of the Chinese." This unfortunate miscalculation, which some other high-ranking advisers of the government endorsed as their independent judgment, hustled the army into a foolhardy action in NEFA the following year.

Mullick's assessment was formally accepted at another secret meeting attended by Nehru, Menon, Thapar and a few senior civil servants, and on November 2, 1961, the Prime Minister formally issued an order.

Nehru's order was balanced and by no means lacking in caution. Also it was precise and clear. It dealt with each of the three sectors of the India-China border separately. With respect to Ladakh, which had been the scene of much of the Chinese intrusion up to the time, the Prime Minister said that "we should patrol as far forward as possible and establish posts to check and dominate their existing posts without getting involved in a clash." Creation of posts similarly in the Central and NEFA sectors was ordered and this was designated as the "forward policy." Significantly, in an introductory clause to the order, Nehru clearly suggested "major concentration of our troops at places conveniently situated behind the forward posts." And this "concentration" was precisely what the army headquarters neglected to carry out.

Nehru's order visualized establishment of forward posts adequately supported by bigger bases behind them, a kind of stretching forward of fingers linked properly to the palm of a strong hand. The army headquarters, however, took prompt action to set up new posts to dominate existing Chinese posts and send out patrols "as far forward as possible," but did little to build the essential "major concentration" of troops behind them. A field commander in Ladakh protested against the establishment of additional posts without proportionate increase in the base behind them and pointed out in a blunt communication that "there is no short cut to military preparedness." But the army headquarters tersely reminded him that there was "small chance of a large-scale Chinese reaction."

Thanks to this careless reading of Nehru's instructions and an almost childlike faith in the accuracy of the Intelligence Department's assessment of how the Chinese would react, by the middle of 1962 India had acquired a rickety fence comprising small posts, each manned by a handful of men, inadequately equipped and often lacking logistic support of any kind. Many of them had no line of communication with the base, and their supplies of food and ammunition had to be air-dropped. They established Indian presence in the previously "unadministered area," but the Chinese detected their vulnerability and clearly saw behind them vast stretches of undefended territory.

As this fence lengthened, the resolve explicit in Nehru's directive to the army to avoid getting involved in clashes seemingly weakened. In any case, as both sides raced to establish new footholds, confrontation and conflict became increasingly difficult to avoid. Both armies were operating in an area which they claimed was theirs by right. The Chinese troops—or Border Guards, as they were called—were fortified in their action by Communist-style indoctrination. Unlike their adversaries, the Indian soldiers were not abounding in confidence, for they saw their unpreparedness, but were moved by a certain degree of patriotism and were additionally being prodded into forward action by a public which, unaware of their handicaps and limitations, was anxious to salvage national territory and pride.

It was a measure of the public ignorance of the country's state of military unpreparedness that on September 13, 1962, when the news came that the Chinese had surrounded the Indian post at Dhola in NEFA, there was a marked display of aggressive confidence on the part of Indian political writers. After warning the government of the maliciousness of the Chinese intentions, a *Statesman* commentator wrote: "While India's defense forces were nowhere in Ladakh when the Chinese began their intrusion, NEFA and the rest of the eastern sector of the border has always been claimed to be well defended. Instead of marching forward blithely, as they did in Ladakh, the Chinese may, therefore, be forced to have a showdown with India fairly early in their advance across the McMahon Line." The showdown came fairly soon, but the eastern sector, contrary to official claims, was anything but well defended.

Newspaper commentators could perhaps be excused for their reliance on official statements of what had been done to protect the border and the consequent tendency to indulge in chest-thumping but, curiously, many even in high authority had apparently become victims of their own propaganda. Otherwise there was no reason why the government should have decided, as it did a week later, to evict the Chinese from the Dhola area. Aside from the exaggerated claims that Menon had been making about his achievements in equipping the armed forces through indigenous production, there were political pressures and certain personal considerations. Parliament and the bulk of the Indian press, which were always suspicious of Menon, were berating the government for poor judgment in choosing its friends and demanding stern action against the unprincipled Communist rulers of China. The attack on Menon was particularly sharp and persistent, and many in the country sincerely believed that his left-wing political beliefs blinded him to the menace from the direction of Peking. The publication of a photograph of Menon clinking his glass in a toast with Marshal Chen Yi, the Chinese Foreign Minister, at a reception in Geneva some weeks earlier had caused a storm of public anger. Menon had also invited Chen Yi to breakfast, at which he must undoubtedly have tried to sound him out about his government's intentions on the border, but such fraternization with the Chinese at a time when they had spilled Indian blood shocked Indians, many of whom questioned the validity of such diplomatic bonhomie and doubted Menon's motives. One national newspaper remarked tartly that one did not see Menon "sharing a cosy meal with Chaudhri Mohammed Zafrullah Khan [the Pakistan representative at the U.N.] during a debate on Kashmir." By adopting a stern, uncompromising posture against the Chinese intruders, Menon could remove all suspicions against him and prove that his intentions were bona fide. It would also end, or at least soften, the criticism against Nehru for having misjudged the Chinese and lost thousands of square miles of Indian territory in the vain hope of appeasing a bully. Yet another advantage from adopting a policy of firm action in NEFA would be the burnishing of Kaul's image as a brave warrior and the filling of a serious gap in his service record, thereby qualifying him for appointment as the Army Chief, a post that Menon doubtless had in mind for his friend. When he chose Kaul for the NEFA assignment—and the decision in the matter was entirely his—Menon presumably believed that the two hundred Chinese who had menaced the Indian post at Dhola would be evicted in a short, swift action and that Kaul would return to New Delhi covered with martial glory and public approbation to resume his prestigious post as the Chief of General Staff, soon to be entitled to quick promotion to higher positions.

All this planning on the part of Nehru, Menon and Kaul, if it took place, made a basic assumption—that the Chinese would not react with undue belligerence to an Indian move. Much of what had happened in Ladakh thus far was a game of bluff and bluster, with the Chinese trying to scare the Indians into withdrawing rather than using military force for the purpose. There seemed no reason why they should adopt different tactics and techniques in NEFA. In his talks with Chen Yi in Geneva, Menon claimed that he had received no indication that the Chinese were contemplating any major military moves to secure their territorial objectives. He was strengthened in his assessment of the Chinese strategy by what had happened in Galwan Valley, where the Chinese soldiers had lifted the siege of the Indian post after encircling it threateningly for some time. In fact, during the siege they cooperated with Indians to the extent of retrieving and handing over any supplies that were mistakenly air-dropped away from the beleaguered post. Foreign Secretary Desai, moreover, claimed that he had had unmistakable indications from Soviet diplomats that Peking was unlikely to react strongly to an attempt to assert India's rights in NEFA. At the September 22 meeting at which the "eviction" order was issued to the army, Desai pointedly disagreed with the military assessment and argued that a few posts might be attacked and the Chinese might protest loudly, but their reaction to the Indian move would not be in strength. Mullick similarly dismissed the possibility of a large-scale outburst of Chinese anger. In his view, the Chinese strength in Tibet, though large, was so deeply committed to putting down the Khampa rebellion that it would hesitate to entangle itself with the Indian Army. Khera, the Cabinet Secretary, who—like Desai and Mullick—was known to enjoy Menon's trust, presented a similar assessment of how the Chinese might react. The two countries were thus set on a collision course on the border.

An account of how the Defense Ministry set about the task of clearing the Thagla Ridge area of the intruders would read much like the Mad Hatter's party if it were not for the fact that some of its actions, foolish and comical by themselves, led to tragic results involving the loss of thousands of lives. Seldom has a military operation been planned and discussed so publicly as the one that India decided on September 22 to launch. Important decisions that should have been kept secret were leaked to the press. The Defense Ministry was previously so secretive that in July, when the Chinese had surrounded the Galwan Valley post, it would not even disclose the height at which the post was located—a fact known to the enemy—but by September it had suddenly become strangely lax about keeping its secrets. The decision to clear the area of the intruders was reported in *The Times of India* five days after it was formally communicated to the army. But this was obviously not a case of a newspaper acting without due regard to national security, for only three days later Menon himself declared in a speech that "the Government's policy is to make an impact on the Chinese in NEFA before they settle down for the winter." From the point of view of warning the enemy of India's intentions, the statement could not have been clearer. The creation of a new corps for the task and Kaul's appointment as its commander on October 3 was prominently reported by the *Statesman* and *The Times of India*. The day the news appeared, Menon invited a group of senior Indian journalists for a private talk in his room in the ministry, but far from admonishing them for the leakage of what was essentially an operational matter of considerable importance, Menon, who had previously never missed an opportunity to berate the press for "its anti-national hunger for headlines," seemed distinctly pleased with the publicity that Kaul and his ministry had received. Talking to reporters before leaving for Ceylon on a state visit, Nehru himself publicly acknowledged that the "army has been ordered to clear the Thagla Ridge of the Chinese." The only possible explanation for such official behavior on the brink of hostilities is that the government did not think the fight would be a serious operation and was deliberately indulging in saber-rattling in the hope that the intruders would be awed into pulling back from Dhola and that Parliament, due to meet shortly, would be impressed by the government's ability to deal sternly with the Chinese.

If the leaders' public references to the impending operations showed gross indiscretion on their part, the way the operation was actually launched reflected a measure of nonchalance unsuited to a grim undertaking of this kind and an amazing lack of realism.

The Dhola post, which sparked the conflict, was situated on the McMahon Line, which India regards as its legal and traditional border in that sector with Tibet. The post was established as part of the "Forward Policy" to mark India's presence in the farthest part of its territory. The headquarters of the 33 Corps, responsible for the area's defense, questioned the exact location of the post, but despite the obvious importance of the inquiry, Army Headquarters never answered it. After waiting in vain for guidance, the men on the border duty put the post in position. Such negligence apart, when a group of Chinese soldiers surrounded the post, the decision was taken almost at once to clear the area of the intruders. How quickly—and unthinkingly—this momentous step was decided upon is evident from the fact that the Eastern Command ordered local commanders the very next day to prepare to move forward and deal with the Chinese. Later, when the logistical problems involved in the task were fully appreciated, a new corps was created to accomplish it and placed under the command of Kaul, who had no battle experience of any kind, let alone fighting in the kind of hazardous terrain that the Thagla Ridge presented. His inexperience apart, Kaul had been away on a long vacation and was not aware of the various developments, political and military, that had taken place in the weeks preceding his appointment.

From the moment he accepted the new post, Kaul displayed total ineptness as a general. He later was to complain that the corps placed under his command hardly existed when the battle started—a true enough claim, but one that disregards how little he himself did to make sure that the necessary equipment and organizational structure were provided before the corps went into battle. As Chief of General Staff, a post that he had held for almost eighteen months before accepting the NEFA post, Kaul was responsible for planning operations, intelligence, issue of battlefield equipment and final coordination of the activities of the various branches of the army. In that position he supposedly had his finger on the army's pulse; yet the state in which he found the army units in NEFA came to him as a demoralizing surprise. It was stated in the Henderson-Brooks probe that two battalions which had been on their way to a peacetime station and which were suddenly directed to NEFA arrived with no winter clothing. There were only 50 rounds of small-arms ammunition per man, a 100-round backing for each 4.2-inch mortar, only ten-minute firing capacity in the case of 3-inch mortars, one hand grenade and two blankets per soldier, only one week's food supply, and tents for only 300 men. To most of the small posts—part of a rickety defense line set up earlier in the year—supplies had to be air-dropped, but the air-drop zone was situated at a height of 14,000 feet and in a terrain of deep ravines and sharp cliffs. As much as 50 to 70 percent of the supplies fell outside the zone and could not be retrieved. To maintain extensive and tortuous supply lines required 12,000 one-ton trucks and 9,000 porters, by Kaul's estimate. Even if this requirement was exaggerated, the real need was obviously considerably greater than the 300 vehicles actually available.

In these circumstances, it was not surprising that the Chinese forces should sweep down within a month from Dhola, a couple of miles from the border, to Bomdilla in the foothills of Assam; that Nehru should address the nation on November 19 as if the fall of the entire state of Assam into Chinese hands was virtually a foregone conclusion; and that on November 20 a beaten and disconsolate Kaul should sit lonesomely in his office room in Tezpur all night apparently waiting for the Chinese to arrive.

What happened in the western sector, where (as Thapar had also predicted) the Chinese launched a massive attack, was not much different from the events in NEFA, but the Chinese had to fight much harder than in NEFA. The Indian Army units in Ladakh did not retreat in confusion and panic, abandoning their arms and equipment to the Chinese, who were far superior in numbers as well as arms and supplies. India's defense line in Ladakh was as weak and flimsy and its men as poorly equipped as in NEFA, but the army leadership there, less divided and more experienced, was able to mitigate some of the handicaps under which it functioned through better teamwork and a more thorough study of the battleground terrain.

In retrospect, the shock that the army and the nation suffered at the hands of the Chinese was something of a blessing. Nothing short of a traumatic experience of this type would have shaken the government and the people into awareness of the moth-eaten state of the country's armed forces and dislodged Menon and others who were responsible for it. Only a debacle of this magnitude and the sense of national outrage it created would have pushed Menon out of effective power. Beyond forcing the exit of Menon, Thapar and Kaul, it ended the government's penny-pinching attitude toward the question of equipping the military and removed the various management defects from which defense production was suffering.

Once Indian leaders and civil servants had overcome the mental hurdle in the way of seeking foreign arms assistance, their demands were loud and prodigious. In this, they were encouraged by the warmth and urgency with which the initial request for small arms was fulfilled by the United States and Britain. The Defense Ministry, no longer under Menon and thus not inhibited by his personal prejudices, prepared a list so formidable that the U.S. authorities tartly noted it would require an outlay of several billion dollars. Later, when the Chinese withdrew to their earlier positions in NEFA and the India-China war was reduced to diplomatic bickering, the Indian demands for Western arms aid became less exacting and the Western attitude of concern for India's security, too, underwent some second thoughts. Anxious though they were to see that India did not knuckle under to Chinese pressure, Britain and the United States obviously had also other considerations to keep in view. Neither apparently wished to get involved too deeply in India's defense, given the magnitude of such a commitment, or to be pitched directly against an adversary such as Communist China. Besides, there were Pakistan's fears, some real, some imaginary, to consider in the matter. Even if Britain and the United States were convinced that India would not use their military assistance against Pakistan, it was undeniable that an increase in Indian power would enable it to adopt a sterner posture over Kashmir and in other Indo-Pakistan disputes. It was, therefore, not surprising that some of the Western promises to India were not fulfilled. At their Nassau meeting, President Kennedy and Prime Minister Macmillan resolved to provide India with arms assistance to the extent of 60 million dollars each. Presumably because of Pakistani diplomatic pressure, the U.S. promise remained unfulfilled to the extent of over 20 million dollars. Equipment for six divisions for high-altitude warfare was supplied, but, significantly, only one of the six ordnance factories that the United States and Britain had agreed to set up in India was actually established.

India's own determination to increase its military strength, however, did not decline similarly. With Menon's exit, some of his favorites who had been placed in positions of authority in defense production were moved to other posts or agreed to have their performance measured in terms of concrete results rather than their personal influence. The Ishapur rifle factory and the tank factory at Avadi solved their chronic problems with amazing speed and went into regular production soon after the NEFA debacle. The rifle produced at Ishapur is acknowledged to be among the finest in the world, and Indian tanks have stood the test of battle alongside others imported from Britain and the

Soviet Union. The Finance Ministry overcame much of its previous reluctance to allocate funds for defense, and it is a measure of the jolt that Peking gave India that the national defense budget, which was less than 600 million dollars in 1962, was increased almost threefold the following year. With the additional money provided for defense, India bought weapons from abroad expeditiously and not unwisely. With Western powers unwilling to alter the balance of power between India and Pakistan through massive aid or a liberal arms-sale policy, the country turned to the Soviet Union for its supplies and found accommodating terms.

Fortunately for India, the period of its defense rehabilitation coincided with the Soviet estrangement with China. During the war with China, Moscow sat on the fence. Faced with the embarrassing dilemma of choosing between a "socialist brother" and a "nonaligned friend," Khrushchev procrastinated for several weeks while India waited anxiously. Even an earlier promise to provide a squadron of MIG-21 supersonic aircraft was obscured by the haze of political indecisiveness in Moscow. Happily for the Indian leadership, this stage did not last long, and that Moscow had chosen to stand closer to India became clear by the middle of February 1963, when a ship carrying six MIGs arrived in Bombay. From then until some time toward the end of 1965, when the Soviet Union decided to adopt a neutral posture toward Kashmir, India received sizable help in strengthening its armed forces. On Soviet insistence, the nature and size of its military aid are kept secret, but it is known that besides help worth an estimated 300 million dollars in the establishment of the MIG aircraft factory, India has purchased a large number of Soviet helicopters, transport aircraft, light and heavy tanks and some electronic equipment.

3: *Showing Strength* . .

Ironically, India's endeavor to mend its fences and add to its military strength was one of the principal factors that involved it in another brief but equally gruesome war with another neighbor, Pakistan, three years later. That a large number of paramilitary personnel from Pakistani-held parts of Kashmir crossed the 1949 cease-fire line and infiltrated into the Kashmir Valley, with Pakistan's active complicity in the operation, is acknowledged by the U.N., but what motivated the rash and hazardous Pakistani action can only be surmised. The most plausible explanation, with which most neutral observers tend to agree, is that Pakistan had grown apprehensive of India's increasing strength and sought a military solution of the Kashmir problem before the advantage that the availability of sophisticated U.S. military equipment offered it was neutralized by India's hectic efforts to repair its defenses. It is also possible that what India genuinely regarded as defensive preparedness seemed offensive preparations when viewed from Rawalpindi. Fear of India and help from the United States had given Pakistan an unduly large military force. According to the Institute of Strategic Studies, by 1964 India had narrowed the gap between its own and Pakistan's military strength and had publicly announced its intention to continue its efforts to enlarge and modernize its armed forces. For Pakistani leaders, who had rejected the Indian proposal for a no-war pact and thus tacitly reserved their country's right to go to war over Kashmir, time was obviously running out. Somewhat typical of Pakistani thinking at the time was the remark by a commentator in the *Pakistan Times* in the summer of 1965. "Foreign Powers are pumping arms and ammunition into India," he said. "Five years hence the Indians will be very strong." Apparently, it was considered necessary to strike before that stage was reached.

The skirmishes that Pakistan had with India in the Rann (marshland) of Kutch in April 1965 have been described by foreign observers as a Pakistani way of testing India's responses and military potential. That Pakistan should suddenly precipitate a crisis over a dispute so trifling that an Indian communication about it sent six years earlier had gone unanswered confirms this view. But it was not only the Indian reaction that Pakistan wished to test. Before launching any major operation over Kashmir, it was important for Pakistani leaders to know how the U.S. government would react to the use of American arms given to Pakistan as a CENTO ally—arms that Eisenhower had expressly assured Nehru would not be used against India.

If Kutch was indeed the testing ground for contemplated aggression, Pakistan received ample encouragement. Taken by surprise in a distant, marshy, uninhabited corner of the country involving territory of little real value to either country, the Indian Army once again seemed to act nervously and gave the impression that it was unable to meet a challenge effectively, even from a smaller neighbor. The Indian Army had been entrusted with the task of defending the Kutch border only on April 7—previously the border had been guarded by a small contingent of the Gujarat state police—by which time the Pakistani armed forces had not only occupied a slice of Indian territory but also made adequate preparations for any Indian reaction. In certain ways the situation was very similar to the Chinese challenge three years earlier. Pakistani bases were much closer to the border than Indian bases. Maler cantonment in Sind, which served the area, was only about fifty miles from the disputed territory, while the nearest railhead on the Indian side was more than a hundred miles away. By the end of May the Rann would be underwater for six months, and the terrain was such that the Indian side of the border would be submerged first.

The Indian Army, therefore, had reasons for acting diffidently. Despite provocation and some sneering from both sides of the border, General Chaudhri, then the Army Chief, resisted the temptation to send in Indian tanks to battle with the Shermans that Pakistan had moved into the area. The vagaries of the monsoon could have created a watery grave for the Indian armor much more easily than the Pakistani tanks or fighting potential. Chaudhuri's advice to Shastri was that it was futile to fight at a place of Pakistan's choosing and that its challenge must be met elsewhere. Harold Wilson's intervention in the dispute as a mediator and the agreement reached later made it unncessary for India to open a second front and for the army to demonstrate how it would fight at a place of its choice. Thus, the world in general and Pakistan in particular were left with the impression that the Indian Army was a force of no significant courage and fighting capabilities. *Dawn,* a leading Pakistan daily, which usually influences and echoes official thinking in Pakistan, crowed on May 19 that Pakistan had won "easy victories" and that the Indians "would hardly ever allow themselves to get too close to the Pakistanis." In describing the confrontation to a group of Pakistanis in London during his visit to attend the Commonwealth Premiers' conference, Ayub reportedly remarked with contempt that he had ordered the Pakistani soldiers to show restraint in pursuing retreating Indians, but "even so, they are squealing like they did after the conflict with China." *Dawn* and Ayub could be forgiven for their disdain, for many in India then also felt that the Indian Army had once again failed the country.

What Pakistan learned about U.S. reaction to the use of its arms against India must also have been equally reassuring. After a brief display of disbelief, seemingly for form's sake, the United States accepted the Indian charge that U.S. equipment, notably tanks, had been used in Kutch in clear violation of the assurance that India had been offered at the highest level. *The Hindustan Times* reported on the basis of "authoritative diplomatic reports" that the "U.S. Government had lodged a strong protest with the Pakistan authorities against the use of American military assistance equipment in the current fighting in Kutch." But apparently the protest was not so strong as was reported, for Pakistan took no notice of it. It declined to allow U.S. military personnel to visit the area of operations as it was obliged to do under the terms on which U.S. arms were supplied. The State Department took no further action, thereby leaving the Pakistani leaders to infer that by using American arms in a larger conflict with India they would invite upon themselves no U.S. wrath.

It is possible that if the U.S. government had taken a stern view of the Pakistani violation of Eisenhower's assurance to India and effective measures to prevent future use of U.S. arms in an attack on India, or if the Indian Army had given a more convincing account of itself in Kutch, Pakistan would have been discourged from launching its plan to capture Kashmir four months later.

The political misjudgments on the part of the Pakistani leaders that paved the way for the twenty-two-day war and also their military miscalculations were of serious consequence. That the Indian Army did not achieve any signal victories in Kutch and hesitated to open another front encouraged Pakistan's leaders to think, as Ayub's disdainful remarks in London suggest, that the Indian Army was lacking not only in muscle but also in courage. A second miscalculation was Pakistan's assumption that India would confine the war to Kashmir and would not retaliate across the international frontier. Similarly, India's hesitation to employ its air force in 1962, even when the Chinese seemed on the verge of capturing not merely NEFA but also Manipur, Tripura and the entire state of Assam, prompted Pakistan to assume that, as in the Chinese conflict, India would fight a war limited to the ground.

For Shastri and his colleagues the fact that India had never crossed the international border and not used its air force added to the enormity of the decisions that they had to take. When several thousand Pakistani agents and guerrilla forces were discovered to have infiltrated into Kashmir from across the cease-fire line, the army was summoned to help the police in rounding them up. But when it was realized that Pakistani trained guerrillas were continuing to enter Kashmir through passes held by Pakistani forces, India took offensive action to capture and seal the passes. In thus crossing the cease-fire line to occupy such strategic posts as Kargil, Uri and Haji Pir, India's political leadership clearly visualized a situation in which the air force might have to be summoned and the war enlarged to cover areas beyond the international border. General Chaudhuri as well as the Air Chief, Arjan Singh, unambiguously outlined the hazards involved in capturing the vital passes on the Pakistani side of the cease-fire line and the extent to which the war might be escalated. When he indicated in Parliament that Indian forces might occupy further strategic positions—as they actually did the same afternoon—Shastri was well aware of the possibility that he might have to order a total war with Pakistan.

For those who knew Shastri—somewhat superficially—it was hard to believe that he could take such militant decisions. Meek and humble, with no experience or understanding of a war situation, a man who had failed to discipline traders and hoarders over food prices and who was constantly accused of being a "prisoner of indecision," Shastri would normally have been expected to act so haltingly as to lose the situation through vacillation or to permit the army to dictate to him. Neither likelihood happened.

What was not realized by Ayub was that Shastri and his Cabinet colleagues, for all their background of Gandhian nonviolence, needed to prove themselves even more than the armed forces. The charge that the government was a prisoner of indecision had hurt them because it came too near the bone. Shastri knew that he lacked Nehru's stature and charisma to be able to survive a bad compromise or an adverse trial of strength with Pakistan. He was also disillusioned about Ayub's profession of eagerness to establish friendly ties with India. Impressed by Ayub's cordiality earlier that summer at a meeting in London, Shastri had spoken to him frankly, almost indiscreetly, of his difficulties at home and his personal thinking on Kashmir, but later he learned, to his discomfiture, that about the time he was sharing his confidences with Ayub, the latter was actively launching his plan to annex Kashmir through guerrilla warfare. Shastri thus came to believe that there could be no meaningful talks nor a reliable understanding with the Pakistani leaders, and that the challenge in Kashmir must be met with as much strength as India could muster. In this approach Shastri was supported by his principal Cabinet colleagues.

On the morning of September 1, 1965, the day after Pakistani tanks had crossed what India regarded as a sector of the international border (as distinct from the cease-fire line) but before the

Indian Army had been ordered to put its plan into action, Home Minister Nanda called at the Prime Minister's house to urge him to order the army to go ahead. Alternatively, he suggested, Shastri and he should resign to make room "for others whose response to the challenge had not been blunted by age." Chavan, then Defense Minister, was also in favor of action, but expressed himself with greater restraint and tended to speak of the hazards of an all-out, protracted war. Indira Gandhi had by then drifted away from Shastri, but as a member of the five-member Emergency Committee of the Cabinet stood firmly committed to strong military action. She was the first among the senior ministers to raise the alarm about the magnitude and nature of the Pakistani invasion. The politicians thus needed no pressure from the army to act as they did.

The decision to employ the air force was probably the most difficult for Shastri and the one on which he showed the greatest degree of hesitation. During the war with China, India had held back its air force, partly owing to its operational limitations and partly in the hope of restricting the scope of the conflict. By acting similarly, India might avoid escalation in the war with Pakistan. On the other hand, as India had subsequently learned through Western intelligence sources, the Chinese air force was in no position to retaliate and if the IAF had gone into action in support of the ground forces, the outcome in 1962 might have been less ignominious. Shastri was particularly worried about the security of New Delhi and Bombay and asked for a careful assessment of the relative strength of the two air forces. Could the oil refinery, the nuclear reactor and other important installations in Bombay be saved from Pakistani air attacks? Could Delhi's civilian population be guarded against Pakistani air raids? These were questions he repeatedly asked in the last few days of August. Arjan Singh's advice to the Prime Minister was that the air force could be deployed with advantage even though Pakistan possessed more sophisticated aircraft, and that to keep India's air arm out of the war would be to repeat the mistake of 1962. He could not guarantee total protection for New Delhi against

Pakistani air raids, but was confident that the damage, if any, would be small.

The air force was ordered into action when—in obvious retaliation against the Indian action in occupying Kargil, Uri and Haji Pir—Pakistan launched a massive tank and infantry attack in the Chhamb-Jaurian area in the southwest of Jammu and Kashmir. This was a vital point, for it is here that the Kashmir cease-fire line ends and the international border between the two countries begins. Through this area also run two important roads, one linking the northwestern parts of Kashmir with India and the other providing the country's only line of communication with the valley. If Pakistani forces could reach Akhnur only twenty miles inside Indian territory and destroy or capture the key bridge over the Chenab and then advance to Jammu and control the Pathankot-Srinagar road, India would lose its only road link with Kashmir.

When they met at Tashkent in January 1966 during the Indo-Pakistan peace talks, Indian newsmen were surprised to find that their Pakistani counterparts sincerely believed that Pakistan's army had inflicted a crushing defeat on India, and that it was India which was beseeching early return of its territory. In all situations of this kind, both sides tend to make exaggerated claims and reaching the truth is hard, particularly when, as in Pakistan, the press is controlled. In India the area of ignorance was smaller, but it existed. Till almost the end of the fighting, the public in India did not know, for example, that at Khemkaran on the southern end of West Pakistan's border with Punjab, the Pakistani forces had launched a furious armored attack on September 8 and had come fifteen miles inside Indian territory before being pushed back. Not many facts of any importance have, however, remained hidden for long. A broad assessment of the Indian Army's performance is, therefore, possible.

More than occupying Pakistani territory or menacing its security, the Indian objective was to blunt the sharp edge that U.S. arms and equipment had given to Pakistan's sword. The Indian Army had for long stood in secret awe of the F-104 supersonic fighters and the allegedly invincible Patton tanks that Pakistan had secured from the United States. Though these were given as part of its SEATO and CENTO obligations to contain Communist threats, Pakistan had seldom hesitated to flaunt them in the context of the conflict in the subcontinent. At the end of the fighting, Pakistani losses in tanks were estimated by competent neutral observers at over 400. A London *Times* correspondent reported that India had lost 200 tanks and Pakistan twice that number. *Time* Magazine reported that Pakistan had lost "Over 500 tanks." In the big battle of Khemkaran alone, as many as 180 Pakistani tanks were believed to have been damaged. Of these, 97 were left on the battlefield and are still kept there as an Indian war trophy. Whatever the precise Pakistani loss in tanks, the toll was considerable for a country that before the war reportedly possessed a total tank strength of 1,000.

The Indian Army's principal gain from the Indo-Pakistan war was its rehabilitation in its own and the people's eyes. It regained the self-respect and self-confidence that it had lost during the years of Menon's overlordship of the Defense Ministry and the war with China. If the conflict with China disclosed the extent to which it had been allowed to run down, the war over Kashmir offered the assurance that the efforts to restore India's defense forces to their former state of health were proceeding along correct lines.

The efforts to improve the combat efficiency of the Indian Army, Air Force and Navy have become even more brisk since 1965. It is now a force of considerable size—nearly one million regular men in the three services—and its training and equipment, far more modern and streamlined than at any time since independence, have made it a formidable fighting machine.

Though India still relies rather heavily on the Soviet Union for the supply of its arms and equipment, it has been moving rapidly toward self-sufficiency in arms manufacture. In fact, since 1968 it has been selling certain quantities of arms to others in the region.

India still does not have the nuclear bomb and is formally

committed to not producing one, though most foreign military and scientific experts acknowledge that India has the capability of developing nuclear power. This realization, combined with the country's stubborn refusal to sign the Nonproliferation Treaty, has left India open to suspicions of future aggressive designs on its part. Such suspicions at present seem uncharitable. India disassociated itself from the Nonproliferation Treaty because it found the treaty an unequal one, placing few real restrictions on the big powers while asking the non-nuclear nations to renounce their rights. Nor has India wished to close its options in the matter while China, which offers the principal threat to its security, is building a large arsenal of nuclear weapons and is not a signatory to the treaty.

VII

ECONOMICS: THE RACE
WITH CATASTROPHE

1: *Socialism, Indian Style*

BEFORE INDEPENDENCE, nearly every Indian schoolchild was required to read a textbook that devoted an entire chapter to enumerating what were described as the "blessings of the British Raj." The British, it was stated, had built railways, dug canals, laid roads and enforced law and order. The chapter suggested fairly explicitly that Indians should be grateful to the British for the enormous economic benefits that India enjoyed.

That the British accomplished much of what the textbook gave them credit for is undoubtedly true. Compared to other colonial powers of the time, the British displayed remarkable benevolence toward the people they ruled. They not only built railways and roads but also introduced a modern system of education in India and laid the foundation for parliamentary institutions. India was spared the type of intellectual and economic backwardness from which, for example, some of the Belgian colonies seemed to suffer at the time of independence.

Yet it would also be true to say that the British action was motivated not so much by a consideration for the people they ruled as by the need to consolidate their political power in a distant land and further Britain's own economic interests. If the railways facilitated communications and travel, they also enabled the alien government to maintain a tight military rein on a far-flung colony. The roads supplemented the railways in transporting raw materials for British industry from rural India to the ports. Even the digging of canals was not devoid of ulterior purpose. The canals and the economic growth that they represented were concentrated largely in areas amenable to British influence and power. The Punjab irrigation system was a case in point. The province (later divided between India and Pakistan on a religious basis) had what was then believed to be the finest network of canals in Asia, perhaps in the world. But the canals drawn from rivers flowing in the Hindu-majority part of the province provided irrigation in the western half, which had a Muslim majority and was dominated by feudal elements on whose loyalty the British could depend. The Bhakra irrigation project, which would have served the Hindu peasantry in the eastern part of Punjab and had been visualized as early as the beginning of the century, was not implemented until after independence.

Such political bias aside, economic development under the British was limited in scope. According to a survey published in 1944, which undoubtedly reflected the extraordinary growth of the war years, undivided India had 65,000 miles of paved roads. Even if unpaved roads were taken into account, there were 62 miles of road for every 100,000 inhabitants. The comparable figures then for the United States were 2,500 miles and for Japan 850 miles. The railways, the principal means of transportation, were more extensive. There were nearly 42,000 miles of broad- and meter-gauge railway track. But roads and railways were designed to serve the security and economic interests of the British, and their range did not correctly reflect the strength of India's economy. A more accurate index of the plight of the country was the estimate of national income offered by Sir James Grigg, Finance Member of the Central Government, in his budget speech of 1938. He assessed the per-capita annual income in India at fifty-six rupees, or a little over four British pounds then. Indian economists pointed out that this income was enough to feed only two of every three Indians at a level of bare subsistence and with little left for clothing, housing or education. Sir Alfred Watson, editor of the *Statesman,* a leading Indian newspaper which was then British-owned, told the Royal Empire Society in London in 1933 that unless India could undertake industrial development "on a wholly unprecedented scale," its "appallingly low level of subsistence" would "fall below the starvation point." This is a far cry from the recorded remark of another soldier of the Empire—Lord Clive—who, when he entered the city of Murshidabad in Bengal in 1757, wrote that "this city is as extensive, populous and rich as the city of London." A century earlier the French traveler Bernier felt that Bengal was richer even than Egypt. Another European traveler who visited India in the seventeenth century, Tavernier, recorded that "even in the smallest of villages rice, flour, butter, milk, beans and other vegetables, sugar and other sweetmeats, dry and liquid, can be procured in abundance."

Nor was the starvation, malnutrition and economic stagnation witnessed in the first half of the twentieth century the unavoidable result of limited resources. Sir George Watt, an agriculture expert, reported to the Indian government in 1894 that "few countries in the world can be said to possess so brilliant an agricultural prospect" as India. The American Technical Mission that assessed India's economic potential in 1942 gave an impressive list of the country's mineral resources. It described the iron-ore reserves as "probably the largest in the world" and "superior in quality to those of any other country." In his lecture to the Royal Empire Society, Sir Alfred Watson referred to India as "a land of missed opportunities" and remarked that the "main blame for this rested heavily on the British." According to an account of the lecture in *The Times* of London, Sir Alfred reported that "though India possessed in abundance all the conditions for a great industrial country, she was today one of the backward nations of the world economically and was very backward industrially." He felt that "we had never tackled seriously the problem of developing India's undoubted capacity for industry." As editor of a newspaper owned wholly by British commercial interests and addressing a gathering as conservative as the Royal Empire Society, Sir Alfred would not have been blaming the British government of India needlessly.

The Indian people as well as the leaders who took power in 1947 needed no foreign technical missions or journalists to remind them of how the country had suffered at the hands of the colonial rulers. Under the British, India's economic interests had been unabashedly subordinated to those of Britian. The industrial revolution, which had contributed much to Britain's own greatness, was calculatedly allowed to pass the subcontinent by. India merely produced the raw materials—cotton, jute, oilseeds, minerals—that British industry needed. At the same time, it served as a vast market for finished products, ranging from biscuits to railway engines. For what they produced, Indian farmers received a pittance while British-owned firms in Calcutta and Bombay reaped sizable middleman's profits. Even Indian agriculture was permitted to stagnate in most parts of the country. Canal irrigation was the exception, not the rule. Farmers were offered no encouragement to discard the primitive implements they had traditionally used. The land-tenure system was oppressive in most parts of the country and the government's primary interest in rural areas was to collect land revenues.

If they saw selfishness and callousness on the part of the former rulers, Indian leaders also felt assured of the country's capacity to pull itself up. Instead of disheartening them, the enormity of the task of economic development spurred their imagination. Anger over the selfishness of the colonial rulers created a sense of urgency and the desire to make up for lost time. The nationalistic fervor and a genuine belief in the vastness of India's resources combined to give their thinking on economic issues an added, if somewhat unreal, dimension.

There was a tendency, particularly on Nehru's part, to be impatient and set goals unrelated to the country's technical and administrative competence. He would respond testily to any suggestion that India must learn to walk before it could run. His speeches in the early years of independence were full of economic rhetoric about the great future that awaited India and the rapid strides that the nation must make to reach it. He seemed to chafe at the realization that in the middle of the twentieth century India was still in the bullock-cart stage and was edging toward what he once described as the "bicycle age."

Nehru therefore tended to think in grandiose terms. The emphasis in Indian economic planning, particularly in the first decade, was on large, monumental projects that would satisfy national pride and demonstrate India's rapid progress. The accent was on a few multipurpose irrigation and power projects rather than on numerous minor irrigation schemes, on gigantic steel plants rather than on smaller and more feasible units. Typically, work on the Bhakra project, which involved construction of what was then the world's highest straight-gravity dam (740 feet high), began in 1948; the million-ton Rourkela steel plant, the first of the four state-owned units, was conceived in 1953; the Indian part of the border state of Punjab, which had lost its capital to Pakistan at the time of partition, was allowed to build a new, modern city planned by no less a personage than Le Corbusier.

In these circumstances it was inevitable that the process of economic planning which Nehru initiated should be on an ambitious, somewhat idealistic basis. The Planning Commission, a high-power body, was set up in March 1950 and entrusted with the task of devising the strategy for the country's rapid and extensive economic progress. To emphasize its role and importance, Nehru himself chose to be its chairman.

Starting in 1951, the Commission prepared four Five-Year Plans. The first three were implemented one after the other, without interruption, but the fourth started only in 1969. Between the third and the fourth plans, for three years India was faced with a marked depletion of resources owing to a protracted drought and the war with Pakistan. During this period, therefore, long-term planning was rendered impossible and the Planning Commission lived virtually from hand to mouth and planned on a yearly basis.

The concept of five-year plans was obviously taken from the Soviet experience, but it was trimmed to match India's mood for democracy. Indian planning required the state to play an active role, but did not seek to replace normal market mechanisms with an authoritarian central body thinking and acting arbitrarily. The state was supposed to use—and in practice it actually did use—market mechanisms to achieve many of the goals set out in the various Plans.

As was but natural, economic objectives varied from plan to plan. The first plan provided for an investment equal to over eight billion dollars (at the then prevailing exchange rate) and was aimed principally at mitigating the shortage of food and essential consumer goods and helping the rehabilitation of those who had migrated to India as refugees. The second plan was twice the size of its predecessor, and it shifted the emphasis from agriculture to industrialization, particularly development of basic and heavy industries such as iron and steel, chemicals and machine-building. By the time the third plan was to be launched, planners had realized that they had moved from agriculture to industrialization a little too soon. The new plan, therefore, again stressed greater food production. But it also provided for further expansion of the already established heavy industries so that the country could be almost self-sufficient with respect to future industrialization. The fourth plan is, in terms of rupee value, six times the size of the first plan. Its size represents a victory for those in India who believe India's problems and needs are so big that if an economic disaster is to be averted, it must plan its development effort on a big scale. They scoff at those who suggest that India must plan according to its limited resources or that after three plans there should be a pause in planning. The fourth plan aims at reduction of the country's dependence on foreign aid through development of internal resources, provision of wider employment opportunities and implementation of population control as "a program of highest priority."

The ideological force expected to catapult India from colonial stagnation to vibrant modernity was socialism. India's professions of faith in socialism are loud. Many in the Western world view it with considerable suspicion, even hostility. Nehru and many other senior leaders spoke constantly of socialism as a panacea of India's ailments. At every annual meeting the Congress Party ritualistically reiterated its faith in socialism, which in fact was manifested in occasional sweeping actions such as the nationalization of insurance companies in 1956 and of private banks in 1969. At its Jaipur session in 1963 the party preeningly claimed that over the years it had moved steadily and consciously toward socialism. Yet, from the very start, Indian socialism has been rather superficial. It has been more a political slogan intended to serve as an opiate for the poverty-stricken masses than a chosen form of action.

Nehru's preference for socialism was genuine. Marxist writings and the Soviet success in overcoming backwardness had influenced his thinking. But his temperament, particularly his readiness to compromise, had given his faith a Fabian character. His principal colleagues in the government, however, did not share his enthusiasm even for a diluted kind of socialism. Sardar Patel, Deputy Prime Minister in the first Cabinet and the party strong man, had no time for socialism. The first three Finance Ministers after independence as well as the first Deputy Chairman of the Planning Commission were generally known to have no left-wing predilections. In fact, all four of them were technocrats and three of them had earned knighthoods from the British rulers. Later Morarji Desai, who held the Finance Portfolio for an aggregate of eight years under Nehru and Mrs. Gandhi, was an acknowledged conservative. The Congress Chief Ministers who exercised power in the states, almost without exception, were devoid of socialistic leanings. Of the people in authority at the Centre since independence, the only ones harboring varying

degrees of leftist beliefs were Krishna Menon, T. T. Krishnamachari and K. D. Malaviya. The first two had no following in the
party and no political base worthy of the name, and all three had
to leave the government in unedifying circumstances.

If, despite their total lack of faith in socialism, most prominent
party leaders accepted it as an article of basic policy, it was
partly because they did not wish to challenge Nehru on this
point and partly because it offered them a useful slogan to
counter the appeal of the Communist and other left-wing parties. They also stood secure in the belief that in actual practice
they could dilute the element of socialism in official decisions
and, if necessary, sabotage their implementation.

Land reform is a case in point. Even before freedom, the
Congress Party had committed itself to abolishing absentee landlordism and ensuring for the actual cultivator security of tenure
and a fair share of the crop. In Nehru's home state of Uttar
Pradesh, the party had enacted legislation for the abolition of
the "zamindari" some years before independence while it held
office under the Government of India Act of 1935. The law protected the cultivator from the landlord's highhandedness by as-
suring him permanence of tenure as long as he paid a reasonable
rent for the holding. He was also offered the option to own the
land he tilled by paying moderate compensation to the absentee
owner.

After independence, however, there was much talk about land
reforms, but effective action was limited. The party's national
council regularly passed resolutions on the subject, the Centre
issued stern directives, and the state governments applied themselves to the task with seeming earnestness, but improvement in
the economic status of tenants was marginal in most states.

The land-tenure system in almost all parts of the country was
antiquated. Social inequities created by feudalism had been
deepened by the colonial rulers, who enlarged and sustained a
class of big landlords in return for loyalty and political support.
The system of tenure varied from area to area, but the exploita-

tion of the peasants was uniform. They were at the mercy of exacting, capricious landlords, few of whom actually worked on the land or even supervised farming. Most tenants enjoyed no security of tenure and paid as much as 70 percent of the crop as rent. Where land was directly owned by the tiller, division of property over generations had fragmented the holdings into uneconomic sizes, reducing the peasant to penury and helplessness. Of India's fifty-five million holdings, over 70 percent were less than five acres. Over 20 percent of the rural population had neither a plot of their own nor any regular tenancy and were forced to work as landless labor. Most of those who worked on land thus had neither the incentive nor the resources to make any investment in land beyond their daily labor.

Curiously, Uttar Pradesh was virtually the only state where land reforms were purposeful. After an investigation which took him to various parts of India, Wolf Ladejinsky, a Ford Foundation consultant, reported that "only in Uttar Pradesh has well-thought-out, comprehensive legislation been enacted and effectively inplemented." He had undertaken the study at the request of the Planning Commission in 1963. That land reforms in Uttar Pradesh were initiated before independence may explain why they conspicuously lacked the element of spuriousness. Before 1947 the Congress Party was a mass movement and not the Establishment. Its sense of social justice was strong and its concern for the underprivileged in the rural areas genuine. The landlords then stood by the side of the British government. The dividing line disappeared after independence, when the big landowners and others wielding economic power in the villages rapidly built bridges with Congress leaders. In most states the party itself met them more than halfway. Few political organizations which launched a fierce and protracted freedom movement have converted themselves into the Establishment so quickly and effortlessly as the Congress Party. The Uttar Pradesh reforms had gone too far to be rendered innocuous, but other states that undertook land legislation after independence willingly responded to the demands of the party's new alliances. Pre-independence commitments loudly proclaimed for years had to be honored, but the state governments (in whose domain the constitution had placed land reforms) consciously built loopholes into the land legislation.

The changes in the economic pattern of rural India caused by these reforms were anything but revolutionary. Every landlord was permitted to select thirty acres (more in some states) of his holding for "self-cultivation." What was more, the law permitted him to parcel out his property—on paper only—to members of his family. In terms of the reform he was thus able to retain many times the permissible limit. As a corollary to the concept of self-cultivation, he was allowed to eject the tenants from the portions he had chosen to till himself. He brought in tractors to replace labor or retained his ejected tenants as landless laborers. Instead of bringing the real cultivators of land greater security, the reforms only added to the numbers of landless peasants and sharecroppers. Most state governments conveniently looked the other way while this process was occurring.

Sixteen years after independence, Ladejinsky found that all over India the landlord's right to "resume" land for self-cultivation had tended to defeat the provision for security of tenure. "It would be in the best interest of agriculture, therefore, to restrict resumption severely: no resumption should be permitted to absentee owners and others whose principal occupation is not cultivation," he said. In Tanjore district of Madras, described as the rice bowl of south India, Ladejinsky found that "about half the owners hold 2.5 acres or less while the top 4 percent, who own more than thirty acres each, hold 45 percent of all cultivated land." Tenants paid 60 to 65 percent of the crop as rent. In the area he visited in the adjoining state of Andhra, Ladejinsky learned that while two years previously 75 percent of the land was cultivated by tenants, "it was much less now because a large number of tenants had been ejected recently." In his opinion, the land legislation in Punjab, agriculturally the most progressive part of India, "is extremely defective and needs complete overhauling." In Bihar the law in force was still the Tenancy Act of 1885, with some modifications which, he felt, were "wholly inadequate."

Criticism did not come only from foreign experts or others unsympathetic to the party that had wielded effective power at the Centre and in most states for the first two decades of independence. A thirty-member party panel on economic affairs that Mrs. Gandhi appointed in December 1969 pleaded for a major program of land redistribution "to deliver the soil to the tillers." Implicit in this recommendation was admission of the failure of land reforms not only during Mrs. Gandhi's four years as Prime Minister, when allegedly she was hamstrung by the conservatives in the party, but also during her father's seventeen years as the country's supreme leader and Shastri's brief reign.

When it came to a battle over matters involving ideology, the right wing in the ruling party was uncomprising, and Nehru was insufficiently assertive. In January 1959 he succeeded in persuading the Congress Party to accept a gradual move toward cooperative farming as a goal. At the Nagpur session of the party, where the issue was raised, its opponents fought tenaciously and, even while bowing to Nehru's wishes, reduced the whole thing to a paper exercise. In the years that followed, Nehru did little to see that the concept, though watered down, was administratively implemented. Even the structure of economic development that his government built was patently designed to help the upper crust of the rural society. It was the top 10 percent, owning 56 percent of the cultivable land, who derived the principal benefits from the various ways in which the government offered assistance to agriculture. They, and not the small owners or tenants, had the capacity to buy the subsidized fertilizers or enough collateral to use the credit facilities organized by the state. Even the rise in food-grain prices helped them exclusively, for the peasant who owned less than three acres of land or the tenant who retained only about 35 percent of the crop as his share scarcely had any surplus to bring to the market.

In the urban sector of the economy, the practice of socialism was marked by an equal measure of halfheartedness and readiness to compromise. Certain steps that seemed to fit into a copybook concept of socialism were taken. Fairly soon after independence, private airlines operating on various domestic routes were nationalized to form a state-controlled corporation with a monopoly of internal air traffic. Insurance companies were nationalized similarly to form another corporation, and the nationalization of banks was finally ordered by Mrs. Gandhi. As Minister for Oil, K. D. Malaviya, one of the few leftist members of Nehru's Cabinet, worked relentlessly to restrict the growth and profits of foreign oil companies while preparing the ground for state ownership and exploitation of India's oil and gas resources. But these were either symbolic gestures or the result of the tenacity of certain individuals; they did not represent the character of the ruling party or its real economic policies. It is doubtful that the airlines would have been acquired if they had not been as decrepit and inefficient as they were or that the insurance industry would have been nationalized if so stubborn a person as T. T. Krishnamachari had not been the Finance Minister. The severe curbs on the oil companies were, similarly, the result of Malaviya's left-wing predilections, without which the oil policy, though clearly defined, would have suffered the fate of the land reforms. Even nationalization of banks—twice proposed, but shelved in Nehru's time—was essentially a part of the tactics that Mrs. Gandhi employed to oust and discredit the conservative section of the Congress leadership.

In fact, while there was much public talk about socialism, the industrial policy officially propounded the concept not of socialism but of a "mixed economy" in which the private sector shared the areas of activity as well as profits with the state. A Cabinet resolution adopted in 1948 had listed six industries—coal, iron and steel, aircraft manufacture, shipbuilding, mineral oils and production of communication equipment—in which all future expansion would be undertaken by the government. This list was enlarged by the Industrial Policy Resolution of 1956, which added atomic energy, defense production, manufacture of heavy machinery and air transport to the state preserve. The resolution also defined a second field in which both government and the private sector might operate side by side. The rest of the industrial field was left exclusively to private enterprise.

The area that the government allocated to itself covered either defense-oriented industries or industries requiring large investment but offering small and delayed dividends. In the field of common activity were such major industries as mining, machine-tool production, aluminum, drugs, plastics, fertilizers and road and sea transport. This dual system was really the most realistic approach to India's industrial development, in view of its limited resources. Typical of the manner in which the public and private sectors were meant to share the field in 1951–61, the first decade of planning, was the arrangement by which three steel plants of one-million-ton capacity each were set up in the public sector, but two existing, privately owned steelworks of 1.5-million-ton capacity were permitted to double their capacity. In the second Five-Year Plan (1956–61) the public-sector investment in industry was nearly 1.6 billion dollars, but the investment in privately owned industries was higher by 160 million dollars. In the next plan, the proportion of the private sector's share declined, but only slightly.

No leadership, irrespective of its ideological compulsions, would have adopted a radically different policy. The realities of the Indian economic situation allowed the government and the planners only limited room for maneuver. A country with meager resources, an underdeveloped private sector, sharp memories of foreign economic exploitation and eagerness to industrialize rapidly had no choice but to let the state build the basic infrastructure. The role allotted to the private sector may have been small in terms of its expectations, but it was in reasonable proportion to its capabilities. At the time of independence, India's private industrial sector was unimpressive. Barring a few big industrial families such as the Tatas and the Birlas, there was no acknowledged tradition of initiative and enterprise by private industrialists. Those who may be described as "captains of industry" could be counted on the fingers of one hand. Much of the so-called private sector in Indian industry had grown up during the years of World War II; nurtured on a diet of high and easy profits, it had never developed genuine muscle and a pioneering spirit. If the principal burden of industrializing India had been entrusted to it, the private sector would have had no option but to look beseechingly toward foreign collaborators for capital, technical support and management and happily accept the position of a junior profit-sharer. Circumstances, more than ideology, thus prescribed the nature of the economic policies followed during the first two decades of freedom.

Actually, what is described as socialism in India is little better than a limited form of "state-ism" practiced in a rather inefficient way. What an Indian industrialist finds particularly odious about socialism is its tendency to place seemingly needless obstacles in his way. Even with respect to the industries clearly allocated to the private sector under the Industrial Policy Resolution, the government exercises considerable regulatory authority in the form of licenses and permits that an entrepreneur must obtain at every stage of the establishment and growth of an industry. Whether it is the original decision to set up an industrial unit or the importing of raw materials or the conclusion of a foreign trade agreement, the government's approval is essential and entails frustrating, costly delays. These obstructions were partly due to the inefficiency and the traditionally negative outlook of Indian bureaucracy and partly the result of the general psychology of hostility toward the capitalist created by the incessant talk of socialism. Such controls were perhaps justified in the initial years of planning, when the private sector lacked resources as well as experience in tackling problems of the magnitude of those facing the country. They could have been relaxed in later years and the role of the state reduced progressively as free-market forces were able to operate over larger areas of economy. But that did not happen because such a shift involved

a serious political issue. In a country which is genuinely democratic, where economic disparities are pronounced and where
the masses, a large proportion of them illiterate, have long been
fed on socialistic jargon, any politician who suggests greater lati-
tude for private enterprise in the economy is likely to be accused
of having sold his soul to the capitalists. Political leaders must
not only continue to reiterate their faith in socialism but must
also support their words occasionally with such acts of "expro-
priatory socialism" as nationalization of banks or cancelation of
the pensions of the deposed princes. Mrs. Gandhi's order for the
takeover of private banks, announced in the midst of her power
struggle with the syndicate, won her a tremendous public ovation. Her opponents were acknowledged conservatives, and her
action marked her as a progressive. Significantly, after it broke
with her, the syndicate itself announced a ten-point economic
program designed primarily to mitigate its right-wing reputation.

2: *The Balance Sheet*

At the end of nearly twenty years of planning, India presents
a curious picture of mingled economic achievement and failure.
Food production has grown by almost 90 percent; between 1950
and 1967 power generation increased sevenfold, and industrial
production rose by 7 percent annually. Enrollment in schools
almost tripled in this period. The commission headed by Lester
Pearson which studied the economies of developing countries on
behalf of the World Bank reported in 1969 that India's achievements have been "dramatic and important."

At the same time, there is much to justify disappointment
with India's performance. Despite long years of planning and a
considerable increase in food production, India is not self-
sufficient and is still vulnerable to nature's vagaries. The rate of
net increase in its population growth is as high as 2.5 percent
annually, which nullifies much of the increase in food production and national income. Its hard-currency resources have been

badly depleted, and for further development it depends heavily on foreign assistance. Dr. William Paddock, an agriculture expert and co-author of the book *Famine: 1975,* took such a pessimistic view of India's capacity to feed itself that he argued against further U.S. assistance. He listed Pakistan among the countries which, if helped, could stave off extensive famine.

Dr. Paddock's assessment was unduly dismal and perhaps not free from political prejudice. India has failed to achieve self-sufficiency in food, but its accomplishment is not so meager as to justify prediction of inevitable disaster. During the first half of the century, Indian agricultural production was virtually static. Under the British, population was growing without any increase in food. When planning was launched, this trend was reversed; and for the first time in decades food production pushed a little ahead of population growth. The increase in national income over the pre-independence period was even more marked. Under the British it had risen a bare 1 percent annually; in the fifteen years following the creation of the Planning Commission, national income grew at the rate of nearly 4 percent per year.

India's performance has been somewhat below the average rate of growth of non-Communist underdeveloped countries. Certain other countries such as Taiwan, South Korea, Israel and Mexico have done substantially better. Even Pakistan is often described as a more convincing example of economic growth than India. But such comparisons overlook the magnitude of India's problem and its conscious preference for certain political processes and values. Almost all countries that have made impressive progress are small in size and population. Israel's population is below 3 million; South Korea's, below 30 million, while Mexico's is 42 million. India's population at the time of independence was over 350 million, and in 1970 it was estimated to be over 540 million. India thus has the population of the continents of Latin America and Africa combined and adds to it every year the equivalent of an Australia. It is nearly one-third the size of the United States, but has almost three times its population. It does not enjoy the benefits of religious cohesion that a country like Pakistan does. Also, unlike most countries credited with dynamic growth, India has endeavored to overcome its problems through genuinely democratic institutions and processes. The concept of five-year plans may have been taken out of a Communist copybook, but the entire process of economic development that the plans represented was subjected constantly to public debate, Parliamentary supervision and scrutiny by the press. It was also exposed to regional pulls and pressures that often slowed down planning markedly. Whether establishing a shipyard, a steel plant, a coal washery or part of an aircraft production complex, the government's decision about its location was usually delayed in an endeavor to bring about a compromise among rival claims from various states. The government has also conspicuously lacked any authoritarian power to punish failures in execution.

Besides taking into account the enormity of India's tasks and the limitations imposed by its political institutions, one must judge the results in the context of the objectives that its planners had placed before themselves. India wished to achieve self-sufficiency in food, but it also wished to grow—and grow rapidly —into an industrial nation. Its leaders, notably Nehru, were not content with securing for the country only a flourishing agricultural economy. The prosperity, freedom from foreign dominance, and power in today's world that they envisioned for India called for the creation of an effective industrial base. But even agricultural well-being could not be achieved without an extensive network of industries. With over 70 percent of the population engaged in agriculture, land was heavily overburdened, and unless industry drew some of this work force away from the villages, emphasis on agriculture could at best achieve marginal improvement in national income. The first among India's economic objectives, therefore, was to strike a balance between agriculture and industry.

Equally pronounced was the desire to attain a self-reliant economy and end India's dependence on foreign assistance as early as possible. An essential feature of the national mind soon after the exit of the British was a rather exaggerated sense of self-respect. Years of heavy dependence on foreign aid, need for large food imports to ward off starvation, and the almost annual spectacle of Indian ministers pleading with donor countries for grants of assistance have dissipated some of that sensitiveness, but in 1950 the thought of seeking loans from abroad was repugnant to many in India. When it became obvious that reliance on foreign help was unavoidable, the realization was accompanied by a minor shock and a sense of humiliation. Even those in authority who were not moved by post-independence euphoria and examined these issues dispassionately were averse to excessive or long-term reliance on foreign aid. Even dependence on purchased imports of certain essential goods such as machinery, tools and steel or components for industrial products was considered a challenge to national dignity and self-respect. The aim, therefore, was to attain self-sufficiency quickly and over as wide a field as possible. India had to produce enough food to feed itself and manufacture many of the industrial products that it needed. It even had to be able to manufacture the machinery required for its expanded industrial base. Nearly all essential imports would have to be replaced by indigenous production.

Basically, this was a sound approach. A country of India's size and population must aim at a balanced growth in all segments of its economy and must meet the essential requirements of its vast domestic market without banking too heavily on others. That India should have concentrated principally on the development of agriculture, as was suggested by some foreign experts, was an unrealistic approach. It could not have financed its import of consumer and other industrial products through export of traditional raw materials unless it was reconciled to a fairly low standard of living for its people. A small country—such as Kuwait—with limited population but vast reserves of some essential, valuable raw material can manage without diversifying its economy, but not a country like India, whose import requirements are tremendous and whose traditional exports (e.g., tea, jute, oilseeds) were faced with such uncertainties as price fluctuations, saturation of demand and development of synthetic rivals.

For all its problems, India suffered no paucity of natural resources. Her natural wealth—much of it yet unexploited—is truly enormous.

India has the world's largest iron-ore reserves. Estimated at nearly 22 billion tons, they account for nearly one-fourth of the total world deposits. The country is also acknowledged to be rich in manganese ore, lead zincs, bauxite (half of it described as high-grade) and other industrial minerals such as mica, ilmenite and gypsum. The proven gold-ore reserves in the Kolar and Hutti goldfields in Mysore are about 4 million tons. As far as its power resources are concerned, its coal reserves are estimated at about 120 billion tons. The search for oil started only after independence, and government experts tentatively believe that over one million square kilometers may prove to be oil-bearing. The country's hydro-electric potential is placed at 41 million kilowatts at 60 percent load factor. (Of this only one-third was being exploited in 1970.) Nearly half of the country's total geographical area of 800 million acres is cultivable.

In terms of the size of its resources and enormity of the needs of its people, India's economic progress since freedom does not seem impressive. But for a country whose capital and technological resources were also known to be meager, it has collected some magnificent statistics of growth. The Pearson Commission, which unreservedly endorses India's basic strategy of import substitution and creation of a capital-goods industry, testifies to its dramatic achievement. Taking 1950, when the process of planned development began, as the base year, the Commission reports that up to 1967–68 the gross national product per capita rose by 1 to 1.5 percent per year. The average annual rise in exports was 2 percent. Pig-iron production rose from a mere 1.69 million tons to nearly 7 million tons annually. Cement production was nearly doubled during this period. After producing only 54,000 radio sets in 1950, the country was manufacturing one million of them annually by 1967. Power generation increased almost seven times. The production of railway wagons rose from less than 3,000 to nearly 12,000 a year.

Statistics apart, there is little doubt about the strides that Indian industry has made and the size of the new area it has covered. Organized industry and mines employ nearly five million persons, while three times as many are engaged in small-scale ancillary enterprises. A country that at the time of independence imported even toothbrushes and could not produce an entire bicycle was exporting, within two decades, not merely routine consumer products such as textiles, sewing machines and shoes, but heavy machinery and capital goods such as power-transmission towers to the United States, locomotive gearboxes to Canada, and railway engines and wagons to several countries. In 1969–70, India was also producing its own supersonic fighter aircraft and manufacturing 85,000 vehicles annually, so it was close to self-sufficiency in motor cars, jeeps and trucks.

Even in the field of agriculture, where its dependence on foreign help continues, progress has not been minimal. Grain production rose from 51 million tons in 1950 to nearly 96 million tons in 1968. The availability of irrigation facilities more than doubled during this period. Even before the introduction of the Mexican variety of seeds that ushered in the "green revolution," the increase in agricultural output was reasonable. Up to 1965, when India suffered the worst and the longest drought in more than a century, it recorded a 3-percent average annual agricultural increase.

Where India's performance has been deplorably poor, however, and where negligence—more than failure—has wiped out much of the economic gains is in the field of population control. The enormity of the problem and the utter meagerness of the endeavor to tackle it cause—and justify—the type of pessimism about India's future that Dr. Paddock expressed. The Ford Foundation, which has taken much interest in studying this problem in India, believes that the country's "current population of 540 million will increase to 695 million by 1981." More disturbing is the Foundation's belief that this figure will be attained "even if the program [for population control] is successful in meeting its targets." The family-planning work in India, even the optimists admit, will almost certainly not achieve its targets, in which case the country's population in 1981 may be markedly higher than 695 million.

Except for the first decade of the century, when, for reasons not convincingly explained, the population actually declined, Indians have been growing steadily in number. In 1941 the population of undivided India was 319 million; in the following ten years India more than made up the numbers it lost due to the creation of Pakistan. The net annual rate of increase, which was only 1.25 percent before independence, had almost doubled by 1970, due to the decline in the death rate. To the satisfaction of those who administered health programs, but to the dismay of those who studied demographic charts, life expectancy in India had risen during this period from 32.5 years to 53.2 years. Inevitably the additional mouths ate up much of India's economic gains.

According to the Ford Foundation analysis, the Indian government "was among the first to recognize the long-range implications of unchecked population growth on economic and social development." It gives the government credit for starting the family-planning program as early as 1951. But this assessment seems excessively charitable, for if the government saw the serious implications of rising population, precious little was done about it. The first Five-Year Plan, launched in 1951, provided less than a million dollars for the task of preventing unwanted and needless births in a country of India's size. What was more, the task was assigned to a very junior official in the Health Ministry.

The government then had neither any concept of what it should do nor how it should go about doing it. It halfheartedly toyed with the rhythm method based on the concept of "safe" days for sexual intercourse. The method was far from foolproof, and little effort was made to introduce it on a reasonably extensive scale. Nor was anything done to change social attitudes on the subject. For the poor, illiterate masses of India an additional child represented an additional mouth to feed but also an added source of labor which sometimes brought welcome extra income. Besides ignorance and poverty, there were factors rooted in the Indian mind that resisted suggestions about preventing births. In a country where there were no provisions of any kind for old-age security (there are still almost none for the majority of the people), Indian parents have traditionally valued sons on whom they might depend in their declining years. For most people, having just one or two sons was not adequate security. A son might die prematurely or turn out to be undutiful or a parasite. The Indian couple's endeavor, therefore, was to have several sons, and if in this process they collected a large family, they accepted it philosophically, often with some satisfaction. Such deep-seated beliefs and values could obviously not be changed when budget provisions as well as the ruling authority's sense of purpose were utterly meager.

By the time the fourth plan was introduced in 1966–67, funds for fighting population explosion appeared adequate. The same, however could not be said of the enthusiasm of political leaders. In 1969, India spent 56 million dollars on persuading people to restrict their families to no more than three children. A factory has been set up for production of condoms, which are distributed virtually free and may be obtained from the village grocer or even the postman. Besides this conventional method, the choices offered are insertion of intra-uterine devices for women and sterilization for men. Mobile health clinics move from village to village offering their facilities to those who might like to take advantage of them. Financial and administrative bottlenecks in the way of a massive effort to control population have thus been removed, but not the diffidence of political leadership. Family planning is still part of the Health Ministry, which is headed by a minister ranking fairly low in the Cabinet. Few politicians seem to realize the enormity of the task and the gravity of the consequences should it be performed indifferently. India aims to reduce the present birth rate to almost half by 1980. For this, nearly 60 million births must be "prevented" by persuading 50 to 60 percent of the couples in the productive age group to practice contraception. Even if this target is somehow achieved, India's population will have risen to nearly 700 million, neutralizing much of the gain made in industry and agriculture. Not many within the government seriously believe that the targets will be reached. Other experts privately express the fear that even if the program succeeds entirely, disaster may not be averted. In their view, India lost precious years before taking up the task in earnest and has allowed a "virtually hopeless" situation to develop.

Their failure to give adequate and timely attention to the question of population control was undoubtedly the biggest error of judgment that Indian leaders made, but they committed other serious, if relatively less costly, mistakes.

The Pearson Commission, which regards some of those mistakes as inevitable, described the state of India's economy in 1964 in rather grim terms. The performance of agriculture, it said, was "poor; large-scale public industry did not yield the profits expected; most industry had extensive idle capacity; exports had been virtually stagnant for a decade; the exchange rate [of the rupee] was seriously overvalued; the import-allocation system was cumbersome, capricious and not price-responsive; and savings and investments had remained unchanged as a percentage of GNP for three years."

This sad state was due at least partly to the sudden and heavy burdens placed on the country by the Chinese invasion of the border region in 1962. Until the war with China, India was spending about 600 million dollars annually on defense. Its policy of befriending China was designed to avoid having to spend excessively on military equipment, but once hostilities broke out and revealed grievous neglect of national security, the government moved to the other extreme and hastily trebled the defense budget. This step inevitably necessitated some drastic pruning of expenditures in many other fields. Economic priorities had to be redrawn. Even essential industrial imports were curtailed, causing idle capacity and wastefulness. To purchase needed arms quickly, India drew heavily on its foreign-exchange reserves, which dipped to a record low of a mere 500 million dollars—a condition that further weakened the rupee and paved the way for its devaluation in June 1966.

The economic implications of the added defense demands, however, should not be exaggerated. The state of messy stagnation in which the economy found itself in 1964 was largely the result of mistakes not all of which were "inevitable." The heavy expenditure on arms and military equipment undoubtedly aggravated problems of financing certain fields of development, but it also gave a spurt to certain defense-oriented industries and provided additional employment. It was thus not an unmitigated economic disaster. Many of the difficulties that the economy ran into, the outcome largely of weaknesses and inadequacies that had developed long before 1962, would have been there even if the war with China had not caused a costly shift in priorities.

3: *Unsteady Hands at the Wheel*

The most severe infirmity afflicting India's economic effort was its leadership. Though Nehru and many who were around him or ruled the states had earned wide public respect for their roles in the freedom movement and should therefore have been able to move the country to stern self-discipline and a heroic effort, most of these leaders had curiously lost the magic touch by the time planned economic development was initiated. Nehru himself was widely loved, but his understanding of economic issues was pathetically superficial. For his economic thinking he seemed to rely heavily on outdated concepts that he had picked up during his visits to Europe years earlier or advice from a few academicians who had somehow elbowed their way to his ear. Most of them were Western-trained and did not understand the peculiarities of India's problems or the temperament of its people. Principal among the handful of economists who influenced Nehru were Dr. P. C. Mahalanobis, a leftist professor who headed the Indian Statistical Institute in Calcutta; Tralok Singh, a member of the Indian Civil Service, who worked as Nehru's secretary immediately after independence; and Dr. S. S. Bhatnagar, an educator of only moderate ability. Their contribution to the process of planning often disclosed their predilections and limited experience, and to that extent hampered India's economic effort.

Political leaders had almost no role to play in devising the economic strategy. Significantly, when the Planning Commission was first set up in 1950, it did not include the country's Finance Minister, even though the portfolio then was held by Dr. John Mathai, a man of acknowledged intellectual stature. The Deputy Chairman of the Commission, Sir V. T. Krishnamachari, was supposed to be its executive head, but his forte was administration, not economic planning. Other ministers were appointed to the Planning Commission, but they were too involved with their own departments to make worthwhile contribution to the thinking on economic issues or to provide dynamic leadership in the execution of the policies that the Commission proposed. In the initial years, India's leadership showed signs of having been exhausted by the long-drawn-out independence movement and largely seemed content to enjoy the fruits of power that freedom brought. In later years, those who assumed power at the Centre and in the states were too involved in factional fights within the party to be able to attend purposefully to economic problems. Nehru himself was singularly reluctant to prod his fellow leaders into action, although he was in a position to do so. At one stage, for example, Nehru suggested that in view of the importance of agriculture, the portfolio should be held in every state by the Chief Minister himself—a step that would have demonstrated the gravity of the food problem, reduced ministerial red tape and goaded the bureaucracy into greater action. But although he repeated the suggestion several times publicly, he exerted no pressure to secure its acceptance. The Chief Ministers, almost without exception, continued to hold administrative and politically more profitable portfolios while agriculture was allocated to relatively junior ministers often lacking political muscle and administrative authority.

The state Chief Ministers were consulted—if only ritualistically—in the preparation of the plan, but the involvement of politicians at the lower levels in economic thinking and action was virtually nonexistent. The task of catapulting the country into the advanced stages of the industrial revolution required an enormous effort and, if it was to be performed through democratic methods, a national consensus. The importance of the latter was never realized. The Congress party organization had units existing at all levels, from national to village, but little effort was made to involve this vast structure in the undertaking. Bold economic decisions must enjoy political sanctions. Political mobilization is essential for their successful implementation. No administrative machine, however efficient, is a complete substitute for political fervor—a truth that eluded Nehru as well as those who dominated the Planning Commission.

The primary responsibility for executing the plans was placed on the bureaucrat, who had traditionally kept his distance from the people and seldom made any effort to understand their problems. In some states, such as Punjab and Uttar Pradesh, a number of political workers were associated with the development program, but this was done by absorbing them into the bureaucracy as paid employees of the government to reward them for services in support of the ruling faction rather than to seek their help in spurring the people to resolute action. Thus, if the masses lacked a sense of involvement in planning and if economic progress suffered in no small measure, it was because those who came to guide them were not of them. Even the village-level worker that the government appointed spent only the minimum of his time in the rural area and tended to rush off to the nearby town as soon as he could.

The British built India's bureaucratic structure, from the lower-division clerk to the senior secretariat official, largely to maintain law and order and collect the revenues. They were suspicious of the few individuals who attended to public welfare with conspicuous zeal. Ruling a vast and somewhat hostile country with only a handful of trusted men, they warily built into the administration numerous checks and balances intended to dampen individual enthusiasm and keep a civil servant on the straight and narrow path of routine administration. Elaborate rules and regulations were prescribed to cover virtually every aspect of daily administration, and their disregard by a bureaucrat was frowned upon. Decision-making was restricted to a few at the top. Knowledge of rules and their wooden application was considered a merit among juniors. By tradition, therefore, the average Indian civil servant was excessively rule-bound and unwilling to act on his own initiative.

Inheriting power when the country was in a state of serious turmoil, Nehru and other Congress leaders were grateful for the existence of trained cadres of bureaucrats accustomed to obeying the political authority. The civil services performed a near-miracle in restoring order in a country overwhelmed by religious hatred and coping with the movement of millions of refugees. But while the bureaucracy was experienced in dealing with civil disorder of the kind witnessed at the time of partition, it was out of its depth when called upon to execute a massive program of economic uplift. Political leaders made no effort to change the attitudes and reflexes of the bureaucrats. Recruitment to the ICS, the principal instrument of British power, was stopped even before independence, but its members—often criticized for their distance from the Indian masses—continued to hold all top administrative positions at the Centre and in the states for over two decades after freedom. The Indian Administrative Service, organized as the successor service, was virtually patterned on the ICS. Its members were no more dedicated to the welfare of the common man than those who had been recruited by the imperial rulers of earlier years. Enthusiasm for socialistic activity was conspicuously lacking among the senior civil servants. S. S. Khera, who retired from service as Cabinet Secretary, frankly confessed in a book that socialism was a "dirty word" among the senior services.

The Indian people themselves suffer from prejudices and inhibitions which prevented them from enjoying the full benefits of economic development. In most parts of the country, the people are singularly averse to self-help or collective action. An Indian tends to be individualistic and self-centered. He is habitually reluctant to do anything that does not benefit him directly, and even if it does, he is less likely to do it himself if he can expect the government or the society to do it for him. His loyalty is to himself and his family or, at most, to the caste group in the village to which he belongs.

Thus, a great deal that could have been accomplished without official direction and financial help remained undone. Leaders' constant appeals for donation of personal labor found little response. Even such elementary tasks as the deepening of a village pond remain undone until the authorities prod the villagers into action. A choked storm-water channel skirting the village may cause flooding every year, but will not be cleared up unless and until the irrigation department chooses to undertake the task. India's irrigation projects are impressive examples of engineering skill, but are shamefully underutilized because under the law the channels from the feeder canals to the fields must be dug by the peasants concerned, and these remain undug. The average Indian's sense of maintenance, furthermore, is shockingly poor when it comes to handling public property. For months after purchasing a bicycle, a villager may be loath to remove the paper wrapped round its tubings for fear of scratching the paint, but he will scarcely worry if through rough handling he damages the community radio set and deprives the village of one of its very few diversions. Consequently, even when the government builds schools, roads and community centers, these have to be maintained by official agencies or face rapid deterioration. At the beginning of the first Five-Year Plan, Alipur, a large village ten miles outside Delhi, was given a road linking it with a national highway. Completion of the road was marked by much publicity, but a few months later it was virtually unnegotiable because the villagers whom it served did not look after it.

The constrictions on India's economic growth caused by the

inadequacies of leadership and the imperfection of the tools it employed were compounded by certain marked misjudgments. That the backwardness of Indian agriculture was a serious problem was realized, but few in the government or the Planning Commission or even among the intellectuals seemed to visualize it as an Achilles' heel. In the early Fifties, Nehru spoke often about the gravity of the food problem and the government's determination to solve it, and he even fixed firm dates by which the country must attain self-sufficiency. His appeals for self-discipline gave rise to many ideas—some reasonable, some little better than gimmicks—aimed at ending India's dependence on others for food. Various foods such as sweet potatoes and tapioca were suggested as substitutes for basic cereals. Efforts were made even to change Indian food habits in the hope of lessening the demand for scarce foodstuffs. People of southern India were urged to eat more wheat to reduce the demand for rice, which was their staple diet. A movement was launched to persuade everyone to miss one meal every week and thus reduce consumption. But these plans and movements were implemented halfheartedly and abandoned unceremoniously if the sponsor did not receive the personal rewards that he might be expecting.

The planners themselves lost much of their ardor as soon as remarkable weather conditions produced good crops for two successive years. The targets in the first plan were set rather low. It was proposed, for example, that annual food production should be raised in five years from about 55 million tons to 62.6 million tons. When these modest targets were reached, the problem was considered to have been brought under control and the authorities turned their attention in the second plan (1956–61) to industrialization.

The resources for agriculture development were reasonable even under the second plan. The 20 percent of the total plan resources that had been allocated to it would have maintained a moderate rate of growth if the field had continued to receive its share of administrative vigilance. But authority at the Centre and in the states was so engrossed in setting up big industrial plants that various aspects of the agricultural problem received uneven attention. Big irrigation projects were completed, but the drive to dig the channels to link the canals with the farmers' fields was lacking. Targets for fertilizer production were low and even those remained unachieved. Importation of fertilizers was restricted because scarce foreign exchange was needed for industrialization, but even the limited quantities of fertilizer available often did not reach the farmer at the time he needed them.

The government's inability to understand the psychology of the farmer probably contributed in no small measure to India's indifferent performance in agriculture. An economic survey of India produced by General Motors' overseas division in 1945 recorded that it is "fatally easy in many parts of India to just maintain life." All that a villager needed was "a handful of rice, a cotton rag, a mud hut and dung cakes for fuel." The report went on to note that the "most desired luxuries are the opportunity to lie in the shade and sleep and smoke or to squat by the road and gossip." This was a typical Western view of the mind of the Indian villager, who had customarily been described as totally devoid of ambition and whose effort was circumscribed by his caste affiliations and the general Hindu faith in the doctrine of karma and the inevitability of what is preordained.

It was a measure of their divorce from reality that Indian planners accepted this assessment without serious question. They took it for granted that profit through higher prices for his produce would not be sufficient incentive to shake the peasant out of his supposed lethargy. A slow and lengthy process of education was, therefore, considered the answer. While the farmers were being "educated" into making new responses, food prices were calculatedly kept low—a situation that satisfied the relatively small urban population but helped cause agriculture to stagnate. The fallacy of this evaluation of the farmer's mind was demonstrated after 1965, when price incentives were finally offered. The "ignorant" peasant responded to them as readily as his counterpart in the more materialistic West would have. He took readily to unfamiliar tools, new varieties of seed and other

aspects of modern technology without any mental or social inhibitions when he discovered that they would bring him higher
profits.

The miscalculations on the industrial side were more numerous. Several assessments turned out to be overoptimistic and
goals unreal. But the principal weakness in this area was poor
management. Few public-sector projects were completed on
time. Many worked below capacity and showed sizable losses.
Also there was a noticeable tendency on the part of leaders to
frown upon foreign investments despite an obvious limitation of
indigenous capital resources.

Over the years, Indian leaders had reconciled themselves to
the need for large-scale foreign aid, but on the question of private capital from abroad they preserved some massive mental
road blocks. Foreign capitalists, they feared, would subvert the
country's freedom if allowed to invest extensively. The background to these apprehensions, of course, was the memory of
how the British had come to trade but had stayed to rule. Such
suspicions were entertained not merely by socialistically inclined
leaders such as Nehru but also by many others, even those who
favored Indian big business and worked for the advancement of
its interests. In 1966, when India's food situation was precarious
and the importance and urgency of undertaking extensive production of fertilizers was widely realized, a government move to
relax the terms for foreign investment to attract capital in this
field invited a storm of protest. At the Jaipur session of the Congress, C. Subramaniam, the Food Minister, was attacked derisively by nearly all sections of the party for his support for the
policy, which many described as a charter to foreign companies
to exploit the country. Even the party president, K. Kamaraj,
angrily suggested at a closed-door meeting of the executive that
Subramaniam should resign if he was so indulgent to foreign
capital.

In earlier years the Indian attitude at the top was marked by
even greater hostility and cynicism. At the end of the first fifteen
years of independence, foreign investments were only about 1.5

billion dollars, which, considering the country's needs as well as its economic potentialities, was unimpressive. Even if the terms offered to investors were reasonable, the atmosphere was not propitious. The firms already established were treated suspiciously and were under constant pressure from the government to Indianize their senior executive cadres; new investors were placed under a virtual strait-jacket of administrative checks and regulations.

Public-sector undertakings suffered similarly from official interference, though for different reasons. Under the mixed-economy concept of planning, most of the basic industries were set up by the state itself. In theory they were public corporations with considerable autonomy. Actually, most of them were run like subordinate departments of the government. Central ministers and civil servants and local politicians constantly meddled in their administration and tended to treat them as preserves for personal and factional patronage. Instead of being assigned to those with drive and acumen for business management, the top positions in most corporations became the resting places for weary civil servants after they had retired from regular service. Thus, the public-sector undertakings that were supposed to provide the foundation for the country's rapid industrialization offered a sad story of delayed installations, unachieved targets and poor or nonexistent profits. The combined output of the three new steel plants at Bhillai, Durgapur and Rourkela in 1960–61 was only 600,000 tons instead of the expected 2 million tons. The expansion of the state-owned Sindri fertilizer factory and of the ammonium-chloride plant at Benaras was nearly eighteen months behind schedule. The three fertilizer factories at Nangal, Rourkela and Neyveli, the heavy electrical project at Bhopal and heavy machinery, mining machinery and the foundry forge projects all suffered long delays in installation, and the actual cost of many projects proved considerably higher than estimated. The second plan's expenditure for industry, for example, proved nearly 30 percent higher than originally planned.

For a country with limited resources, it was doubtful wisdom

to invest so heavily in slow-gestation projects like big multipurpose dams and massive steel plants but worse to manage them
lackadaisically and starve the rest of the economy for avoidable
additional periods. Investment in the state-owned sector of industry rose from less than 60 million dollars in 1950 to over 3
billion dollars in 1955. It covered such items as steel, heavy
engineering, petroleum, mining and minerals, chemicals and avi-
ation. In its socialistic zeal the government set up a State Trading
Corporation and even entered the hotel trade. The Durgapur
steel plant functioned below installed capacity for years after
completion. Because of indifferent or inexperienced management, the performance of many units varied from year to year.
The Indian Airlines, with a monopoly of domestic traffic, made
a small profit in 1965–66, but lost heavily the following year.
Others that saw profits turn into sizable losses were the National
Coal Development Corporation, the Hindustan Shipyard, and
the Fertilizer Corporation. An official report for 1966–67 listed
seventeen public undertakings that incurred losses during the
year. The Ashoka Hotel, situated in New Delhi's posh diplomatic enclave, started as a five-star establishment, but because
of indifferent management it lost that distinction some years
later.

The management of India's precious foreign-exchange resources was hardly more efficient. In 1948 India's currency balances, built during World War II, were estimated at the prevailing rate of exchange at over four billion dollars. By the end of
the third plan in 1966 they had dwindled to around 600 million
dollars, just enough to provide the statutory cover for its currency. Besides exhausting its reserves by the end of 1969, India
had accummulated over nine billion dollars in foreign debts, the
bulk of which have to be repaid in hard currencies. The gravity
of the foreign-exchange position began to be fully realized only
in 1957, when steps were taken hurriedly to conserve what was
left. But by then a serious proportion of the resources had been
squandered on avoidable, often wasteful, low-priority expenditures like the importing of cosmetics and other luxury goods or

such needless "industrial investment" as the purchase of trade-mark rights for a well-known brand of women's undergarment. The depletion of reserves and heavy indebtedness exposed Indian leaders to the very economic dependence and political pressures that they had hoped to avoid through a major development effort. With billions invested in projects offering poor returns, mobilization of resources for further growth was greatly handicapped. At the same time, the industrial units already established needed heavy imports of machinery, spare parts, steel and certain raw materials to keep them in production, and thus placed further strains on the country's meager resources. The stagnation of agriculture, aggravated by the unprecedented drought, created a gigantic task of feeding the people through imports. The United States had by the end of 1967 accumulated over four billion dollars in rupees for the food grain it had supplied under Public Law 480, which authorized the sale of farm produce for local currencies. As *The New York Times* once pointed out, the United States could create economic chaos for India if it chose to draw and spend its rupees.

The use of the PL-480 rupees is governed by specific conditions to guard against unhealthy pressures on Indian currency, but there are other ways by which India can be subjected to economic pressure. In accepting the Tashkent agreement in January of 1966, for example, Shastri was seemingly influenced by the realization that disregard of Kosygin's "persuasion" was liable to cut the supply of Soviet arms that India received under favorable barter terms as well as affect the completion of the big steel plant at Bokaro being built with Russian aid. Similarly, despite his sense of personal hurt over the brusque "postponement" of his visit to the United States in the summer of 1965, Shastri agreed to visit Washington the following spring—his death intervened—because the suspension of U.S. economic assistance after the war with Pakistan that year had created an intolerable situation for the Indian economy.

Even devaluation of Indian currency in June 1966 is generally believed to have been caused by World Bank pressure. Both

India and the Bank vehemently deny that any pressure was exerted. The Bank and the U.S. aid agencies merely pointed out that the rupee was overpriced and "advised" the Indian government to bring it down to a more reasonable level. Asoka Mehta, the Minister for Planning, who visited Washington shortly before devaluation, argued in the Lok Sabha that India's creditors "are entitled to say that they will not be prepared to give us any more credit." But when a country is so completely dependent on foreign aid as India was in 1966, any "advice," particularly when combined with hints that aid may stop if it is not heeded, acquires a mandatory character.

4: *Uncertain Prospects*

At the beginning of the Seventies, India appeared to be running neck-and-neck with disaster. Its food production is growing, but so is its population. It has acquired a sizable industrial base, but the problem of unemployment—over 15 million are jobless—is truly gigantic. Its economy is within sight of the takeoff stage, but most aid-givers whose help facilitated past progress are losing some of their earlier zeal. After three Five-Year Plans, India is capable of benefiting from its experience, but its political leadership is weaker and more divided than in the earlier years of independence.

In the opinion of the Pearson Commission, Indian agriculture should have several years of "rapid growth" if the policies it adopted around 1965 continue. In its view, an annual increase of 4 to 5 percent is feasible. Since the drought year of 1966, when India imported over 10 million tons of food, its dependence on others has declined markedly, and the official claims of approaching self-sufficiency by 1971 do not appear totally unrealistic.

Factors that combined to brighten the prospects of Indian agriculture were the two-year (1965–66) drought and the development of the high-yielding varieties of food grains. The drought, generally described as the worst in over a century, dropped the annual output of food grains from 89 million tons in 1964 to 72 million tons and exposed a population of nearly 100 million to varying degrees of malnutrition and starvation. Even though deaths from starvation were averted, the drought dramatized the vulnerability of the country's food position and infused a sense of purpose and urgency that had been conspicuously lacking among government personnel in this field. In official thinking and action, emphasis quickly shifted back to agriculture. Instead of being bound by ideological theories, the government for once chose to follow pragmatic policies and seek quick and concrete results. Prices, previously kept low, were allowed to attain a more reasonable level and thus offer the farmer the incentive he needed. Manufacture of fertilizers, which had suffered from neglect in the past, was given urgent attention. Pending development of indigenous production, the government undertook massive importing of fertilizers. Happily, the development of the high-yielding Mexican variety of wheat coincided with this new sense of realism in Indian agriculture. Traditionally, the per-acre yield in India has been the lowest in the world. Much of the increase in production in the first fourteen years of planning was achieved through cultivation of additional land, but the stage was fast being reached when there would be little new land to be brought under the plow. The "green revolution" has made it possible for food production to increase without having to reclaim further territories. Several million acres have already begun to produce nearly twice their previous output through the introduction of the new seeds. By 1974, over 30 million acres of agricultural land with assured irrigation are expected to be covered by the high-yielding varieties which, the planners hope, would enable India to reach the annual production target of 129 million tons.

The situation is considerably more forbidding in regard to unemployment. Already over 15 million Indians are unemployed or underemployed—figures that do not take into account millions of peasants who produce only one crop a year and are always underemployed. The present rate of population increase adds nearly 5 million annually to the country's labor force, not all of whom can be absorbed in industry. Those among the unemployed who remain in the rural areas place additional burdens on land; those who flock to the cities add to its social inequalities and tensions. After eighteen years of planned development, tens of thousands still sleep on the pavements of Calcutta, Bombay and Delhi. In the national capital, a night shelter charging less than two cents for its use remains largely untenanted, while the penniless sit on the nearby footpaths huddled together in the cold.

In the coming years, economic activity must strike a deft balance and attain diverse, sometimes opposing, objectives. In order to provide work for the growing mass of unemployed it must emphasize projects employing extensive labor, even if returns from such undertakings are small and slow. At the same time, India must produce and export more to make up for the inevitable decline in foreign aid. Its industry has already attained a measure of sophistication that enables it to compete with Western industrial establishments in fields ranging from textiles to surgical instruments and heavy machinery, and to collaborate in setting up new plants in such countries as Yugoslavia, Malaysia, Brazil and Ethiopia. One of the largest paperboard factories in Canada has been set up by an Indian industrialist. In recent years India has even entered the highly competitive area of arms manufacture and is unobtrusively supplying some Asian nations. Following Mrs. Gandhi's goodwill tour of nearly a dozen Latin American countries in 1968, Indian industrialists have been seeking—with some success—new contacts in the Western Hemisphere.

These heartening developments indicate the country's capabilities, but they will need to be enlarged into serious undertakings through judicious planning and much rigorous discipline. India's industry may have developed some advanced skills, but it still suffers from many notable weaknesses. There has been some effort lately to improve the management of public-sector undertakings through employment of managers from private industry, but by and large they still suffer from the bureaucratic stranglehold. And private industry, which shines only by comparison to the state-run units, has led a highly sheltered life: the total ban on imports and a vast domestic market have allowed it to disregard quality and fall prey to the inefficiencies customarily bred by monopolistic operation. In many industries, notably automobiles, drugs, sugar and synthetic fibers, the costs of production are notoriously high and greatly limit the capacity to compete with rivals abroad. Industry will have to alter its way of life and impose upon itself stern financial discipline and improve its management before it can withstand the rough winds of international competition.

Even the satisfaction over the success of the "green revolution" hides some serious uncertainties. The breakthrough in high-yielding grain varieties has come only in wheat, which constitutes only about 18 percent of the country's total food-grain output. The "miracle" varieties in rice have so far not succeeded in India. Current research may develop suitable strains of rice, but until then the "revolution" remains limited in scope and the danger of population outstripping food is as real as ever. Singularly little has been done to improve the yield of the coarser grains like bajra and jawar, which sustain a large segment of the Indian people, or of cash crops like sugar cane, jute, tea and oilseeds, which comprise the bulk of Indian exports. Indian attitudes toward research are strangely cavalier. The number of agricultural research workers in India per 100,000 persons is the lowest in the world. Japan, which has a similar problem of feeding a large and growing population, has twenty persons engaged in research for India's one.

But the largest uncertainty in India's economic future is the caliber of its leadership. For the type of difficulty facing it, India needs leaders with the wisdom to understand the real nature of the problems and to prescribe the right solutions as well as the personal forcefulness to make the people implement them zealously. Unfortunately, among the top people currently at the

Centre there is no one who genuinely understands economic issues. Several states—including West Bengal, with the largest concentration of industry—are politically hostile to the Centre. Political considerations blatantly outweigh the demands of economic reality. After she dismissed her Finance Minister, Morarji Desai, in a party rift, Mrs. Gandhi did not fill the post for nearly a year. The ministry, which is the hub of national economic activity, was run on an *ad hoc* basis by junior ministers who carried little weight. Y. B. Chavan, whom she finally chose for the post, has almost no experience in finance and reportedly moved from Home Affairs to his new portfolio with some reluctance. Neither he nor anyone like him is likely to prove the master architect of India's economic edifice. Mrs. Gandhi's other actions, too, have indicated a tendency on her part to rely more on vague promises and political slogans than on positive programs. She has nationalized banks, which had already been functioning as quasi-public institutions, and threatened to discontinue payment of nearly seven million dollars annually as privy purses to former princely rulers. These attract public attention and make her appear as an opponent of the vested interests, but their actual contribution to India's economic progress is small. Such actions may win her party some temporary public acclaim and burnish her socialistic image, but will not go far in solving any of India's colossal problems. What is more, few in authority seem to realize that India can ill afford to make mistakes or even experiment with unproven ideas, for time is not on India's side.

VIII

NEIGHBORS

1: *A Misunderstood Friend*

FOR A COUNTRY that has constantly longed to be understood and that has supported other nations' causes, often at a time when they were considered almost lost, India cuts a strikingly lonesome figure in Asia today.

In 1948, when the Dutch arrested all principal Indonesian leaders, it was India, itself only in the second year of its independence and faced with towering problems of its own, which angrily denounced the Dutch attempt to reassert its colonial power; yet, except for a brief period during the early years of the nonaligned group, Indonesia has looked at India with a marked lack of cordiality. Later, India worked zealously to secure membership in the United Nations and a seat in the Security Council for Communist China, only to be charged with all the unsocialistic sins that Peking could list and to have its territory invaded by China's "border guards." Nehru valiantly stood up for the Arabs over Suez in 1956 and later offered them unreserved support on all issues—from Palestine refugees to the Jordan waters—on which the Arab governments felt strongly. But in 1965 at their meeting in Casablanca the Arab leaders, instead of offering India sympathy over the Pakistani attack in Kashmir, very nearly accused India of committing aggression. When King Tribhuvan of Nepal, father of the present ruler, fled from his country, where he was a virtual prisoner of his Prime Minister, India gave him asylum and helped him return to his throne as a free man, but Indo-Nepal relations, too, have witnessed extensive periods of suspicion bordering on hostility. Burma, despite its cultural ties with India, has always remained aloof, while Ceylon has consistently criticized India for its allegedly unhelpful attitude on the issue of repatriation of Indian settlers. Iran, which had no visible reason for being hostile to India, surreptitiously sold nearly 100 aircraft to Pakistan immediately after the Indo-Pakistan war, an act that the government and people of India regarded as unfriendly. Even the tiny Himalayan State of Sikkim, an Indian protectorate which depends for its security entirely on India, has often acted waspishly toward New Delhi.

A certain degree of hostility on the part of neighboring countries could be attributed to India's size and population. However friendly and reassuring India's policies, its dimensions must cause some nervousness to countries like Nepal, Ceylon and even Pakistan. But there must also be something in India's diplomatic style that has deepened suspicions and made other peoples forget friendship and support.

A retrospective examination of India's relations with its immediate neighbors in Asia discloses two principal flaws. First, too much of its foreign policy centered around Nehru's personality, his whims and his prejudices. Too often his personal friendship with the head of another country formed the total basis of India's relationship with that country. The relationship thus fluctuated as cordiality between the two leaders waxed or waned. The personal understanding at the top was not buttressed by a measure of political give and take or an economic relationship of mutual advantage. Indonesia, for example, was one of the early members of the nonaligned group, but few economic or political ties were created between the two countries. Over the years the relationship markedly reflected the distaste that Nehru developed for Sukarno's personal behavior, particularly his sexual propensities and the sheer vulgarity of his demands when visiting another country. Nehru, Nasser and Tito formed an impressive trio of nonaligned leaders, but it was only in 1966, two years after Nehru's death, that action was initiated to give India's ties with the United Arab Republic and Yugoslavia some economic substance through preferential tariffs and the exchange of technical skills. Nehru and Prime Minister U Nu of Burma knew each other on a basis of personal cordiality for several years, but as soon as U Nu was deposed by a military junta, Burma promptly retreated into a shell of isolation.

Secondly, India has too often been reluctant to act generously where no conflict of national interest is involved. At the same time, it has been halfhearted in the exercise of its power when flexing of muscles was considered necessary. It has tended to offer friendship in a niggardly manner. In the personal struggle for power in Nepal between King Mahendra and his Premier, B. P. Koirala, Nehru's sympathies were with the latter, owing, presumably, to his temperamental antipathy toward princes and the feudal approach to politics that they represent. During a state visit to Nepal he demonstrated his aversion to the King sufficiently to earn his hostility, but did not support Koirala adequately to help him to power. When Koirala was imprisoned, some of his associates fled to India and organized commando-style raids on Nepalese government buildings from across the border. Indian authorities were implicated in the raids inasmuch as they were aware of them and did not object to the use of Indian soil for the purpose. Typically, the attacks were enough to irritate the King but not to push him into doing what India favored.

India has often made concessions, but seldom with a show of spontaneity and large-heartedness. In 1964, during Shastri's Prime Ministership, New Delhi made sizable concessions to Ceylon on the question of future status of Indian settlers there, yet these fell somewhat short of what would have impressed

India's small neighbor. India rushed in with massive economic aid and technical assistance for Nepal, but only when Peking had agreed to link Nepal's capital, Kathmandu, with Lhasa and firmly established its presence in the kingdom; moreover, the Indian government has quibbled with avoidable bureaucratic pettiness for years over the Susta forest, a 170-acre border tract that Nepal claims as its own and that is of no strategic or economic value.

In its relations with Pakistan and China, too, India has at times acted with inadequate firmness or generosity, but other more powerful factors, deeper hostilities and certain basic historical facts were far more decisive in molding the country's relations with its two principal neighbors. Perhaps, as many a Western observer suggested at the time, India should have challenged Peking's action in sending its armies into Tibet in 1951 instead of quietly accepting the loss of Tibet's autonomous status. Similarly, it should have transferred the small enclave of Berubari to East Pakistan, as it had agreed to, and ratified in 1961 the agreement which provided Pakistan with a rail link between its two wings. Yet on the issue of division of the Indus Basin waters—a matter that one Pakistani Prime Minister, H. S. Suhrawardy, once described as of greater importance to Pakistan than even Kashmir—India acted with acknowledged generosity, but the goodwill it created, though seemingly tremendous at the time, was short-lived.

The capacity of India and Pakistan to direct their mutual relations has been limited. Much of the time the leaders and the people of the two countries were buffeted almost helplessly by forces of deep-seated religious animosity, the bitterness of ancient as well as recent memories, the compulsion of circumstances and the pressures of world powers. India was partitioned on the basis of communal hatred, not of mutual understanding. In the riots that occurred in both countries in the weeks before and immediately after independence, hundreds of thousands were killed barbarously, and several million Hindus and Muslims were forced to leave their ancestral homes and migrate to the other side of the border. Such peoples could not be expected to live next to each other in total peace and on the basis of magnanimity and understanding.

At the time of partition it was agreed by the Congress and Muslim League leaders that minorities would stay in India and Pakistan as loyal citizens of the country in which they resided. As a corollary to this assumption, Hindu legislators whose constituencies formed part of Pakistan stayed there to function in the provincial legislature elected the previous year under British supervision. Similarly, Muslim League leaders who hailed from the Hindu-majority areas joined the Constituent Assembly in New Delhi in its task of framing the constitution of the new India. But within weeks it became apparent that this was an unrealistic arrangement. The massacres at the time of partition had denuded West Pakistan of its entire population of Hindus and Sikhs. Muslims had been similarly driven out of the eastern part of Punjab. There was no point in legislators staying on when those whom they represented had fled across the border. The Hindu members of the assemblies of Punjab, Sind and North West Frontier Province, therefore, soon migrated to India. On the Indian side, even after the partition exodus, over thirty million Muslims were still left there, but most of their leaders fled to Pakistan, sometimes openly but often surreptitiously. The action of Khaliqu Zaman, a prominent Muslim League leader, was typical. At the transfer-of-power ceremony, he solemnly affirmed his allegiance to India, but after a few weeks he quietly migrated to Karachi. Actions such as Khaliqu Zaman's demonstrated the psychology of mass fear and distrust that pervaded the subcontinent then and has persisted since.

The condition of the millions of Muslims who stayed behind was unenviable. They remained partly because Indian authority was able to offer them some measure of security, but largely because economic compulsions made it impossible for them to migrate. Thousands had gone to Pakistan, but had reluctantly returned to their original homes and property when they found the new "homeland" economically inhospitable. In India, even when there were no riots, they were the victims of what might be described as "psychological violence" from the majority community. The Hindus regarded them with open belligerency and contempt, asking why they did not go to the separate homeland they had demanded. Nehru's insistence that the Muslims had as much right to stay in India as the Hindus only added to the anger. The Hindus had always regarded themselves as a tolerant and fair people. By insisting on separation, the Muslims had challenged that belief and questioned the majority community's capacity to be fair to non-Hindus. The very existence of Pakistan also represented a kind of defeat. Just as the Hindus were about to secure a position of dominance after centuries of subservience, the creation of Pakistan had restricted the area of their paramountcy. Thus, even those who were rational enough to rule out a future reunification of the two countries tended to regard Pakistan as an affront. Friendship and neighborly amiability were considered out of the question.

On the other side of the border, fears and suspicions were equally strong. Hinduism, it was argued, had always tried to emasculate Islam, and a Hindu India would similarly try to smother what had become the home of Islam in the region. If any argument was needed in support of this fear, the Pakistani leaders reminded themselves that Nehru had accepted partition without conceding the Muslim claim to be a separate nation. This grudging attitude, in their view, constituted a dangerous mental reservation on the part of the Hindus and India's leaders.

A state of hostility toward India and a tendency to shout "wolf" constantly also served a useful political purpose for the Pakistanis. It kept together a people who had just acquired a name but had yet to develop a distinct national identity. Beneath the general umbrella of Islam there were some marked social, economic and cultural diversities in Pakistan. The people of Sind, Baluchistan and NWFP resented the dominance of the economically prosperous Punjab. The eastern wing of the new state was a thousand miles away geographically, and even further ethnically and culturally. Unlike India, where Hindu refugees had come as destitutes and wielded little power, those who had migrated to Pakistan had provided the leadership of the partition movement and consequently they dominated the new state. Jinnah, who became Pakistan's first Governor-General, came from Bombay. The first Prime Minister, Liaqat Ali Khan, belonged to Uttar Pradesh. The resentment against the domination of Pakistan by "outsiders" was considerable. Besides, economic problems confronting the new state were even more serious than those facing its larger neighbor. Its economy was backward and its resources meager. The rehabilitation of five million refugees presented a much bigger challenge to it than the arrival of a similar number in India. In these circumstances, a state of constant hostility toward India and the creation of a sense of being besieged and threatened took people's minds off their internal disputes and difficulties and lent the new nation a certain cohesiveness.

Over the years, the physical links between the two countries have tended to shrivel up. The bridges between them were either deliberately demolished or have collapsed through lack of maintenance. Despite the Kashmir war and the bitter memories associated with the partition, the contact between India and Pakistan did not end wholly in 1947. This was due to the necessity of completing the lengthy and cumbersome process of division. Economic and cultural ties between the two areas formed a crisscross pattern and could not be snapped instantly. But the two countries have deliberately drifted away from each other. The trade agreements concluded in the earlier years have lapsed through lack of renewal. The jute mills of India have started growing their own jute rather than depend on the supply from areas in East Pakistan. Pakistan has started buying coal from distant countries rather than get it from the traditional source in Bihar. The flow of visitors has dwindled to a mere trickle. Governments are unwilling to issue visas to visitors from across the border, and when permits are issued, travelers are treated with discourtesy and subjected to humiliating restrictions. There is no cultural exchange between India and Pakistan.

Even newspapers are not allowed to be imported. The through train service stopped soon after partition; the air service was stopped in 1965 after the war over Kashmir. Pakistan International Airlines flies over Indian territory when traveling between the two wings of the country, but does not touch down at any Indian airfield; Air India, similarly, is allowed over-flight facilities, but does not land anywhere in Pakistan. The promises that the leaders of the two countries made at Tashkent in 1966 in regard to normalization of relations have not been fulfilled.

The element of irrationality is thus obvious in the Indo-Pakistan relations, and it is only that irrationality which might explain the bitterness of their conflict over Kashmir.

2: *Kashmir: Asia's Switzerland*

Perched atop the map of the subcontinent like a crown, Kashmir is over 80,000 square miles in area, nearly as large as the United Kingdom. It touches Soviet Turkistan in the north and China's Sinkiang province in the east and is thus contiguous to two major powers besides India and Pakistan.

In the past, its beauty more than its strategic location has invited invaders. Its written history dates back well beyond the Muslim period that began in the fourteenth century. Emperor Ashok introduced Buddhism into Kashmir in the third century B.C. Akbar's forces occupied the state in 1586 A.D., and Moghul rule was followed by the Pathan invasion from Kabul. At the beginning of the nineteenth century, it was occupied by the Sikh rulers from the adjoining Punjab, who later lost the territory to the British. The British, in turn, handed over virtual control of the state to the Hindu Dogra rulers in 1846. It was Hari Singh, the fourth Dogra ruler, who was on the throne a century later and was required to make the difficult decision about Kashmir's future.

Its natural isolation from the rest of the subcontinent and the fact that much of its territory is comprised of high, uninhabitable mountain ranges have kept Kashmir's population low. At the time of independence, the population was only four million, nearly 75 percent of whom were Muslim; the rest were Hindus, Sikhs and Buddhists. Significantly, the state had seen almost no communal tension until some years after independence. This is the only area in India where Hindus and Muslims may sometimes have common caste or surnames. A Kaul, for example, may be a Hindu Brahmin or he may be a Muslim. As a people, the Kashmiris are mild and gentle with an acknowledged claim to excellence in handicrafts. During the long winter months, when work ceases in the paddy fields, the Kashmiri peasant becomes an artist and produces some of the world's finest silks, carpets and wood carvings.

What is generally described as Kashmir, however, is only the valley. In his book *The Valley of Kashmir* the British author Walter Lawrence describes it as "a white footprint set in a mass of black mountains." The Jhelum River runs through the valley, which is over eighty miles long and nearly twenty-five miles wide —an oval plain that lies at an average height of six thousand feet above sea level and is the principal area of dispute between India and Pakistan. (A U.S. Embassy handout in New Delhi once described the valley as a "piece of real estate," much to the annoyance of the government, which believes it is fighting for a principle, not for valuable property.) Range after range separates the valley from Jammu, the state's southern province; in Jammu, closer to the plains of Punjab, the Hindu Dogras predominate. On the northern side, the valley is similarly separated from Ladakh, land of Buddhist monasteries, where, until India's conflict with China, thousands of Buddhists lived in serene isolation. Though scenically beautiful (it is often described as Asia's Switzerland), Kashmir is vital to neither India nor Pakistan. The Muslim League leaders had visualized the state as part of their new country and were unhappy when it was not included, but there were other areas besides Kashmir which Britain did not concede. Three of Pakistan's rivers—the Indus, the Jhelum and the Chenab—originate in Kashmir, but in other parts of the world, upper and lower riparian countries have lived without coming to blows. India's stakes in Kashmir are even shallower. The sources of its rivers are not located in Kashmir, and the state offers little that is essential to India's economy or culture. Yet India and Pakistan have fought two bloody and costly wars over Kashmir, and the government in either country would run a serious risk of being overthrown if it appeared ready to compromise on this issue.

It is not the common acquisitive instinct that prompts the average Indian to refuse to part with Kashmir. To most people, even in north India, Kashmir means little emotionally. It is Pakistan's involvement as an adversary that makes Kashmir's future such a volatile matter. If in the normal course Kashmir had acceded to Pakistan, few in India would have been upset about it. The majority of its people were Muslims and since the state was contiguous to Pakistan, yoking it to that country would have been considered logical when the entire subcontinent was being divided on the basis of religion. What gave the matter a different complexion, however, was the invasion of the state by Pakistani tribesmen. Under the partition plan, the decision about the state's future rested with the ruler, and by unleashing armed tribesmen into Kashmir, Pakistan, it was felt, was not playing the game according to the prescribed rules. To many in India, the tribal raid was an instance of Pakistani arrogance, similar to that displayed by the Muslims before independence, which, if not challenged immediately, would manifest itself even more blatantly in the years to come. What seemed important then, and still does twenty-three years later, was not the acquisition of territory by India but stopping Pakistan from enlarging its boundaries. In subsequent years, public consciousness of Kashmir's strategic importance has grown, but that is still not the basic consideration influencing the Indian mind in the matter.

The blame for creating so volatile a situation rests in large measure with the British government, which displayed excessive regard for the letter of its treaties with the Indian princes (see pp. 31–32) and declined to transfer its paramountcy over the

Indian princely states to the successor dominion governments of India and Pakistan. Instead, it allowed the paramountcy to "lapse," thereby creating a politically anachronistic situation in which all such states (including some no more than a few hundred square miles in area) became independent unless they acceded to one or the other newly created country. If the principle of division on the basis of religion had been applied as it was elsewhere, the bulk of Kashmir would have gone to Pakistan since, though ruled by a Hindu Maharaja, the majority of its people were Muslims. But by withdrawing paramountcy, the British government created a a power vacuum in a large and strategically sensitive area, thereby encouraging territorial ambitions all around and leaving the decision about the state's future with an individual who had neither much political wisdom nor any sizable popular support. It was perhaps natural for Maharaja Hari Singh to dream of independence for the state and of continuing personal power. Kashmir was as large as many a European country and was endowed with remarkable scenic beauty. If Switzerland could preserve its neutral, independent existence in a warring Europe, why could not Kashmir exist similarly between India and Pakistan? But Hari Singh, according to those who knew him personally or worked under him, was cut in the traditional mold of Indian princes, given to autocratic, often unwise exercise of authority, lacking in consideration for his subjects and insatiable in appetite for pleasures of the flesh. He had neither the intelligence nor the experience to discern the political forces in the subcontinent and elsewhere that would make the state's independent existence impossible.

Even if he had been a wiser, more judicious man, the Maharaja would have found it hard to take the right decision. As a Hindu, he should personally have been drawn toward India and away from Pakistan, which was being created as a homeland for the Muslims. But his relations with those who were assuming power in India were strained, and their ideology of democracy and socialism left no room for princely power. In Nehru, whom he had imprisoned only a year earlier for entering Kashmir in

defiance of his orders, Hari Singh saw an enemy who now had
the inclination and the power to settle some old scores. Pakistani
leaders had been beckoning the Maharaja to accede to the new
country, but the problem was rendered more complicated by the
religious composition and political preferences of his subjects.
Though Muslims comprised nearly 80 percent of the state's
population, the political movement in Kashmir, particularly in
the valley, was dominated by the National Conference, which
drew its inspiration from Nehru and would have liked to see the
Maharaja's autocratic rule ended and the state linked with India.
In these circumstances, Hari Singh vacillated, and a month after
the end of British power he still had not acceded to India or
Pakistan. If he had acceded to either country on the eve of partition, the subcontinent might have been spared much bloodshed
and bitterness.

In the series of acts of short-sightedness—British failure to
arrange a complete partition and the Maharaja's hesitance—the
next was committed by Pakistan, when it let loose hordes of
Pathan tribesmen into Kashmir from the Pakistani side of the
border. Later, when India took the issue to the U.N., the Pakistani government pleaded innocence of the charge of having
connived at Kashmir's invasion. The presence of Pakistan's
armed forces in Kashmir was acknowledged only after successive teams of observers had visited the subcontinent and denial of
Pakistan's role in the invasion had become pointless and uncon-
vincing. To Indian leaders and many impartial observers, however, the Pakistani hand behind the invasion was visible from
the very start. Pathan tribesmen are ferocious fighters, but those
who know them would readily testify that they were incapable of
organizing the logistics of an operation of this size. That Pakistan exercised control over the raiders was indicated by a remark Jinnah made in a meeting with Mountbatten, which the
latter's Press Secretary, Alan Campbell-Johnson, records in his
book *Mission with Mountbatten*. At the meeting which took
place in Lahore only a few days after India had sent its forces to
fight the tribesmen, Jinnah proposed a simultaneous withdrawal

of the Indian Army and the raiders. When Mountbatten inquired how the withdrawal of the latter could be assured, Jinnah, according to Campbell-Johnson, remarked, "If you do this, I will call the whole thing off."

The Maharaja's ill-trained Army retreated in total disarray, as Pakistani leaders had presumably expected, but the Maharaja did something that they had not foreseen. He applied for accession to India and asked for its military protection.

Why Pakistani leaders pushed the Maharaja into Indian arms in this manner is difficult to explain. Their desire to acquire Kashmir was inherent in the concept of the homeland that they demanded. The original demand that Jinnah put forward included Kashmir as an integral part of Pakistan. When it became a reality, Pakistan lacked not only large portions of the provinces of Punjab and Bengal but also the entire state of Jammu and Kashmir. When the British plan was outlined to him some months before partition, Jinnah noticed the gap between what the Muslim League had demanded and what was being offered him, and reportedly he angrily remarked that he was being given a "moth-eaten" Pakistan. If Pakistan had waited patiently, the Maharaja might have chosen to accept the attractive promises of maximum autonomy and maintenance of personal power that Jinnah had publicly made to the princes. In any case, Hari Singh had no reason to be drawn to Nehru and the Congress Party, whose antagonism to him was no secret. Apparently, Jinnah and his advisers calculated that, despite the League's friendly attitude toward the princes, the Maharaja would feel less vulnerable as part of the Hindu-majority India than in Pakistan. The fact that politics in Kashmir was then dominated by Sheikh Abdullah and his National Conference, which was opposed to the Muslim League approach, was also considered likely to propel the Maharaja toward India. On the other hand, it was perhaps hoped that if a major threat to Kashmir materialized from the Pakistani side, the Maharaja would capitulate and sign the accession papers in return for the withdrawal of the bloodthirsty raiders. If these were the Pakistani calculations, they misfired.

Pakistan has charged India with securing Kashmir's accession through fraud and violence and has even accused Mountbatten of conniving to secure Kashmir for India. Nehru's Kashmiri ancestry and his unwillingness to make compromises and concessions in the Kashmir dispute have often been mentioned as evidence of India's acquisitive designs on the state. In fact, Nehru's first reaction to the Maharaja's request for accession was markedly lacking in enthusiasm. As published and some private records of the period show, Nehru agreed to the accession only under pressure from Sheikh Abdullah, who was anxious to secure India's military assistance in fighting the raiders. Kashmir Premier Mehr Chand Mahajan, who brought the Maharaja's appeal to New Delhi, tried to hustle Nehru by stating that he had orders to go to Pakistan if India's response was not immediate. Nehru responded by angrily telling Mahajan to "go away" and calmed down only when Abdullah, who was sitting in an adjoining room and listening to the exchange, sent a hurried note to Nehru urging him not to refuse the Maharaja's offer of accession. Even later, when Abdullah pleaded for the dispatch of troops, Nehru brushed aside the accession request as routine and unimportant and told the Kashmir leader with characteristic impulsiveness, "You go and fight the invaders. We will help you."

The "help" involved India in a war within weeks of becoming independent and placed a heavy strain on both countries. It ended only when the U.N. was successful in persuading the parties to accept a cease-fire nearly fifteen months later. By then India had established control over two-thirds of the Kashmir's territory by pushing out the tribal raiders and the Pakistani armed personnel. But the rest of the state remained with Pakistan. The cease-fire drew a dividing line which cut across natural features and in defense of which nearly one-third of India's army was perpetually engaged.

At the time the Indian Army was sent into Kashmir, it was Mountbatten who pointed out that India could not do so unless the state legally became a part of the country, and that formal acceptance of accession by India was essential. Without accession, India had no right to intervene in a matter which concerned Kashmir and, allegedly, Pakistan. For his advice to Nehru on the question of accession, Mountbatten has earned Pakistani wrath. Mountbatten, many in Pakistan feel, plotted to secure Kashmir for India because it was he who advised the Indian government to accept accession and thereby provided the legal basis for Kashmir's integration with India. Those who level this charge against Mountbatten obviously speak in anger and frustration. No Governor-General, unless he had been deliberately mischievous or dishonest, would have done anything but what Mountbatten did. It was his duty to point out to the country's Prime Minister the legal and constitutional proprieties involved in the situation. Nehru himself would have realized the need for formal accession once the mood of impetuousness—and such moods were usually short-lived—had given place to his customary deliberativeness. In any case, his Cabinet colleagues —notably Sardar Patel, who held the States Portfolio—and senior official advisers had insisted on accession with equal firmness. Actually, critics of India's Kashmir policy have as much reason to blame Mountbatten as did the Pakistanis, because it was the Governor-General who urged Nehru to make his acceptance of the Maharaja's request subject to subsequent referendum or reference to the people of Kashmir. In gratuitously offering to hold such a referendum or plebiscite, Nehru went well beyond the contitutional requirements involved in the state's accession to India. This offer has caused India more embarrassment during the past twenty years than any other single act of the government. Even the decision to refer the Kashmir complaint to the Security Council in January 1948, which many in authority in India regret with good reason, was made on Mountbatten's advice.

India's actions over Kashmir are replete with instances of hasty resolves, unsound advice and faulty assessments. But those who exercised power at the time were inexperienced and immature. The leaders, particularly Nehru, were also in an ideal-

istic frame of mind. India had won freedom from a powerful
master and a new nation with a vital role to play in the world
had risen. This euphoria was heightened by the feeling that not
only India but the entire world was beginning a new age in
which wars of destruction were seemingly behind mankind. In
these circumstances and in this mood, the Pakistani action in unleashing—or at least actively abetting—a barbaric attack on
the people of Kashmir appalled Nehru. To him it seemed nega-
tion of the spirit for which the U.N. stood that any nation should
resort to aggression in the unabashed hope of annexing territory.
Resistance to aggression of this kind it was felt, was India's
moral duty, and if fulfillment of that duty necessitated acceptance of accession, then the Maharaja's request must be accepted.

In that atmosphere of self-confidence and self-righteousness,
neither Nehru nor his advisers realized that the offer of a plebiscite would hang around India's neck like a millstone. The offer
to ascertain the will of the people was gratuitously made because
Indian leaders were conscious of Sheikh Abdullah's charismatic
hold over the people of Kashmir and his preference for joining
India. They, therefore, had no doubt about the outcome of the
verdict. If a plebiscite had been held soon after the accession,
the Kashmiris would almost certainly have favored India, but
Nehru could not imagine that other considerations—personal
and political—might gradually emerge to lessen Abdullah's
ardor for union with India. Nor did he foresee, as he perhaps
should have, that the U.N. was to prove a forum influenced by
political factors and that its judgments would not be handed
down on a strictly legal and moral basis.

The mistakes that Nehru committed with respect to the domestic aspect of the Kashmir problem were even less pardon-
able. In the first instance, while accepting the state's accession
he allotted it "a special status." Unlike other princely states that
acceded to India—and some were as big and populous—Kashmir ceded authority to the Centre only for Foreign Affairs, Defense and Finance. It retained its own flag, chose its own head of

state, elected its own constituent assembly and drew its own constitution. For years even Indians could not enter Kashmir except on the basis of an official permit, and a virtual customs barrier existed between the state and the rest of India. In this concession, more than anything else, lay the seeds of separation which, in the years that followed, grew like a vicious weed. While the Indian Army was fighting the tribal raiders and protecting the Kashmiris from looting, rape and other barbaric acts, the state's anxiety to become a part of India and its loathing of Pakistan were unreserved. If, like other states, Kashmir had been integrated fully then, the Kashmiris would have settled down to their life as Indians. But with the assurance—implied in the plebiscite offer—that the accession was subject to popular ratification (and therefore temporary) and the granting of special privileges distinguishing the state from other parts of the country, it was natural for the leaders and the people of Kashmir to acquire a sense of self-importance and to come to think of separate independence as an attainable objective. It was equally natural for them to respond to the religious pull from Pakistan once the atrocities committed by the raiders were forgotten. As long as the promised referendum was postponed, it was not unrealistic for Kashmir to contemplate secession from India.

Over the years, Kashmir's special status has been slowly liquidated. It was only in the 1967 general election that the election laws of the union were fully extended to Kashmir. The President's authority over the state government was extended only in 1964. Even today the integration is not complete, and certain special privileges remain sacrosanct. An Indian citizen, for example, may buy property in any other part of India but not in Kashmir unless he is a Kashmiri by birth and residence. Even Nehru, notwithstanding his ancestry, could not have bought a house in Kashmir if he had wanted to. With the curtailment of every privilege came Pakistani protests in the U.N. that India was hustling Kashmir's integration and trying to settle unilaterally a dispute which was before the Security Council. At the same time, a sizable section of Kashmiris resented the erosion of their autonomy and demonstrated against it loudly.

The second mistake that Nehru committed was the failure to integrate the state's political institutions or exercise any stern supervision over those to whom he entrusted power in Kashmir. Instead of merging with the All-India Congress Party, as similar organizations in other princely states had, the Kashmir National Conference, which formed the government following accession, was allowed to preserve its separate identity for as long as seventeen years. As a local party with no precise organizational links with any national party, the Conference was subject to no discipline from outside.

Nehru was never regarded as a good judge of men, and those he chose to trust in Kashmir fully reflected his poor judgment. The two men in whose hands he placed almost total power were either vainglorious and arrogant, as Abdullah was, or corrupt and unscrupulous, as was Bakshi Ghulam Mohammed, who succeeded him. Five years of power had changed Abdullah considerably. "A comrade of twenty years," as Nehru sadly referred to him after the former's dismissal and arrest in August 1953, had acquired new horizons of personal power. The common belief is that Abdullah was contemplating an independent status for Kashmir—a vision in which he was allegedly encouraged by Western powers anxious to exploit the state's strategic location in the cold war. There were, however, enough indications at the time that Abdullah's affection for India had weakened considerably. His relationship with Nehru lacked its former cordiality and trust. It is perhaps true that in no public statement has Abdullah demanded independence for Kashmir, but many of those who met him at the time, including Indian and foreign journalists, received the impression that Abdullah's thinking about Kashmir's future—and his own position in it—coincided with what Hari Singh had planned in the weeks preceding the end of British paramountcy. The emphasis in Abdullah's remarks, of course, varied according to his listeners. If he spoke to an Indian, he would express his apprehensions over manifestations of Hindu communalism in certain parts of the country, which made the Kashmiri Muslims wary of India's claim to be a secular state. But this hint of disenchantment on the part of Kashmir was accompanied by his pledge to be loyal to India and reiteration of his personal faith in Nehru's leadership. In talking to foreigners, he stressed not his loyalty to Nehru and India but the fact that Kashmir's accession was an open issue. If he spoke to a mass meeting where there were few pressmen who understood Kashmiri, he would condemn India for not ascertaining the will of the Kashmiri people and allude in scarcely veiled language to a "third alternative" to joining India or Pakistan.

While they caused much annoyance and worry to New Delhi, these visions of personal glory and snappishness with Indian leaders would not have led to Abdullah's downfall if he had not at the same time alienated himself from most members of his Cabinet and large sections of the National Conference. A man of remarkable courage—as his defiance of the Maharaja and later of the government of India clearly demonstrated—and mass appeal, Abdullah also exhibited enormous conceit and a disdain of his associates and colleagues. Recalling the situation several years later, a senior Kashmiri leader remarked, "He treated us like dirt. He behaved as if he had overthrown the Maharaja singlehandedly." When, therefore, Indian leaders came to the conclusion that time had come to dismiss Abdullah, they found all his principal colleagues willing and anxious to form the new government without him.

Abdullah's successor, Bakshi Ghulam Mohammed, did even greater damage to India's cause in Kashmir and its case in international forums. The authorities in New Delhi appeared to have learned little from the discomfiture that Abdullah's waywardness had caused them. As in the case of Abdullah, power was placed in Bakshi's hands with almost no local checks and balances or supervision from the Centre. The state's political institutions were allowed to continue their independent course. Funds were channeled into the state for economic development, but emphasis was placed on organizing small, local projects rather than integrating the economy with that of the entire country. Nor was disbursement of the money that India poured into Kashmir scrutinized with care. If, as was widely alleged by responsible observers, a large proportion of it went into individual pockets or was used for political corruption, the Indian government conveniently looked the other way.

Until 1963, when he was eased out of office after ten years in authority, Bakshi was a byword for corruption and nepotism. His technique was simple. He either bribed his opponents or made them submit through strong-arm methods. He rewarded loyalty and support generously. During his years of power, his brothers and son grew from penury to unusual affluence. Many in the state believed that his influence extended even to those who were avowedly with Pakistan. Whenever the government in Delhi seemed inclined to cast a critical look on Bakshi's methods, agitation for the state's merger with Pakistan would flare up, forcing the Centre to retreat and stand nervously behind its man in Kashmir.

If the Centre naïvely went along with the Bakshi regime, it was because many in the Centre's own agencies in Kashmir were affected by the state leaders' capacity to pander to their personal weaknesses and shower on them and members of their families expensive gifts and services. Even some senior responsible Indian journalists were similarly corrupted into echoing the views that Bakshi wanted conveyed to New Delhi. In fact, Bakshi's decade in power offers a sad story of how, with only a few exceptions, senior visiting newsmen accepted lavish hospitality (some spent weeks holidaying with their large families entirely at state expense) and allowed their professional conscience to be smothered. Instead of drawing attention to the state government's questionable methods and its unpopularity with the people, such newsmen praised it for maintaining law and order. The net effect of all this was that while the people of Kashmir came to associate the state's links to India with corruption and tyranny, the government in New Delhi and the people in other parts of the country were led to believe that sternness was the only way to keep the state within India. This created a vicious circle in which firmness led to Kashmiri resentment and the tendency to look toward Pakistan, which in turn called for greater repression on the part of the authority. The gap between the people of Kashmir and the Indian government thus widened steadily.

It was only toward 1960 that Nehru became conscious that the people of the state were being denied a clean administration and certain basic personal rights. But Kashmir was too much in international limelight for the Prime Minister to deal with Bakshi abruptly. Abdullah's dismissal and his unsuccessful prosecution on charges of corruption and political conspiracy—the trial lasted years and had a phony air about it from the very start—had brought India and its tactics in Kashmir much adverse attention abroad. Summary action against Abdullah's successor would have been greeted in Pakistan with glee and interpreted as a further indication of the untenability of India's position in the disputed state. This ruled out straightforward action to remove Bakshi from power. Not until 1963, therefore, was Nehru able to depose Bakshi as part of the Kamaraj Plan (see pp. 138–42), under which a dozen state Chief Ministers and Central ministers were prodded into resigning office.

Constitutionally and legally, India's position in Kashmir—the state's accession and the dispatch of the Indian armed forces to defend it—was above reproach. And that it voluntarily offered to hold a plebiscite in Kashmir was cited as adequate evidence of India's good faith. Circumstances, however, conspired to rob this action of the conviction that it should have carried with the country's foreign critics. The plebiscite was never held, and in answer to a question at a press conference on July 19, 1961, Nehru curtly remarked that "there is no question of any plebiscite in Kashmir, now or later." The U.N. resolution of 1951 provided for the holding of a referendum, but such a reference to the people was contingent upon the withdrawal of the Pakistani forces from the part of Kashmir that they held. India accepted the resolution and if, as the resolution required, Pakistan had withdrawn its forces, the plebiscite would almost certainly have been held then. But Pakistan never fulfilled this condition —a fact that most foreign observers tend to overlook when blaming India for not fulfilling its pledge.

What weakens the Indian stance on this controversial point is its argument that what was promised was not plebiscite but, in Menon's words in the Security Council on February 8, 1957, "a reference to the people." Actually, in the complaint India made to the Security Council on January 1, 1948, its pledge was specifically described as "a plebiscite or referendum." Apart from this verbal inaccuracy in the official assertions, India has argued unconvincingly and, what is more, needlessly, that a "reference to the people" was implicit in the three elections that Kashmir has held and in which the National Conference, supporting accession to India, was returned to power. The Conference undoubtedly was returned to power, but it never contested the elections on the issue of accession. Also, the fairness of the Kashmir elections has been challenged extensively in India and abroad. In the 1962 elections, for example, of the state's seventy-five constituencies, more than half returned a candidate without any contest.

After two wars in which many thousand lives were lost on both sides, the Kashmir dispute between India and Pakistan has reached the stage where it seems almost beyond settlement in the foreseeable future. Both sides have invested far too much in it in terms of money, political prestige and human lives for them to make any concessions. In fact, though attempts have been made at several points during the past twenty-two years to resolve the problem, the Indian and Pakistani positions have all along been too far apart for any reconciliation.

The fundamental point about the problem is rather simple. India holds the really valuable part of the state, and what it is prepared to concede to Pakistan in terms of territory falls considerably short of what Pakistan is prepared to settle for. India has offered to take into account what it describes as the "realities of the situation" and abandon its claim to the part of Kashmir occupied by Pakistan, in return for a permanent settlement on the basis of the present cease-fire line. This position does not satisfy Pakistan, which has set its heart on the bulk of the state, particularly the valley. In the minister-level talks held at the initiative of the United States and Britain in the beginning of 1963, India offered to "rationalize" the cease-fire line and in the process concede a further 2,000 square miles of territory to Pakistan. But Pakistan insisted not only on getting the entire valley but also the bulk of the Jammu province, which has a Hindu majority and direct geographical and cultural ties with adjoining parts of India. There was, thus, no meeting ground. Even in the early years of Ayub's power, Pakistan's concept of a settlement called for the bulk of what India held. In fact, Ayub also hinted, much to Nehru's irritation, that Pakistan might turn to China if it did not get satisfaction over Kashmir.

The causes of the dispute go much deeper than ordinary covetousness over land. Kashmir undoubtedly embitters Indo-Pakistan relations, but it is also a manifestation of certain basic hostilities and suspicions that exist between the two peoples. Other problems, such as refugee rehabilitation and exchange of evacuee property, have been settled by time. And the World Bank's generosity in helping Pakistan develop alternative irrigation works has ended the dispute over the Indus Basin waters. Trade links that mutual distrust tore apart have been replaced by a new pattern of commerce with other countries. Kashmir is the only major dispute that has persisted in a form that mirrors the historical and political factors which led to India's partition and which are still valid sources of bitterness.

The two countries were born with a deep sense of hostility. Indian leaders and many among the country's intellectuals believed at the time of partition—and still believe—that Pakistan was created by the imperialists in Britain to weaken the new Indian nation and prevent it from becoming a powerful factor in Asia. British sympathy with Pakistan over Kashmir has given this belief substance in Indian minds. Typical of this conviction were the remarks in a speech by Sardar Patel in June 1948. "No dispassionate student of recent Indian history can fail to be convinced," he said, "that the partition of the country and the attendant disasters were brought about by the disruptive activities of the group of which Mr. Churchill was the inspiration and spokesman."

The class structure of the leadership of the two countries encouraged hostility. The leadership in India was drawn principally from the urban, Hindu middle classes, while Pakistan was led largely by rich, feudal elements from among rural Muslims. This antipathy was deepened by Nehru's contemptuous belief, shared by many among the top Indian leaders, that those who had inherited power in Pakistan had come by it without struggling for it and thus could not be expected to exercise it judiciously.

Even before the idea of a separate homeland took root, Muslims endeavored to secure parity with the Hindus in matters of political power. In the quarter-century preceding independence, while British rulers doled out constitutional reforms and political offices, Muslim leaders insisted on an equal division between the two principal communities, notwithstanding the enormous disparity in their size. Jinnah adopted the same attitude when the interim government was formed on the eve of independence. Since partition, in carving out its place in the new world as an independent nation, Pakistani leaders have been obsessed with the idea of parity with India.

Pakistan's foreign policy reflects the search for parity in status and power with India—a goal that the realities of the world situation do not justify. Those who run Pakistan did not accept the dominance of the Hindus or even acknowledge their superior position before independence, and they are now unwilling to concede a more important role to India in the power balance in the subcontinent. This is a position which to India, nearly 85 percent Hindu and holding power for the first time in nearly a thousand years, is irksome and unacceptable.

Challenge and hostility were inherent in the Muslim demand for a separate homeland. The essential argument of the Muslim

League leaders was not, as is often claimed, that Muslims were a separate nation that must have its own homeland, but that they were not Hindus and could not share the country with Hindus. The basic urge was never for unity of Muslims—despite common Islamic bonds, Pakistan has never regarded the adjoining Afghanistan as part of the same nation—but for separation from the majority community. In this approach lie the seeds of antagonism and distrust prevailing in the subcontinent. If the Hindus could not be trusted to give the Muslim minority its due in an undivided India, they could not be relied upon to let Pakistan play its fair role on the world stage. If Pakistan is not vigilant, its leaders have seemed to feel, Hindu-dominated India will smother it.

The Hindus, on the other hand, accepted the country's division not because they regarded Muslims as a separate entity entitled to a homeland, but as a way of ending a long-lasting grievance. Barring a small section of right-wing Hindus, few in India have desired reunification of the two countries with any degree of earnestness. Once the initial shock of partition and the communal massacres that accompanied it were absorbed, the average Hindu tended to regard the whole thing as a painful but unavoidable operation. In Muslim-majority areas, the Muslim next door had often lived aggressively, with a marked penchant for bullying tactics; separation from him was not unwelcome. The Hindus in India, however, were not prepared for continued Muslim accusations and aggressive acts even after partition. Consequently, when Pakistanis snarl at them, they react much more sharply than they would to similar provocations from another direction. It is typical of this exasperation and resentment toward Pakistan that the proposed transfer to it of a small border enclave, Berubari, caused such a political storm that the government had virtually to rescind its agreement, and yet continued occupation by the Chinese of nearly 15,000 square miles of what India considers as its territory has been calmly accepted.

Mutual suspicions and hostilities make India and Pakistan assess each other's moves in the worst possible light. Pakistan joined Western defense pacts to seek security against a big and hostile neighbor; India was convinced Pakistan's aim was to secure arms to alter the power balance in the region. India invited Pakistan to sign a declaration that the two countries would not resort to war against each other; Pakistan alleged India was trying to deprive it of the right to go to war over Kashmir and thereby perpetuate India's hold on the state. Pakistan proposed a joint defense with India, but the latter saw the suggestion as a sinister move to bring it indirectly within the orbit of Western defense pacts that it had declined to join.

In such an atmosphere of mutual distrust, foreign-policy options open to the two governments are singularly few. Much of what they do is to react to what happens on the other side of the border rather than to shape policies to any significant extent. Nehru could not persuade the public to honor his commitment with Pakistan over a trivial matter like the transfer of Berubari even when he was at the peak of his power. Ayub took power reportedly with the sincere intention of coming to terms with India, but soon he was as helpless a prisoner of circumstances as the selfish, hapless politicians whom he had deposed. General Yahya Khan may be equally anxious to establish peace with India, but he, too, has proved unable to swim against the current. If, for example, his difficulties with East Pakistan do not ease substantially, Pakistan's complaints against India are likely to acquire a regional orientation. Kashmir seems remote to the people of East Pakistan, and the distribution of the Ganges waters, an issue in which they have a major stake, may replace Kashmir as the country's principal dispute with India. Pakistani leaders are likely to charge loudly that India, as the upper riparian, is denying East Pakistan its rightful share of the waters and starving its development projects.

Peace and understanding will come to the two countries only when Pakistan acquires a positive *raison d'être* and reconciles itself to a relatively smaller role in the region and when Indian Hindus overcome their sense of apprehension and of inferiority to the Muslims. This may take a long time. After all, it took

Germany and France over two centuries and three major wars to settle their border dispute. Even the United States and Canada, with no history of religious strife, needed almost three generations to learn to live with each other in peace.

3: *Colliding Giants*

In the early evening of November 19, 1962, almost every functioning radio set in India had been switched on. The war with China had entered its second month and the Prime Minister was due to speak to the nation about the latest situation. That the situation was grave was no secret to the people. Even the state-controlled All-India Radio, anxious though it always was to protect the government's reputation and preserve public morale, had acknowledged the virtual collapse of Indian defenses in the northeastern sector and the lightning-like advance of the Chinese forces into Indian territory. Walong, Tezpur, Se La and other names mentioned in connection with the war were unknown to the vast majority of the Indian people, and to many even the state of Assam was a vague, distant entity; but this unfamiliarity did not prevent them from sensing the catastrophe which had befallen the country.

When he came on the air, Nehru made no attempt to hide or minimize the seriousness of the situation. He looked haggard and drawn as he arrived at the AIR studios to make the broadcast. He sounded even worse. There was no evidence of the chin-forward kind of style in which he customarily spoke to the people when confronting a difficult problem. His delivery was halting and his voice heavy, at times even hoarse, at points trailing off into a near-whisper—as if he found the task of speaking too burdensome—and conveying to millions of illiterate Indians crowding around community radio sets the Prime Minister's despondence and despair.

He enumerated the setbacks that India had suffered, and spoke of the "huge Chinese armies" that had penetrated deep into Indian territory, and of "several reverses" that India had suffered. There was an element of resignation in his reference to the people of Assam. "I can well understand what our friends in Assam must be feeling," he said, "because all this is happening on their doorstep, one might say. I want to tell them that we feel very much and that we shall help them to the utmost of our ability."

This was obviously no Churchillian performance. There were passages in the speech in which Nehru spoke of the country's determination not to waver and to "fight to the end—and that end is going to be a victory for us"; but the tone belied the words. The Chinese soldiers were still only at Bomdila, in the foothills of Assam, but, as his reference to the people of Assam indicated, Nehru had presumed that the invaders would quickly sweep across the vast, oil-rich state. In the earlier phases of the war, as the Indian Army retreated in the face of the Chinese aggression, Nehru's public remarks had reflected shock and anger. On November 19 the sense of shock had deepened perceptibly and anger had apparently given place to hopelessness. For one who had an impressive record of personal courage, such despondence was unusual.

Later that evening Nehru did something even more uncharacteristic of him and against the political philosophy to which he had tenaciously adhered since independence. He summoned U.S. Ambassador John Kenneth Galbraith and handed him a personal letter for President Kennedy requesting massive help in meeting the Chinese threat. Appeals for help had been made earlier to the United States, Britain and other friendly countries, but what was exceptional in the communication that he sent to Kennedy on November 19 was the fact that for the first time Nehru sought an arrangement involving the posting of U.S. combat personnel on Indian soil. Wary previously of even unarmed U.N. observers in Kashmir, Nehru in his letter to Kennedy actually pleaded for Americans to defend Indian cities and join the Indian Air Force in combat with the Chinese over Indian areas. The letter painted a highly pessimistic picture of what was happening. A serious threat, Nehru informed Kennedy, had developed to the Digboi oilfields in Assam. Also, with the advance of the Chinese in massive strength, the entire Brahmaputra Valley was threatened, and unless something was done immediately to stem the Chinese tide, the whole of Assam, Tripura, Manipur and Nagaland would also pass into foreign hands. He had previously refrained from seeking more comprehensive assistance, particularly air assistance, because of the "wider implications" of such help in the global context, but now the situation was really desperate. Nehru then listed the minimum requirements of the Indian Air Force: twelve squadrons of supersonic all-weather fighters to be manned by U.S. Air Force personnel while Indians were being trained in their use.

What staggered Galbraith, as he told Nehru immediately and confessed to some senior embassy colleagues later that night, was not the quantity of military hardware requested, but the political implications of Nehru's action. The apostle of nonalignment was virtually renouncing that creed and was seeking to involve the United States in what might well develop into a major war. His own assessment, which Galbraith reportedly offered Nehru, was that the Prime Minister was taking an excessively gloomy view of the situation. In his advice to Kennedy he similarly urged caution and warned against hasty decision.

The Chinese decision two days later to declare a unilateral cease-fire made any response on Kennedy's part unnecessary, and those in Nehru's secretariat who knew of the existence of the document—and their number was singularly small—thought of it later with much embarrassment.

At seventy-three, Jawaharlal Nehru could not be expected to display the spirit and confidence of his earlier years, but it was distressing to see Nehru's morale sag so noticeably in Parliament and other arenas. He looked as if he had personally lived through the ordeal of every border reverse and died the death of every Indian soldier in the two theaters of the war with China. Even after the Chinese had withdrawn to the other side of the McMahon Line and the danger of their sweeping down to the

Assam plains had been averted, Nehru bore the look of a tired, defeated man who carried a heavy load of sorrow and an overwhelming sense of failure.

The Chinese attack on India in October 1962 did mark the failure of Nehru's China policy—a policy supposedly aimed at securing accommodation with the Communist regime in Peking and making China a factor for Asian stability. That many abroad, particularly in the Western world, had predicted the failure of this policy added to the humiliation that came with its ultimate collapse. It also brought Nehru a feeling of political vulnerability at home. Many in India used to fear what would happen when the protective canopy of Nehru's leadership would be there no longer—speculation that suggested their total reliance on him. But apparently the conflict with China had undermined confidence in him so sharply that a vocal group within his own party succeeded in compelling him to dismiss his close associate and Defense Minister, Krishna Menon. His arm had never been twisted that way before.

Nehru came to be criticized for being unduly naïve in accepting Chinese professions of peaceful aims, for misreading history, for ignoring the warnings of the past regarding China's expansionist tendencies, for condoning, if not indirectly abetting, the Chinese occupation of a defenseless Tibet and thereby allowing the traditional buffer between India and China to disappear, and for neglecting to secure recognition of India's border by Peking. For some, criticism of India's attempts to seek a period of peace with Communist China is only a corollary to their disapproval of India's—or Nehru's—policy of nonalignment. Although Nehru undoubtedly made some grievous mistakes in dealing with Peking, a more charitable assessment of his performance might conclude that anyone else, without benefit of hindsight, would probably have committed most of those same errors.

Nehru did not, for example, overlook the expansionist nature of the Chinese character. He did not speak about it in public and probably did not visualize the extent to which that expansionism would be compounded by the impact of international Communism, which itself has marked expansionist impulses. But he was not unaware of this danger. After the Chinese attack, he denounced the Communist regime as the "grossest form of imperialism functioning across our borders" and on another occasion as "a powerful and unscrupulous opponent," but it was not adversity alone that had brought him this knowledge.

K. M. Panikkar, an eminent historian who was India's first Ambassador to Communist China, had warned as early as 1947 in a magazine article that, with the growth of air power, the Himalayas could not be an effective barrier against a potential enemy from the north. Some of the important foreign-policy decisions that the Indian government took after the Chinese Communist takeover in 1949 clearly suggest that Nehru, who held the Foreign Affairs portfolio, realized that the Himalayas were no longer an impregnable defense. In the latter half of 1949, India had concluded a new treaty with Bhutan under which the Himalayan kingdom agreed to be guided by India in its foreign affairs. This was followed by a treaty with Sikkim reaffirming its status as India's protectorate. Nepal, the largest of the countries situated between India and Tibet, signed a treaty of friendship with India on July 31, 1950. Besides the treaty, Nehru and King Tribhuvan exchanged letters—as yet confidential—in which it was agreed that any threat to Nepal's security would be considered a challenge to India's security. (On November 27, 1959, when Nehru asserted in the Indian Parliament, much to his listeners' puzzlement, that aggression against Nepal would be regarded as aggression against India, he had in mind the commitment made in those letters.)

India in fact went beyond mending its fences with the three kingdoms. Unlike the British, who had administered only fitfully and indifferently the North-East Frontier Agency (NEFA) comprising four tribal divisions bordering Tibet and Burma, the government of independent India took early measures to bring the area under its regular administrative control. Under the British, district officials would visit some of the distant border regions perhaps once in many years, but an administrative service specifically for the border regions was organized by India long before the Chinese challenge had developed. The army, similarly, was instructed to extend its posts to the limits of the Indian territory in this region. Again, in 1949 India supplied a sizable quantity of small arms to Burma to combat insurrectionist elements on its northern borders. These were by no means the decisions of a government which, as is often alleged, fell victim to its own public declarations of long-standing friendship between India and China and overlooked the warning that history had to offer it.

Even the charge that India allowed Tibet to disappear as a buffer between itself and an aggressive neighbor is based largely on ignorance or prejudice. Indian authorities endeavored to put some muscle in Tibetan leadership but did not succeed. H. E. Richardson, a British official who headed the Indian Mission in Lhasa for some time even after the end of the Empire and who should have no reason to distort history in favor of independent India, records in his book *Tibet and Its History* how India offered to supply arms and ammunition to Tibet and to train its army, but the Tibetan government declined. In the beginning of 1951, when the Chinese occupation of Tibet seemed imminent, the Indian government is believed to have sent emissaries to the Dalai Lama's brother, Norbu, and some of his other associates who were then in Calcutta to determine their plans to meet the threat from Peking. According to private, unpublished records, the people around the Dalai Lama, though much concerned about the Chinese designs on Tibet, had neither a plan of action nor the unity and sense of purpose essential to meet the challenge. They were riven by petty jealousies and moved by small, selfish aims. India's advice in the circumstances was to avoid precipitating the conflict and to endeavor to salvage as much of their autonomy as possible. It is not clear if India then refused to give the Dalai Lama asylum, but it certainly held the view that his departure from Tibet would give the Chinese the excuse they sought to extinguish Tibetan autonomy. India exerted whatever diplomatic and political influence it had at the time—and that was precious little—to save Tibet's autonomy. In the preceding year, following Peking's abrupt summons to the Tibetan leaders to send a delegation to negotiate their country's "liberation," India sent at least three formal communications urging China to settle the problem peacefully and desist from steps that might make the Communist regime unwelcome to the family of nations. On October 21, Panikkar presented Peking with an *aide-mémoire* recording India's concern over the entry of Chinese troops into Tibet. In another note ten days later India reminded China of Tibet's rights and objected to any move aimed at a unilateral abrogation of the privileges that India had inherited in Tibet from the British.

These were admittedly half-hearted gestures. But what influenced Nehru's position most adversely was the attitude of other world powers who seemed unwilling to get involved. Tibet's cause seemed lost from the very start. When Tibet could not resist Communist pressure and agreed to send a delegation for talks, it was anxious to negotiate on neutral ground for fear its representatives would be subjected to intolerable pressure in Peking. It reportedly favored Hong Kong as the venue for the talks, but British authorities displayed marked reluctance in issuing the necessary visas to the Tibetans. The talks were then started in New Delhi. Later, none of the principal powers came forward to sponsor Tibet's complaint to the United Nations, and it was left to El Salvador to place the issue on the U.N. agenda. At about the same time, a Communist Chinese delegation arrived at the U.N. to present a complaint against the United States for alleged aggression in Taiwan. Here was an excellent opportunity for those sympathetic to Tibet to undertake behind-the-scenes negotiations with Peking's representatives. Secret talks reportedly did take place, but they related to the possibility, then being openly discussed, of Chinese entry into the Korean war and not to Tibet's autonomy. Tibet's case was allowed to drop by the wayside. The writing on the international wall was thus clear to India, which saw no reason why it should involve itself in a conflict with an immature, arrogant power. Even in the beginning of the century, when Britain was at the zenith of its power and China a decrepit entity, London had constantly warned its Viceroy in India against allowing himself to be provoked into precipitate action in Tibet. In 1950, already engaged in a war with another neighbor, India rightly refused to be drawn into a seemingly hopeless war in defense of a cause to which others were prepared to give nothing more than lip-service.

Once India had accepted the inevitability of Chinese domination of Tibet, the surrender of its own privileges was only a matter of time. Few in the government or the country then seemed to care much about their loss. Besides its diplomatic representation in Lhasa, India under the British had maintained its own communications, certain nominal forces, a few "dak" bungalows (rest houses) and some exclusive trading facilities. Most of these rights had been rendered anachronistic by time. Indian leaders, therefore, needed little persuasion from the Chinese to agree to withdraw the military escorts and hand over Indian facilities to the Chinese authorities.

But the surrender of special privileges was only a part of the Indian move to normalize its relations with China in Tibet, an effort that culminated in the famous and much-criticized Panch-Sheel Agreement of 1954. By referring to Tibet as the "Tibet Region of China" in the preamble to the treaty, India tacitly acknowledged Peking's supremacy over the area. The preamble also enunciated the Five Principles of coexistence (hence the Hindi name of "Panch-Sheel"). If the description of Tibet as a region of China offered assurance to Peking, China's willingness to accept the Five Principles was taken by Nehru—though many in the Indian Parliament were skeptical—as an indication of its peaceful intentions.

Perhaps it was wrong on India's part to formally acknowledge China's sovereignty over Tibet and thereby deprive itself of a major bargaining point. Perhaps all along India had displayed excessive eagerness to befriend China and appreciate its viewpoint, seemingly asking for nothing in return. And for his efforts, the official Chinese journals were denouncing Nehru as a "running dog of imperialism" and bracketing him with Chiang Kaishek, Bao Dai, Syngman Rhee and others as "dregs of mankind."

To suggest that Nehru ignored these personal insults and continued to work gratuitously to promote China's cause because he was moved by an overpowering desire to be a bridge between China and the West is to oversimplify the situation. Nehru undoubtedly saw himself in the role of a peacemaker. He believed that India, as a democratic, nonaligned Asian country familiar with Western political institutions, was qualified to help Communist China and the Western world understand each other. But in addition he was moved in his task by his assessment of India's own interests and certain compulsions of world politics as they affected Asia.

India's principal need in 1950 was a period of peace. With its economy in a primitive stage after the long spell of colonial rule and from the blow it had suffered as a result of partition, India required peace not only with its neighbors but also in the South Asia region. Even if no solution of the Kashmir dispute had been found, at least a cease-fire had been accepted by India and Pakistan by then. India's endeavor, therefore, was to avoid a confrontation with its other big neighbor. For the first time in a long while China was ruled by a strong central government, and if Nehru noticed the menace that that development presented to others in Asia, he also tried to understand the causes that prompted it to act provocatively and aggressively—among them, the immaturity of the regime, the arrogance that success in a long-drawn-out internal struggle had given it, and the continued U.S. hostility, as manifested by its refusal to grant the legitimacy of the Chinese government and by maintenance of bases in Japan. Nehru's endeavor, therefore, was to assure China of India's wish to live in peace and convince it that the country was not, as the Chinese Communists suspected, a front for neo-imperialists. Neither the world situation nor its own interests prompted India to make an issue of Tibetan autonomy with

China. Thus, if India was not prepared to go to war with China —and it would have been extreme foolishness for the Indian leaders to contemplate such a course of action—it seemed best to accept the Chinese position with a show of friendliness rather than risk igniting the kind of tensions that were to come a decade later.

In return for giving up India's traditional rights in Tibet, lobbying constantly for China's admission into the U.N., watching over Peking's security interests in Korea with acknowledged zeal and endorsing Chinese occupation of Tibet, it is often argued that Nehru should have insisted that the Communists formally accept the McMahon Line as the Indian border with Tibet in the eastern sector and offer similar satisfaction in regard to the rest of the long frontier. By not doing that early enough and instead merely stating the Indian position from time to time in Parliament and other forums at home, the Indian government exposed itself to the Chinese claim to nearly 50,000 square miles of territory in NEFA in the east and in the Ladakh region of Kashmir in the north. In signing the 1954 agreement over Tibet, Nehru adopted the attitude that India's border with China was clearly defined by tradition and history, and since it had no doubt about the position, it saw no reason why it should needlessly reopen a settled issue and thereby invite challenges. As early as November 1950 Nehru stated that, "map or no map, the McMahon Line is our definitive frontier." Having said this and repeated it on several occasions in the following years, he presumably believed that if any party had a divergent viewpoint, it should come forward to raise the issue.

The Indian case on the border has been based on usage, natural features such as watersheds of principal river systems, and certain specific treaties. Besides the agreement arrived at in Simla in 1914, which drew the McMahon Line and which, much later, Peking denounced as an imperialist perpetration, India has extensive documentary data, some going as far back as the middle of the nineteenth century, to support its claim on the eastern sector. They include annual reports of the region's political officers, police records and reports of survey parties. On the Ladakh side, the Indian title to the area which China claimed and surreptitiously occupied is based on treaties going back to 1684. Another treaty was concluded in 1842 following a war between Kashmir (of which Ladakh is a part) and Tibet. Tibet was assisted in the war by China, and consequently the second signatory to the treaty on the Tibetan side, confirming the earlier boundaries between Kashmir and Tibet, was the Emperor of China.

Still, there were indications—which undoubtedly look more significant in retrospect than they did at the time—that the Communist rulers of China had the same attitude toward Tibet and India as the previous regimes. Maps were frequently published officially and circulated in China and abroad in which nearly 35,000 square miles of NEFA and about 15,000 square miles of the Aksaichin region of Kashmir were depicted as part of China. Indian apprehensions over this "cartographic aggression" were, however, readily lulled by the explanation that the maps were old ones, stemming from the nationalist government's times, which the Communist government had not had the time to correct. Nehru raised the question of erroneous maps with Chou En-lai in October 1954, but felt reassured by the reply blaming their inaccuracy on the previous regime. When uncorrected maps continued to be issued, Nehru discussed the matter again during Chou's state visit to India in the winter of 1956–57. As he reported to Parliament later, Chou advised him that China accepted the McMahon Line "in consideration of the friendly relations between India and China." Significantly, however, when Nehru sent the minutes of this conversation to the Chinese Premier, confirmation never came. Indian eagerness to place faith in the Chinese word at this stage was conspicuous. This was the phase of India-China relations when the Peking propaganda machine was no longer denouncing Nehru as a lackey of the imperialists, when Chou was being charming to Asian and African nations ("The Chinese delegation has come to Bandung to seek unity and not to quarrel"), when Peking

startled even the United States by offering to discuss measures to
relax tension in the Taiwan area, and when the Eighth Congress
of the Communist Party of China formally acknowledged nonaligned nations as a force for world peace.

It was with considerable disbelief, therefore, that India heard
the news in September 1957 that the Chinese had built a motor
road through the hump of Aksaichin to link Tibet with Sinkiang.
India protested against this major encroachment of its territory
and violation of its sovereignty several months later. In reply,
Chou stated blandly that "the Sino-Indian boundary has never
been formally delimited."

China, by then no longer needing India to do its international
chores, deliberately and consciously turned toward it a face of
hostility. At home Mao's "hundred flowers" had bloomed but
only briefly, and the cry against revisionism had already been
raised. Chinese adherence to the principle of peaceful coexistence had seemingly been a temporary tactic that had served its
purpose.

The verbal war between China and India was fought with increasing vigor in the three years that followed. Chou, who had
dismissed the Chinese maps as errors of the previous regime,
now bluntly endorsed all the claims they made. John Rowland, a
former member of the U.S. Foreign Service, states in his *History
of Sino-Indian Relations* that "Peking had its reasons for claim-
ing more than 50,000 square miles of Indian territory. But the
reasons, based partly on Communist doctrine and partly on
more traditional Han expansionist tendencies, bear little relationship to the pseudo-legal case argued with India. Part of
China's case had an air of plausibility when viewed in the context of erroneous assumptions and accommodating definitions;
much of the case is spurious, regardless of context. Only a small
part could serve as a legitimate basis for meaningful boundary
negotiations with India."

While challenging the Indian position and making counter-
claims, China also steadily consolidated its hold over Aksaichin
and extended its control well beyond the road that it had built.
The Tibetan revolt against the Chinese occupation in 1959,

which led to the Dalai Lama's escape to India, gave the quarrel a new dimension. With the Dalai Lama's arrival in India and the hospitality that Nehru and his government extended him, India's dispute with China had reached the point of no return, at least for the foreseeable future. The stage was set for the massive armed conflict that came in October 1962.

Perhaps even the most farsighted of administrators would have been a similar victim of circumstances, but today it does seem indefensible that in the first half of the Fifties, when India was supposedly concentrating its energies on consolidating its position in the NEFA sector, it neglected the Ladakh sector to such an extent that the Chinese were able to construct a major motor road across a large segment of its territory without being detected.

Only a few weeks before the Chinese attack materialized, Nehru pointed out in Parliament on August 22, 1962, that "our judgment of the situation was that the danger lay in the NEFA border . . . that before the Chinese came to Tibet, we could not hold them at the frontier. The one border which we protected more or less adequately was the NEFA border." Subsequent events show how ill-informed Nehru was about Indian defenses.

The failure of Indian defenses was the result of a combination of several factors (see pp. 215–26). Most of the weaknesses were visible even to casual observers and were often pointedly discussed by the press and Parliament between 1958 and 1962. But apparently Nehru and the China experts in the Foreign Office had noted the enormous domestic problems that faced China's Communist leaders and argued that for a considerable time after the takeover they would be too involved at home to undertake any adventurous action against a neighbor of India's size. They lulled themselves into a state of mind in which danger signals went unnoticed. In their evaluation of the Chinese provocations on the border (the first one occurred immediately after the Five Principles agreement of 1954) they tended to give the aggressors the benefit of the doubt.

In minimizing the Chinese potential for aggression, Nehru

and Menon were also encouraged by the cordial relations that existed at the time between India and the Soviet Union. In July 1960 the Russians had abruptly withdrawn their technicians from China, thereby indicating that stresses and strains were developing in Sino-Soviet relations, but it was not foreseen that soon Peking would challenge the Soviet position as the leader of the Communist world. After 1958, when the Chinese reverted to their former attitude of hostility toward India, the Indian leaders relied heavily—and, it appears in retrospect, pathetically—on Soviet capacity to keep Peking's provocative actions within bounds. During his visit to India in 1955, Khrushchev had publicly supported India's title to Kashmir, and it seemed logical that in the dispute over Ladakh, which was a part of Kashmir, the Soviet sympathies would lie on the Indian side. There were other portents to hearten Nehru and Menon. In the beginning of 1960, when the verbal war between the two countries was at its worst, Moscow sent a high-ranking delegation to New Delhi to attend India's tenth-anniversary celebrations. The following month Khrushchev himself dropped by for political talks with Nehru. Indian leaders, eagerly looking for support and understanding, interpreted the two visits as an indication of the Soviet backing for India, and it strengthened their hope that the Soviet Union would place a restraining hand on China.

When the attack on Indian territory came, the Soviet attitude greatly disappointed the Indians, as did that of the country's non-aligned friends such as Yugoslavia, the United Arab Republic, Burma and Ghana, for their hesitation and tardiness in offering India even moral support in its hour of distress. Far from restraining Peking or even speaking out in India's defense, the Soviet Union sided with the aggressor for the first few crucial days of the conflict. On October 25, a week after the Chinese attack, *Pravda* and *Izvestia* praised the Chinese peace proposals that India had found too humiliating for acceptance, and tartly urged New Delhi to accept them. There was no criticism, implied or otherwise, of the Chinese action in trying to settle a dispute through force. The previous day the official journals of the Soviet Union had printed the Chinese proposals, but no space was found for the Indian viewpoint. Even on October 30, by which time the Chinese troops had crossed several Himalayan ranges on the Indian side of the border and Nehru was compelled to declare a state of national emergency, Moscow continued its pro-Peking stance. Speaking in the U.N. General Assembly, Soviet Deputy Foreign Minister Valerin Zorin advised India to make peace with China on the latter's terms.

The Soviet attempt to lean on the Chinese side in the opening phase of the border war is generally attributed to Moscow's involvement then in the Cuban crisis. Khrushchev apparently did not want the Communist ranks divided while he was engaged in a confrontation with the United States. As soon as Khrushchev's confrontation with Kennedy came to an end, Moscow moved from a pro-Peking to a neutral and later to a somewhat pro-India posture. The acid test of the Soviet attitude was the delivery of the MIG-21 aircraft and some helicopters that India had contracted to buy from it. Ten days after the beginning of the fighting, a Soviet military spokesman, according to *The New York Times,* endorsed the Chinese territorial claim and announced his country's inability to provide arms to India. The MIGs were of little use to India in the conflict at the time, for neither side was using its air force, but their supply according to schedule would have indicated Soviet support for India and conveyed a warning to Peking. It was only on November 10 that Nehru was able to inform a parliamentary committee that the eagerly awaited signal had finally come. A month later, addressing the Supreme Soviet of the U.S.S.R., Khrushchev reminded China that "even the most complicated negotiations are better than war." It was not clear to Indian observers, however, whether the Soviet Premier was supporting India or using India as yet another stick with which to beat China in his ideological dispute with Mao.

Why did China invade Ladakh and NEFA? In the years since the Sino-Indian war the theories and surmises have multiplied. The late Kingsley Martin, who visited India immediately after the beginning of the hostilities and wrote extensively in the *New Statesman* then, believed that by routing the Indian Army,

Peking wished to humiliate India in the eyes of the smaller
Asian nations and demonstrate where real power lay. Others
have argued that the conflict was the inevitable by-product of
the ideological rivalry between the two countries. India and
China are prototypes of two different political systems for
emerging Asian and African nations, and the Indian system was
inviting greater appreciation—an intolerable situation to China.
While the Communist "leap forward" had failed, India had held
three general elections and had implemented three Five-Year
Plans and thereby proved that a backward Asian people could
achieve economic development without sacrificing democracy
and individual freedom. By compelling India to triple its defense spending, China, it is argued, placed crushing burdens on
India's economy to ensure the failure of the Indian experiment
in democratic planning. Some argue with a slight variation in
emphasis that the attack was intended to cut India to size, for
in China's view, Nehru was assuming too much importance in
world politics. Many feel that the attack was launched in the
confident belief that military reverses would bring about the collapse of the Nehru government and pave the way for a more
amenable regime. The aggressors withdrew hastily and in an unprecedented manner when their attack had the opposite effect of
uniting the Indian people behind Nehru and pushing the nonaligned government almost into the Western camp.

Alternatively, of course, it is possible that the Chinese did not
think in these elaborate terms of political cause and effect and
merely acted in straightforward anger over India's action in
offering asylum to the Dalai Lama and hurriedly extending its
lines of military control on the border. Having made their point,
the Chinese withdrew from the area since they did not immediately need it, and controlling it would have extended their lines
of communication and supply excessively. Toward the end of
1959 and at the beginning of 1960, when the Chinese intrusions
into Indian territory had increased markedly in the wake of the
Tibetan revolt, Nehru often expressed the belief that the border
violations were somehow linked with developments in Tibet. It

is possible that the Chinese attack of 1962 similarly grew out of the Tibetan revolt. In any event, it had the added advantage of putting a virtual end to India's "Forward Policy," by which India was establishing military posts perilously close to the Chinese posts and often even crossing what Peking regarded as its line of actual control. In the brief war, apart from giving expression to its annoyance over India's "imperialistic" role in Tibet, China had demolished the offending posts.

The conflict over ideology and the rivalry for Asian leadership is probably yet to come. The impact of Chinese expansionism and Communism on India may be considerably greater in the next decade or so if India is able to establish itself as a democracy of some durability and chooses to obstruct China's political and territorial plans. China's obsessive concern about its security and its feeling of ideological claustrophobia—fed by democratic India and "revisionist" Soviet Union as its neighbors and the presence in Japan and Taiwan of the "imperialist" United States—may drive it toward a much bigger military adventure than the border attack of 1962. The Chinese occupation of Tibet was apparently motivated not merely by the need to reduce the population burdens on the mainland but also to ensure that the "roof of the world" would not fall into hostile hands. The Chinese leaders may similarly come to the conclusion that control over the kingdoms of Nepal, Bhutan and Sikkim on the southern slopes of the Himalayas is essential for the security of Tibet. In the past, Peking has shown considerable interest in extending its influence to these small states and declined to accept India's claim of special position in the area. Should China choose to subvert the kingdoms (the medieval state of their society and politics would make Communist subversion comparatively easy), India would be faced with the difficult choice of going to war in fulfillment of its pledges or stoically accepting a situation in which the Gangetic plains, its heartland, would be exposed constantly to the threat of Chinese power.

INDIA AND THE BIG TWO

1: *Cold Line to Washington*

AT A SEMINAR in Washington in 1959 on India–U.S. relations, an American speaker remarked angrily that "American backs have been put up time after time . . . by assumptions made by Indians, questioning our motivations, seeing us as war-mongers and that sort of thing." Another speaker indignantly asked if India believed "that it is a part of this struggle between what we call freedom and Communism," and he asserted that when he raised the question, he was "talking about the morality of the issues."

The seminar was no routine gathering. Among its eighty-eight participants were such distinguished observers of international politics as John F. Kennedy, Richard M. Nixon, Chester Bowles and Barbara Ward. Nor were those who cashiered India for its lack of understanding of U.S. motives the isolated voices of straggling cold-war soldiers. Almost throughout the twenty-two-year relationship between the United States and independent India, many responsible, sober men in both countries have frequently suffered mutual exasperation and complained bitterly, though sincerely, of lack of understanding on the other side. It is a fact that India has not shared the U.S. enthusiasm for the fight against world Communism. Few in India regard it as a holy crusade or accept the premise that abstaining from it involves surrender of moral values. But it is also true that Indians have often bluntly chided the United States for acts the like of which they have conveniently overlooked when committed by the Soviet Union. India has not stopped at merely denying the United States the understanding and support to which Washington considered itself entitled from another democracy in its confrontation with the Soviet Union; India has frequently appeared to stand closer to the latter.

In the minds of most Western critics, India's observance of a double standard is typified by its role in 1956 over Suez and Hungary. When British, French and Israeli forces marched into Egypt to occupy Suez, India denounced their aggression in blunt, angry words and worked actively at the United Nations for condemnation of the action. But when Soviet tanks entered Hungary to crush a popular uprising against Russian domination, Nehru temporized distinctly and, instead of condemning the aggression, appeared to speak of it somewhat apologetically. At the U.N. the Indian delegate opposed the move for a plebiscite in Hungary and virtually supported the Soviet position.

This tendency on India's part to pull its punches where the Soviet Union is concerned and give them an extra measure of thrust when dealing with the United States has been apparent on other occasions. As U.S. Congressional leaders, authors and newsmen frequently point out, the enormous amount of aid that India has received from their country over the years has elicited scant thanks, but a relatively small packet of assistance from the U.S.S.R. is widely lauded in India. The Soviet decision in 1960 to sell six MIG aircraft to India was hailed as a tremendous gesture of goodwill, but Eisenhower's offer of sizable military aid in his letter to Nehru of February 24, 1954, was regarded as an affront and spurned summarily. In 1962, following the Chinese attack on India's borders, for a brief but crucial period

Moscow stopped the delivery of the tanks that it had contracted to sell India. Indian leaders waited anxiously but offered no criticism. But in far less grim circumstances in 1966, when President Johnson appeared to dawdle over the dispatch of food grains, the Indian reaction was sharp and vocal. The Soviet decision to adopt a neutral posture in the India-China conflict was greeted in India with relief, but the U.S. resolve to act similarly during the India-Pakistan war caused dismay and anger. The ruthless dictator Stalin, who treated independent India rather contemptuously, was given fulsome praise on his death in India's Parliament, but the death of John F. Kennedy ten years later in deeply tragic circumstances did not cause in New Delhi a demonstration of sorrow of the kind that might have been expected for one who was generally acknowledged as a genuine friend of India.

The Indian elite that came to power after independence was Western-oriented in its thinking and way of life. English, which it spoke fluently and wrote expressively, offered it a valuable link with the United States, as did its dedication to principles and institutions of democracy. Some bonds of sympathy had been created even before 1947, when President Roosevelt risked the ire of a major war ally by urging Britain, then led by Winston Churchill, a hardened Tory, to hasten the process of Indian independence. It was perhaps a measure of Nehru's sentiments toward the United States that he raised India's mission in Washington to a regular embassy even before the British had formally left India.

If relations between India and the United States were cool and punctuated with minor irritations soon after 1947, the fault lay on both sides. Each suffered from ignorance of the other, and whatever little knowledge of each other they had was colored by strong prejudices.

The mental horizon of the educated and politically dominant class in India scarcely extended beyond Britain. With the English they had formed a love-hate relationship. They fretted and chafed under British domination, but they also greatly admired its literature, culture and political institutions. Their understanding of British personality, character and attitudes was fairly deep, but beyond Britain they saw things shrouded in a thick haze. Their exposure to the Americans was limited to the few missionaries who worked in India or the soldiers who were posted in various Indian cantonments during the war. The former were greeted with suspicion, as almost all foreign missionaries were, and the latter with hostility for being allied to the British colonial power. The vague picture of the United States that the average Indian had formed in his mind in the Forties was of a country that was a sort of distant cousin of Britain but rather naïve and often uncouth, for all the riches it had struck. Hollywood, which had a large market in India, offered a harsh, overdrawn picture of the United States. American society appeared not to have come to terms with itself yet. The Americans were not admirable because in their behavior, mannerisms, even in the way they spoke English, they were so different from the British. To this unflattering image were also imparted elements of ill-will by such works as Katherine Mayo's *Mother India,* which Gandhi sorrowfully described as "a gutter inspector's report." The book was widely read, caused deep resentment and invited a rejoinder by an Indian author who raked muck about the United States equally unashamedly, to the malicious glee of Indian readers.

The American understanding of India was not much better. If Indians knew Americans as Hollywood presented them, the latter tended to look at India largely through British eyes. In the early years of Indian independence it seemed that the United States had accepted not only the British assessment of the subcontinent but had also acquired Britain's prejudices and misconceptions about the area. In adopting these images secondhand from India's former rulers, the Americans often also tended to oversimplify the picture.

The British in India had usually entertained a favorable, somewhat romantic, view of the Muslims, who, according to the British, were straightforward, dependable and brave, while

Hindus were devious, calculating and generally poor soldiers. This assessment undoubtedly had an element of truth in it. The average Hindu is more complex than a Muslim and often tends to be rather calculating in his actions, but the British evaluation of the characteristics of the two communities was obviously exaggerated and colored by the Britons' political predicament in the subcontinent. Hindus, who took to Western education long before the Muslims, imbibed modern political ideas and a preference for democracy and freedom sooner. Inevitably, they formed the backbone of the independence movement. Muslims, on the other hand, tenaciously stuck to their feudal attitudes and values, and their leaders were readily induced by political favors to act as loyalists rather than as challengers of foreign domination. In recruitment to the Indian Army, which until independence was, for all practical purposes, an army of occupation, the British relied heavily on Muslims for obvious reasons. That Islam is a monotheistic religion while Hinduism accommodates a complex hierarchy of divine powers and seemingly conflicting dogma also deepened the British prejudice against the latter.

Such exaggerated bias admirably served the purpose of a colonial ruler intent on dividing the people of India in order to maintain his tenuous hold on the country. Reflecting on the period, U.S. diplomats and foreign-policy specialists admit that, unfamiliar as they were then with the region, they tended to be influenced and guided by their British colleagues, who were supposed to be experts on the area. British prejudices, of course, were translated into terms suited to the constitutional changes that had taken place in the subcontinent. India was regarded as a "Hindu country," while Pakistan was a "Muslim nation." The latter was a "dependable" ally, while the former tended "not to be helpful." In his report on June 1, 1953, after his travels in the area, John Foster Dulles praised Pakistan for "the strong spiritual faith and martial spirit of the people." Several others in the Department of State and the Pentagon had firmly held a similar view of Pakistani Muslims even earlier. A leading American journal, *U.S. News and World Report,* described the Pakistanis as "a warrior people . . . tough . . . mainly six-footers . . . tall, rugged eaters of meat and wheat" and thus indirectly scorned the Hindu preference for rice and a vegetarian diet. The logic of the argument is not clear, but somehow it was also believed that "a good Muslim would find difficulty in being a good Communist," and this alleged immunity, at that stage of anti-Communist hysteria in the United States, was considered a major asset. Dulles himself stated that Pakistanis could be "a dependable bulwark against Communism." All these beliefs and prejudices bore a striking resemblance to what a retired British member of the Indian Civil Service might have said while musing back over his colonial career in a London club.

The pronouncements and actions of Indian leaders and the policies of the new government only deepened American suspicions about India's dependability as an ally. India, believed to be "soft" on Communism, was the second non-Communist country to accord formal diplomatic recognition to Red China. In fact, it was during a state visit to the United States in 1949 that Nehru proclaimed India's intention to recognize the Communist regime in China. To policy-planners in the U.S. government this must have appeared a calculated affront. India went much further, actively lobbying for Red China's admission into the U.N. and chiding the United States for its unrealistic attitude on this important issue. In American eyes this unfriendliness on the issue was further compounded when in the beginning of 1951 India, along with a Soviet-led group of U.N. members, opposed a resolution censuring China for its role in the Korean conflict.

U.S. diplomats in India at the time, presumably reflecting State Department views, often inquired, with a touch of exasperation, "Why doesn't India see the threat to its security and its institutions that Communism poses?" To them it seemed an act of suicidal folly that India should surrender its privileges in Tibet and virtually pave the way for China's occupation of what the British had studiously preserved as a buffer between the two countries. Indian leaders also appeared to disregard the traditional threat to national security from the Russian side. The considerations that prompted the British viceroys of India at the turn of the century to take elaborate measures to guard against the danger from the direction of Czarist Russia had become doubly valid with the rise of Soviet power, yet Indian leaders, Western diplomats argued, seemed oblivious to the peril.

India's decision to stay nonaligned was greeted with equal suspicion and resentment. Its firm refusal to be counted on the American side in the confrontation with the Soviet Union caused the U.S. government dismay and annoyance as well as a measure of puzzlement. A country so burdened with overwhelming economic and political problems as India should have looked around eagerly for allies who could lighten its load and offer it a sense of security. As a state that had adopted a parliamentary form of democracy, it should have regarded the United States as a natural ally or at least viewed U.S. actions with sympathy and understanding. Instead, it categorically refused to make a deal and seldom missed an opportunity of snapping at the United States and its allies in international forums. In his speech at the National Press Club in Washington on October 14, 1949, Nehru, on his first visit to the United States, reviewed his discussions with the American leaders and asserted that "there is no question of a deal." Such declarations, combined with India's behavior in the U.N. in championing Red China's cause, presumably confirmed the Western impression of Hindu India's "undependability" as an ally.

Dulles' widely quoted remark that nonalignment was "immoral" reflected the Eisenhower administration's anger over the Indian posture during the Fifties, but it also shows how insensitive the U.S. leaders could be to views of a country whose assessment of the global situation and its own national interests did not conform entirely with American thinking. Averell Harriman told the 1959 Washington seminar held at the close of the Eisenhower era that he did not "know any country that ought to be more understanding of nonalignment than the United States, which for nearly a century and a half went on a course of its own." India's international posture on becoming independent was remarkably similar to what the U.S. stance had been on achieving its freedom. The United States had refused to be involved in the disputes between Britain and France, and, as Nehru and Krishna Menon did to America and the Soviet Union in the cold-war years, lectured world powers rather freely while going about its business. Chester Bowles, who has spent more time in India than any other U.S. Ambassador to that country, reminded the seminar of the words of George Washington that "an attachment for one nation or another produces a variety of evils. It is our true policy to steer clear of all foreign entanglements." These words, Bowles said, could easily have been uttered by Nehru. But voices like Harriman's and Bowles's were lonely ones. Bowles, appointed U.S. Ambassador in New Delhi in 1951, was convinced of the genuineness and strength of India's desire to remain nonaligned. He made a determined effort to make the policy-framers in Washington and the people of America conscious of Indian sincerity, but in the atmosphere of almost obsessive fear of Soviet Russia and the hectic marshaling of "dependable allies" that marked the period, his failure was complete and inevitable.

Suspicion, impatience and inability to appreciate the other party's viewpoint were not confined to the American side. India had its own blind spots and ideological angularities—an undoubting faith in its own wisdom, and a tendency to bristle with self-righteous indignation over even minor matters. Its leaders habitually spoke in a highly moralistic tone guaranteed to pique friend and foe alike.

If the United States derided India for refusing to place itself clearly on the side of freedom and fight the forces of servitude, India regarded U.S. actions as thinly camouflaged efforts to establish itself as the new dominant power in Asia. To a people who had suffered at the hands of a colonial power and who had vowed to help end that form of tyranny anywhere in the world, it came as a deep shock that France and the Netherlands should have the benefit of U.S. arms and political support in their endeavors to resurrect the empires in Southeast Asia that they had lost to the Japanese during the war. When Nehru spoke angrily against the Dutch in 1948 for imprisoning the principal national leaders of Indonesia, his wrath was directed at least partly against the United States, whose military and material support had aided the Dutch.

This suspicion of U.S. motives in Asia was deepened by the fact that, by and large, Indians did not share the American assessment of the threat from communism. Indian leaders had long felt admiration for the Soviet Union, even if they did not agree with its system of government and some of its practices. The Indian attitudes were influenced by the success that Communist Russia had achieved in industrializing a backward, long-exploited country. In Soviet achievements, Indian leaders hopefully saw a parallel with the plight and problems of their own country. Nehru wrote excitedly of what he saw when he visited Russia in 1927—a time when the hopes Communism had raised and the discipline and social order it had imposed were visible but the tyranny and suppression of human dignity were yet to come. At home, the Communist Party had been, at least briefly, part of the freedom movement—in fact, it was a small wing of the Congress Party—and the untenability of the creed that it believed in was obscured by its enthusiasm for national independence. To Indian leaders, the Communists at home did not appear a menace. They were, for the most part, a group whose creed differed from theirs only in regard to the nature of the political structure to be set up after independence. Their betrayal of the movement in 1942 had caused irritation, but in the satisfaction following attainment of freedom there was a tendency not to blame the Communists excessively. It was known that they believed in violence as a means to power, but the Communist Party of India was so puny in size that it was difficult for Nehru and his colleagues in the Congress Party—barring the few belonging to the ultraconservative wing—to imagine that the CPI could pose a serious challenge at any time. The CPI had backed a peasants' "uprising" in the Telengana region of South

India in 1948, but that was put down quickly and effectively. Though for a brief period soon after independence the CPI was outlawed, the action reflected the personal conservativism of Sardar Patel, the Home Minister, rather than any serious and widespread concern on the part of the government regarding Communist intentions and capabilities.

Unlike the U.S. leaders, those who came to power in India in 1947 had led a rather sheltered life as far as international Communism was concerned. No confrontation between Indian leadership and the Soviet Union seemed to be in the offing. There was nothing in India's national experience to substantiate the Western accusation that international Communism stood for the extinction of freedom—of nations or individuals. It was sometimes suggested that the CPI acted under Moscow's direction and received assistance from it, but somehow the CPI's poor performance in Telengana deprived such assertions of credibility. Reports of Stalin's cruel purges did not shock Indian opinion as much as they should have, partly because they were viewed with a measure of suspicion as Western propaganda. Just about the time the Stalinist purges were taking place in the Soviet Union, a number of European countries were swept up by Fascism. The fact that Fascists in Germany, Italy and Spain stood in uncompromising hostility toward Communism apparently excited Nehru's sympathy for the Soviet Union.

Thus, Indian reaction might have been predicted when the United States appeared to be helping former colonial powers to revive their empires in postwar Asia while the Soviet Union was offering, if nothing else, at least verbal support for the independence of Indonesia, Malaya and Indo-China. Could it be, many in India wondered, that the Western powers were acting aggressively even in Europe and that the Soviet Union was prompted in its moves by genuine considerations of national security? Even those who did not question U.S. motives seemed to think that the United States was overreacting to the Communist challenge and was employing faulty methods to meet it. Communists might infiltrate and subvert a society, particularly one suffering from social and economic inequalities, in the hope of making it a political vessel, but they were unlikely to commit formal aggression against it. To Indians, therefore, it appeared rather naïve that the United States should place so much emphasis on erecting military barriers against the advance of Communism in Asia while virtually neglecting the political aspirations and economic needs of the Asian people. U.S. aid—direct or indirect—in enabling the former colonial rulers of Asia to re-establish their authority or to prop up unpopular, if indigenous, regimes as part of an Asian security plan struck most thinking Indians as shortsighted and futile.

It was not this divergence in the assessment of the character of international Communism, however, or a feeling of distaste for U.S. association with the former colonial powers that propelled India closer to the Soviet Union despite its official policy of nonalignment. In its readiness to see the Soviet viewpoint, stand by it in the U.N. and overlook Moscow's acts of international misdemeanor, India was moved primarily by consideration of its own interests and security objectives. Nehru's self-righteousness and Krishna Menon's needless vituperation in the U.N. combined to give the impression that in their foreign-policy formulation Indian leaders were moved unduly by sentiment, that they followed an unrealistic course of action and that they paid inadequate attention to the country's real interests. In reality, India followed as practical a policy as international circumstances permitted it to. Some argued that India's endeavor to play an independent role in world politics was unrealistic in light of the limitations of its power and resources as well as the enormity of its own problems. According to this line of reasoning, if India had placed itself clearly in the Western camp, the United States and Britain would have poured billions of dollars in capital and technical know-how into the country to bring it prosperity, offered it effective security against aggression, and even supported it on the issue of Kashmir. This argument makes certain obvious assumptions regarding the selflessness of Western intentions and overlooks the price in national self-respect and sovereignty that India would have had to pay for such an arrangement. Those who chide the Indian leadership for spurning the role of Western satellite also overlook the mood of the country in the years following independence. A people who had fought for decades for their sovereignty, who in the process had acquired a somewhat exaggerated sense of pride, and who, unlike Pakistan, suffered from no obsessive, unnatural fear of a neighbor, would have rejected any political arrangement suggesting diminution of their role and freedom. If in the first decade of its independence India seemed to strut unnecessarily on the international stage or to aspire to a diplomatic role totally out of proportion to its military power, it was largely an expression of the sense of grandeur under which its people labored at the time.

Once it was decided that India should not become the camp-follower of any big power, most of its other foreign-policy postures developed as corollaries. Nehru could have been less pompous in his pronouncements on international developments and Menon could have been less abrasive in dealing with Western delegates in the U.N., but the effect of such restraint on their part would have been only marginal. India's claims to Kashmir, for example, were not notably better appreciated by the West when India was represented in the Security Council debates by Gopalaswami Ayyangar and M. C. Chagla, who in personal style and ideological beliefs could be described as the antitheses of Menon. Nor would John Foster Dulles likely have hesitated to supply U.S. arms to Pakistan if Nehru, without giving up India's nonalignment, had chosen to play a somewhat less conspicuous role in the cold-war politics of the time. Both countries were moved by what they regarded as their national interests. There was cordiality and cooperation between them when these interests coincided, as in 1962 at the time of the Chinese attack on the Indian border, but they tended to be irritable and sensitive when their interests diverged.

Far from being excessively idealistic and unrealistic, Indian foreign policy has often been coldly practical, almost cynically so. Whatever the formal official explanation for it, India's stand over Hungary in 1956 was dictated by anxiety to protect its position in Kashmir. What the Soviet Union did in Hungary went against all that India had stood for and what Nehru had preached, but India's delegate at the U.N. voted against the Western move for a referendum in Hungary since that step might have paved the way for a similar ballot on Kashmir. By then Indian leaders had clearly resolved not to accept a plebiscite in the state. If they had supported the right of self-determination for the people of Hungary, they could not have effectivly resisted the Pakistani demand that the Kashmir accession be put to a popular vote.

Compulsions of national interest also made Nehru overcome his strong personal distaste for military regimes and establish ties of close friendship with the United Arab Republic under Nasser and generally support the Arab cause against Israel. The consistent Indian advocacy of the Arab viewpoint was intended not only to secure Arab support on Kashmir, as was often officially claimed, but also to thwart any Pakistani plan to organize a Muslim bloc in West Asia. Such a bloc, if it had come into being, would have posed a threat to India's security and influence.

Even Nehru's advocacy of Afro-Asian solidarity and subsequent disenchantment with the cause were motivated by national and regional interests. He worked enthusiastically for unity among newly emerging nations in Asia and Africa up to their first meeting in Bandung. But he soon cooled off visibly when he found African and Asian leaders immature, confused and too often moved by ideas of personal glory. What made him drag his feet even more noticeably was the danger of the Afro-Asian alliance coming under the domination of Communist China. At Bandung in 1955, where he introduced China to other Asian and African nations, he found that Chou En-lai had cast a powerful spell on his listeners. Seeing a danger signal for India, he preferred not to help cast Chou as an Afro-Asian Pied Piper.

If Indians displayed an exaggerated sense of pride and a tendency at times to view the world situation with a limited perspective, the U.S. leadership showed little capacity to understand the sensibilities of a newly independent people and make allowances for their seeming brashness. To the United States, supreme international power came suddenly and unsought. America was like an inexperienced player being called upon to play the leading role without having had the time to rehearse the lines. Its movements were therefore jerky, and it tended to miss cues. The circumstances in which international power was exercised, had changed radically, as had its idiom. The world was no longer divided between colonial powers and subject peoples. Many who belonged to the latter category were still weak, but they had become independent and sensitive. Power still decided all arguments between nations, but it had to be exercised more subtly than in the days of European dominance—a reality inadequately understood in Washington. Moreover, to most Western leaders, Asians were still inferior to Europeans. In these circumstances, it was one thing to urge the British idealistically to grant India its freedom and help set up the United Nations, and quite another to establish a working relationship with an independent India based on mutual understanding and respect. The U.S. policy-makers were also undoubtedly influenced by their wartime experience: it was an Asian nation that had drawn their country into the war while all their principal allies were Europeans. Therefore what appeared to the Indian eyes as American attempts to prop up colonial institutions in Asia seemed to the United States a natural obligation toward those with whom it had long-standing cultural and political ties.

The Calvinistic vigor with which the United States endeavored to contain the Soviet Union and Communism made cordial relations with India even more difficult. The way the United States stubbornly refused to acknowledge the emergence of a Communist China and clung to the illusion that Taiwan was the real China seemed a strange—even childish—way of conducting foreign policy. To the United States, on the other hand, any tolerance of Communism or suggestion of coexistence with it seemed political cowardice. Those who declined to fight against

Communism were shirking their moral responsibility—and, certainly, untrustworthy.

Having thus dismissed India's nonalignment as "immoral," U.S. leaders looked for friends in Asia whose hearts would be stout even if their shoulders were not broad enough to carry the burdens of keeping the Soviet Union and Communism at bay. In the Indian subcontinent, they quickly and inevitably found such an ally in Pakistan.

No action of the U.S. government has caused as much resentment and bitterness in India as its initiative in building military pacts anchored around Pakistan and the bilateral mutual-security agreement of 1954. Moved as they were by deep-seated animosities rendered more acute then by a territorial conflict in Kashmir, both India and Pakistan regarded the U.S. maneuver as essentially an act of partisanship in the subcontinent, not as a move to contain China and the Soviet Union. The existence of sophisticated U.S. arms in Pakistan were to the Indians a constant reminder that the United States had deliberately chosen to side with India's principal enemy. The hostility engendered by this policy could not be mitigated by the genuine display of sympathy and understanding on the part of U.S. Ambassadors to India such as Chester Bowles, Ellsworth Bunker and Sherman Cooper, who worked for extensive economic aid to the Indian people. The mutual-security arrangement with Pakistan adversely affected not only the left-wing elements and men like Krishna Menon, who had a pathological distrust of the U.S., but even conservative parties like the Jana Sangh, which would normally have pleaded for a close relationship with the United States. To most Indians, regardless of party, the policy seemed to involve a bargain between the United States and Pakistan in which the former acquired valuable military bases and in return agreed to give the latter arms in full knowledge of their importance in altering the balance of power in the subcontinent. Indians could not imagine that the United States would make a decision of that magnitude without realizing its full implications. Chester Bowles, who was the U.S. Ambassador in New Delhi from 1951 to 1953, argued emphatically against establishment of military links with Pakistan and testified to the sincerity of India's nonalignment. Even George Allen, who succeeded him in the New Delhi post and was a Dulles nominee, reportedly warned the State Department toward the end of 1953 of the anger that an arms pact with Pakistan was likely to cause in India. In Washington, criticism was voiced by Senator J. William Fulbright, who believed the decision to supply arms to Pakistan was "an unfortunate mistake."

The U.S. argument that arms were supplied to Pakistan for use against Communist aggression did not carry conviction with Indian leaders. In fact, they did not believe that Americans themselves took that assurance seriously. The hostility between India and Pakistan was so intense that to suppose, in a conflict between the two, Pakistan would scrupulously lay U.S. arms aside and fight only with arms acquired from other sources was to be naïve beyond words. In the earlier phase of the pact, Pakistani leaders were discreet in their public utterances on the subject, but in private conversations they were frank enough to admit that their purpose in acquiring U.S. arms was different from what was professed in the pact. In November 1953, some months before the agreement was formally concluded, *The New York Times* reported from Karachi that "Pakistan is more inclined to build her military strength as a bargaining factor in dealing with India on the Kashmir issue than as a defense against other countries, including the Soviet Union. This is a common admission, privately expressed." Eisenhower's assurance to Nehru in his letter of February 24, 1954, that the supply of arms to Pakistan was "not directed in any way against India" brought little consolation to New Delhi. Indian fears were to prove correct. In the spring of 1965, when Pakistan sent in its forces to settle a border dispute with India on the Kutch border, it openly used U.S.-supplied tanks. India was right also in predicting, as it did in the course of diplomatic exchanges following the arms pact with Pakistan, that the United States, notwithstanding Eisenhower's solemn assurance, would be able to do nothing to stop Pakistan from using U.S.-supplied arms against India. The U.S. Ambassador in Pakistan, Walter McConaughy, conveyed to the Pakistan Foreign Office the sense of embarrassment in the U.S. A sharp reprimand of the kind India sought was obviously not possible, because the operative clause in the agreement provided for the use of U.S. arms by Pakistan for "legitimate self-defense," and what Pakistanis regarded as "legitimate self-defense" need not tally with the view in Washington.

The psychological impact of the U.S. arms supply to Pakistan on the Indian mind was even more harmful. Not only Menon and people of his persuasion but many others believed that India was being punished for refusing to line up obediently behind the United States in the big-power confrontation. In *Harper's* magazine in July 1966, Selig S. Harrison referred to a briefing that Richard Nixon, then Vice President, had held in 1954 in which he described the military pact as an opportunity to build a counterforce to Nehru's neutralism in the Indian leader's own backyard. This view of the Eisenhower administration's thinking on the delicate issue is also recorded in the biography of Nixon by Ralph Toledano. In his Senate speech opposing the arms pact, Senator Fulbright argued that the supporters of the agreement had probably "laid the basis for the belief by Mr. Nehru that this arming of Pakistan is designed to force his hand." Most Indians, however, needed no testimony of this kind to convince them that arms to Pakistan were intended to penalize India for its stubborn refusal to toe the American line.

In the early Fifties, when the arms policy was taking shape, there were many in Washington who, unlike Senator Fulbright, believed Nehru had done much to deserve having his hand forced, if not slapped. India's advocacy of the Communist Chinese cause had been so enthusiastic that in later years India itself came to regret it. When the Korean war started, India condemned North Korea as the aggressor; but even before the applause for its action in Western circles had died down, it began urging a cease-fire and a negotiated settlement of the conflict.

Nehru sent identical letters suggesting as much to Stalin and Truman, thereby virtually equating the aggressor with the aggrieved in Korea. Dean Acheson, then Secretary of State, rejected the suggestion. Senator William F. Knowland and others in the U.S. Congress mounted a sharp attack on India and its unhelpful attitude. *The New York Times* wrote that Nehru's criticism was "obstructive" and his "policy is appeasement." The *Times* felt certain that "history will condemn the Nehru policy as well-intentioned but timid, shortsighted and irresponsible."

Such rebukes apparently did not deter Nehru. When U.S. forces were moving toward the 38th Parallel in Korea, Nehru and the Indian delegates at the U.N. repeatedly warned against crossing it for fear of inviting Chinese retaliation. Later when, disturbed by the massive Chinese intervention, the U.S. strategic thinking favored a peace treaty with Japan, India opposed it vigorously on the plea that a peace conference of the kind the United States was proposing would be pointless without Chinese attendance. India's "obstructionist" role drew further angry retorts from the U.S. press and politicians. *The New York Times* described Nehru as "the lost leader." By contrast, the Pakistani attitude was the last word in cooperation and understanding. Instead of lecturing his American hosts on the importance of recognizing Communist China, as Nehru had during his visit to the United States in October 1949, Pakistani Prime Minister Liaqat Ali Khan expressed his country's determination to oppose aggression. Visiting America on the heels of the Indian Prime Minister, Liaqat Ali described Communism as incompatible with Pakistan's Islamic way of life and even offered blandishments to American private capital. Later, Pakistan vigorously supported the U.S. position in Korea. At the San Francisco conference on the signing of the Japanese peace treaty, Pakistan's representative, Sir Mohammed Zafrullah Khan, hailed the treaty enthusiastically. All this had the expected effect of highlighting Pakistan's friendliness and exaggerating India's intransigence. The United States had found a "trustworthy" friend in the subcontinent, and if display of cordiality toward it upset India, the U.S. Administration was not overly bothered by the prospect.

In these circumstances, it was natural that the United States should stand closer to Pakistan than to India in the dispute over Kashmir. But at no stage during the dispute did the United States exert excessive pressure on India on this issue. Pakistan may have hoped that acquisition of U.S. arms would enable it to wrest Kashmir from Indian hands, but the United States offered it neither military help nor diplomatic support in measures that might have settled the issue against India. There was much needling of India, and the United States frequently refused to see what India regarded as the justice of the case. But there were also occasions when the United States genuinely tried to restrain Pakistan. Truman and Attlee suggested arbitration to resolve the dispute—a proposal implying that Kashmir's accession to India was not final, for, as India argued, an integral part of a sovereign country cannot be the subject of arbitration. In 1962, when India was suffering reverses in the war with China, the United States and Britain pushed a reluctant Nehru into bilateral talks with Pakistan to resolve the Kashmir dispute. Three years later, Pakistan's action in sending several thousand armed personnel into Kashmir across the cease-fire line to organize an "internal uprising" earned it no Western rebuke.

At the same time, however, when India refused to accept U.S. advice in the matter or knowingly thwarted a Western move for a settlement, the reaction in Washington seldom went beyond mild annoyance. If in 1962 Kennedy had forced India into talking terms with Pakistan, he had earlier strongly urged Pakistan's President Ayub Khan to observe a "freeze" on the cease-fire line in Kashmir while India was engaged in repelling the Chinese aggression. U.S. and British diplomats stood in the wings anxiously as the Indo-Pakistan talks continued for months, but India's firm refusal to budge from its known stand and make any new concessions to Pakistan brought it no punishment from those who had sponsored the reconciliation move. Similarly, the United States, while it did not condemn Pakistan for sending raiders into Kashmir in 1965, was prompt in suspending all military and economic assistance to the subcontinent—a step that hurt Pakistan much more than India.

The ambivalence that the United States displayed in its attitude over Kashmir typifies almost the entire area of its relations with India. In the letter in which he assured Nehru that U.S. arms to Pakistan would not be used against India, Eisenhower also offered similar arms assistance to India. But in the years that followed, the administration repeatedly turned down Indian requests for permission to "buy" arms. The Indian government had set its heart on, among other things, F-104 supersonic fighter aircraft like those the United States had supplied to Pakistan, but U.S. authorities persistently argued that India did not need such sophisticated aircraft. To Indians it seemed strange that Pakistan required the fighter aircraft for its defense against an apparently nonexistent threat from the neighboring Communist powers but that India, actually engaged in a serious confrontation with China since 1958–59, was not considered entitled even to purchase them. At the time of the Chinese border attack, India turned to the United States and Britain for urgent help. The response was magnificent and touched many an Indian heart. But the supply of arms dwindled as soon as the fighting stopped. Even the sixty-million-dollar assistance that Kennedy had reportedly resolved to provide at his meeting with Macmillan in Nassau was not given fully, presumably owing to Pakistani protests. In 1965, following the India–Pakistan war, the United States suspended assistance to both countries on the ground that it could not tolerate a situation in which two peoples were frittering away its aid in needless mutual strife. In the spring of 1967, however, the decision was modified to permit purchase of spare parts. This step had the effect of helping Pakistan, whose military equipment was almost entirely of U.S. manufacture, and thereby depriving India of the superiority in military equipment that it had achieved by causing heavy damage to Patton tanks and other U.S.-supplied hardware in the 1965 war.

Much of this seeming ambivalence in U.S. policy is due to what Indian leaders regard as an American endeavor to balance

Pakistan against India even though India is three times Pakistan's size in area and five times in population. The economies of both countries are backward, but India's, despite its enormous food problem, is much less so. It has a considerably larger industrial base than Pakistan, and its political institutions are more modern and forward-looking. It is inevitable that India should exercise markedly greater influence and power in the region than its hostile neighbor. The United States realizes India's importance—otherwise it would not have offered India over four billion dollars in economic aid and supplied over four billion dollars' worth of food grains against soft-currency payments since 1950. In 1965–66, when India was in the grip of the worst drought of the century and nearly 100 million of its people were faced with starvation or serious malnutrition, the United States supplied India as much as twelve million tons of food grains. Even if it refused to fit itself into the U.S.-designed security plan for the region, India's political stability and economic viability were important to a U.S. concerned over Communist expansion in Asia. Yet, instead of allowing Pakistan to evolve its own power equation based on natural factors, successive U.S. regimes appeared to encourage Pakistan to challenge India and create artificial conditions of stability in the subcontinent. But what chance was there that two peoples with disproportionate strength would come to an arrangement on the basis of the realities of the situation if the weaker of the two contrived to acquire extra muscle temporarily? The situation would have been more graphic for the United States if, for example, its territorial dispute with Mexico had occurred in the middle of the twentieth century and a third party had been there to commiserate with Mexico and give it encouragement and arms to keep the tension alive. Even such an analogy would not have reflected the emotional pressures of the dispute between India and Pakistan, for the clash between the United States and its relatively smaller neighbor was not marked by the elements of historic bitterness that exist between India and Pakistan. There was no comparable background of religious hatred, nor a territorial division that uprooted millions of people and took countless lives.

U.S. preoccupation with the Soviet challenge and the consequent need for operational bases in Pakistan continued to affect the relations between the two countries even after the Eisenhower–Dulles period. Genuine realization of India's importance as a viable nation in Asia was evident in the measure of economic assistance that India received from the United States in implementing its various five-year plans. India, on the other hand, was conscious of its economic difficulties and its dependence on Western—particularly U.S.—assistance in overcoming them. But this awareness was balanced in part by India's seemingly compulsive desire not merely to be independent in its foreign policy but also to appear convincingly so. Though it dragged the country into a interminable commitment in Vietnam, the U.S. concern over Chinese expansionism was not strong enough to justify building up India's military potential. Even after the Chinese attacked Indian borders in 1962 and India unabashedly sought assistance, the United States carefully avoided offering India sophisticated fighter aircraft and tanks and was noticeably niggardly in giving much-needed electronic equipment. Against nearly 1.5 billion dollars' worth of arms given to Pakistan, Kennedy's military assistance to India in 1962 was no more than 80 million dollars. And what was equally significant, as the Indians were quick to notice, U.S. assistance tapered off rather sharply, soon after the Pakistan government lodged a protest about it. Consequently, Indo-U.S. relations fluctuated within certain limits. They never became warm, but they did not develop any serious or durable tensions.

In the economic field, U.S.-India cooperation has suffered from similar ambivalence and predilections on one side and sensitivity and suspicion on the other. Up to the end of September 1970, India had received 4 billion dollars in U.S. aid. In addition, it had been given nearly 60 million tons of American food grains under Public Law 480. The terms on which the assistance was offered compared favorably with aid from any other external source. India was the largest recipient of U.S. aid, the "service charges" on that aid were low, and the arrangements for re-payment easy. PL 480, under which it was able to import large quantities of food grains against rupee payments, was tailored to suit the financial limitations of countries such as India. It not only paid for the purchases in its own currency, but the United States was virtually debarred from spending the bulk of what it "earned" from such sales. Except for the U.S. shipments, food prices in India, around which the entire price structure of its economy is built, would have attained chaotic levels. Besides, without U.S. help, the Indian government might not have suc-ceeded in averting widespread starvation and consequent politi-cal disaster during the 1965–67 drought.

Yet the total political impact of U.S. aid was not as deep as it should have been. For one thing, Indians tended to compare the aid with similar help given Pakistan and to read motives and meanings into the U.S. actions that were not always there; for another, the U.S. effort reflected needless ideological inhibi-tions.

India undoubtedly is the principal beneficiary of U.S. eco-nomic assistance, but this fact loses some of its impressiveness in Indian eyes when it is realized that Pakistan received larger per-capita assistance. The United States has also insisted on offering its loans for development in the private sector. For a country conducting an experiment in mixed economy and devel-oping some of the basic industries such as steel and fertilizers in the state-owned sector, this provision placed a tremendous re-striction on India's deployment of its national resources accord-ing to its own lights. Britain, West Germany and the Soviet Union each helped in establishing a steel plant, but despite the energetic support of U.S. Ambassador Galbraith, a U.S.-financed plant did not materialize. India argued that no one in the private sector had the financial resources to set up a gigantic steel plant. Its contention was supported by some of the leading Indian industrialists themselves, but that did not overcome American reluctance to assist a public-sector steel project. Such U.S. hesitation in associating itself with one wing of India's economy has also had the effect of creating a major bottleneck in the growth of the fertilizer industry. Inevitably, U.S. reservations with respect to the public sector of India's industry influenced the World Bank's attitude. Until the last few months of George Woods's term as its president, the Bank took a rigid stand against helping anything but private enterprise in India.

The United States had good reasons for acting in this manner. It was influenced by its own experience and history. Also, the inefficiency of some of the state-owned undertakings in India justified wariness in the matter of investing American capital. But to a people who wore their socialism as a badge and who were encouraged by their leaders for years to think of state ownership as a panacea for their political and economic ills, such insistence on capitalism seemed to have a sinister motive. Many in India, including some who were not admirers of the Soviet system, believed that the U.S. posture was designed to pave the way for massive U.S. investments at the grass-roots level of the Indian economy. The Indian government itself regarded the U.S. insistence on helping the private sector as a way of pressuring India into opening extensive pastures of exploitation for American corporations. The resentment that this suspicion caused was widespread.

Quite apart from India's sensitiveness on the point, the U.S. style of economic assistance made its effort look much less impressive than it actually was. At times the Soviet assistance, much smaller in volume, appeared more imposing to the public eye. The steel plant at Bhillai with a 2.5-million-ton capacity that the Soviet Union had helped set up seemed a more convincing example of its participation in India's economic growth than the numerous smaller industrial undertakings that the United States had floated in collaboration with private Indian capital. Again, in a country where the average agricultural holding is less than five acres per family, the state-owned Suratgarh farm stretching over 30,000 acres of Rajasthan's arid land was a better showpiece for Russian participation than the millions of tons of food grains from the United States, which India undoubtedly needed but which it knew were surplus to the American farm economy.

Even the U.S. emphasis on modernization of India's agriculture has caused misunderstandings. Many have viewed it suspiciously as an attempt to keep the country's economy tied to the land and, consequently, backward. Under Nehru's leadership, India had set its heart on becoming an industrial power. It was aware of its food problem, but by 1956, following some providentially good monsoon years, its planners mistakenly believed the food situation was virtually under control and shifted the emphasis in the second Five-Year Plan to industry. The United States, however, was unconvinced that the food problem was solved and continued to tie the bulk of its aid to improving seeds, implements and farming methods rather than to the establishment of new industrial plants. Events proved the American experts to be right, but until that happened in 1965 and India once again turned its energies to agriculture, many in India resented the U.S. accent on the rural sector of the economy.

2: *The Bear Bites, the Bear Hugs*

For a country with strong cultural and commercial links to the West—and some of its basic political values—India has developed a relationship of remarkable harmony with the Soviet Union.

In 1947 the Russian understanding of India's impulses and aspirations was no greater than that of the United States. In fact, in the years following India's independence, the Soviet prejudices about the country were deeper and more irrational than those which even the most biased among the Western observers had ever entertained. The Soviet Union pointedly refused to acknowledge India's independence. The news of the transfer of power in the subcontinent, an event which drew scores of Western journalists to New Delhi, was never published in the Soviet press. In October 1947, several weeks after Indian independence, CPSU Secretary Andrey Zhdanov, in a speech in Moscow, chided the "imperialist and antidemocratic camp" for keeping India in "obedience and enslavement." Gandhi, whom millions in India idolized, was described by the Russians as "a reactionary Hindu leader." *Pravda* considered the news of his assassination worth no more than two sentences. Stalin had nothing but scorn for India's freedom movement and contemptuously regarded its leaders as agents of Indian bourgeoisie who wanted to rule India on behalf of their British masters. The Indian claim of being nonaligned was thus regarded as too ridiculous to be taken seriously. During this period the Soviet Union took little interest in India's dispute with Pakistan over Kashmir. In referring to the Pakistani invasion of Kashmir, the Soviet news media were interested not in highlighting the aggression but in the fact that the raiders were organized by a British general. In 1951 the Kashmir debate dominated the proceedings of the U.N. Security Council, but the Soviet delegation took almost no part in it.

Even the Communist Party of India, taking its cue from Moscow, gave Nehru and other Indian leaders considerable grounds for annoyance. The CPI had betrayed the freedom movement at a crucial juncture in 1940 by offering to cooperate with the British in the war effort. It compounded its offense by loudly echoing Stalinist contempt for national leadership and organizing the abortive but vexing uprising in the Telengana region of South India in 1948. Even as late as April 1954, Nehru castigated the CPI for having "extraterritorial loyalty." The Communists, he declared at a public meeting, "are born in one country, but their fatherland is elsewhere."

These are obviously not sentiments of the kind on which durable amity can be based, yet from about the time in 1954 when Nehru was denouncing the CPI to the beginning of 1966 the two countries maintained a relationship notable for mutual understanding and the consistency of their endeavor to stand by each other.

There are several reasons why the earlier suspicions and antagonisms were overcome quickly despite sharply divergent ideologies. For one thing, the Soviet attitude did not suffer from ambivalence of the type that sometimes marred U.S. relations with India. When Soviet leaders scorned India, they did so openly and completely. During Stalin's time they looked down upon India and made no secret of it. As India's Ambassador to Moscow, Mrs. Vijayalakshmi Pandit, Nehru's own sister, was not permitted to meet Stalin. Later, when Soviet leaders chose to befriend India, they did so without any mental reservations and offered wholehearted support to the Indian position on various issues. The national interests of the two countries, moreover, developed along courses that were parallel, often identical. Though for different reasons, both were interested in limiting the U.S. presence in Asia, checking the flow of American arms to Pakistan, opposing SEATO and CENTO and, at a later stage, restricting China's power. Almost throughout the first two decades of its independence, India has thus had a sense of common purpose with the Soviet Union. Even during the early years there were issues to which they had a common approach. Both were interested, for example, in securing Communist China's admission to the U.N. and opposing the re-establishment of colonial power in south Asia. In denouncing the Dutch and French efforts to reassert sway over their colonies in the region, Nehru was moved by the facts of India's own recent history while the Soviet Union was driven by cold-war compulsions; but, whatever their motives, their positions were highly compatible.

Indo-Soviet relations have passed through three distinct phases. After the opening years of Soviet aloofness and the Indian effort to be accepted in Moscow as a country with a mind of its own, there was a decade or more of remarkable bonhomie when the Soviet Union was India's principal source of strength in international affairs and a major supplier of its defense needs. In the latest phase, which began with Khrushchev's fall in 1964, the distance between them has increased somewhat. India still relies heavily on the Soviet Union for military hardware and for sustaining its position on Kashmir in the Security Council, but

Moscow has adopted what may be described as a less committed posture in the subcontinent. Its actions in supplying arms to Pakistan has created a measure of wariness in India that may, in years to come, develop into bitterness.

A few months before the actual transfer of power, when he formed the interim government, Nehru bracketed the U.S.S.R. with the U.S. in describing them as great powers. He offered greetings "to that other great nation of the modern world, the Soviet Union, which also carries a vast responsibility for shaping world events." His personal approach to the attitude that independent India should adopt toward Moscow was clearly reflected in his remark in that address: "They [the Russians] are our neighbors in Asia and inevitably we shall have to undertake many common tasks and have much to do with each other," he said.

The Soviet Union established diplomatic relations with India with reasonable promptness, but made no other gestures of cordiality. There was nothing that it approved of in the India of 1947–48. The democratic socialism that the Congress Party had aspired to, as well as the policy of nonalignment that Nehru had honed into shape for India, were subjected to strong, often vicious criticism. These objectives, as Soviet leaders saw them, were designed merely to create a socialist camouflage for a regime capable only of functioning as a camp-follower of imperialist powers. The Indian "revolution" was not completed with the exit of the British, and the Indian Communists, who had approved of the transfer of power earlier, presumably received their signal to resume their "revolutionary" activities.

Some of the reasons for Soviet hostility can be surmised. The process of peaceful struggle by which Indian leaders had won freedom from Britain did not quite fit into the Communist pattern of political change. How could an imperialist power decide to hand over power without a bloody conflict? The entire drama of the withdrawal of the British Raj from India—successive negotiations with Indian leaders, the country's partition through

agreement and even the setting of a firm date for the subcontinent's independence—had no relation to what the Soviet leaders
had experienced in their own country. There seemed to be a
certain phoniness about the transfer of power, therefore—a way
to deceive the Indian masses. Authority had merely passed into
the hands of those who acted under Britain's direction and were
committed to safeguarding its imperialist interests. Gandhi, with
his blend of religion and politics, and Nehru, with his aristo-
cratic upbringing and background of British education, seemed
typical agents of a foreign power.

It is doubtful that the Soviet leadership made any serious
effort to evaluate the character of the authority that had succeeded Britain in India. In 1947 it had little time for India. In
the wake of World War II, two power blocs had been formed,
and the arena for the trial of strength between them was obviously Europe, not Asia. A divided Europe, a divided Germany
were valuable gains that the Soviet Union had to consolidate
and, if possible, enlarge; there was no point in expending its
energies in Asia, where Western power was on the decline
anyway. The creation of NATO not only made the Soviet task
of consolidating its position in Europe more difficult, but also
posed a threat to its own security. There was, therefore, little
inclination on the part of Stalin and his associates to understand
the phenomenon of Indian independence.

Some of India's actions soon after independence only confirmed the Soviet suspicions that it was a handmaiden of Western colonial interests. Nehru's decision to continue its membership in the Commonwealth surprised and distressed many in
India. If any corroborative evidence was needed to convince the
Kremlin that its assessment of the true character of independent
India was correct, it was probably offered by the fact that British
investments in India continued to flourish and even dominate
certain sectors of the Indian economy. India's unsuccessful attempt in the autumn of 1947 to contest, with U.S. support, a
Security Council seat generated further hostility.

After his 1927 visit to Moscow, Nehru had written: "The

U.S.S.R. is a large country sprawling half over Asia and Europe. Between two such countries as India and Russia, there can be amity or enmity. Indifference is out of the question." The period of Indo-Soviet amity began around 1955. In fact, Nehru's second visit to Russia in June 1955 and the return visit to India by Bulganin and Khrushchev in the winter of the same year marked a watershed in Soviet-India relations. The thaw in the relations had, of course, started much earlier. Signs of lessening hostility had been noticeable as early as the latter part of 1949, when India signed the first of a series of trade agreements with countries in the Soviet bloc. The agreement provided India with 220,000 tons of Soviet wheat and maize in return for raw jute and tea. On January 25, 1950, on the eve of the inauguration of India's new constitution, the Kremlin chose to send warm felicitations, thereby signaling that it no longer regarded India a British vassal. India's efforts as a peacemaker in the Korean war, particularly its opposition to the crossing of the 38th Parallel by the U.N. forces, seemingly mellowed the Soviet leaders' mood and prompted them to reconsider their earlier assessment. What was perhaps the ultimate gesture of Soviet "acceptance" of India came in April 1952, when Stalin, who had not met any foreign diplomats for nearly two years, consented to receive the retiring Indian Ambassador, Dr. Sarvapalli Radhakrishnan. These developments aside, the period of purposeful understanding between the two countries truly began only after Khrushchev's rise to effective power and the exchange of state visits by the leaders.

State visits are usually tedious affairs dominated by protocol and generating limited and short-lived goodwill. But sometimes they crystalize a national mood or dramatically demonstrate it. Queen Elizabeth's visit to India in 1961 and even Harold Macmillan's visit in 1958 were marked by tumultuous public welcomes, but had no lasting impact on Indo-British relations. The exchange of visits by Nehru and Khrushchev, however, carried landmark significance, as did Eisenhower's visit to India in 1959.

Just as the Eisenhower visit marked the end of Dullesian rejection of nonalignment, the invitation to Nehru to come to the

Soviet Union and the tremendous ovation that the Russians gave him during his fortnight's stay demonstratively closed the chapter of Soviet antagonism and indifference toward India. By the beginning of 1955 the leaders of both countries had realized that they could cooperate to their mutual advantage.

The stage for Nehru's visit was elaborately set. The figure of Gandhi, whom the Russians had denounced as a "reactionary Hindu leader," was not only rehabilitated but elevated to a status equal to Lenin's. A member of a Soviet cultural delegation touring India in December 1954 penitently announced that the Soviet encyclopedia, which had denigrated Gandhi, was in error. A few weeks earlier, at ceremonies on the occasion of the thirty-seventh anniversary of the October Revolution, India headed the list of non-Communist countries and was even mentioned in the slogans as an upholder of world peace. In February 1955 the Soviet Union went beyond verbal eulogy and signed an agreement with India that set the pattern of Indo-Soviet economic collaboration in the years to follow. By the agreement, the Soviet Union undertook to set up a modern steel plant at Bhillai in India, thereby underscoring, if only by implication, American unwillingness to aid India in setting up state-owned heavy industries.

The reception accorded Nehru was indeed impressive. He was virtually the first non-Communist leader of any stature who had visited the country, and, in the words of a correspondent of a Washington newspaper, the Russians spread for Nehru "the reddest of red carpets." He traveled extensively and saw a great deal. He was even shown the atomic power stations, which until then the Russians had permitted no foreigners to see. If the Russian aim was to impress Nehru with the country's technological achievements, it succeeded. In addition, Nehru was convinced of the earnestness of the Soviet desire for peace. Moved by the warmth of his reception, he remarked at the time of his departure that he was leaving "a part of my heart behind."

The Moscow visit enabled the Indian Prime Minister to speak of Soviet intentions with confidence and authority. After the talks with Bulganin and Khrushchev, India was heard by Western powers with greater respect and credibility. India's status in international politics was undoubtedly enhanced, but the dividends that the visit of Bulganin and Khrushchev later that year brought India were considerably more sizable and concrete.

The "two traveling salesmen" as *The New York Times* rather churlishly described Bulganin and Khrushchev, spent three weeks in India during November–December 1955 and spared no effort to woo the nation. As they talked to Nehru or traveled through India, Bulganin performed routine protocol functions and uttered the customary platitudes, while Khrushchev, by then clearly established as the effective power in the Kremlin, made all policy pronouncements and commitments. From India's point of view, the most important of these commitments was the Russian pledge of unreserved support to its claim to Kashmir. As in other fields, Soviet indifference and ambivalence on Kashmir were disappearing steadily since Stalin's death, but it was only during their visit to India that the Soviet leaders categorically and publicly endorsed the Indian stand. A visit to Kashmir was not included in the itinerary that the Indian government had drafted for its guests, but, significantly, they insisted on an opportunity to spend some time in the state. And it was in a speech in Kashmir's capital, Srinagar, on December 10 that Khrushchev spelled out his country's new policy on Kashmir. The Kashmir question, he declared, had been settled finally by the people of Kashmir when they decided to join the Indian Union. The Soviet Union accepted their verdict, he added. On their return to Moscow, the report of the two leaders to the Supreme Soviet declared that the people of Kashmir "regard themselves as an integral part of the Republic of India" and that the Soviet government "supports India's policy on the Kashmir issue because it fully accords with the interests of peace in this part of Asia." On other occasions during their travels in India, the Russian leaders attacked Portugal for refusing to withdraw from Goa, its tiny colony on the southwest coast of India, and emphatically supported India's claim to it.

Apart from winning some immediate public goodwill in India, Khrushchev's basic endeavor was to assure India and its leaders that they could live in friendship with the Soviet Union without fear of ideological domination or subversion. The Russian "bear hug" was not the frightening phenomenon that it had traditionally been made out to be. India's nonalignment, suspect in Western eyes, was wholly acceptable to the Russian leaders. They even acknowledged that the Russian experience might not be relevant to the Indian situation and genius. Khrushchev expressed this belief when he quoted a Russian saying that "it is impossible to force the buffalo to eat meat; it is impossible for the tiger to eat grass." Even Soviet aid was offered without any apparent strings. The Soviet Union would gladly help India's industrialization, but they saw no reason why India should not also continue to receive aid from capitalist countries. India and the U.S.S.R. could be friends without having to share friends. Khrushchev also publicly wondered why only five countries—the permanent members of the Security Council—were regarded as great powers. In his view, India too was a great power and should occupy a position of pre-eminence in world councils. Such words were, of course, music to the ears of a people who have traditionally had a somewhat exaggerated view of their own importance.

What India gained from the Soviet Union during the Khrushchev era, however, was much more than a verbal pandering to its ego. The relationship brought concrete advantages ranging from support in the Security Council to the establishment of a gigantic complex to manufacture MIG supersonic fighter aircraft. During this period India's Kashmir policy existed under the umbrella of the Soviet veto in the Security Council. The potential Soviet veto, in fact, spared India considerable embarrassment in the U.N. not only over Kashmir but also when its armies marched into Goa in December 1961 to forcibly end Portugal's colonial rule in that tiny Indian enclave. That the protection of the Soviet veto was available at a time when other big powers, notably the United States and Britain, viewed the Pakistani position on Kashmir and the Portuguese position on Goa with sympathy made the Soviet veto all the more valuable to India. But for the Soviet intervention, India would have been branded as the aggressor over Goa. Soviet help was even more welcome on the three occasions when Pakistan took the Kashmir dispute to the Council. In January 1957 Pakistan objected to India's plans to proceed with the constitutional integration of Kashmir with the rest of the country. In the U.N. debate on the issue the Anglo-American bloc was conspicuously lined up on the Pakistani side, but the Soviet delegate offered its government's unreserved support to India. At a subsequent meeting the Soviet veto defeated a resolution sponsored by Britain, the United States, Australia and Cuba recommending the use of a U.N. force to hold a plebiscite in Kashmir. The Soviet veto defeated a similar plebiscite move at the beginning of 1962. India by then had withdrawn its offer to hold a referendum in Kashmir, pleading that the circumstances in which the offer was made had altered radically. The Soviet delegate echoed this view and reminded the Council that the U.N. resolution on the plebiscite had been adopted in quite different circumstances. He also argued, much to the satisfaction of the Indian government and people, that the withdrawal of the Pakistani troops from the entire territory of Kashmir was an important prerequisite prescribed in the plebiscite resolution and had never been fulfilled.

Compared to Western aid, Soviet economic assistance to India was considerably smaller and covered a rather limited sector of the economy. By the end of 1969, Soviet loans and other forms of assistance had totaled about one billion dollars—about 25 percent of the aid that the United States had extended. The terms on which Soviet aid was offered were reasonably lenient but not so attractive as those governing U.S. assistance. The period for repayment to the Russians, for example, was as short as twelve years compared with forty years followed by a possible grace period of ten years allowed by the Americans. The usual Soviet rate of interest was 2.5 percent. But the psychological impact of Soviet aid on the Indian mind was considerable—in fact, out of proportion to its size and terms.

Perhaps fortuitously, the beginning of the Soviet aid program coincided with the Indian government's second Five-Year Plan. The policy formulation, which for the first time since independence enunciated objectives and prescribed guidelines, presented the concept of mixed economy in which private as well as public sectors were assigned roles. Partly for ideological reasons and partly in view of the limited resources of Indian industrialists, basic industries such as steel, heavy engineering, machine-tool manufacture and electronics were assigned to the state-owned sector. At the same time, in the second plan (1956–61) emphasis was calculatedly shifted from agriculture to industrial development. The Soviet Union, for obvious reasons, had no hesitation in offering assistance in the establishment of public-sector industries. Besides the steel plant at Bhillai, its finances and technical help were available to India in creating a fairly large complex of basic industries manufacturing heavy electrical equipment, mining and allied machinery, precision instruments, drugs and aluminum. Other areas of Indo-Soviet collaboration have included power plants, oil exploration, oil refineries, and iron-ore mining. Like American aid, the Soviet aid is tied to purchases and services available in Russia, but the interest charges are tied to purchases being made from India—a concession not offered by Western nations. In 1963, when the United States finally declined to help India in setting up its fourth public-sector steel plant at Bokaro (the earlier three were contributed by the U.S.S.R., Britain and West Germany), the Soviet Union rushed forward to take on the responsibility of finding credit and technical assistance for it.

Quite apart from rescuing the Bokaro steel plant (and reaping much political benefit at the expense of the United States), the Soviet Union successfully demonstrated that effective and mutually beneficial economic links can be established between a highly advanced country and a technically backward one. The Soviet Union did buy certain raw materials from India, but it also purchased sizable quantities of manufactured and semiprocessed goods. The volume of Indian exports to the U.S.S.R. rose from nearly 5 million dollars in 1955 to more than 100 million dollars in 1963. Over 40 percent of Indian exports in 1963 comprised manufactured and consumer articles, ranging from razor blades, knitted wear, cosmetics, shoes and artificial silk to medical equipment, motorcycles, scooters, machine tools and railroad wagons. In January 1965 the Soviet Union abolished tariff levies on exports of developing countries, bringing India additional economic benefits. The offer of two-way "tied" economic aid and purchase of Indian manufactured goods, of course, was not motivated entirely by philanthropic considerations. Besides securing valuable political dividends in the form of keeping India away from Western domination, the Soviet Union drove a fairly hard bargain over the pricing of goods. What India bought from Russia with the loaned rubles could have been purchased at a somewhat lower price elsewhere, while the payments it received for its own exports were often lower than the world prices. India, however, benefited inasmuch as this arrangement lessened the burden on its meager hard-currency resources. By the middle 1950s, India's foreign-exchange holdings had dwindled alarmingly, and any relief was welcome, even if the price paid for it was rather high. At the same time, the Indo-Soviet trade arrangement enabled India to find a market for some of its manufactured goods that attracted few buyers in the West.

As far as supplying military equipment was concerned, the Soviet Union during the Khrushchev regime caught India on the rebound. In organizing and equipping its armed forces, India traditionally followed the British pattern, and Britain was its main source of military supplies. But in the years following independence, owing presumably to its quarrels with Pakistan and related political reasons, Britain seemed reluctant to meet India's demands. Trained in Sandhurst, most senior officers of the Indian Army entertained a strong preference for British weapons, but successive Chiefs of Army Staff reported to the Cabinet British diffidence in supplying India with arms. In the secret in-

quiry held after the 1962 war with China, British unwillingness
to help India modernize its army was cited as one of the major
reasons for India's failure. Its armored wing was based on Cen-
turion tanks and its artillery used principally the British 25-
pounders of World War II vintage. That the United States was
supplying highly sophisticated arms to Pakistan stimulated India's desire for better weapons, but also restricted Western desire to meet its demands.

India inevitably turned to the Soviet Union for help and received a good deal of it. Much of the arms transaction is
shrouded in secrecy—any newspaper report about Russian supplies has always led to a strong Soviet protest to the Indian government—but the volume of the supplies is known to be large.
When India was frustrated in obtaining F-104 aircraft, it found
Moscow willing to offer the MIG-21, modify the aircraft to give
it longer range to meet India's peculiar border requirements, and
later help in setting up a factory to manufacture the planes in
India. The first consignment of six MIGs arrived in 1963, and
by the middle of 1969 the Indian Air Force was known to possess 120 of them. By then the armored division boasted a fleet of
450 T-54 and T-55 Russian tanks and nearly 350 light tanks,
while the artillery units had 300 100 mm. and another 140 even
larger guns from the U.S.S.R.

But the important thing about the Soviet economic and military assistance has not been its volume but its timeliness and the
absence of any political quibbling on the part of the Russians.
Soviet leaders did not question India's intention to set up heavy
industries, nor doubt the ideological wisdom of mixing state
ownership with private capital, nor subject India's desire for
supersonic MIGs to an expert's critical scrutiny. It willingly
offered India what was sought and fulfilled its commitments
without any seeming foot-dragging. The Russian veto on Kashmir came to India's rescue when it was needed most. The price
that Russia sought was relatively small. If in 1956 Nehru pulled
his punches over the Soviet action in Hungary, it was not because Khrushchev was twisting his arm but because support of

the Western demand for a U.N.-supervised referendum in Hungary would inevitably have lent strength to Pakistan's demand for a similar plebiscite in Kashmir. Khrushchev sought no precise *quid pro quo* for Soviet economic and military assistance and the use of the Soviet veto. He urged no special socialization of Indian policies. In fact, Nehru constantly castigated Indian Communists during this period and showed them scant mercy. The Communist ministry that came to power in the small southern state of Kerala in the 1957 general elections was ousted from office by the Congress Party with the Central Government's active help and the use of methods some thought were not entirely democratic. Such sternness on Nehru's part in dealing with the Communists at home apparently brought no protests from Soviet leaders. Under Khrushchev, the Russians' interest was not that India should become a Soviet satellite but, negatively, that it should not become a Western camp-follower. By the mid-1950s, despite denunciation by Dulles, nonalignment had attained respectability as an international policy and the number of its practitioners had grown. As Harold Macmillan once stated, Khrushchev was the first Communist leader to realize that Marx was a pre-atomic thinker and that war with capitalist society was not inevitable. He also realized before the Western world that nonaligned nations were not necessarily shirking moral responsibilities and that they could be a force for peace. In this approach he received a quick and enthusiastic response from Indian leadership. In defending India's nonalignment, the Soviet Union was even ready to undertake ideological polemics with a "Socialist brother." Mikhail Suslov, one of the leading theoreticians of the Communist Party of the Soviet Union, presented a report to the party Central Committee in February 1964 in which he chided China for "allowing its relations with India, which as everybody knows is not a member of military blocs, to deteriorate sharply." He also rebuked Peking for friendship "with Pakistan, a member of SEATO and CENTO."

Curiously, the winds of change began to affect Indo-Soviet relations within weeks of the Suslov statement. Moscow, which had previously condemned Pakistan for its military alliance with the Western bloc, showed a marked interest in establishing a close association with Pakistan. Since the beginning of 1955 India had found the going so harmonious as far as the Soviet Union was concerned that the change, when it came, had to be sharp. In the type of situation prevailing in the subcontinent, the Soviet endeavor to improve relations with Pakistan unavoidably meant a lessening of its cordiality to India.

The beginning of the change is usually associated with the downfall of Khrushchev in October 1964, but there is evidence to suggest that the Soviet effort to move away from a position of total commitment to India had started some time before that. In June 1964 the then Soviet President, Anastas Mikoyan, told Shastri during a visit to New Delhi that it was time for India and Pakistan to seek to settle their differences. There must have been other, even more disturbing, indications of declining Soviet support that prompted India to seek renewed assurance on this point during Radhakrishnan's visit to Moscow a month before Khrushchev's unexpected fall. It is claimed that in private talks the assurance was given, but, significantly, the official communiqué issued at the end of the Indian President's stay contained no mention of Kashmir.

In the years that followed, the U.S.S.R. did not at any stage alter its stand on Kashmir. On the record, it still stands committed to Kashmir as a part of India and opposed to any referendum there. But it has singularly refrained from reiterating its stand publicly. Indian leaders and diplomatic representatives have frequently claimed that the country enjoys unreserved Soviet support on Kashmir—a view that has not been denied by Russian spokesmen but also has not been endorsed in any responsible forum or official document. In private parleys Kosygin and other Soviet leaders have informed Mrs. Gandhi that they regard Kashmir as part of India and that they would favor a solution of the dispute in accordance with the Indian suggestion that the state be partitioned between the two contenders along the present cease-fire line.

Indians claim, furthermore, that the Soviet veto would be available on their side should the Security Council adopt a resolution unacceptable to India. Visible evidence, however, does not justify this sanguine Indian view on the Soviet veto. Since 1965 Moscow has adopted a convincingly neutral posture in Indo-Pakistan disputes. It was unwilling to take sides when the two countries clashed briefly over a marshy tract in Kutch on their western border. Immediately after the Kutch episode, Shastri paid his first state visit to Russia and sought the customary assurance of support against Pakistan. Kosygin remarked, somewhat tartly, in his Kremlin speech that "when the Soviet Union is striving to improve its relations with a third country, this does not have to be at the cost of Soviet-Indian friendship." The Soviet Union was striving so hard to improve its relations with Pakistan that when Mrs. Aruna Asaf Ali, a well-known Communist sympathizer in India, was in Moscow to receive the Lenin Peace Prize, the *Pravda* report of her speech on the occasion carefully deleted all references, even innocuous ones, to Kashmir. *Pravda* also censored heavily a resolution passed by the National Council of the Communist Party of India criticizing Pakistan for aggression in Kashmir in September 1965.

During the Security Council debate in September 1965 on the India-Pakistan war, the Soviet delegate struck a studied pose of neutrality and voted with the Western resolution for an immediate cease-fire. Later, when Shastri and Ayub met in Tashkent at Kosygin's invitation, the Soviet leaders exerted considerable pressure on the Indian Prime Minister to bring him closer to an acceptance of the Pakistani viewpoint.

In their present phase, Indo-Soviet relations have also undergone a subtle but significant change. In terms of power and influence, there was always great disparity between the two countries. Yet, for some years following 1955 the relationship was maintained virtually on the basis of equality. The Soviet Union seemed as anxious to retain India's goodwill as the latter was to preserve Russian friendship. Nehru was treated with marked deference and the Indian view was given much importance.

There was seldom any attempt to tell Indian leaders how they should manage their affairs. The situation has changed since 1964. In the post-Khrushchev period, there has been a distinct tendency on the part of the Russian authorities to speak to the Indians bluntly. The Soviet Embassy in New Delhi and Russian technicians associated with various industrial undertakings in India have spoken impatiently and often brusquely of Indian shortcomings in the management of these projects. Such expressions of criticism were unknown in previous years when the Indian administration of Soviet-aided projects was no more efficient. In private talks during a visit to New Delhi in 1968, Kosygin even ventured to complain to Mrs. Gandhi that India had not set its house in order in Kashmir—a problem that embarrassed the Soviet Union. He was referring to the political agitation by Sheikh Abdullah and certain pro-Pakistan elements in Kashmir. This kind of unrest and challenge to Indian authority had marked the situation in Kashmir since 1952, but, in view of India's sensitivity on the point, the Russian leaders had never previously referred to it.

The principal demonstration of Soviet insensitiveness to Indian sentiment has come in the form of arms aid to Pakistan. As part of their endeavor to normalize their relationship with Pakistan, the Soviet authorities started to supply military equipment to Rawalpindi in 1967. As they argued to the United States when it signed the mutual-defense treaty with Pakistan, Mrs. Gandhi and others in the Indian government believe that any arms provided to Pakistan are liable to be aimed at India. Many public figures in India have expressed deep concern over the implications of the Soviet action, but Soviet leaders have remained unmoved. They have assured India that the supplies are in small quantities and of a type that would not affect India's military superiority in the subcontinent. Significantly, the exact volume of Soviet assistance and the nature of the arms supplied have not been communicated to the Indian government.

From its own sources, however, India has a fairly accurate idea of what Russia is supplying to its neighbor and in what quantities. Toward the end of 1970, Indian leaders did not think the Soviet aid posed a threat to the country's security, but some nervousness on their part is unmistakable.

The Soviet Union's efforts to bring Pakistan closer to it is motivated by consideration of its own national interests, just as was the change in its attitude toward India in 1955. Following Indian humiliation in the war with China and in view of the decline in Nehru's influence at home and abroad and the stodginess of Indian economic planning, Soviet leaders must have begun to doubt India's capacity to meet the challenge of Chinese power, lead the nonaligned bloc of nations and help curb Western influence in Southeast Asia. Pakistan's growing contacts with China constituted a new dimension to the problem of Chinese influence, but at the same time Pakistan's disenchantment with its Western ties also offered the Soviet Union a new opportunity. The most convincing evidence of the success of the Soviet diplomacy was the Pakistani action in serving notice to the United States to close down its big secret base at Peshawar, where the U-2 flights over Russia used to originate and where electronic equipment enabled it to eavesdrop on Russia constantly. Pakistan served the required one-year termination notice on the United States in the summer of 1968, at just about the time the supply of Soviet arms to Pakistan came to be known publicly. The U.S. urged the Pakistanis to reconsider their decision, but without success, and the base was duly closed down.

Pakistan has obviously not ended its Peshawar base agreement and earned the United States' displeasure merely for some transport vehicles and a few medium tanks that the Soviet Union is known to have given it so far. Pakistan's interest is to continue its confrontation with India, and to succeed, it must either have the Soviet Union's diplomatic help in securing Kashmir or enough arms to enable it to achieve its purpose. Kosygin and Brezhnev were undoubtedly aware of Pakistani ambitions when they embarked on their policy to win it over.

India's own sentiments on Kashmir remain strong. Since the 1965 war there is little tendency in India to make any concessions to Pakistan. If there is any attempt, however oblique, on the part of the Soviet Union to put pressure on India concerning Kashmir, the public reaction will be so adverse that no government, however left-oriented, will be able to ignore it. Even the limited supplies of Soviet arms that have so far reached Pakistan have caused extensive resentment in India. Any seeming use of Soviet influence in favor of Pakistan is bound to intensify serious annoyance in India. Even economic pressures—and the Soviet Union is in a position to exert them—are unlikely to overawe India on Kashmir. They will only quickly consume the reserves of public goodwill accumulated over the years.

EPILOGUE

ONE WOULD have to be utterly brash or blessed with the vision of a seer to hazard a guess about India's destiny in the coming few years. As it enters the Seventies, there is much in India to justify hope and confidence about the country's future. But there is also much which gives rise to despair and despondence. It is difficult to determine which side would outweigh the other because a society as large and complex as India's must involve many economic, political and psychological imponderables.

The next decade may carry for India bigger dangers and uncertainties than those it has encountered in the past. Some of the major challenges appear to be ahead, not behind. In fact, so far India has led what a combination of circumstances has made a rather sheltered, unreal life. Nehru's personality gave India an exaggerated, almost artificial sense of national unity. Under his leadership, the Centre exercised authority that was warranted neither by the Constitution nor by Indian temperament. His presence sustained political institutions, administrative practices and social attitudes that were foreign to the land. Besides

Nehru's dominance, other advantages that India enjoyed in the early years of independence have been dissipated by now. The euphoric self-confidence created by the success of the freedom movement is gone; so is the stimulation that the economy received from World War II and the accumulation of enormous sterling resources. The administrative structure that it had inherited from the British is still there, but the once-streamlined instrument of power has grown into a vast, amorphous bureaucracy that has obstinately retained some of the negative attitudes cultivated during the days of the Raj but has acquired few positive virtues suited to the needs of the new society.

It was not until well after Nehru's death that India slowly started the process of coming to terms with its true self, its politics began to find its real level, and its institutions and practices were molded to match the country's special character. It will be several years before the change is completed—an interim during which the capacity of India's leadership, the strength of its administration and economy and its instinct for survival will be subjected to severe strains. It may be apparent only toward the end of the Seventies whether India will succumb to regional and parochial pulls or continue to live as a united nation and, if the latter is the case, whether it will grow into a modern-minded, prosperous nation.

The country's political prospects present what is probably the least depressing aspect of the picture. After Shastri's sudden death in the beginning of 1966, India appeared to be without a nationally accepted leader. Mrs. Gandhi, who succeeded him as Prime Minister, was unsure of herself and, though respected as Nehru's daughter, was not considered a leader in her own right. Others behind her could at best command local and regional followings. Since her confrontation with the right-wing "syndicate" in her party, however, Mrs. Gandhi has appeared to be growing into a leader of national stature. She is still nowhere near the position that her father held or that Shastri won for himself through his leadership during the war with Pakistan. But she is no longer a helpless front for a clique of political operators, as she seemed to be for the first three and a half years of her Prime Ministership. In her struggle for effective power she has displayed remarkable shrewdness in assessing her opponents' strengths and exploiting their weaknesses, as well as a capacity for daring action. Time will tell whether she can also acquire a sense of national purpose and commitment of the kind her predecessors in office had.

Outside the legislature, the task before Mrs. Gandhi or any other leader who might come to the top is less overwhelming than it may seem. Indian masses do not make exacting demands on their leaders. Once a leader's *bona fides* are established, Indians give him their affection and trust in generous measures, and their capacity to overlook the leader's mistakes or shortcomings is considerable. In the hands of a strong leader whose integrity is not doubted, such a people can be strongly directed to positive action. Some of the causes for divisiveness, moreover, appear to be subsiding. The dispute over national language, for example, has lost much of its earlier virulence. A certain amount of regional aloofness and arrogance remains, but nowhere has it grown into even a vague desire for separation. The people of Bengal, for example, may take pride in the richness of their culture and look contemptuously at other parts of the country, but there is no descernible sentiment among the Bengalis for an independent political identity. Sections of the Tamil-speaking people of Madras at one time raised the slogan of separation, but since 1967, when their party, the DMK, won control of the state government, this demand has been completely abandoned. Acquisition of office has neutralized their hostility to such an extent that it manifests itself only in such harmless moves as changing the name of the state from Madras to Tamil Nadu.

Political power, in fact, may also offer the solution to the problem of religious confrontation between Hindus and Muslims. Much of the Hindu chauvinism in recent years has been practiced by parties like the Jana Sangh and groups like the RSS and Shiv Sena, which, owing to the Congress Party dominance, were virtually excluded from the exercise of power. As the Congress Party's strength declines and the non-Congress Hindus edge closer to office, they may begin to think and act with greater restraint. That Muslims, though a small minority (11 percent of the total), should match the majority community's aggressiveness with equal fanaticism is also due probably to their sense of political deprivation. For years after independence, Indian Muslims had no effective leaders. Most of their leaders had migrated to Pakistan, and those who remained did not enjoy the community's confidence. The Muslims, therefore, voted listlessly for the Congress because its secular ideals mitigated their feeling of insecurity. Only since 1967 have the Muslims started looking around for accord with other groups in the hope of sharing power. A slice of political power should widen their economic opportunities, add to their self-assurance and enable them to come to terms with other communities around them.

The economic challenges that India will have to face in the coming years are considerably more serious than the political ones, and the hopeful signs in this area are more scarce.

The development of the new, high-yielding varieties of wheat have created a sense of optimism in India about its economic future. Given a fair monsoon, India should soon produce an annual harvest of 106 million tons of food grains—enough to achieve self-sufficiency in food for the first time since independence. This would be a welcome development, but its significance should not be exaggerated; nor should attention be distracted from some of the truly grim aspects of the situation. The breakthrough in the development of superior seeds covers only wheat, while India's principal need is for rice. The "green revolution" has so far been confined to areas that were already irrigated; it must now move to other areas. Extension of assured irrigation facilities as well as production of fertilizers must proceed rapidly—developments that will require considerable organizational skill and financial investment on India's part. Unless this effort is forthcoming, India's food production may settle on a plateau while its population and food requirements continue to rise rapidly.

The rise in population and unemployment are the real problems India must confront successfully in order to survive. It must stablize its population at around 700 million by 1980. This is the least that it must achieve in order to keep its head above water. But, while acknowledging the earnestness of India's current efforts in this regard, many experts doubt the likely efficacy of the population-control program.

With the increase in population, the spread of literacy and the urbanization of the society, the dimension of India's unemployment problem has grown enormously. No precise data is available about the number of the unemployed, but it is generally conceded that the problem is severe and that it has worsened despite the three Five-Year Plans. The impact of Western ideas and extravagant political promises since independence have eroded the average Indian's capacity for stoic acceptance of what strike him as injustice and economic hardship. In the coming years, therefore, armies of the unemployed may seriously threaten India's social stability, particularly in its slum-abounding cities.

Unless drastic remedial action is taken soon, India's administration may collapse under its own weight. The central and state governments, state-controlled corporations and various local administrations now employ nearly eleven million officials— several times the size of the bureaucracy at the time of independence. Government involvement in the lives of the people has increased markedly since the time of the British, and it was inevitable that the number of its functionaries should grow. But the increase has been far out of proportion to the increase in their responsibilities—and certainly to their productivity.

Administrative experts have often bemoaned the Indian bureaucracy's tendency to obstruct rather than facilitate the process of governance. Mrs. Gandhi herself has spoken with unconcealed exasperation about being hamstrung by the officials around her and her helplessness to prod them into purposeful action. Few administrations are so paper-bound as India's. Most civil servants have a Brahminical penchant for theorizing and a marked aversion to action. Under the British, the average official was expected to quote rules and regulations and then await direction from the top. He still retains that colonial attitude of mind and will not make a decision if he can maneuver someone above him into giving him an order. As under the British, he tends to play it safe and devotes time and energy to protecting himself against any possible criticism rather than to making a sensible decision quickly. That members of Parliament often ask searching questions about official actions and legislative bodies sometimes probe them with almost judicial thoroughness has only added to his nervousness and desire to shield himself completely before taking even a small step. The result is a constant shuffling of official files from table to table, interminable interdepartmental conferences in an unabashed bid to diffuse responsibility, and over-all delays of a kind that a country with so much to accomplish cannot afford.

While refusing to shed some of its outdated methods and habits, the bureaucracy has shown an enormous appetite for personal power and, particularly at lower levels, a distressing capacity for graft and corruption. In the name of socialism, the civil service has usurped a sizable area of national activity as its exclusive preserve and then proceeded to administer it indifferently and unenthusiastically. Barring a few exceptions, the numerous semi-autonomous corporations created to administer important economic projects have been placed under civil servants who, after retirement from regular service, needed lucrative, comfortable berths for themselves. In today's India, bureaucracy affects nearly everything, from the importing of sophisticated machinery by a private industrialist in Bombay to the distribution of fertilizers to a small farmer in a remote village. The magnitude of its role combined with its ponderousness and lack of commitment gives the bureaucracy a near stranglehold on the country.

Yet, notwithstanding its mistakes and inadequacies, one must not judge India with undue harshness. What it has set itself to accomplish is a truly enormous task. It is trying to bring about a virtual revolution without the kind of convulsive upheaval usual in an underdeveloped society seeking to become a modern nation almost overnight. It is hoping to achieve in two or three decades what others lingered over for centuries, and it intends to do so without bloodshed or impairment of personal liberties. In Britain, devolution of political power started with the signing of the Magna Carta in the thirteenth century; the process was completed only at the beginning of the twentieth century with the rise of the Labour Party. In India, power has passed in twenty years from princes and the Western-educated urban elite to the lower middle classes—and now seems within reach of the factory worker and the peasant. The caste system and other social structures that had remained unchanged for several thousand years have developed serious cracks since independence. That India should be manufacturing its own supersonic fighter aircraft while the bullock cart, the traditional symbol of its backwardness, is nowhere near obsolescence yet characterizes the size of the task before India as well as the measure of success it has so far achieved.

Index

KRISHAN BHATIA

Krishan Bhatia was born in 1925 and, after earn-
ing his Master of Arts degree in English at Forman
Christian College in Lahore, joined the Associated
Press of India in 1946, a year before the nation
became independent. His first reportorial assignment was to cover Mahatma Gandhi's temporary
residence in New Delhi, where the leaders of the
new country came for consultation during negotiations with the British. Later he traveled extensively
with Prime Minister Nehru. Mr. Bhatia has held
several of the top positions in Indian journalism.
He was the Political Correspondent and chief
of the News Bureau of *The Statesman,* an influential English-language daily published in New
Delhi and Calcutta. He then served as Editor of
The Hindustan Times, another leading national
daily; since 1967, he has served as that newspaper's Special Correspondent in the United States.
Mr. Bhatia resides in a suburb of Washington,
D.C., with his wife and two children.